THE BODY LEGAL IN BARBARIAN LAW

The sixth to ninth centuries saw a flowering of written laws among the early Germanic tribes. These laws include tables of fines for personal injury, designed to offer a legal, non-violent alternative to blood feud. Using these personal injury tariffs, *The Body Legal in Barbarian Law* examines a variety of issues, including the interrelationships between victims, perpetrators, and their families; the causes and results of wounds inflicted in daily life; the methods, successes, and failures of healing techniques; the processes of individual redress and public litigation; and the native and borrowed developments in the various 'barbarian' territories as they separated from the Roman Empire.

By applying the techniques of linguistic anthropology to the pre-history of medicine, anatomical knowledge, and law, Lisi Oliver has produced a remarkable study that sheds new light on early Germanic conceptions of the body in terms of medical value, physiological function, psychological worth, and social significance.

(Toronto Anglo-Saxon Series)

LISI OLIVER was Greater Houston Alumni Chapter Endowed Alumni Professor in the Department of English at Louisiana State University.

LISI OLIVER

The Body Legal
in Barbarian Law

UNIVERSITY OF TORONTO PRESS
Toronto Buffalo London

© University of Toronto Press 2011
Toronto Buffalo London
utorontopress.com

Reprinted in paperback 2022

ISBN 978-0-8020-9706-4 (cloth)
ISBN 978-1-4875-4770-7 (paper)

Toronto Anglo-Saxon Series

Publication cataloguing information is available from Library and Archives Canada.

University of Toronto Press gratefully acknowledges the financial assistance of the Centre for Medieval Studies, University of Toronto, in the publication of this book.

We wish to acknowledge the land on which the University of Toronto Press operates. This land is the traditional territory of the Wendat, the Anishnaabeg, the Haudenosaunee, the Métis, and the Mississaugas of the Credit First Nation.

University of Toronto Press acknowledges the financial support of the Government of Canada, the Canada Council for the Arts, and the Ontario Arts Council, an agency of the Government of Ontario, for its publishing activities.

This study is dedicated

to

Ben Guelfo
Louisiana Personal Injury Lawyer Extraordinaire

and to

Sadie and Jasper

without any of whom the book would have been completed much more quickly,
but with far less laughter.

Contents

List of Illustrations, Maps, and Tables ix
Acknowledgments xiii
Abbreviations xvii

Introduction 3
1 Barbarian Laws in Context 8
2 Process and Procedure 26
3 The Head 72
4 Torso, Arms, and Legs 112
5 Hands and Feet 137
6 Insult and Injury 165
7 Assaults against Women 180
8 Assaults According to Rank (Nobles and King's Servants, Freedmen, Slaves, Clerics, Foreigners) 203
9 Summary: A Review of What Personal Injury Tariffs Have Told Us about Transmission of Law 227
Conclusion 238
Appendix: Tables of Injury Laws by Territory 247

Bibliography 263

Index 285

Addendum: Additional information can be found in online appendices at http://www.utppublishing.com/The-Body-Legal-in-Barbarian-Law.html.

Illustrations, Maps, and Tables

Figures

Figure 3.1   Skull from Grave 506, Halifingen (Kreis Tübingen, Germany).   77
Figure 3.2   Skull from Grave 234, Kirchheim/Ries (Ostalpkreis, Germany).   78
Figure 3.3   Difference in spall between direct and tangential wounds to skull.   81
Figure 3.4   Skull from Grave 561, Weingarten (Kreis Ravensburg, Germany).   83
Figure 3.5   Skull from Grave 410, Kirchheim/Ries (Ostalbkreis, Germany).   85
Figure 3.6   Skull from Horrheim, Germany.   94
Figure 3.7   Non-sensory organs regulated in barbarian laws.   100
Figure 3.8   Relative functional value of teeth.   103
Figure 3.9   Chart of relative value of teeth by territory.   105
Figure 4.1   Regulations on injury to torso.   115
Figure 4.2   Femurs from Greisheim Grave 226.   118
Figure 4.3   Fragment of mosaic from Cathedral of Lescar in southern France showing prosthetic leg.   119
Figure 4.4   Femurs from Grave 57, Kirchheim/Ries (Ostalbkreis, Germany).   121
Figure 4.5   Ulnae from Grave 363, Weingarten, Kreis Ravensburg. Artistic reconstruction of cause of injury.   125
Figure 4.6   Ulna and radius from grave in Eichstätten, Kreis Breisgau-Hochschwartzwald.   126
Figure 4.7   Forearm bones from grave in Balingen/Zollernalbkreis.   127

x   Illustrations, Maps, and Tables

Figure 4.8   Collarbones of adult male from Grave 45, Nusplingen, Zollernalbkreis.   131
Figure 5.1   Warriors wielding spears and swords. Franks Casket, 8th century.   144
Figure 5.2   Configurations of throwing hand for spear warriors.   146
Figure 5.3   Anglo-Saxon archer. Franks Casket, 8th century.   149
Figure 5.4   Charts of finger values in descending order of functional accuracy.   154
Figure 5.5   Charts of toe values in descending order of functional accuracy.   159 and 160
Figure 5.6   Prosthesis in situ, Grave 248, Bonaduz, Switzerland.   163
Figure 5.7   Schematic of stump and prosthesis from Bonaduz, Switzerland.   163
Figure 9.1   Tabulations for 'Matthew limbs' and sensory organs.   228
Figure 9.2   Tabulations of valuation of teeth, toes, fingers according to functional worth.   229
Figure 9.3   Tabulation of valuation of torso.   231
Figure 9.4   Tabulations of regulations for damage to genitals, arms and legs, internal organs.   232
Figure 9.5   Terms for fingers.   234

Maps

Map 1.1   Spread of laws by century of promulgation.   15
Map 1.2   Languages of the laws.   20
Map 3.1   Regulation of sensory organs.   97
Map 3.2   Regulations of teeth according to physiological value.   107
Map 4.1   Regulations on injury to torso.   113
Map 5.1   Assessment of 'Matthew limbs.'   139
Map 5.2   Distribution of terminology and functional approximation for fingers.   155
Map 5.3   Distribution of functional approximation for toes.   161

Tables

Table 1.1   Possible influences on composition of personal injury laws.   17
Table 1.2   Languages of the laws.   19
Table 2.1   Commutations in kind.   48
Table 3.1   Skull injuries in barbarian laws.   86

Table 4.1 Relative assessment of damage to major limbs for 'major four' territories. 134
Table 4.2 Relative assessment of damage to major limbs for secondary territories. 135
Table 5.1 Assessment of 'Matthew limbs.' 138
Table 8.1 Compensations for Bavarian freeman compared to Bavarian freedman. 208
Table 8.2 Compensations for Lombard freeman vs freedman and house-slave. 211
Table 8.3 Values of slaves. 213
Table 8.4 Compensations for Lombard freedmen/house slaves vs. field slaves. 214–15
Table 8.5 Compensations for slaves in Lombardy, Ripuaria, Bavaria. 216–17
Table 8.6 Relative compensations for Bavarian freeman, freedman, slave. 218–19
Table 8.7 Compensations for male religious. 223

Acknowledgments

It is a fashion among many academics to treat the daily horoscope as if it were simply an entertainment feature. However, the real and obvious influence that the stars can exert over our earthly lives is clearly demonstrated by my horoscope of 7 June 2008, printed in the Baton Rouge *Daily Advocate*:

> You might find some exceptional thinkers at your disposal with whom you can discuss some complicated issues; they will help explain things most people wouldn't understand.

The startling perspicacity of the zodiac in this respect can be seen in the following list of exceptional thinkers who have helped me at many stages of the production of this book. Not only scholars but also non-academic specialists in various fields have been extremely generous in giving of their time and expertise to aid me in the analyses presented in this study. The following list of experts in wide-ranging fields of knowledge only begins to acknowledge my debt to the multitude of friends and colleagues who have patiently listened to and commented on my attempts to elucidate the social world hinted at in the early medieval personal injury laws. Those named below have all contributed in many areas beyond their listed specializations. If I have inadvertently omitted any from this list, I beg their forgiveness and thank them here. Any errors remaining in the analyses must be laid to my account: these exceptional thinkers have done their best to inform my scholarship.

- *Medieval law*: Marianne Elsakkers, Stefan Jurasinski, Andy Rabin.
- *Medieval history and historical analysis*: Kent Hare, Tom Lambert, Sue Marchand, David Rollason.

- *Contemporary law*: Stuart Green, Ben Guelfo.
- *Medieval medicine*: Rolf Baumgartner, Florence Eliza Glase, Markus Hedeman.
- *Contemporary medicine and dentistry*: Toby Charamie, Jim McIlwain, Susan Postell, Ricardo Rodriguez, Cameron Rose, Elizabeth Strother, Jennifer Szurgot, Ken Wilkinson.
- *Linguistics and translation*: Ben Fortson, Maria Mahoney, Calvert Watkins, Ryan Williams.
- *Sports technology*: 'Coach Hat' Bachar, Peter Clayton, Amanda Harmata, John Woosley.
- *Rhetoric, theory, and argumentation*: Lilian Bridwell-Bowles, Stefan Jurasinski, Malcolm Richardson, Brooke Rollins.
- *Medieval religious theory and practice*: Maria Mahoney.
- *Research support*: Bob Doyle gave me my best graduation present from Harvard University: a day of photocopying whatever I wanted from the collection in Widener Library. This enabled me to bring to Louisiana copies of all the Germanenrechte editions of barbarian laws, without which this project would not have been possible.
- *Scholarly approach and editorial assistance*: To the anonymous readers assigned by UTP to comment on drafts of this manuscript; they have helped tremendously in shaping the final appearance of this book. I thank them for steering me from errors and towards solutions.
- The many libraries, museums, and photographic collections that provided the images produced herein. I am particularly grateful to Alfred Czarnetzki and his collaborators in the excellent exhibition and accompanying catalogue of *Menschen des Frühen Mittelalters im Spiegel der Anthropologie und Medizin* which provided invaluable archaeological evidence from medieval gravesites.
- Most importantly, to my editor at University of Toronto Press, Suzanne Rancourt, who believed in this book from the beginning, saw me through the dark ages of doubt, and is primarily responsible for bringing this book to conclusion. Every author should be so lucky to have such an editor, but very few are.

Further, I owe a tremendous debt of thanks to my students at Louisiana State University who have provided help in the collection, organization, and interpretation of the data incorporated in this study. Although many remain unnamed for reasons of space, particular credit must go to those who helped organize the data: Sally O'Rourke, Greg Molchan, Caroline Newman, and – far more than any citation can credit – Candice Scott.

Also to Melissa Norman, who prepared the initial index, and Joshua Hamburg, who helped bring it to conclusion. And, finally, to numerous neighbours and friends who have listened to me work out problems which must have seemed both arcane and boring during long walks with our dogs.

For financial support, I would like to thank Louisiana State University, in particular, the Department of English, for providing me with a semester's research leave and subsequently with a sabbatical leave (supported by the College of Arts and Sciences) to collect the data underlying this study. I also thank the Medieval Centre at the University of Toronto for a generous grant to subvent the publication, and the National Institutes of Health/National Library of Medicine for underwriting an extended teaching release which allowed me to complete the manuscript. Funding for this Scholarly Works project was made possible by grant 1 G13 LM009300-01 from the National Library of Medicine, NIH, DHHS. The views expressed in any written publication, or other media, do not necessarily reflect the official policies of the Department of Health and Human Services; nor does mention by trade names, commercial practices, or organizations imply endorsement by the U.S. Government.

Abbreviations

Edict Roth.	Laws of Lombards. See Friedrich Bluhme, ed. *Leges Langobardorum*.
Forum Iud.	Laws of Visigothic Spain. See Karl Zeumer, ed. *Leges Visigothorum*.
Kent.	Laws of Kentish kingdom. See Lisi Oliver, ed. *Beginnings of English Law*.
Lex Ala.	Laws of Alamanns. See Johann Merkel, ed. *Leges Alamannorum*.
Lex Baiu.	Laws of Bavarians. See Johann Merkel, ed. *Leges Baiuwariorum*.
Lex Cham.	Laws of Chamavan Franks. See Rudolf Sohm, ed. *Lex Francorum Chamavorum*.
Lex Fris.	Laws of Frisians. See Karl von Richthofen, ed. *Lex Frisionum*.
Lex Rib.	Laws of Ripuarian Franks. See Franz Beyerle and Rudolf Buchner, eds. *Lex Ribvaria*.
Lex Sal.	Laws of Salian Franks. See Karl August Eckhardt. ed. *Lex Salica, 100-Titel Text*.
Lex Sax.	Laws of Saxons. See Karl von Richthofen and Karl Friedrich von Richthofen, eds. *Leges Saxonum*.
Lex Thur.	Laws of Thuringians. See Friedrich von Richthofen, ed. *Lex Thuringorum*.
Liber Const.	Laws of Burgundians. See Friedrich Bluhme, ed. *Leges Burgundionum*.
Wessex.	Laws of West Saxons. See Felix Liebermann, *Die Gesetze der Angelsachsen*.

Introduction

This is a book about laws, bones, and related stories emanating from western Europe in the sixth to early ninth centuries. The primary focus is on the personal injury tariffs included in the legal codes established for the various continental kingdoms and dukedoms ranging from Visigothic Spain in the west to Bavaria in the east, from Italic Lombardy in the south to Saxony in the north, and incorporating the Anglo-Saxon island regions of Britain.[1] The discussions which follow present a wide variety of pictures: the causes and results of injuries inflicted in private altercation; the evidence for methods and successes (or lack thereof) of healing techniques; the process of individual redress or public litigation; and indications of how the early medieval laws either drew upon native tradition, borrowed regulations from other regions, or innovated when need arose in particular cases. The primary data for this study are drawn from the terse formulations assessing fines for inflicting injury contained in the territorial laws. To flesh out these skeletal legal stipulations, I have incorporated anthropological evidence from gravesites; literary evidence from histories, lawsuits, hagiographies, sagas, and poems; visual evidence from illustrations and sculptures; and the occasional modern parallel from our own contempor-

---

1 This study concentrates on the group of laws referred to by legal scholars as 'barbarian' – that is, the laws of the peoples speaking a Germanic dialect who recorded their territorial laws for central, western, and southern Europe in the sixth to ninth centuries. I have excluded discussions of Irish and Scandinavian laws, except where evidence from these territories may help explicate ambiguities in the barbarian laws. The reasons for these exclusions are specific to the two regions: Ireland recorded its laws in a non-Germanic vernacular, and the regions of Scandinavia committed their laws to writing several centuries after the period under consideration in this analysis.

ary life. This study draws upon the remaining fragments and traces left to us in a wide range of physical and literary evidence to depict a picture of how early medieval society understood the anatomical consequences of wounds to the human body, the varieties of practices available to heal such injuries, and the legal process of obtaining compensation for temporary or permanent incapacitation.

Why are these injury tariffs relevant to us today? Recently a Louisiana State University student, riding her bicycle to school, was hit by a car and lost her left arm. This presented a problem not uncommon to insurance companies and personal injury lawyers: namely, what is the value of the left arm? Is it worth less than the right arm? Is it worth more or less if she is left-handed? Is it worse to lose an arm than a leg? An eye? The sense of smell, with concomitant loss of taste? Furthermore, to what extent should cosmetic damage be valued? What is the value of any particular body part in both physiological and psychological terms? How does an injury affect the ability of the wounded to provide for the family?

Such problems are directly addressed within the Germanic personal injury tariffs, which are the focus of this study. But the investigation extends to detailed examination of the rulings on assault elsewhere in the laws. These examinations raise many other issues which we continue to struggle with today. For example:

- To what extent should damages be awarded according to the profession of the victim?
- Should all rapes require equal restitution? What if the woman is pregnant? Married? Underage?
- What is lost when oral transmission is converted to writing? To what extent does inherited wisdom continue to be transmitted from master to apprentice?

These questions – individual, personal, physiological, and societal – plagued our ancestors, and continue to plague us today. These are among the questions this study addresses.

Although the specific cases raised in this investigation are contained within narrow geographical and chronological parameters, they present wide-ranging implications. First, I would like to think that this examination will help lay to rest the use of the adjective 'medieval' often employed in modern prose to represent 'uninformed.' The following chapters demonstrate that the Germanic peoples possessed knowledge of functional anatomy far beyond the average perceptions of my own contemporaries.

The student discussed above was strapped to a gurney which was immediately rolled into an ambulance and thence to an emergency ward, where the injury was operated on by white-coated professionals using expensive technical equipment. Had she incurred a similar injury in early medieval Europe, the healing process would have involved a communal endeavour, taking place with the assistance of family, friends, and neighbours. Early medieval communities had a much greater understanding of the immediacy of wounds and the requirements for cure than we possess in this era of medical specialization. Today, healing is usually relegated to designated doctors or surgeons, although there has been a recent resurgence in home care for medical needs such as birthing, hospice, or even preparation for burial.[2] The Germanic territories provide a model for such communal health practices, as they directly involved family, doctors and priests.

Second, and closely allied to the first consideration, is the fact that the knowledge of anatomy demonstrated by the 'barbarian' laws is considerably more extensive than it has previously received credit for. Before undertaking this study, I had no understanding of the anatomical structure of the skull, or what 'water on the knee' actually was. The following chapters demonstrate that legislators in the early Middle Ages show an awareness of how the body functions far beyond what is generally assumed for that period.

Scholarly Context of the Current Study

Recent years have seen an explosion of monographs examining the relationship of attitudes towards the human body in a range of fields of contemporary societal study (for example, Turner, *The Body and Society*; Hyde, *Bodies of Law*). This focus on the body has spread to early medieval studies (as in the collection of essays edited by Withers and Wilcox, *Naked Before God*; Williams, *Death and Memory in Early Medieval Britain*). In general, investigations of the understanding of the body in the Middle Ages have concentrated on medical knowledge (see Bonser, *The Medical Background of Anglo-Saxon England*; McKinney, *Early Medieval*

---

2 Recent scholarly studies have addressed attitudes towards death and caring for the dying. For comparative surveys, see Ariès, *Western Attitudes toward Death*, and *The Hour of our Death*. For detailed analyses focused on a particular period in the history of the United States see Faust, *A Riddle of Death*, and *This Republic of Suffering*. More directly pertinent to the period under study in this monograph is Williams, *Death and Memory in Early Medieval Britain*.

Medicine; more recently, Glaze, *The Perforated Wall*).³ The evidence provided by legal treatises has been either overlooked or summarily addressed. An exception to this generalization is provided by the works of Annette Niederhellmann, who carefully examines the medical nomenclature used in the laws, but does not expand her investigations beyond legal texts.⁴

Previous scholarly works concentrating on the laws themselves can be divided into five major categories. The first approach presents comparative studies of all facets of the laws (such as the classic, comparative works of Grimm, *Deutsche Rechtsalterthümer*, and Brunner, *Deutsche Rechtsgeschichte*; more recently Drew, *Law and Society in Early Medieval Europe*; and Lupoi, *Alle radici del mondo giuridico europeo*). Recent scholarly research has addressed anthropological approaches to legal procedure and dispute resolution (notably Falk Moore, *Law as Process* and Roberts, *Order and Dispute*; this study has been taken up by medievalists with a more narrow focus (see Davies and Fouracre's collection of essays, *The Settlement of Disputes in Early Medieval Europe*; or Brown, *Unjust Seizure*). The third approach examines the laws of individual territories (including Brown's *Unjust Seizures*, concentrating on Bavaria; Wormald, *The Making of English Law*; Costambeys, *Power and Patronage in Early Medieval Italy*). Most recently, attention has turned to genres of law outside the codes themselves (such as Rosenwein, *Negotiating Space*; Rio, *Legal Practice and the Written Word*; Fulk and Jurasinski, *The Old English Canons of Theodore*). Finally, recent years have seen a flurry of publications on those who were previously considered liminal in scholarship on the laws. The ground-breaking work of Christine Fell, *Women in Anglo-Saxon England and the Impact of 1066*, has been followed by excellent (although sometimes contradictory) studies on the position of women in early Germanic legislation by, among others, Marianne Elsakkers, Carole Hough, and Anne Klinck; later in chronological focus, although dealing with many of the same issues is Sara M. Butler, *The Language of Abuse*.

---

3 This list of monographs is summary; the investigation of medical practice in early medieval Europe has produced many excellent studies not included in this list. See, for example, the citations in Pilsworth, 'Could you just sign this for me, John?' n. 4. A good list pertaining specifically to medical studies of the barbarian laws, albeit now somewhat outdated, can be found in 'Der Medizinhisstorische Hintergrund,' and 'Krankheiten,' in Niederhellmann, *Arzt- und Heilkunde*, 39–57.

4 For a good overview of earlier investigations of medical information provided in the individual *Leges*, see 'Forschungsstand' in Niederhellmann, *Arzt- und Heilkunde*, 19–29. One of the many strengths of Niederhellmann's work is her comparative approach towards this data.

Expanding beyond the field of women in law is Hans-Werner Goetz's *Frauen im frühen Mittelalter*. Other studies have concentrated on the legal position of slaves (early on, Nehlsen, *Sklavenrecht zwischen Antike und Mittelalter*; more recently Pelteret, *Slavery in Early Medieval England*; Hammer, *A Large-Scale Slave Society of the Early Middle Ages*; and the collection of essays edited by Frantzen and Moffat, *The Work of Work*).

This monograph merges six approaches – medical and anatomical, legislative, anthropological, territorial, genre-based, and societal. The focus of this study aligns most closely to the genre-based approach, but ranges widely outside its particular parameters. Beginning with the specifics of compensation for personal injury, the discussions expand to consider how evidence from all facets of early medieval society – legal, archaeological, literary and pictorial – allow us to draw a fuller picture of how early medieval Europe understood the workings of the human body. Despite its narrow temporal and geographic focus, this study should provide all scholars interested in the analysis of societal approaches towards the human body with a significant collection and interpretation of data from which to expand their own investigations.

1 Barbarian Laws in Context

As the Roman Empire spread north from the Italian peninsula, it subjugated or affected most of the widely spread Germanic peoples of central Europe, bringing literacy to cultures that had previously transmitted their literary, religious, and legal traditions orally. Because of this, the sixth to ninth centuries saw a flowering of written laws by and for the early Germanic peoples.[1] A salient feature of all these collocations is the table of fines for personal injury, which provide insight into the anatomical and physiological knowledge of early Germanic peoples. Despite the fact that literacy increasingly replaced oral transmission for the preservation of legal mores, we have few written texts other than the laws from these territories in the early medieval period, and dismayingly few which deal specifically with anatomy, physiology, or the economic ramifications of physical incapacitation. For this reason, these tables of fines provide our best starting point to examine not only the physiological knowledge displayed by the laws, but also to address the practices of healing and the legal processes for resolving conflict.

In general, these laws should not and cannot be seen merely as a repository of ancient Germanic legal traditions. For many centuries, the Germanic

---

1 Many excellent recent monographs and articles address the development of the Germanic territories and their laws in this period of emergence. I cite only a few examples, as a complete bibliography would fill the pages of this book. For historical surveys of the development of the Germanic kingdoms and the notion of ethnicity, see Innes, *Introduction to Early Medieval Western Europe, 300–900*; Geary, *Before France and Germany*, and *The Myth of Nations*; and Lupoi, *Origins of European Legal Order*. For surveys of the early history of barbarian laws, see Bloch, *La Société Féodale*, 173–84; Drew, *Law and Society in Early Medieval Europe*; and most recently, Wormald, 'The *Leges Barbarorum*.'

peoples had been living under Roman rule, which meant Roman law. When the barbarian peoples came to write their own laws, all except the Anglo-Saxons across the Channel used the Latin language; furthermore, they assessed fines according to the Roman monetary system. Conversely, for example, in Early Irish laws compensation for injury is regulated in *cumal*s, an earlier designation for slave girl. This term came simply to mean a financial amount which could be substituted for by, among other property items, various types of bovine, including bull, year-old heifer, or a cow after having given milk – that is, old enough to have produced offspring.[2] Although the Irish laws specifically designate repayment in goods rather than coin, commutation from the monetary fine stipulated in Roman *solidi* – a *solidus* being a coin containing 4.48 grams of pure gold[3] – to tangible property was also possible in the Germanic territories.[4] The legal model was Roman, but the implementation was local.

The process of writing itself demonstrates Roman influence in the local Germanic communities. Although many early medieval European cultures had experimented with writing systems such as Germanic runes or Celtic ogham, the Latinate practice of recording words in ink on parchment or papyrus came to be the predominant method for preserving legal practice. Recording scribes were trained in Latin, and most probably were familiar with Roman law – some of them may even have been Roman.[5] However, these laws were designed to govern Germanic peoples.[6] The designation 'Germanic' is a linguistic appellation: these peoples separating themselves from the dominance of the Roman Empire spoke natively either a western or eastern dialect of the linguistic category reconstructed by scholars as Proto-Germanic.[7] The Latin literary convention in which

---

2 Binchy, *Críth Gablach*, 81–2.
3 Bloch, *Esquisse d'une Histoire Monétaire de l'Europe*, 12, within an overview of the early medieval monetary system in western Europe discussed on pages 11–24. For Charlemagne's reorganization, in which one pound of silver equalled one *solidus*, see Becher, *Charlemagne*, 112.
4 See Table 2.1.
5 Wormald, '*Lex Scripta* and *Verbum Regis*.'
6 Two territories, Visigothic Spain and Burgundy, establish separate codes (*Lex Romana*) for governing the Romans living in their lands. These are not aimed at the Germanic peoples, and do not include personal injury tariffs. For both these reasons, they are excluded from this study.
7 The designation of 'Germanic' applies to all dialects of Proto-Indo-European that underwent the consonant shift known as 'Grimm's Law.' See Fruscione, 'Eine philologische Schlussbemerkung.'

most recorded their laws was at best a second, if not a foreign, language to those for whom the laws were set. (An analogy is provided by those Roman Catholic religious communities which continue to say mass in Latin, no longer the native language of any of their congregants.) Despite the influence of the Latin language, the barbarian laws exhibit a distinctly Germanic remnant of earlier legislation in their personal injury tariffs.

These laws are not simply copied from Roman models. Written codifications of barbarian law often demonstrate a sense of territorial self-identity, and sometimes the influence of contemporary political relationships with other Germanic peoples. Furthermore, a strong central authority – king or overlord – could leave his mark on a text. (The copy of *Lex Salica* in Manuscript San Gall 731 contains a miniature of a crowned lawmaker;[8] the *Forum Iudicum* of Visigothic Spain either labels a clause *antiqua*, 'ancient,' or heads it with the name of the lawgiver to whom it is attributed.) These territorial laws are thus compilations, neither directly inherited nor directly mimicked codes.[9]

One common thread unites them, however, distinguishing them significantly from their Roman predecessors. Roman law was what we might term 'top-down' – that is, the fine for any crime or tort was paid to the ruling authority. The Germanic personal injury tariffs, in contradiction, require that the primary payment for personal injury be rendered to the victim and the family. Legally, injury was no longer a governmental, but a personal affront, and compensation was accordingly assigned directly to the kin-group, although an additional fine payable to the common coffer could be assessed as a penalty for disturbance of the peace to offset the costs of the trial. Furthermore, punitive damages for insult to honour were often added to the compensatory damages due for the assault, thus requiring extra recompense for the affront of visible damage as a surcharge to the fine for the injury itself. These legal peculiarities of the Germanic laws allow us a unique insight into the private and professional relationships of those living in the Germanic territories.[10]

---

8 http://www.e-codices.unifr.ch/en/list/one/csg/0731.
9 For overviews, see Wormald, '*Lex Scripta* and *Verbum Regis*,' and 'The *Leges Barbarorum*.'
10 An overview of the Roman system can be found in Harries, 'Violence, Victims, and the Legal Tradition in Late Antiquity.' For the comparison to Germanic practice see discussion in Wormald, 'The *Leges Barbarorum*,' 28–32.

Ethnogenesis in Early Medieval Europe[11]

Affiliation to a people or a place is a shifting and amorphous concept; it is not primarily biological, but is deeply affected by territorial and political alliances. Prominent examples are provided in Anglo-Saxon England by the last non-Christian king of Kent, the father of the lawgiver Æthelberht, who bore the Frankish name Eormenric; or the first known Anglo-Saxon poet Cædmon, who composed in Old English despite his Welsh name; or the Scandinavian Maccus who fought on the Anglo-Saxon side at the battle of Maldon.[12] Unfortunately, our scanty historical records provide no further elucidation for any of these anomalies.

The patterns of my own life furnish a better-documented, albeit contemporary, example, demonstrating the range of complexity that may determine ethnicity. I could serve genealogically as a prototypical WASP – White Anglo-Saxon Protestant – although my father's family claims to come from Ireland. A DNA analysis would place my bloodline securely within Germanic and subsequently English origins. This contradicts my paternal claim to an Irish background. Unfortunately, what constitutes homeland is often defined by the current inhabitant: my father's ancestors were part of the English settlement in Ulster, the political fallout from which continues to the present day. I was born in the Federal Republic of Germany, a happenstance which still allows me to claim German citizenship. My childhood was spent between Germany and Washington, DC; the peripatetic nature of this youth led me to consider myself 'from' Massachusetts, the home of my grandparents, despite the fact that I only spent vacations with them as a child. My claim to New England heritage was bolstered when I spent my undergraduate and graduate years in or near Boston. But now that I teach at Louisiana State University, all my legal documents indicate that I am subject to the laws of the State of Louisiana. When I travel, I return to Baton Rouge: this must signify that I am now 'from' Louisiana. When I stand in line to vote, my fellow Louisianians consist of various biological admixtures of

---

11 Patrick J. Geary has provided several important studies on the process of Germanic self-identification: 'Ethnic Identity as a Situational Construct in the Early Middle Ages'; *Before France and Germany*; *The Myth of Nations*. Other important recent investigations include Goetz, Jarnut and Pohl, *Regna and Gentes*; and the series on Germanic ethnogenesis published by Boydell, for which a representative example is Hines, *The Anglo-Saxons from the Migration Period to the Eighth Century*. See also Fruscione, 'Zur Rolle von Ethnologie.'

12 For the second two examples, I am indebted to an anonymous reviewer of this manuscript.

Cajun, Creole, Houma, French, or Spanish, but also English, German, Russian, Vietnamese, and many others. At the time of this writing, the governor of Louisiana comes from an Indian background.

This brief autobiography provides an apposite metaphor for the changing boundaries and allegiances that characterized western Europe as the Roman Empire gradually lost hegemony and power in the second to fourth centuries CE. New confederations rose to combat Romans or fellow barbarians as a result of competition to annex abandoned or weakened territories. Some of these coalitions retained ancient names, some took regional appellations, and some were known by designations fashioned by the Romans. Shakespeare's query 'What's in a name?' is appropriate indeed – the term 'Germania,' first popularized by the Roman historian Tacitus, was never used by the Germanic tribes as a self-determination. Neither was 'barbarian,' which originally just meant a non-Greek speaker whose speech sounded like a continuous *bar-bar-bar*.[13] This designation eventually came to refer primarily to the central and northern European peoples with their strange Germanic tongues, although many of the new alliances incorporated Celts and Slavs.[14] Nor can Romans be counted out of this mixture: barbarians often served in the Roman military, and Romans conversely acted as administrators for barbarian rulers. Finally, intermarriage between Frank, Lombard, Burgundian, Slav, Celt, or Roman also changed the face of personal affiliation. No longer was race the determining factor, but the more complicated notion of ethnicity, dependent on place and politics. The Alamanni seem to have been particularly cognizant of this development, as their name simply means 'all men.'

Despite the established scope of Roman legislation, individual Germanic cultures developed their own communal identities and social expectations. One of the most important monuments of barbarian independence from Rome was the establishment of their own regional laws. (Semi-)autonomously, the Burgundians, Merovingians, Visigoths, Kentish folk, and Lombards drew up written texts under which the peoples in their territories were to be governed. As the Merovingian and later Carolingian Franks

---

13 However, in one passage, *Lex Salica* equates the legal position of 'free Frank' and 'barbarian who lives by Salic Law' (ingenuum Francum aut barbarum, qui lege Salica vivit). See discussion in Wormald, '*Leges Barbarorum*,' 31.

14 Differing definitions of 'barbarian' are used by historians. Although some scholars include the Celts and the Scandinavians, legal historians tend to limit the term to those peoples of Germanic origin living in western and central Europe and, later, in Britain. Throughout this study, I employ this latter definition.

gained in power, they imposed regional laws on Ripuarian Francia, Alamannia, Bavaria, Saxony, Frisia, Thuringia, and Chamavan Francia, collocations that drew upon Roman, Frankish, and local legal custom. The great seventh-century scholar Isidore of Seville delineates thus the difference between old and new:

> *Etymologiae* V.iii. All jurisprudence consists of laws and customs. A law is a written statute. A custom is usage tested by age, or unwritten law, for law (*lex*, gen. *legis*) is named from reading (*legere*), because it is written. But custom (*mos*) is a longstanding usage drawn likewise from 'moral habits' (*mores*, the plural of *mos*). 'Customary law' (*consuetudo*) is a certain system of justice established by moral habits, which is taken as law when a law is lacking; nor does it matter whether it exists in writing or reasoning, since reason also validates law.[15]

With the power of customary law in mind, this study concentrates on the schedules of personal injury tariffs: systems of monetary compensation designed as an alternative to bloodfeud.[16] This characteristic distinguishes the Germanic laws from imperial legal codes: no Roman laws after the archaic Twelve Tables (for which we have only fragmentary remains) provide such tariffs. In these personal injury clauses, then, we must consider the possibility of customary law, which may have been in effect before the arrival of literacy. Non-literate societies obviously do not lack legal resources to regulate communal behaviour; the precedents are retained in legal memory (Isidore's *mos*) rather than written records (Isidore's *lex*).[17] Several early Germanic peoples had a functionary known as the 'lawspeaker,' whose job it was to accurately transmit orally preserved law.[18] Certain parts of the barbarian laws could thus considerably predate their commission to writing.

There is no better place in barbarian law than the schedules of compensation for injury to look for what Isidore termed 'customary law' – new in their written instantiations but conceivably old in actual practice. We must also, however, consider the possibility that these tariffs include regional

---

15 Isidore, *The Etymologies of Isidore of Seville*, ed. Barney et al., 118.
16 These tariffs do not necessarily replace bloodfeud, which continues to exist throughout the European Middle Ages. See, for example, Brown, *Unjust Seizure*, 30–72; Hyams, *Rancor and Reconciliation in Medieval England*; Fletcher, *Bloodfeud*.
17 For cross-cultural discussion, see Falk-Moore, *Law as Process*.
18 See Oliver, *The Beginnings of English Law*, 34.

innovation. No two schedules demonstrate complete agreement, leading Patrick Wormald to suggest that these tariff structures may have served the barbarian regions as markers of individual identity.[19] One facet of this monograph is to examine what comparative analysis of the injury schedules can tell us about the intermixture of political influence and regional self-characterization in the various kingdoms and dukedoms of early medieval western Europe.

Parameters of the Data

The first question we must address is: who were the 'Germanic' peoples, and when did they commit their laws to writing?[20]

- The earliest laws were set in Salic Francia sometime between 507 and 511; they are followed closely by the compilation established in Burgundy in 517.
- The seventh century saw (in approximate order) laws established in Kent (c. 600), Alamannia (beginning of the seventh century), Lombardy (643), Ripuarian Francia (c. 623, as an extension and emendation of Salic law), and Visigothic Spain (654).
- Added to these in the eighth century were laws for the territories of Bavaria (c. 745) and Saxony (c. 785), both heavily influenced by Francia.
- The laws of Frisia (785 x 803) straddle the eighth to ninth centuries.
- Early in the ninth century, Frankish overlords also oversaw the compilations of laws for Thuringia (802 x 803)) and the Chamavan region of Francia (c. 813; this territory had almost surely previously operated under Salic law). The final efflorescence of personal injury tariffs appears in the later ninth-century laws of Wessex, promulgated under King Alfred the Great (890 x 901).

---

19 See Wormald, 'Leges Barbarorum,' 41.
20 The earliest code recorded in a Germanic territory was that of the Visigothic king Euric (466–84), which survives only in a palimpsest. This law, however, is heavily Romanized and contains no personal injury clauses; it is thus irrelevant to this study. (See Wormald, 'Leges Barbarorum,' 26–7.)

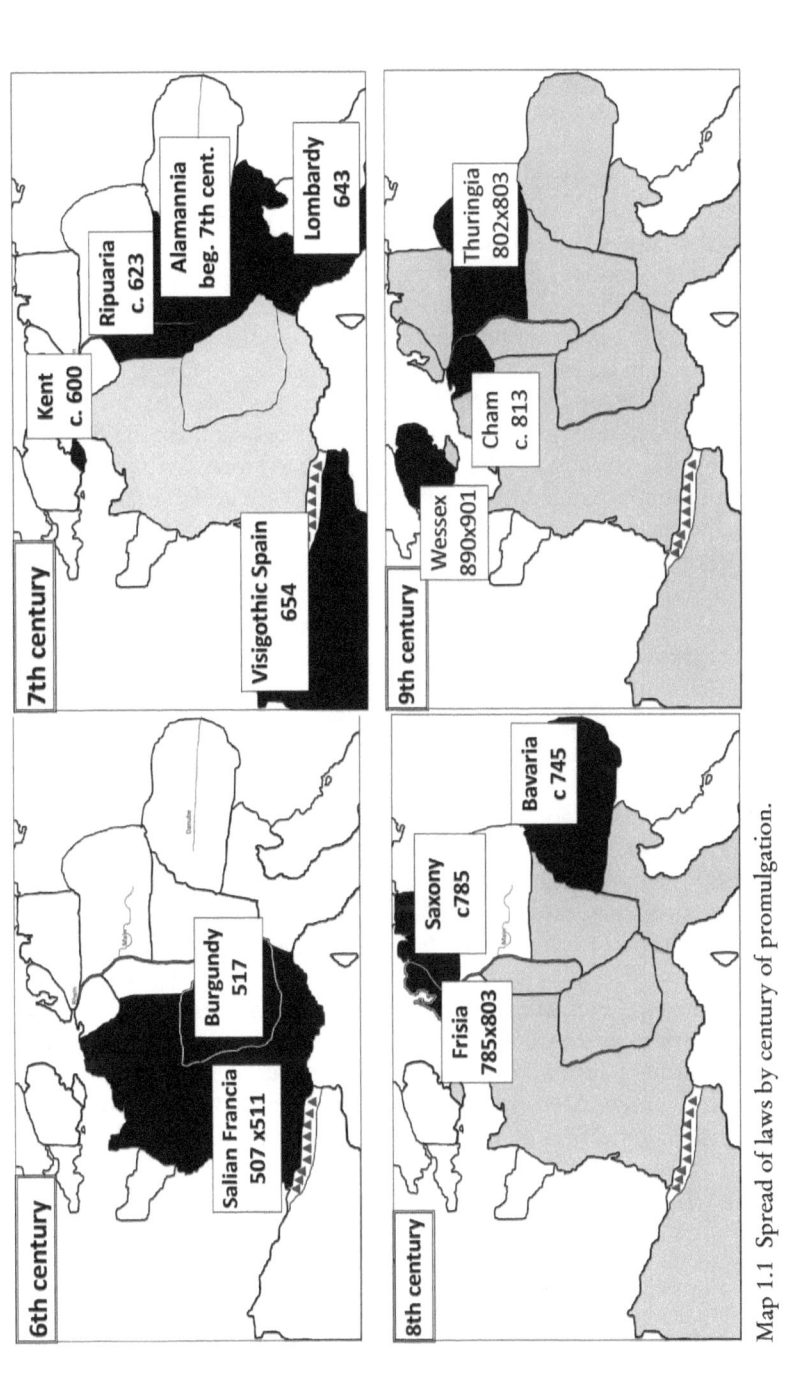

Map 1.1 Spread of laws by century of promulgation.

The compendium of Map 1.1 illustrates that the locus of spread originated in the eastern and southern territories of Salic Francia and Burgundy, expanded first across the south and then proceeded in a generally northeast direction. Another possible way of looking at this is that the earliest laws were set in territories closer to the legal centre of the old Roman government, demonstrating a tradition of written legislation, and then gradually spread to more distant regions. These maps provide a visual image of this percolation according to the century of promulgation. Crucially, throughout this study the maps do not indicate political or geographical reality at any one point in time – for example, the insular kingdoms of Kent (governed by the laws of Æthelberht)[21] and Wessex (governed by the laws of Alfred the Great) were separated by two and a half centuries, and the latter eventually came to subsume the old territory of the former. The Saxons relocated to the south to aid the Lombards in their territorial expansion, but returned to the north when they refused to be subjected to Lombard laws. Many other examples could be adduced to exemplify the fluctuating boundaries established and reformed by the coalitions established in the early Middle Ages. The maps included in the following chapters – the boundaries on which provide the basis for illustrating various data throughout this study – are meant to serve as only a schematic, showing approximate geographical locations at the time of the promulgations of the laws.

Map 1.1 demonstrates not only the chronological spread, but also the geographic proximities that may have led to areal influence. Four factors must be considered in looking for any influence of one code on the rulings contained in another: three of these are general, while the fourth pertains specifically to the personal injury tariffs. The first is simple chronology: one set of laws that postdates another may have been affected by the earlier collocation, but cannot have had any effect upon it. The second is geographic proximity: certain practices could have spread beyond territorial borders and been incorporated into the legal rulings of neighbouring regions. Both these considerations have been visually presented in Map 1.1. The third issue is political dominance. The authority of the Frankish territories over several of the surrounding kingdoms or dukedoms at the time of the codification of their laws surely permitted some legislative control. These political relationships are laid out in the right-hand column in Table 1.1.

---

21 The subsequent laws of Hloþhere and Eadric and those of Wihtred are not included here, as they lack any regulation on personal injury.

Barbarian Laws in Context   17

Table 1.1
Possible influences on composition of personal injury laws

Date of promulgation	Possible textual influence from other barbarian laws	Political influence from other Germanic territories
Salian Francia [507–11]		The first of the Merovingian laws
Burgundy [c. 500]		Recording of earlier rulings that predated Salic Laws
Kent [c. 600]	First of the Anglo-Saxon laws written in Old English	Marriage of King Æthelberht to Merovingian princess leads some scholars to propose Frankish influence.
Ripuarian Francia [c. 623, rev. 770–803]	Some textual influence from Burgundian law.	Early assimilated into the Frankish empire. Law imposed by Merovingian Franks ▲ possible influence from *Lex Salica*.
Alamannia [beginning 7th century]	*Pactus* shows textual influence from *Lex Salica*.	Law imposed by Merovingian Franks ▲ possible influence from *Lex Salica*.
Lombardy [643]		
Bavaria [c. 745] (or perhaps closer to date for Alamannia)	Textual echoes from Lombard *Edictus Rothari*; *Lex Salica*; *Lex Alamannorum*.	Law imposed by Franks ▲ possible influence from *Lex Salica*.
Saxony [c. 785]		Law imposed by Franks ▲ possible influence from *Lex Salica*.
Frisia [785–803]	Textual echoes from *Lex Alamannorum*.	Law imposed by Franks ▲ possible influence from *Lex Salica*.
Thuringia [802/3]		Law imposed by Franks ▲ possible influence from *Lex Salica*.
Chamavan Francia [c. 813]	Textual echoes from *Lex Ribuaria*.	Law imposed by Franks ▲ possible influence from *Lex Salica*.
Wessex [890 x 901]	Alfred states in prologue that he consulted laws of Æthelberht.	

18   The Body Legal in Barbarian Law

All three of these factors could be investigated for influence on the laws as a whole. This study, however, concentrates on the limited sections of the codes containing the personal injury tariffs. Nonetheless, we must also take into account other portions of the complete texts which seem to imply a cross-territorial model; that is, two codes which demonstrate similarities outside the schedules of personal injuries may equally share rulings within these tariffs. The indications of cross-territorial textual influence, as postulated by the respective editors of the laws in the Monumenta Germaniae Historica series, are charted in the right-hand column of Table 1.1.[22] We must, however, always be cautious in assuming that the later of two similar rulings copies the earlier: such echoes might also stem from a common source, perhaps even one rooted in the Roman territorial laws to which so many Germanic peoples had been subject for many centuries.

Linguistic clues provide further crucial data as to possible areal or inherited influence. Similar phraseology or striking, shared word choices can link two clauses across regions. But this approach presents a particular problem for the barbarian laws, as few are recorded in a Germanic vernacular. Several of the continental Germanic laws were promulgated when the territories were *foederati* – that is, allied states – of the Roman Empire, and thus the legal statutes were preserved in Latin, the imperial language of Rome; this model was later followed by the other continental regions. A salient exception to this is provided by the insular Anglo-Saxons, who recorded their laws in the Old English vernacular. Table 1.2 displays the underlying vernacular of the territories in question, and the language in which their laws were recorded.

The major linguistic break occurs between the territories on the continent, whose laws were written in Latin, and those on the island of Britain, which employed Old English. However, many of the continental statutes incorporated vernacular terminology. In the case of the Salic laws, these native words are deliberately set off from the Latin in the nature of a gloss, preceded by the phrase *mallbergo*, 'per *mallberg*' (the language of juridical terminology). Other continental laws simply insert Germanic terms (often morphologically Latinized) into the text for lack of a precise Latin equivalent, such as the Frisian *granones*, 'mustache.' Furthermore, when Lombardy

---

22 See 'Quellen' in Niederhellmann, *Arzt- und Heilkunde*, 5–18.

Table 1.2
Languages of the laws (colour-keyed to Map 1.2)

Vernacular Branch	Language of Composition			
	Latin	Latin with some vernacular terms	Old English	Greek
West Germanic				
Frankish	Ripuarian Chamavan	Salic Alamann Bavarian		
Anglo-Frisian		Frisian	Kent Wessex	
Other	Saxon Thuringen			
East Germanic	Burgundian Lombard* Visigoth			Lombard

(*Lombard laws employed Germanic terms, but not within the schedule of personal injury tariffs.)

was allied with the Byzantine Empire in the ninth century, the Lombard laws were translated into Greek; this does not represent original composition but translation from Latin (which itself may represent translation from an oral vernacular original). Geographically, the East Germanic vernacular dialects (Burgundian, Lombard, and Visigoth) are all located in the south; the Anglo-Frisian (Kentish, Frisian, West Saxon) in the northwest; while Frankish dialects dominate the centre, as indicated by Map 1.2.

Frisia inhabits a liminal position not demonstrated by Map 1.2. Although the language is linguistically grouped with Old English in an intermediate Anglo-Frisian node, the written practice associates itself with Frisia's continental neighbours, all of whom recorded their laws in Latin. As we will see in the later investigations, this dichotomy is echoed in the structure of the personal injury tariffs, in which the Frisian laws at some times ally themselves with their linguistic relatives in Britain, but at others reflect the norms of other continental regions.

20   The Body Legal in Barbarian Law

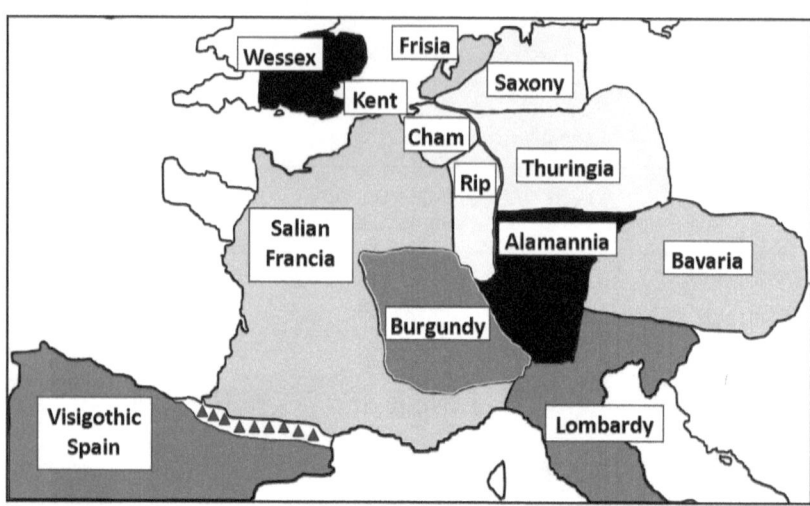

Map 1.2 Languages of the laws.

Linguistic Affiliation	West Germanic	West Germanic	East Germanic	Old English
Language of Composition	Latin	Latin with vernacular terms	Latin	Old English

The Manuscript Evidence[23]

The importance that barbarian laws held for the Germanic peoples and their descendants can be seen by the continuity of the textual transmission. This study draws its data from the earliest existing attestations. No single original source for the issuance of any of these laws remains extant. We have a smattering of manuscripts from the eighth century, and many more from the ninth when the rulers of Carolingian Francia re-examined and sometimes restructured the individual collocations. Many of these codices contain collections of laws from several regions, indicating the ongoing interest in territorial individuality.

The oldest surviving manuscript records the Lombard *Edict of Rothari*, produced in 670 x 680, perhaps in Bobbio. It is now divided into San Gall

---

23 For discussion of the manuscript history of individual *Leges*, see ibid.

730 and folios at the Badisches Landesbibliothek in Karlsruhe, the Zentralbibliothek in Zürich, and the public records office of the canton of Zürich. Only fifty-nine folios remain; apparently thirty-four have been lost, including some containing personal injury clauses. The scribe generally uses Germanic terms within vulgar – if not actually debased – Latin: in §41 he writes *axi* for *ac si*.[24] Another early single text can be found in the manuscript of the Ducal Library at Wolfenbüttel 560, which contains an eighth-century copy of *Lex Alamannorum*.

Far more common than individual legal texts are the many collections containing several continental Germanic legal codes, demonstrating an interest not only in the individual laws, but also in the compendium of legal practice throughout western Europe. One of the earliest extant compilations can be found in St Gall 731, containing *Lex Romana Visgiothorum*, *Lex Salica*, and *Lex Alamannorum* (with the name generally rendered as *Allamani* rather than *Alamanni*). The care lavished on the production of this codex is evident in the many coloured initials and the miniature of a crowned lawgiver (mentioned previously). The St Gall manuscript is uncommon in that it provides the name of the scribe – Wandalgario; the date – October, 793; and the place – Lyon. This information makes St Gall 731 the oldest precisely dated manuscript in the abbey library. Unfortunately, not only was Wandalgario an uncertain speller, as indicated by his uncertainty in the copying of the name of the Alamanni, but his Latin is also rather poor.[25]

A somewhat later collocation is contained in Munich Cod. lat. 4115, dating from the end of the eighth/beginning of the ninth century. This contains *Lex Ribuaria* (best extant copy), *Lex Alamannorum*, *Lex Salica*, *Pactus pro tenore pacis*, and three titles of the *Lex Burgundionum*. In the beginning of *Lex Ribuaria* are corrections by other hands, one from the beginning of the ninth century and one from the late tenth or early eleventh century (which brings this A-recension text into line with the B-recension). These emendations demonstrate that, almost five hundred years later, attention was still being paid to details of the laws.[26]

---

24 http://www.e-codices.unifr.ch/en/list/one/csg/0730; this site also provides a digitized image.
25 http://www.e-codices.unifr.ch/en/list/one/csg/0731; this site also provides a digitized image.
26 For dates, provenances, and discussions of manuscripts, see Sohm, *Lex Ribuaria*, MGH *Leges in Folio* V, ed, Heinrich Brunner (Berlin: 1889), 195–202; for editions see 202–7.

Indeed, the enduring interest in early Germanic legislation is evidenced by the steady stream of anthologies of these legal materials. Only two other manuscript collections are mentioned here, as they provide insight into what emendations may tell us about continuing attention placed on these laws. Note, however, that not all territories inspired the same fascination; a mere two manuscripts include *Lex Saxonum*, and *Lex Thuringorum* appears in only one.[27]

The collection in BNF lat 10753 (suppl. lat. 215) from Blois, tenth century, contains *Lex Romana Visigothorum*, *Lex Burgundionum*, and *Lex Romana Burgundionum*, Emendata to *Lex Salica*, *Lex Ribuaria*, *Lex Alamannorum*, and fragments of *Pactus Alamannorum*. *Lex Alamannorum* and *Lex Ribuaria* both have corrections by the same second hand, once again demonstrating ongoing interest in earlier legislation. The poor grammar of the Ripuarian text is not matched in the Alamann, indicating that the two must have come from different exemplars. We can thus infer that various exemplars, either of collections or of individual codes, were still in circulation at the time this collocation (or perhaps its exemplar) was created.

The codex Modena, Cathedral Chapter Ord. I Nr. 2 is assembled from three independent parts of which only the third, folios 9–216, contains laws. The manuscript was evidently written in 991/2, as folio 211r has a Kalendarium for 991. Poems in the manuscript tell us that the exemplar was a legal text written by Lupus of Ferrières for Graf Eberhard von Friaul (829–32). The collection contains the Prologue of *Lex Baiuariorum*, Prologue I, and the beginning of Prologue II of *Lex Salica*, 'Questions and Answers about Law,' an unordered *Lex Salica emendata*, and *Lex Ribuaria* with an index showing 127 titles/chapters in the usual order but with a different division than the usual 124; *Lex Langobardorum* in a completely unordered form; *Lex Alamannorum* with a unique designation of titles but the usual division of titles and text; and *Lex Baiuariorum* with different title/chapter divisions in index and text, and various capitularies. Folio 31 has a picture of Eddana, the author of *Lex Ribuaria*. The variations in order of clauses from the norm for several of these codes indicates that the interest in these laws was still strong enough – either at the recording of the collection or of its exemplar – to change the process of collocation from simple copying to actual re-organizing. Whether we should attribute this editorial work to the period of the collocation itself or to the time that the exemplar was created is impossible to determine.[28]

---

27 Wormald, '*Lex Scripta* and *Verbum Regis*,' 19.
28 A scholarly study of this manuscript, beginning with the 'Questions and Answers' and then investigating the re-ordering of the clauses might provide insight into this question.

Manuscript collections of Germanic laws continue on the continent at least into the twelfth century (represented by a manuscript from Clermont now lost). Although the continental codices do not include insular laws, early medieval England demonstrates a similar concern with preserving its own legal heritage. In the twelfth century, the collator of the *Textus Roffensis* gathered all known Anglo-Saxon laws into one manuscript. This codex contains the only extant copy of the laws of Æthelberht of Kent and the subsequent rulers of this kingdom, written more than half a millennium after the original composition.[29] (The *Textus Roffensis* also includes the laws of Alfred of Wessex. These are, however, also contained in earlier manuscripts, the first of which, the Parker manuscript, CCCC 173, was copied in Alfred's capital of Winchester less than a century after the setting of his laws.)[30]

The advent of printing did not quell European interest in collections of early law. The first printed edition was produced in Basel in 1530 by Johann Sichard: *Leges Riboariorum Baioariorumque quas vocant a Theoderico rege Francorum latae. Item Alemannorum leges a Lothario rege late. Nunc primum vetustatis ergo recusae*. Also in Basel, twenty-seven years later, Johann Herold published *Originum ac Germanicarum antiquitatum libri, leges videlicet Salicae, Ripuariae, Allemannorum, Boiariorum, Saxonum, etc. nunc Wolvgangi abb. princ. Fuldensis benignitate ex superba illa celeberrimi collegii bibl. in lucem prolati opera Basilii Joh. Herold ac collatione exemplariorum, quae vetustissimis nec non ante septingentos annos depictis characteribus expressa erant, descripti, emendati atque in lucem editi*. Herold used several exemplars but greatly reworked the texts. Many readings are attested in Herold alone; at this distance we cannot determine whether these go back to lost manuscripts. According to Rudolph Sohm, the editor of the *Lex Ribuaria*, most differences seem to be mistakes or corrections by the editor.[31] Nonetheless, Herold's 1557 edition remains critically important, as it provides our sole record of the laws of Frisia – first attested more than 750 years after their date of original composition.

Further collected editions based on various sources were published in Paris, 1573 (Jean du Tillet); Frankfurt, 1613 (Friedrich Lindenbruch); Paris, 1677 (Stephan Balzius); Frankfurt, 1720 (Jo. Georg Eccard); Halle,

---

29 See Oliver, *The Beginnings of English Law*, 34–51, for discussion on why we can accept the Anglo-Norman text as reflecting a (generally but not always) modernized version of its original source.
30 See Wormald, *Making of English Law*, 163–5.
31 Sohm, *Lex Ribuaria*, MGH *Leges in Folio* V (Hahn, 1875–89. Reprinted Kraus, 1965), 203.

1738 (Peter Georg); Venice, 1789 (Paul Canciani); Berlin, 1824 (Ferdinand Walter); Paris, 1828 (J.A.F. Peyré); Paris, 1838 (E.A.Th. Laspeyres). The range of both dates and places of publication of these collected laws provides an impressive tribute to their persistent hold on scholarly interest.[32]

In 1819 Reichfreiherr Karl vom Stein founded the Gesellschaft für ältere deutsche Geschichtskunde, which would subsequently begin the publication of the Monumenta Germaniae Historica (MGH). The first collection in the series *Leges in Folio* was Johann Merkel's 1863 edition of the *Leges Alamannorum, Baiwariorum, Burgundionum, Frisionum*. In 1902 MGH launched a second series of editions, *Leges nationum Germanicarum*, beginning with Karl Zeumer's edition of the *Leges Visigothorum*. Both series contain excellent (if now occasionally outdated) scholarly apparatus; most legal and historical analysis is in Latin. Beginning in 1934 the Germanenrechte series provided less extensively annotated editions supplemented by translations into German.

One of the great achievements of the editors of the Monumenta Germaniae Historica series on Germanic laws was to collate and make sense of the bewildering variety of sources from various periods which remain to us.[33] They are the giants upon whose shoulders all subsequent scholars and translators have stood. For the laws of the Anglo-Saxons, a similar service was provided by Felix Liebermann in his great edition and translation of *Die Gesetze der Angelsachsen*, 3 vol. (Halle: 1897–1916).[34] This monograph would not be possible without the thorough foundation of these older editors, and the studies by more recent scholars who have built on their work.

One final consideration concerning manuscript collections pertinent to the following study is that no legal collocations include medical treatises. Several medieval texts – such as the Anglo-Saxon *Lacnunga* or the texts known as *Bald's Leechbook* – suggest healing techniques for various illnesses which must be cured by a specialist in herbal medication.[35] The

---

32 For discussion of printed editions, see ibid., 202–7.
33 See 'Primary Sources' in the bibliography for references.
34 As this book goes to press, *The Early English Laws Project* has undertaken to publish online new revisions of all the laws contained in Liebermann, as well as others recorded in Anglo-Saxon and Anglo-Norman England. The edition of the laws of Æthelberht, Hlothere, and Eadric, and Wihtred will be based on Oliver, *Beginnings of English Law* (2002). The laws of Alfred will be co-edited by Stephan Jurasinski and myself.
35 *Bald's Leechbook* is contained in the mid-tenth-century manuscript London, BL, Royal 12.D.XVII, although the exemplar may be earlier. The collection of remedies and charms known as Lachunga is part of the manuscript British Museum Harley 585. The

laws, however, consider injuries which can only be cured by surgical intervention. While the medical treatises address infection and cure, the legal stipulations pertain to fractures of the skeletal system and the legal responsibility of the perpetrator for inflicting such damage. The first cases involve disability caused by nature; the second wounds caused by human aggression. The manuscript record indicates that these two approaches towards physical infirmity shared a temporal rhetorical space, but did not overlap in contemporary written codices.

The varying collections of legal texts demonstrate a virtually uninterrupted interest in the origins and development of laws in the early Germanic territories. This fascination has continued to the current day, when scholars mine these texts for social and historical information. The schedules of personal injury tariffs within the earliest instantiations of these laws provide the data from which the following discussions will analyse the anatomical and medical knowledge displayed in early Germanic legal rulings.

---

collocation was probably compiled in the southwest part of England in the late tenth or early eleventh century, thus considerably after the period under consideration in this manuscript. However, many of the materials seem to be of much earlier date. Recently, a group of scholars conducted a series of experiments recreating some recipes from the *Lacnunga*, and concluded that 'very few (or none) of them would have been effective, and people would have died or recovered due almost entirely to the actions of their own immune systems.' (See Brennessel, Drout, and Gravel, 'A Reassessment of the Efficacy of Anglo-Saxon Medicine,' 194.) Their critical approach and subsequent analyses have not, however, been universally accepted.

2 Process and Procedure[1]

In order to provide a context for the specifics of bodily injury presented in the chapters which follow, I will attempt to address the issue of how written rulings on personal injury played out in practice. Four reasons dictate why this question is almost impossible to answer for the early Middle Ages.

(1) Overwhelmingly the extant legal records concern property transactions. This is not surprising, due to the difference in prospectivity between injury and property disagreements. If A cuts off the hand of B, the two parties should – by any one of a variety of possible routes discussed below – come to settlement. Once agreement has been reached, the matter is concluded: there are no repercussions which will affect future generations. Recording the judgment on expensive parchment would seem redundant; and if the decision were committed to papyrus, the fragility of the material would predict its disappearance. The implications of property disputes, by contrast, can prove long-lasting. For example, in a case in Lombard Italy in 801, a man gave his son a gift of land. Upon his entry into a monastery, the son turned that land over to the monastery. His paternal uncle contested this donation in court upon the death of his brother, whose heir he was. In this particular instance, the uncle released his claim upon presentation of the pertinent documents.[2] However, a challenge

---

[1] This chapter represents an expansion of Oliver, 'Protecting the Body in Early Medieval England.' I thank the editors of this volume for their careful reading of the initial version.
[2] Hübner, ed. *Gerichtsurkunden der Fränkischen Zeit, Zweite Abtheilung*, B. 14, #678.

of this nature might well initiate a disagreement that could last for years or even through generations, involving repeated court appearances, claims, and challenges. Written records (whether genuine or forged) could be crucial as supportive evidence in property disputes (as they, in fact, were in the case cited above).

(2) Often related to the first, in an era in which literacy was limited primarily to the clergy, self-interest naturally dictated that a preponderance of court cases preserved in writing involve the church, and specifically cases in which the church comes out as victor:[3] as Chris Wickham puts it: 'There was no incentive to keep cases they lost.'[4] Warren Brown suggests that another reason that extant records of cases involving the church far outnumber secular disputes is due to 'institutional longevity.'[5] Indeed, some early cases are even recorded in the margins or endpages of Bibles: the repository of eternal law shelters the record of temporal transactions. An excellent example is provided by the St Chad, or Bangor, Gospels, which contain one of the earliest examples of the outcome of property dispute in Wales recorded in the margins of a manuscript elsewhere notable for its meticulous and expensively illustrated production.[6]

(3) There simply is not much documentation contemporaneous with the barbarian laws. Most of the extant case records date from later centuries. Those we have from the earlier period are often poorly preserved, and many of them, at least from Francia, demonstrate that not much care was given in the original preparation. Often, the quality of the writing surface – whether parchment or papyrus – is poor, the script is sloppy, and in some cases the linguistic formulation

---

3 Paul Fouracre mentions a 'dispute about land ownership between lay persons [in which] no written evidence was mentioned and the case was decided by an oath taken on the cloak of St Martin' (Fouracre, '"Placita" and the Settlement of Disputes in Later Merovingian Francia,' 36.
4 Wickham, 'Land Disputes and Their Social Framework in Lombard-Carolingian Italy, 700–900,' 105. See also Wormald, 'Charters, Law and the Settlement of Disputes in Anglo-Saxon England,' 151; Ganshof, 'La Preuve dans le Droit Franc,' 90–1. Excellent modern studies on land disputes in specific territories can be found in Brown, *Unjust Seizure*, for Bavaria; Costambeys, *Power and Patronage in Early Medieval Italy*, especially at 111–32.
5 Brown, *Unjust Seizure*, 18.
6 See Online Appendices II.2 for an image of the Bangor Gospels with legal memoranda in the margins.

demonstrates grammatical error.[7] With the exception of property disputes, the value of these documents to litigators was to support the immediate right to compensation; once this had been paid, the written record became worthless, and there was no incentive to preserve it. Such documents were basically intended as memoranda rather than permanent records.[8]

(4) Procedure varied to differing degrees from region to region. Included in this variation is the extent of influence remaining from the memory of Roman legislation.

Although presenting any definitive picture of personal injury proceedings in the barbarian territories is thus an unattainable goal, it is feasible to sketch out the probable parameters, drawing on a broad range of materials roughly temporally and locally equivalent to the royal or ducal laws. The following discussion begins with a speculative reconstruction of legal process,[9] continues to look at the sparse evidence that can be drawn from some actual cases which probably involved assault and likely concomitant injury, and finally presents several possible rulings in two hypothetical personal injury cases. These tentative re-enactments do not in any way claim to present an archaic pan-Germanic system: rather, the procedures followed throughout early medieval non-Scandinavian Europe constituted a blending of local and customary practice with the Roman law familiar for centuries in most of the Germanic territories.

Three further caveats need to be considered regarding the necessarily speculative reconstructions presented in the final section below. First, the

---

7 Bergmann, 'Untersuchungen zu den Gerichtsurkunden der Merowingerzeit,' 53–5. A good challenge for a translator seeking to make sense of grammatical carelessness can be found in Zeumer, *Formulae Merowingici et Karolingi aevi*, 182, #51.

8 I borrow the comparison from Bartlett, *Trial by Fire and Water*, 28.

9 An excellent survey of the process of trial in the Merovingian and Carolingian periods is Schmidt-Weigand, *Rechtspflegedelikte in der fränkischen Zeit*. The eminent Frankish historian F.L. Ganshof also presents a reconstruction of legal process in the Frankish regions in 'La Preuve dans Le Droit Franc.' *The Settlement of Disputes in Early Medieval Europe*, ed. Davies and Fouracre, provides a more recent collection of discussions of procedure in several territories in the early Middle Ages. My analysis draws heavily on all the aforementioned. Further evidence is adduced from the excellent (if somewhat outdated) summations of judgments collected and translated by Hübner: *Gerichtsurkunden der Fränkischen Zeit*, B. 12; and *Gerichtsurkunden aus Italien*. Brittany was an independent territory for most of this period, but the examination of the records of the abbey of Redon by Davies in 'Disputes: Their Conduct and Their Settlement in the Village Communities of Eastern Brittany in the Ninth Century,' adds a helpful discussion of procedure as practiced within a single community in Brittany.

overwhelming evidence for case law in early medieval Europe deals with what we might later term civil rather than criminal proceedings. Although these were differentiated in the *Codex Theodosianus*,[10] the great collection of Roman laws compiled between 313 and 438 CE, scholars disagree as to whether or when this distinction was made in the barbarian territories. Our written records do not indicate any procedural difference between civil, criminal, or property hearings, but we necessarily lack the evidence spoken testimony would have provided. As Patrick Wormald points out, 'It is impossible to demonstrate that any law existed in an oral version exactly corresponding to its written form; oral versions are by definition irrecoverable.'[11] Second, the cases below involve freemen of approximately equal status: I do not consider the ramifications of altercations between Germans and Romans or between litigants of greatly differing rank. Finally, the extant written records all come from higher courts. An initial hearing on a personal injury case would have taken place at a local level, and we have no written records which describe this process. Thus the reconstructions below extrapolate a picture of preliminary hearings from the evidence presented to us by contested cases that went to appeal.[12]

Reconstructing Process

The first issue to be considered is who could bring a case to court. The plaintiff had to be a free man, generally of property and of local standing. As a general rule a woman could not plead for herself in court, although she could have an advocate.[13] Slaves were usually represented by their

---

10   Wood, 'Disputes in Late Fifth- and Sixth-Century Gaul,' 10.
11   Wormald, '*Exempla Romanorum*,' 18.
12   As a rule, the Visigothic laws differ greatly from other continental collections, as they are considerably more severe in their approach towards contempt of court. As the *Forum Iudicum* represents an exception to the general approach towards procedure in the Germanic territories, it is excluded in the following discussion except where rulings may shed light on procedural practice employed elsewhere on the continent.
13   Nelson, 'Dispute Settlement in Carolingian West Francia,' 58. Formula #2a of the Avernenses collection 'is a mandate for a man to act as the representative of a woman in legal matters' (Rio, *Legal Practice and the Written Word*, 80). However, Angers Formula #16 records an instance in which a woman did represent herself; she subsequently refused to accept the oath which was sworn, and was thus judged in default as she did not abide by the court's ruling. (See Rio, trans. *The Formularies of Angers and Marculf*, 61–2.) Rabin, 'Female Advocacy and Royal Protection in Tenth Century England: The Legal Career of Queen Ælfthryth.' *Speculum* 84/2 (April, 2009), 261–88, discusses cases in which the later Anglo-Saxon queen Ælfthryth served as *forespeca* or advocate for some women plaintiffs.

masters. A mandate written in the second half of the eighth century in Tours allowed a litigant to name a substitute as his representative in a public hearing in the event that illness prevented his own attendance – the equivalent of modern power of attorney.[14] Several formulae provide templates by which a litigant can name, under any circumstances, a delegate to represent him. In all cases, the impetus for this transference seems to be to assign the case to a representative of higher standing in the community, presumably in the hope that this assignation to a more respected advocate would increase his chances of success in the litigation.[15]

What constituted the court itself was variable, although there were certain common features. In the Salian territories, the judicial assembly was called the *mallus*: the noun is related to the Old English verb *mælan* (to speak), indicating that the function of the gathering was to speak to the legal facts of the matters brought before it.[16] This convocation (similar to the Icelandic *thing*) was a local meeting of freemen. In the Germanic Francian vernacular they were called *rachimburgi*, or – without phonological assimilation of the nasal stop – *rachinburgi* (roughly, judgment-finders),[17] but they were also referred to as *boni homines* or *boni viri* (good men) in terminology borrowed from Roman law. They were summoned to address a variety of administrative business including, but not limited to, legal hearings. The early kingdom of Kent used the cognate term *mæþel* for *mallus*, which implies a comparable institution. Any crime committed during its sitting incurred a double fine, the same penalty which applied to disruption of church services. Saxon law prohibited open convocations on Sundays unless there was urgent need or pressure from an enemy; rather, 'all should hurry to church to hear God's word.'[18] In Visigothic Spain no litigation could be commenced on Sunday or on holy days 'for religion should take precedence of all legal matters.' (If, however, the suit had already

---

14 Hübner, *Gerichtsurkunden aus Deutschland und Frankreich*, #150. For discussion of the later Anglo-Saxon role of *forespeca*, see Rabin, 'Old English *forespeca* and the Role of the Advocate in Anglo-Saxon Law.'
15 Angers # 48 (Rio, trans., *Formularies*, 90); Angers ## 51, 52 (ibid., 93–4); Marculf I, 21 (ibid., 154–5); Marculf II, 31 (ibid., 213–14).
16 See Online Appendices II.3 for an image from the Utrecht Psalter of a Frankish *mallus*.
17 Discussion on the etymology of this term can be found in von Olberg, 'Soziale Schichtung im Spiegel volksprachiger Wörter der Leges,' 103–4. For the position, see Nehlsen-von Stryk, *Die boni homines des frühen Mittelalters under besonderer Berücksichtigung der frankischen Quellen*.
18 *Lex Sax.* §18.

been brought before the judge, it was allowed to proceed – in apparent contradiction to the earlier proclamation – so that 'he who has been sued should not be placed at any disadvantage on account of holidays.')[19] In ninth-century Brittany, courts did not sit on Sundays. It seems likely that similar stipulations held elsewhere in early Christian Europe as well. Although early Kentish law distinguishes the peace of the *mæþel* from that of the church, the fines for disturbance are the same.[20]

The verbs of judging and settlement used in records of Anglo-Saxon legal procedures are nearly always in the plural, demonstrating there as well as in Francia the communal nature of the judicial process.[21] The number of freemen who made up the court was not fixed: although in the Frankish court records there were as few as seven, a case in later Francia was attested to by fifty-two *boni viri*.[22] In Merovingian times these seem to have been local amateurs, although later the position of court participant may have become at least partly professionalized.[23]

Although it originally meant 'brave,' the term 'Frank' came to mean 'free.' The nature of this freedom was to perform military service and to participate in public justice; if for some reason, such as economic, a man could no longer perform as a warrior, he concomitantly lost his judicial

---

19 *Forum Iud* §II, 1, x, trans. Scott, *Visigothic Code*, s.v.
20 I am not sure that Goebel is not himself falling prey to the nineteenth-century romantics' view when he claims that 'so-called church peace (which probably existed even in pagan times as to temples or places of sacrifice) arises out of the belief that the place is under the guardianship of the gods and the special punishments of offenses committed in relation to holy places are laws in aid of the gods. The moot peace bears some relation to the church peace because the meeting place is supposed originally to have been a place of sacrifice as the place of sacrifice has also become a place of meeting. But the sanction here is imposed primarily for a breach of the actual enclosure within which the moot is held, for the mere cutting of the thread encircling the meeting place is treated with particular severity. This fact relates church protection with moot protection because it is demonstrable that ancient magic inheres in the notion of enclosure.' Goebel, Jr, *Felony and Misdemeanor*, 12–13.
21 Wormald, 'Charters, Law and Settlement of Disputes,' 164.
22 Bergmann, 'Untersuchungen zu den Gerichtsurkunden der Merowingerzeit,' 167–9.
23 See Davies and Fouracre, *Settlement of Disputes*, 269, 272, 273; Nelson, 'Dispute Settlement in Carolingian West Francia,' 47; Oliver, *Beginnings of English Law*, 83–4; Davies, 'Disputes in Ninth-Century Brittany,' 73; Wormald, 'Charters, Law and Settlement of Disputes,' 164. Even outside the Germanic territories, in Ireland the very name of the assembly – *airecht* – indicated the freeman – *aire* – who was the constituent of its makeup: see Sharpe, 'Dispute Settlement in Medieval Ireland,' 186.

identity.[24] The members of the court were expected to be men of property and of good character, and conversant with legal custom. Several manuscript collections of barbarian laws appear to have been well-used; Rosamond McKitterick believes this may stem from actual use during the legal proceedings.[25] *Lex Baiuariorum* §2.19 states that 'the count should have in court with him the one who is assigned to judge there and the book of laws, so that they always deliver a right judgment.' In early Francia, the courts may also have had access to formularies – templates designed for creating written documentation in specific cases. Unfortunately, even fewer manuscript collections of these survive than of the laws themselves, perhaps in part because they were seen as individual records and may not have been as consistently or permanently bound together.[26] Despite the fact that only a small percentage of medieval manuscripts have been preserved down to the present time, it seems highly unlikely that most local courts would have had access to a written version of the laws. Tellingly, Visigothic law actually fines the members of the court who fail to arrive at a verdict in a case which had no written precedent, thereby preventing a litigant from avoiding a fine on the claim that there is no punishment stipulated in writing for his precise delict.[27]

In preliminary hearings, then, those sitting in the court not only called upon knowledge of past legal practice, but also served as impartial witnesses to the hearing. Isidore defines the (equivalent) *prudentium* in his *Etymologiae* V.iv as 'experienced people, and arbitrators of equity, who composed and issued instructions of civil jurisprudence by which they might settle the quarrels and disputes of parties in disagreement.'[28] An example is provided by a case from Lucca in 803, in which the defendant bishop accused his fellow local bishops of unjustly removing him from his position on the accusation that he had abducted the nun Gumperga by night from her convent. The twelve *boni homini* all swore against him and he was excommunicated again for exercising his clerical position while

---

24 See Geary, *Before France and Germany*, 113.
25 McKitterick, 'Some Carolingian Law-Books and Their Function,' includes among these BN lat. 4404, BN lat. 4417, BN lat, 4628, and BN lat. 4788. See discussions in Schmitt-Weigand, *Rechtspflegedelikte*, 112–14, 118–19; Wormald, '*Lex Scripta* and *Verbum Regis*.'
26 Rio, *Legal Practice*, 190.
27 Schmitt-Weigand, *Rechtspflegedelikte*, 119–20. Discussion of the tension between orality and literacy in legal procedure can be found also in Costambeys, *Power and Patronage in Early Medieval Italy*, 121–31.
28 Barney et al., *Etymologies of Isidore*, 118.

under the earlier excommunication.²⁹ A different Lombard case implies that an acceptable court-witness must have property worth 150 *solidi*: the wergild of a Lombard freeman.³⁰ The legal age in Visigothic law for serving as a witness is fourteen;³¹ this may be extrapolated at least to Anglo-Saxon England following the clause in the penitentials of Theodore which allow a man to sell himself into slavery at the same age.³² Apparently, fourteen was considered the age of majority in these regions. Returning to Lombard law, it is possible that the acceptable age for a witness was eighteen; this was the age at which a male could undertake legal transactions.³³

We do not know who determined the composition of any particular group of *boni viri*. Both Visigothic law and a later capitulary of Charlemagne prohibited those convicted of certain crimes to serve as part of the court;³⁴ the Visigoths specifically exclude 'murderers, malefactors, thieves, criminals, poisoners, ravishers, perjurers, or those who are addicted to the practice of sorcery or divination.'³⁵ Taking a more positive approach, between 769 and 775 Carolingian laws enumerated those who could validly function as one of the *boni homines*, although it is not clear whether this list applied at the lowest local levels.³⁶

Frankish laws include a sort of precursor to modern habeas corpus: the *rachimburgi* were expected to come expeditiously to judgment. They could be fined three *solidi* each if they did not reach a ruling by the end of

---

29 Hübner, *Gerichtsurkunden aus Italien*, #677. The number twelve occurs frequently both in the composition of the court and in the number of oath-swearers a litigant is required to bring. Neither of these, however, should be seen as fulfilling the role of the modern jury. A good discussion of the differences is provided by Stanley, 'Anglo-Saxon Trial by Jury.' One clear distinction he draws is that the Germanic gathering 'is not what in German is called an *Urteiljury*, a "jury of trial," but it confirms by oath the truth of the evidence of a party to a case: it is a *Beweisjury*, a "jury of proof"' (118).
30 Wickham, 'Land Disputes and Their Social Framework in Lombard-Carolingian Italy,' 106, 111.
31 *Forum Iud.* §II, 4, 1.
32 MacNeill and Gamer, trans., *Medieval Handbooks of Penance*, 209, 211. For discussion on the dating of these Penitentials, see Charles-Edwards, 'The Penitential of Theodore and the *Iudicia Theodori*,' 141–74; also Frantzen, *The Literature of Penance in Anglo-Saxon England*, 63–9.
33 Drew, *Law and Society in Early Medieval Europe*, #4, 20.
34 Davies, 'Disputes, Their Conduct and Their Settlement in the Village Communities of Eastern Brittany in the Ninth Century,' 309 n. 18; Goebel, *Felony and Misdemeanor*, 79.
35 *Forum Iud.* §II, 4, 1; §II, 4, vi. Translation Scott, *Visigothic Code* s. v.
36 Schmitt-Weigand, *Rechtspflegedelikte*, 26.

the first day, and twelve more if the sun set on an undecided case a second time.[37] Furthermore, if the defendant could prove that they had arrived at a judgment which did not accord with the law (*non secundum legem*), they could be charged fifteen *solidi*. Conversely, if such a charge was proven unfounded, the accuser would have to pay each of the *rachimburgi* fifteen *solidi*.[38] This surely protected the jurors by serving as a formidable deterrent against false charges; even if there were as few as seven *rachimburgi* involved in the judgment, the fine could mount as high as 105 *solidi* – more than a half a freeman's wergild – if the ruling was unanimous.

The court was overseen by a presider, whose function was to ensure that both procedure and penalty concurred with written law.[39] Alamann law stipulates that the judge can only be seated if he is appointed by the local ruler and ratified by the local freemen; he could not have been previously convicted of lying, perjury, or taking bribes.[40] The presider would establish the evidence required and call for it to be produced. This proclamation generally occurred at the preliminary presentation; at the subsequent sitting his job was to supervise any necessary oath-swearing; to pronounce on the procedures for judgment; in the case of a delinquent litigant, to establish the required waiting period; to assure that the verdict was in compliance with the law; and, in the event the verdict was divided (*equalis precepcionis*), to determine the evidence to be brought to the higher court of appeal.[41] The judgment as to guilt and fine was arrived at communally by the participants in the court, and ratified by the presider, what Davies and Fouracre call 'collective judgement in an atmosphere of public witness.'[42]

The presider (except, apparently, for local cases in Lombard Italy) could not be a priest, although churchmen could serve in the legal affairs

---

37 Ibid., 10–11. His discussion on Frankish jurors is based on *Pactus Legis Salicae* §57. For comparison to Lombard law, see p. 108.
38 Ibid., 13.
39 Bergmann, 'Untersuchungen zu den Gerichtsurkunden der Merowingerzeit,' 24–8, who points out that occasionally more than one hearing could be held simultaneously. In the royal courts of later Merovingian Francia, the presider is called the count of the palace (Fouracre, '"Placita" and the Settlement of Disputes in Later Merovingian Francia,' 24). One instance in Brittany shows the approximately equivalent position of *machtiern* being held by a woman (Davies, 'Disputes, Their Conduct and Their Settlement in the Village Communities of Eastern Brittany in the Ninth Century,' 294).
40 *Lex Ala.* §41.
41 Bergmann, 'Untersuchungen zu den Gerichtsurkunden der Merowingerzeit,' 27–8, 149.
42 Davies and Fouracre, *Settlement of Disputes*, 216.

of lay people.⁴³ Commonly he was the local nobleman (*comes* or *grafio* in Francia, *dux* in Langobardia, often also termed *iudex*, 'judge'), although as time went on more and more cases were heard by a *missus*, 'envoy,' of the king.⁴⁴ The great Carolingian scholar Alcuin assigned as the most important qualities for this position justice and mercy.⁴⁵ Like the *rachimburgii*, the presider was enjoined to bring his cases to quick and just conclusions: Burgundian law chastised, and Lombard fined, the 'failure of a judge to give judgement within three months,'⁴⁶ which must have been particularly annoying had the verdict already been established by the assembled *boni viri*. Various Carolingian decrees warned against either speeding up the hearing or delaying the court in order to enjoy the hunt or other pleasures.⁴⁷

In earliest times, the court met out of doors, often either in a grove or around a hill – the *berg* of the *mallus*, or *mallberg*, from which the name for the Frankish glosses in *Lex Salica* is taken.⁴⁸ The advantage of a raised barrow was that it might serve as a point for proclamation of judgments. In some instances, the barrow might also be associated with the burial of a past champion, adding historical legitimacy to contemporary function.⁴⁹ The assembly in which Wihtred's laws were set took place in Bearsted in 695; as late as 1897 the vicar cited local lore that 'sessions were formerly held on a moated mound, which has tiers of seats above it, near this

---

43 See ibid., 272–3; Fouracre, '"Placita" and the Settlement of Disputes in Later Merovingian Francia,' 32–3; Davies, 'Disputes in Ninth-Century Brittany,' 79; Wickham, 'Land Disputes and Their Social Framework in Lombard-Carolingian Italy,' 105, 110; Oliver, *Beginnings of English Law*, 84–5.
44 For this role, see Schmitt-Weigand, *Rechtspflegedelikte*, 27; Becher, *Charlemagne*, 108–9; Brown, *Unjust Seizure*, 102–23, traces the career of a specific *missus*, Bishop Arn of Salzburg.
45 Schmitt-Weigand, *Rechtspflegedelikte*, 153.
46 Wood, 'Disputes in Late Fifth- and Sixth-Century Gaul,' 10.
47 Schmitt-Weigand, *Rechtspflegedelikte*, 28. Some details for the presider differ in Langobardia; see ibid., 44–51. For example, the half-wergild fee for delay was later raised in Langobardia to a full wergild and loss of position. In regard to penalties for false judgment or delay in Visigothic law, see ibid., 70–6.
48 That similar geographical features were sought in Anglo-Saxon England can be demonstrated by the name Mettle Hill, which is an exact calque/parallel formation to the Salic *mall-berg*. For discussion of the geographic features of Anglo-Saxon assembly places, see Pantos, 'The Location and Form of Anglo-Saxon Assembly Places'; also Pantos, '"In medle oððe an þinge."'
49 See discussion in Howard Williams, *Death and Memory in Early Medieval Britain*, 207–11.

village.'⁵⁰ Later, it seems that some of these meetings may have been held in churches: several extant cases call for the defendant to appear with his witnesses before the altar, although it is also possible that an altar was especially erected outdoors in the court precincts. In 809 Charlemagne ruled that the place of judgment should be covered with a roof, so it could be used in all weathers. In the seventh-century Anglo-Saxon laws of Hlothere and Eadric, the king seems to have had a permanent hall in London in which cases could be heard.⁵¹

In Bavarian law the court was set to meet every month or more often if necessary, but this varied according to territory: a forty-two day continuance period in other territories may imply that the regular meeting took place every six weeks.

The *mund*, or protection, of the court was taken very seriously. As stated above, in Anglo-Saxon England any offence committed in the *mæþel* required twice the penalty normally stipulated. At a case in later Francia, the defendant was fined fifteen *solidi* for contempt of procedure: ten of these were given to the plaintiff *in exfaida*, roughly, 'to avoid a feud because his word had been wrongly challenged.'⁵² The remaining five went to the king, as the dispute cited took place in the king's court. At a lower level the fine would have been paid to the *comes*.

More personal protection was also provided: in Burgundian law a litigant must pay a triple fine for each blow struck at a member of the court. The normal penalty for a blow was one *solidus*, but for striking a member of the court, a disgruntled litigant had to pay three. This ruling was clearly inserted to prevent altercations arising when the fine was imposed.⁵³ A Carolingian decree in 820 required that a litigant who had been ordered from the court but refused to go had to pay the king's ban of sixty *solidi* for disruption of the peace.⁵⁴ Like the *boni homines*, the presider was individually protected from physical assault: a capitulary of 803 declared that a claimant who approached the presider with balled fist had to be reported to the king, and was also required to pay a tenfold fine of 600 *solidi* (three times a freeman's wergild) for disturbing the peace.

At his first appearance in court, the plaintiff announced his intention to bring the case. Presumably a non-contested case could be settled at this

---

50 Bright, *Chapters in Early English Church History*, 427 n. 3.
51 Oliver, *Beginnings of English Law*, 141–4.
52 Fouracre, '"Placita" and the Settlement of Disputes in Later Merovingian Francia,' 34.
53 Schmitt-Weigand, *Rechtspflegedelikte*, 105.
54 Ibid.

point, although it seems very possible that the parties to such a dispute would previously have reached a private arrangement unless there was disagreement as to the amount of restitution owed.

In certain cases of physical assault, the transitory nature of the evidence would require a speedy hearing. The laws of Alamannia and Salian Francia both differentiate between blows which cause blood to flow and those which do not, the latter presumably leaving only an evidentiary mark of contusion. Kent goes so far as to distinguish between bruises which can be hidden by clothing and those which cannot.[55] These stipulations imply that the first appearance must take place shortly after the incident, since the visible confirmation of assault (such as bruises) would fade over time.[56]

As a rule, an adjournment would be granted while necessary evidence was gathered – in the case of personal injury claims, this proof would rely on witnesses rather than written documents. In some territories this respite may have served a secondary purpose: it was still possible that the disputing parties could reach an out-of-court settlement in the intervening period. (This was not universally true: a case from seventh-century Francia implies that in that jurisdiction once a procedure was set in motion it had to be carried through.[57] The Visigothic *Forum Iudicum* includes a similar stipulation.[58] Presumably the public nature of the proceeding eliminated the possibility of bloodfeud erupting later.) In some regions the process often involved two such postponements if the evidence produced in the second hearing was deemed insufficient or if the verdict of the first finding was divided.[59] At the first appearance, then, the court would establish who would hear the trial, the means of proof, and the period within which the evidence must be brought to a second hearing.[60]

A preliminary hearing in a case of self-defence from Sens around 770 provides a good depiction of this process:

---

55 Kent §61.3; *Lex Ala* §57.1; 4; *Lex Sal* §23.1. *Liber Const* V. I. §§1–3 contain rulings concerning those who strike another with a whip, stick, fist, or kick, which could cause any degree of damage, but certainly does not preclude bruising. For this insight, see Richards, 'The Body as Text in Early Anglo-Saxon Law,' 103.
56 See discussion in Richards, 'The Body as Text in Early Anglo-Saxon Law,' 97–115.
57 See Fouracre, '"Placita" and the Settlement of Disputes in Later Merovingian Francia,' 34–5.
58 *Forum Iud* §II, 2, v.
59 See Fouracre, '"Placita" and the Settlement of Disputes in Later Merovingian Francia,' 35; Wickham, 'Land Disputes and Their Social Framework in Lombard-Carolingian Italy,' 106; Sharpe, 'Dispute Settlement in Medieval Ireland,' 181; Bergmann, 'Untersuchungen zu den Gerichtsurkunden der Merowingerzeit,' 14.
60 Ganshof, 'La Preuve dans le Droit Franc,' 75.

Notice: In what manner and before whom present a certain man named X coming in district X, in the place which is called X, in the public *mallus* before the *comes* X himself or other good men, who have signed below, with his hand placed on the sacred altar, thus the sworn one said: 'Here I swear by this sacred place and God the highest and his sacred power: a certain man named X, stirred with rage, came upon me with his arms and struck me blows; and thus God allowed me forthrightly, that I myself with my arms gave him such blows that he died; and what I did I did for my protection. And today I guarantee myself for exculpation and expiation within 42 nights, as is the law and our custom, with three landholders (*aloarii*) and 12 oath-swearers (*conlaudantes*).' They swore and directed their tongues according to the laws.[61]

Typical of medieval formulae, the past tense shows that this was based on an actual case but the ruling has been generalized by the substitution of X for all names. In the event of a similar case arising later, the appropriate names and locations could be inserted. In this instance, the defendant was given forty-two days – six weeks – to muster his evidence. This case demonstrates that self-defence could be used as an argument in court: Visigothic law proclaims that 'it is no crime to resist another, where the violence of the attacking party is manifest ... because it is more proper for a living person to defend himself against an angry man, than to be revenged after his own death.'[62]

In a case from Tours in the middle of the eighth century, an accused killer was given forty days to find the necessary witnesses to support his claim of self-defence.[63] This same terminus, established in Salic law, overwhelmingly appears elsewhere: for example, in the case of a divided verdict, the litigants

---

61 'Noticia, qualiter et quibus presentibus veniens homo alicus nomen ille in pago illo, in loco que dicitur ille, in mallo publico ante ipso comite illo vel aliis bonis hominibus, qui subter firmaverunt, positam manum suam super sacrosancto altario sancto illo, sic iuratus dixit: 'Hic dico per hunc loco sancto et Deo altissimo et virtutis sancto illo: homo alicus nomen ille, ira factus, apud arma sua super me venit et colappus super me misit; et sic mihi Deus directum dedit, ego ipso de arma mea percussi talis colappus ei dedi, per quid ipse mortuus est; et quod feci super me feci. Et ego hodie ipso facio [in] frodanno et ferbatudo infra noctis 42, sicut lex et nostra consuetude est, apud tris aloarius et 12 conlaudantes.' Iuraverunt et de linguas eorum ligibus direxerant.'

The word before *ferbatudo* is damaged in the manuscript, but Zeumer, taking this to be a Germanic alliterative formula, restores it as above, with a meaning matching Latin *in pace et in expiatione*. *Aloarius* he takes also as a Latinized Germanic term meaning those who own allodial land. Zeumer, *Formulae Merowingici et Karolingi aevi*, 191–2.

62 *Forum Iud*, VI, 4, vi. Trans. Scott, *Visigothic Code*, s.v.

63 Hübner, *Gerichtsurkunden aus Deutschland und Frankreich*, #68.

have forty days to bring additional evidence. Furthermore, the regulation on payment for homicide in early seventh-century Kent was that the first twenty shillings of the wergild must be paid at the open grave, but the kingroup then had forty days to pay the remaining eighty.[64] The forty-day time period may be biblically inspired. However, as discussed above, some regions designate a variation of forty-two days, which may imply that in those territories the court met every six weeks. Another possible interpretation is that the two-day extension to the usual forty-day terminus allowed for the possibility that the assigned date might fall on a Sunday. For example, the suit from Sens cited above allows a man claiming self-defence in a case of homicide forty-two days to appear at the altar with three witnesses and twelve oath-supporters to plead his case.[65] The Frankish *Edict of Chilperic* states that the adjournment in the case of an accused slave is forty-two days, with a possible additional forty-two in the case of excused absence from the court due to illness or incapacity.[66] Finally, Bavaria may have had a larger number of troublemakers than other territories: its law required the court to meet every month, or more often if necessary. No other Germanic region seems to have held such frequent meetings of the *mallus*.

A date would be appointed for the second hearing, to which the two claimants were remanded to appear with the required evidence. The meeting of the *mallus* seems to have been a lively local event, in spirit probably not unlike a regional market and perhaps even associated with it. The Carolingian poet Theodulf, writing in 798, presents a vivid description of these convocations, including the possibility that litigants might attempt to bribe the presider:

> My assemblies are thronged with great droves of people
> Of every age and sex, all with something to ask –
> Little children, old men, youths, fathers, spinsters, bachelors,
> The old and the young, adults, crones, husbands and wives.
> What more can I say? The commoners press upon me promises of bribery,
> Thinking gifts a means of getting whatever they want done.[67]

---

64 Oliver, *Beginnings of English Law*, 66–7, 96–7. Other examples of the forty-day terminus can be found in Ganshof, 'La Preuve dans Le Droit Franc,' 72, 75, and Bergmann, 'Untersuchungen zu den Gerichtsurkunden der Merowingerzeit,' 12, 78, 84.
65 Hübner, *Gerichtsurkunden aus Deutschland und Frankreich*, #97.
66 Wood, 'Disputes in Late Fifth- and Sixth-Century Gaul,' 11.
67 Godman, *Poetry of the Carolingian Renaissance*, 163; for dating, 13. On Theodulf, see also Schmitt-Weigand, *Rechtspflegedelikte*, 156–7.

On the appointed day, both accused and accuser – with their respective witnesses – were expected to show up at the court. Failure to do so was finable in Lex Salica, which also describes processes for 'enforcing judgement on recalcitrant witnesses.'[68] Frankish cases included both a terminus of evening and a period of three days within which the defendant had to appear.[69] Formula #12 from Angers depicts the accuser waiting 'at his placitum from morning to evening according to the laws'; the woman whom he has accused of murder by witchcraft does not appear, and thus loses by default.[70] Visigothic law specifies an adjournment of one day for each ten miles a litigant had to travel to reach the court unless he was detained by 'sickness, tempest, inundation, or snow, or by unavoidable trouble of any kind.' In the event that the litigant won his case, the losing party had to pay him one *solidus* for every ten miles he travelled.[71]

If the accuser did not show up, the defendant was declared innocent and the case was dismissed. Burgundian law imposed a fine of six *solidi* for non-attendance, unless the participant was detained by sickness or business. If he did not come by the sixth hour of the day, the case was concluded in his absence. Extrapolating from a case in which the plaintiff was fined court-costs for presenting a losing case, one can speculate that in some instances he would be similarly charged for bringing a case which he does not appear to prosecute further.[72] Conversely, if the defendant failed to appear (the case noted as *notitia solsadia*), he was considered guilty and assessed the appropriate fine for the *lex loci vestri*, 'law of your place,' presumably upholding the verdict of the lower court.[73]

At this second assembly, then, the litigants arrived with the proofs specified in the preliminary hearing. In the earliest recorded cases, in some territories only the accused was allowed to bring witnesses in his defence; as Ganshof indicates, in a sense these trials were all criminal hearings in

---

68 Further explanation of the points addressed in this paragraph can be found in Wood, 'Disputes in Late Fifth- and Sixth-Century Gaul,' 11, 15. See also Hübner, *Gerichtsurkunden aus Deutschland und Frankreich*, #151 and #197.
69 Bergmann, 'Untersuchungen zu den Gerichtsurkunden der Merowingerzeit,' 112.
70 Rio, trans., *Formulae*, 59–60.
71 *Forum Iud.* §II, 1, xvii; §II, 1, 31. Translation Scott, *Visigothic Code*, s.v.
72 Hübner, *Gerichtsurkunden aus Deutschland und Frankreich*, #158.
73 Ibid., #48 and 49. The citation is from the latter, Zeumer, *Formulae Merowingici et Karolingi aevi*, 67. Similar rulings can be found in Hübner, *Gerichtsurkunden aus Deutschland und Frankreich*, #197 and #151.

which the defendant had to clear himself of the accusation.[74] Later in the Merovingian period, the responsibility of bringing witnesses was expanded to the accuser, which put defendant and plaintiff on more equal ground. In Lombard Italy, a litigant would also need to find a guarantor who pledged for the participant's ability to pay any assessed fine.[75]

In a personal injury case (which would be unlikely to involve documentation), the crux of the proof would rest on the witnesses (*cojuratores*), a group which fulfilled two functions. One was to provide testimony if possible. The other was to support the oath (of innocence in the case of the defendant, or of just accusation in the case of the plaintiff).[76] In this regard, they essentially served as character witnesses. Following Katherine Fischer Drew's analysis: 'The principle seems to have been that if these oathtakers, who were known to be men of integrity in the community, were willing to offer oath for the defendant, then the oathtaker must be convinced that the accused was not guilty of the charge, and therefore the community as a whole (represented by the king's official, the judge) should be willing to accept that judgment also.'[77]

The differentiation in the Sens case cited above between the three property-holders and the twelve oath-swearers is curious (and rare, if not unique). Perhaps the former were meant to present testimony and the latter to support the oath: that is, one group presented evidence while the other provided character witness. This hypothesis is, however, pure speculation. Bavaria seems to have included a ritual in which witnesses were sworn in by pulling on their ears.[78] Presumably this gesture was meant as an admonition to remain true to the evidence that they had heard, that they were about to hear, or that they were about to present to a hearing public. Alice Rio discusses a formula in the collection of the seventh-century scribe Marculf which 'took care to stipulate that half of the oath-helpers were to be selected from a pre-established list of possible candidates, severely restricting the choice of the accused in recruiting them, and suggesting an awareness that the procedure could be open to abuse.'[79]

---

74 Ganshoff, 'La Preuve dans Le Droit Franc,' 76.
75 Wickham, 'Land Disputes and Their Social Framework in Lombard-Carolingian Italy,' 109.
76 Ganshof 'La Preuve dans Le Droit Franc,' 78; Nelson, 'Dispute Settlement in Carolingian West Francia.' *Settlement of Disputes*, Davies and Fouracre, eds, 45–64.
77 Drew, *Law and Society*, #4, 7.
78 Brown, *Unjust Seizure*, 86.
79 Rio, *Legal Practice*, 25.

42   The Body Legal in Barbarian Law

Unique to the personal injury hearings would have been the presence of a doctor, whose testimony under oath established the severity of the wound. As Mary Richards points out, in the case of injury the results

> occur with varying degrees of severity. Someone must render an opinion based upon the examination of the witness and then, with an understanding of what long-term effects such an injury carries in their society, the arbitrator hearing the case can award the damages.[80]

Presumably, if the two parties came to a mutual agreement about the extent of the damage, this testimony could be waived.[81]

The witness-group was generally composed of members of the extended family and particularly close friends. Burgundian law required a freeman rebutting an accusation to be supported in his oath by twelve relatives including his wife and children, or father and mother. This core could be augmented by concerned friends and neighbours.[82] The usual number is twelve, or some multiple thereof. Less commonly the plaintiff or defendant could bring eleven *cojuratores*, using himself to make up the dozen.[83] The oath was sworn on a *res sacra*: an altar, relics, or the like.[84] (An edict issued by King Gundobad in 502 allowed the plaintiff to demand trial by combat in case the defendant chose the option of using oaths: perjury seems to have become common despite the obvious danger to the immortal soul of false witness on relics.)[85] Formula #50 from Angers provides us with a rare look into the actual court proceedings. A man accused of murder is remanded to appear in forty days to swear 'with twelve men, thirteen in-

---

80   Richards, 'The Body as Text,' 113.
81   *Pactus Ala.* §1; *Lex Ala.* §§59–61; *Lex Rib.* §68; *Pactus Lex Sal.* §17.4. See discussion in Niederhellmann, *Arzt- und Heilkunde*, 75–6.
82   See Oliver, *Beginnings of English Law*, 75, note e.
83   Ganshof 'La Preuve dans Le Droit Franc,' 77. In the Kentish laws of Wihtred, the number of oath-swearers for a priest or a freeman is only four.
84   Ibid. See also Oliver, *Beginnings of English Law*, 174–6. Marculf I.40 provides a formula for swearing an oath of loyalty to the king; he sends his own relics brought by his *missus*. Rio states: 'The king's insistence that the oaths should be sworn only on these relics could have been due simply to the practical unavailability of relics in some of the places of assembly, but the king's own relics may also have been more prestigious, which could have given the oath an additional symbolic value (he may also have been guarding against oaths being sworn on unsatisfactory relics belonging to doubtful local cults).' Rio, trans., *Formularies*, 175.
85   Wood, 'Disputes in Late Fifth- and Sixth-Century Gaul; Some Problems,' 16. For trial by combat, see Goebel, *Felony and Misdemeanor*, 121–2, n. 203.

cluding himself, neighbours living close by, of similar status to himself ... that he had never consented to the death of the aforementioned, that he had not killed him, and that he had never known or agreed this should be done.' The document goes on to record the oath which he later swore: 'By this sacred place and the divine protection of all the saints who rest here, with respect to the charge that this man A and his brothers B-C have brought against me, namely that I killed their relative, the late F, or ordered to have him killed: I did not kill him, nor did I order that he should be killed, nor was I ever aware of or complicit in his death; and I do not owe anything in this matter save for this unchallengeable oath, which I was made to give by judgment and completed according to the laws.'[86]

Burgundian law allowed as an alternative to oath-swearing the ordeal by hand/cauldron before three witnesses appointed by the judge. Ripuarian law stipulated that if a foreigner 'cannot find co-jurors in the Ripuarian province, then he must clear himself by cauldron or lot.' Lombard law states that ordeal was the only recourse open to the unfree, unless supported by their masters.[87] Later, Salic and also Ripuarian law prescribed ordeal for theft and false witness: in a sense, the accused hand (which stole the goods or raised itself under oath) must prove its own innocence. The ordeal by cauldron required the defendant to plunge his hand into a deep kettle of boiling water in order to retrieve a ring or a rock from the bottom. If the scalded hand healed after a stipulated period of time, the litigant was proven innocent.

Gregory of Tours vividly describes such a case: the proband 'drew back his clothes from his arm and plunged his right hand into the cauldron ... the fire roared up and in the bubbling it was not easy for him to grasp the little ring, but at last he drew it out.'[88] This ordeal seems to favour assiduous manual labourers: the more calloused the hand, the more likely it was to survive the boiling water. Ironically, the ordeal was the only method of exculpation open to serfs, who, by nature of their occupation, were best able to withstand it.[89] In much later medieval times, a defendant would be exempt from torture on account of physical frailty – for example, pregnant women, young children or the aged – but we find no such exemptions from

---

86 Rio, trans., *Formularies*, 91–3. Angers #10 (ibid., 56–7) provides the oath sworn by a man protesting the claim that he was not of free status.
87 *Lex Rib* §31.5, cited in Bartlett, *Trial by Fire and Water*, 32; for Lombard law see ibid., 33.
88 From *De gloria martyrum*, cited in Bartlett, *Trial by Fire and Water*, 4.
89 See Ganshof, 'La Preuve dans Le Droit Franc,' 78–9; Wood, 'Disputes in Late Fifth- and Sixth-Century Gaul,' 16; Gaudemet, 'Les Ordalies au Moyen Age,' 103.

the earlier ordeal.[90] Presumably God would guard the innocent, and the guilty deserved what they got; it also seems likely that a defendant did not advance to the ordeal unless there was probable cause. *Lex Salica* provided a schedule of repayments by which a defendant could redeem his hand; the cost depended on the severity of the offence. A defendant who swore his innocence but was convicted by ordeal had to pay ninefold compensation in the Burgundian judicial system. Most other Germanic territories lack any mention of this ordeal, which implies that it was of Salic Frankish origin.[91] One wonders if even they themselves questioned the efficacy, since it does not appear in later laws imposed by the Merovingians and Carolingians, even in bellicose Saxony, where we might have expected the cauldron ordeal to be included for its deterrent value.

Both *Lex Salica* and *Lex Ribuaria* added to ordeal by hot water the option of ordeal by lot.[92] Although the latter is not described in the various recensions of either of these texts, contemporary Irish law allowed two methods: either the defendant chose blindly between two (or more) lots indicating innocence or guilt, or his lot was cast upon water in a sink-or-swim demonstration of his culpability.[93] Frisian law, the only other Germanic legal text to mention ordeal by lot, presents an interesting precursor to what would later come to be known as Russian roulette:

> §14: [Proof for a man killed in ambush] Two twigs, which are called *tenos*, are cut from a stick; one of them is marked with the sign of the cross, the other is left unchanged; and they are laid on the altar or the relics wrapped in pure wool; and the priest, if he is present, or if the priest is absent, some innocent boy, should take one of the lots from the altar; and in between God is beseeched, that he should indicate by a visible sign, whether those 7, who have sworn considering the killing, have sworn truly. If he takes up that which is marked with the cross, those who have sworn are innocent; if he takes up the

---

90 Langbein, *Torture and the Law of Proof*, 13.
91 See Bartlett, *Trial by Fire and Water*, 6–9.
92 See Ganshof, 'La Preuve dans Le Droit Franc,' 74.
93 Wood, 'Disputes in Late Fifth- and Sixth-Century Gaul,' 19, suggests that the ordeal by water may have its roots in Roman vulgar law and the ordeal by lot in Germanic tradition. Conversely, O'Flanagan, *The Lives of the Lord Chancellors and the Keepers of the Great Seal of Ireland*, 6, indicates that Irish lore associates the ordeal by lot with 2 Kings, 6:5. Among the miracles of Elisha is the account of a man whose borrowed axe falls into the water. As he laments to Elisha, the prophet throws a stick into the water and causes the iron to float. See also discussion in Gaudemet, 'Les Ordalies au Moyen Age,' 102–3.

other, however, then each of the seven has to put in his lot: that is, a twig from a branch, and mark it with his sign, that he, as well as those standing by, can recognize it; and they shall be wrapped in pure wool and laid on the altar or the relics, and the priest, if he is present, but if not, an innocent boy as above, takes each of them individually from the altar and asks him who recognizes if it is his lot. Whoever's lot remains as last, he is forced to pay the compensation for the killing, while the rest, whose lots were picked earlier, are free.'[94]

A Carolingian capitulary of 816 extends the permissible range of ordeal to trial by combat:

If a party suspects the witnesses brought against him, he can put forward other, better, witnesses against them. But if the two groups of witnesses cannot agree, let one man be chosen from each group to fight it out with shields and spears. Whoever loses is a perjurer, and must lose his right hand; but the other witnesses in the same group can redeem [i.e., pay compensation for] their right hands.[95]

In some senses, this is not very far removed from modern judicial practice, in which both parties to a case select the lawyer strongest in legal argumentation. The judgment may depend on the relative rhetorical strength of the legal champions – that is, trained lawyers – involved, rather than on the actual truth of the case. In cases of contested property, Alamannian law requires the two litigants to duel it out on the land in question. The loser forfeits his right to the land, and pays an additional fine of twelve *solidi*.[96]

We find the ordeal used in a case heard in Frankfurt in 794, which concerned a bishop accused of the betrayal of Hartrad. The ruling was that he must call two or three oath-helpers or that the archbishop of the nearest metropolis should clear him. Unable to find any oath-helpers willing to swear on his behalf, he was forced to rely on a man who underwent the ordeal for him. Presumably this was successful, as the bishop was reinstated by Charlemagne.[97]

---

94 Von Richthofen, *Lex Frisionum*, 667–8.
95 Cited in Nelson, 'Dispute Settlement in Carolingian West Francia,' 47.
96 *Lex Ala.* §86.
97 Hübner, *Gerichtsurkunden aus Deutschland und Frankreich*, #133. For trial by cold water and trial by hot iron as instituted by Charlemagne, see Bartlett, *Trial by Fire and Water*, 10–12.

As Gaudemet points out, proof by swearing and proof by ordeal represent two fundamentally different types of exculpation: the former requires verity whereas the latter demands purity.[98] Bartlett adds the observation that the oath itself 'was, in some sense, an ordeal, but one which relied upon God's eventual rather than his immediate judgement.'[99] A scalded hand provides immediate evidence of guilt, but a perjured soul will find its penalty in the afterlife. However, Nelson's study of 257 ninth-century judgments indicates that in later Francia, oath-helping was rare and the ordeal almost non-existent, an element of juridical theory rather than actual practice.[100] Certainly the possibility of losing your right hand along with the case must have served as a deterrent for more than one potential witness.

In seventh-century Lombardy, on the contrary, oath-helping and judicial duel were the legal norm, and only later emendations allowed for the presentation of witnesses and evidence.[101] However, here there is no record of the Frankish penalty of mutilation for losing a judicial duel. For Anglo-Saxon England, despite the new emphasis on oath-swearing in the early eighth-century laws of Wihtred, we find few oaths in early legal records.[102]

Probably either one or more of the *boni viri* or the presider himself interrogated the witness; unfortunately the Frankish records all use the passive formula *interrogatum fuit ipsius*, 'he was interrogated,' so we do not know to whom and by whom the role of interrogator was assigned.[103] If the judgment was not divided (and it is unclear whether this means unanimous or clear majority) the case would be settled at this point.

In the case of an assessed fine, the responsibility for payment would not rest solely upon the loser of the suit, but would be shared by his kin-group. The legal constituency of this faction might vary from territory to territory. A common genealogical boundary seems to extend to the fourth generation, that is, to the degree of second cousin. This is the same group

---

98 Gaudemet, 'Les Ordalies au Moyen Age,' 100.
99 Bartlett, *Trial by Fire and Water*, 30.
100 Nelson, 'Dispute Settlement in Carolingian West Francia,' 59. See also Schmitt-Weigand, *Rechtspflegedelikte*, 136–7. The same seems to have held from the tenth to the thirteenth centuries: see Bartlett, *Trial by Fire and Water*, 26.
101 Wickham, 'Land Disputes and Their Social Framework in Lombard-Carolingian Italy,' 113.
102 See Oliver, *Beginnings of English Law*, 174–6; Wormald, 'Charters, Law and the Settlement of Disputes in Anglo-Saxon England,' 154.
103 Bergmann, 'Untersuchungen zu den Gerichtsurkunden der Merowingerzeit,' 110.

that would have prosecuted the bloodfeud if the legal alternative had not been instantiated.[104]

If the settlement involved the payment of a fine, this could, of course, be paid in money. However, we find very few coins in early medieval burial sites, indicating that the monetary valuation was generally theoretical rather than actual. *Lex Ribuaria* §40.11 sets a schedule of substitution values for the repayment of wergild; an addendum to the Corbey manuscript of *Lex Saxonum* offers a different set of replacements. Finally, *Lex Alamannorum* presents the respective values of various livestock, and the restitution fee for killing various sorts of slaves.[105] (See Table 2.1.)

The historical records never provide an example in which these exact substitutions are paid, but various case studies demonstrate that these are not the only alternatives. If the one against whom the judgment goes does not have enough monetary wealth, he might, as in a case recorded in 761 from Italy, pay in land.[106] Payment in livestock, such as sheep, horses, and oxen must have, at least in Langobardia, been approved by the presider.[107] Various combinations of property and livestock could make up the sum, as shown by a suit from Freising sometime around the turn of the eighth century, which allowed the defendants to pay the major part of their fine in land, and substitute the value of the remaining seven silver *solidi* with a horse and weapons.[108]

The rate of exchange for the horse – seven silver *solidi* less the value of the weapons – seems low, both in comparison to the options presented in Table 2.1, and in the light of another case from the same year in Italy. The defendant, Audo, was unable to pay the fine of one hundred gold *solidi* for

---

104 On kinship in Germanic law, see the classic study by Murray, *Germanic Kinship Structure*. In relationship to specific territories, for early Anglo-Saxon England, see Oliver, *Beginnings of English Law*, 74–5; Drew, 'Family Institutions,' Part 4 of 'Notes on Lombard Institutions,' chap. 4; 'The Germanic Family of the Leges Burgundionum,' chap. 5; 'The Family in Frankish Law,' chap. 6; 'The Family in Visigothic Law,' chap. 7; and 'The Law of the Family in the Germanic Barbarian Kingdoms,' chap. 8, in *Law and Society*. For quite different kinship calculations in Celtic territories, see Charles-Edwards, *Early Irish and Welsh Kinship*.
105 *Lex Rib.* §40.11; *Lex Sax.* §XVIII.3; *Lex Ala.* §§73–83. For translation, of *Lex Rib.* see Rivers, *Laws of the Salian and Ripuarian Franks*, 185–6. For discussion, see Hüpper-Dröge, 'Schutz- und Angriffswaffen nach den Leges und verwandten fränkischen Rechtsquellen,' 112.
106 Hübner, *Gerichtsurkunden aus Italien*, #639. A case from Redon, Brittany, allows a family to give land in exchange for *wergild* in a case of homicide (Davies, 'Disputes in Ninth-Century Brittany,' 77).
107 Schmitt-Weigand, *Rechtspflegedelikte*, 43.
108 Hübner, *Gerichtsurkunden aus Deutschland und Frankreich*, #191.

Table 2.1
Commutations in kind

Amount	Ripuarian substitution	Saxon substitution	Alamann substitution
1 *solidus*	a horned cow, able to see and healthy		medium quality milk cow
1 ⅓ *solidi*			good milk cow medium quality ox
1 ⅔ *solidi*			highest grade ox
2 *solidi*	a horned ox, able to see and healthy a shield with spear	four-year-old ox	
2 ½ *solidi*		plow ox cow with calf	
3 *solidi*	a mare, able to see and healthy a sword without a sheath	good ox	mare not yet able to foal bull from herd of 12+ cows hunting, herding, or racing dog
6 *solidi*	an untrained hawk a helmet in good condition a pair of leggings in good condition a crane-seizing hawk		mare able to foal lead hunting dog
7 *solidi*	a stallion, able to see and healthy a sword with a sheath		
12 *solidi*	a chain mail coat in good condition a trained hawk		stallion of herd
40 *solidi*			groom for stallion groom for 12 horses pigman for 40 pigs shepherd for 40 sheep supervisor of 12 servants cook overseeing apprentice smith, goldsmith, swordsmith

stealing a horse from the monastery of Farfa. Those deputed to serve for him gave the monastery his property in Malliano. Audo then appeared on this land illegally and forcefully. He was sentenced to service for Lord Giselfus, a duty from which he was allowed to emancipate himself for the price of twenty *solidi*. But he also had to deed to the church the aforementioned property and additionally two serf-holdings (*massaricae*).[109] Stealing from a church was commonly fined higher than from a lay person; nonetheless, it is easy to understand Audo's display of frustration at the enormity of this fine. The most humiliating part of Audo's adventures was predicted in an edict of Chilperic from c. 575:

> If someone commits a crime but does not have enough property to make compensation to the victim, he will nevertheless come before the mallus at three sessions so that his relatives can redeem him by payment. If they refuse to do this, the criminal, after a fourth session of the mallus, shall appear before the royal court, and there it will be decreed that he should be handed over to the victim of his crime who may do what he likes with him.[110]

It is probable that, like Audo, the defaulter would have been pressed into service for the person(s) to whom he owed the fine. He would have remained in that position until such time as he was considered to have completed enough labour to redeem the value of the penalty. This hypothesis is corroborated by a clause that first appears in the *Penitentials of St Columbanus* but is repeated elsewhere; it requires a cleric who has committed homicide to give himself after his penance to the family of the victim for satisfaction. As Stefan Jurasinski remarks, 'It clearly can't be requiring that members of the clergy who have disgraced themselves by committing homicide expose themselves to certain death at the hands of their victims' kin.'[111] Rather, the homicidal cleric must work off his fine in service to the bereaved family. Angers Formula #3 provides a template by which such an arrangement (in this case for restitution for theft) can be entered into the legal record:

---

109 Hübner, *Gerichtsurkunden aus Italien*, #639.
110 Cited in Fouracre, '"Placita" and the Settlement of Disputes in Later Merovingian Francia,' 40.
111 Personal communication; I am indebted to Dr Jurasinski for the data from penitential literature. For St Columbanus, see Bieler, ed. and trans., *The Irish Penitentials*, 98 [cap. 1]; for Frankish penitentials, see Kottje, ed., *Paenitentialia minora franciae et italiae saeculi viii–ix*, 75.

To my lord A and his wife B, I, C. Because all my errors conspired to make me steal your property, and because I am unable to settle this in any other way than to give my entire [free] status over to your service, it is therefore established that I put my entire [free] status into your service on account of this error, not constrained by any power, but out of my own free will, because I have been shown to be guilty of this ... And if anyone, either myself or one of my relatives or any other person, tries to act against this act of sale, which I asked to be made with good will, let him pay *n. solidi* [to be divided] between you and the fisc, and let him be unable to assert his claim, and let this act of sale and my decision remain firm.[112]

Not only does the perpetrator sell himself into servitude, but he also obligates his kin-group to abide by the agreement.

Four final notes on fines. First, it seems likely that some portion of the penalty assessed in the *mallus* went to the presider as a representative of the public coffer.[113] In some instances this was explicitly distinguished from compensatory damages, the surcharge referred to for the upper court as the king's ban and for the lower court as the count's ban (sixty and fifteen *solidi* respectively). The laws of Alfred distinguish between paying *mid were*, 'with wergild,' and *mid wite*, 'with fine,' where the latter is an equivalent to the king's ban.[114] Second, it was not only defendants who could be liable. A Frankish formulary, probably from the eighth century, required the accuser to promise to be able to pay the stipulated fine if he lost his case.[115] Third, as indicated above, Kentish law allowed wergild in the case of homicide to be paid in two installments: 1/5 at the interment and the remainder within forty days.

The fourth consideration – the most important and simultaneously the most impenetrable – is the degree of adherence to the written law in the imposition of penalties. Take, as an example, the tariff set for striking off a hand. As discussed later in chapter 5, this fine was regulated throughout the barbarian territories as a percentage of the wergild. But nowhere is there mention of the difference in value between a predominant and a

---

112 Rio, trans., *Formularies*, 50–1. Similar templates can be found in Angers #2 (ibid., 51–2); Angers #38 (ibid., 79–80); Marculf II, 28 (ibid., 211). See discussion in Rio, *Legal Practice*, 228—37; also Liebs, 'Sklaverei aus Not im germanisch-römischen Recht.'
113 See Schmitt-Weigand, *Rechtspflegedelikte*, 12. For similar rulings in the Anglo-Saxon laws of Hlothere and Eadric, see Oliver, *Beginnings of English Law*, 135–8.
114 Wessex §2.1.
115 Hübner, *Gerichtsurkunden aus Deutschland und Frankreich*, #158.

non-predominant hand. Surely the compensation should be greater for a right-handed man for the loss of his right hand than for the loss of his left? Only the comparatively late Frisian laws made any occupational distinctions, requiring fourfold compensation for injuring the hand of a harpist or goldsmith. But to a woodsman, the loss of the little finger, which enables him to grip his axe, would be far more damaging than the loss of his 'shooting finger.' The two were, however, equal in value in Alamann, Thuringian, and Bavarian laws, and in the laws of Alfred, the *scytefinger* was even ranked higher than the little finger. Visigothic law provides a solution to this conundrum: if a person is wounded in the nostrils, 'iuxta quod deturpationem iudex inspexerit, damnare non morabitur percussorem' (after the judge has examined the deformation, he shall not hesitate to award damages for the blow).[116] No finite amount for these damages is stipulated; presumably the judge must set the fine according to the severity of the wound. Wallace-Hadrill expands this hypothesis to other regions:

> The early barbarian law codes provide, how fully we cannot guess, current tariffs of crimes that were commonly emendable. Their compilers would have seen no necessity to add that there was such as thing as political expediency ... and that kings did in practice interfere to impose severer or lighter sentences than custom allowed.[117]

In the discussion that concludes this chapter, I take as a starting point the supposition that a similar flexibility in emendation applied also to the local courts. That is, the fine assessable for any particular injury could be modified according to the circumstances of the case. Given the percentages of the stipulated fees compared to wergild, I further believe that as a general rule these tariffs represented the maximum possible penalty. This latter inference, however, is even more speculative than the former.[118]

---

116 *Forum Iud.* VI, 4 iii.
117 Wallace-Hadrill, *The Long-Haired Kings*, 112. For specific examples of judicial interpretation in case of property disputes in Carolingian Francia, see Brown, *Unjust Seizure*, chapter 4.
118 I was pleased to discover that Alice Rio arrived at a similar conclusion in regard to clauses outside the personal injury laws: 'Instead of seeing written laws either as recording the doomed efforts of kings at stamping their authority on a resisting population or as attempting to develop measured solutions in response to social practice, it makes more sense to read laws as stating the upper limit of what could be expected from a person by whom one had been wronged – whether this involved marriage

Presiders over the legal process were not immune from criticism. Most Germanic territories had explicit admonitions against *iudices* accepting bribes – the pervasiveness of this temptation was demonstrated in the poem by the Carolingian *missus* Theodulf cited earlier. In an edict of 798, Charlemagne admonished that 'gifts blind the hearts of the wise and twist the words of the just.'[119] The capitularies also warned against influence from friendship, enmity, fear, or consideration for the litigant's appearance.[120] Alcuin grumbled that 'bad judges ... do not complete the hearings until their pockets have been filled; for when they judge, they do not regard the case, but the gifts.'[121] Hincmar, a ninth-century archbishop of Rheims, complained of judges that 'when they hope for profit of some kind, they invoke [customary] law, but when they reckon there's no advantage to be had there, they seek refuge in capitularies [case law]: thus it comes about that neither capitularies nor law are properly observed.'[122] And in Walafrid Strabo's dream vision, when the angel leads Wetti to purgatory with its high mountains and fiery river, he sees a great pile of wealth mounded up by the devil: gold and silver treasures in costly vases, rich clothing, and elaborately equipped horses. The angel informs him that these are bribes that had been taken by judges condemned to tortures in the burning waters.[123] (Note that the nature of these bribes is property in kind rather than coinage.)

The penalty for accepting bribes was often that the dishonest *iudex* either pay his wergild or atone with his life; one assumes the former to have been far more common than the latter.[124] Burgundian law begins with strictures against dishonest and incompetent judges, including that a bribed judge could lose his head even if he judged in accordance with the law, and the obverse, that a judge who judged wrong but had not been bribed had to pay a fine of thirty *solidi*.[125] Visigothic law requires a judge who delivered a false judgment to restitute it with an equal amount of

---

without the consent of the wife's parents or neighbouring landlords competing for manpower' (Rio, *Legal Practice*, 209).
119 Schmitt-Weigand, *Rechtspflegedelikte*, 34.
120 Ibid., 36.
121 Cited in ibid., 153.
122 Cited in Nelson, 'Dispute Settlement in Carolingian West Francia,' 63.
123 Schmitt-Weigand, *Rechtspflegedelikte*, 155.
124 See ibid., 17 for *Lex Rib.*; 18ff. for Merovingian capitularies; 80–1 for Burgundian law; 81–5 for Alamann law; 34–6 and 91–4 for general discussion. In Visigothic law a judge who pronounces a death sentence under influence of a bribe is himself put to death; conversely, if a bribe causes him to set a killer free, he must pay the injured party seven times the normal fine (74).
125 *Liber Const.*, §4 and §9 respectively.

property; if he is not sufficiently wealthy he must be deprived of all he owns, and either submit himself to the litigant in penal servitude or receive fifty lashes in public.[126] Note, however, that this sentence might have been inflicted in the case of incompetence as well as deliberate dishonesty. Certainly a degree of judicial ineptitude is implied by a peculiar fomulary from eighth-century Italy, in which a husband and wife instruct that due to the number of lost written documents, the signed judgment papers should be hung on the church door or in the open market.[127] This seems to have been a viable concern, as formulae from Angers state that, lacking the necessary documentary evidence, a judgment would be considered void.[128]

Either plaintiff or defendant had the right to contest a judgment in the higher court, which equally had the right to refuse to hear it. The privilege of appearing before the king was specifically reserved for those of noble birth and for those of free birth challenging the rulings of lower courts: a litigant could be fined for bringing his suit to the upper court before presenting it at the local *mallus*.[129] Such an appeal could involve a considerable investment, as the first hearing would have been in a locally designated meeting place, whereas the peripatetic king ruled wherever he happened to be. Nonetheless, wherever a litigant came to process, he had the right to be judged according to the law of his own territory.[130] Under Alamann law, if the appeal was upheld, the presider of the lower court was fined twelve *solidi*; if the appeal was struck down, the plaintiff had to pay the same fee to the man who had served as presider at his first hearing.[131]

To flesh out this picture, the following section examines particular cases brought before these upper courts.

Cases Involving Assault

We have no records of cases in early medieval Europe that address the sort of personal injury discussed in the following chapters. However, there are some which either describe or (may) imply assault; these are presented below. I have drawn these from the catalogues of Frankish and Lombard

---

126 *Forum Iud.* II, 1, xix.
127 Hübner, *Gerichtsurkunden aus Deutschland und Frankreich*, #142.
128 Rio, trans., *Formularies*, 62–4.
129 Schmitt-Weigand, *Rechtspflegedelikte*, 52. In both Burgundian and Lombard law, a litigant is also permitted to take his case directly to the higher court if he has made three abortive attempts to have it heard in the local *mallus*. In Burgundian law the fine is twelve *solidi* for going directly to the higher court (56, 80).
130 Ibid., 31.
131 Ibid., 141.

cases compiled by Rudolf Hübner in 1891 and 1893 respectively. Certainly scholarship in the past century plus has increased the number of known cases.[132] Furthermore, Karl Zeumer's edition of formulae from which Hübner drew much of his data often assigned provenances and dates to specific entries which have subsequently been questioned; I have retained these assignations for easy reference, but the reader must keep in mind that they are not necessarily historically accurate.[133] Nonetheless, these collections provide us with a good idea of the types of suits brought to court. I have used a cutoff date of 814, the last year of Charlemagne's reign, to keep the cases roughly contemporaneous with the barbarian laws.

As mentioned previously, an important consideration is the nature of this higher court. These cases involved either high-ranking officials, such as the Bavarian Duke Tassilo,[134] or appeals from split decisions (*equalis percepcionis*) in the lower court. The presiders in the higher court were the king or his emissaries. The rulings were not expected in any way to be rubber stamps: Wickham cites an instance in which a Frankish king in the seventh century provided that if an aristocrat were sent away by the king to fulfil a royal function, 'all his court-cases and those of his friends, sworn dependents, or those in his legitimate sphere of influence' would be suspended until he returned.[135] Presumably 'those under his legitimate sphere of influence' included all his subjects, no matter how low in status. No judgment on appeal could be reached in a case if he were not there personally to rule on the evidence; at the lower level the verdict rested with the court, but at the higher level the presider himself determined the outcome.[136]

---

132 See, for example, the discussion in Bergmann, 'Untersuchungen zu den Gerichtsurkunden der Merowingerzeit,' 48. Brown, *Unjust Seizure*, 31–2, introduces charters of Freising which discuss an attack in which two men are seriously wounded and the son of a third is killed. We do not, however, see the outcome of legal process against the attacker(s); rather, the wounded men hastily donate property to the church to protect their souls and benefit their families. Similarly, 'compelled by the admonition of God and struck down by Count Keparoh with an incurable wound,' a man named Cros donates all his property to a monastery and enters it as a monk (Brown, *Unjust Seizure*, 34). Here we see the common medieval function of the monastery as nursing home. We do not, however, discover what became of Count Keparoh.
133 An excellent introduction to these problems is provided by Rio, *Legal Practice*, the reading of which ought to be a prerequisite for this section of my book; see also discussion in Rio, trans., *Formulae*, 7–8.
134 Hübner, *Gerichtsurkunden aus Deutschland und Frankreich*, #121, 132.
135 Wickham, 'Society,' 90.
136 For Brittany, see Davies, 'Disputes, Their Conduct and Their Settlement in the Village Communities of Eastern Brittany in the Ninth Century,' 304.

Unfortunately, the records remaining to us do not present a picture of the lower, local courts, particularly when the matter comes to unanimous decision. Yet these are precisely the types of hearings in which we would expect disputes on personal injury to be resolved. Rather, the cases of which we have knowledge stem from the higher courts. By far the majority of these deal with property and inheritance. The few we have addressing assault mostly concern homicide, and even those which deal with lesser harm provide no firm information about the amounts of fine actually assessed. Nevertheless, the following case studies remain important, as they provide the only experiential evidence we have to draw on in our attempts to recreate early Germanic procedure in cases of assault and battery.

Cases from Francia

The total number of court records for our period (that is, up to 814, the death of Charlemagne) transcribed by Hübner in his handlist of Frankish cases is 204. The overwhelming majority deal with land ownership, theft, or granting of immunities from public service, but – demonstrating the long-lasting continuity of French priorities – there are also several hearings involving damage to vineyards. A unique case from Reichenau in the eighth century reports the plea of a man whose property has been impounded as a penalty for incest; his request to have the confiscated goods returned is granted.[137] Hübner's full reckoning also includes some procedural issues: the prescription for a judge to call the defendant to court; the decree that a litigant who fails to appear at the *mallus* loses his case and will have this judgment publically announced; the stipulation that an accuser be able to pay the necessary fine in the event that he loses his case; and the possibility to name a permanent power of attorney (the last two having been discussed above).[138] I have excluded these in the total count, and have also eliminated three hearings for treason. This gives a net total of 197 cases, of which those dealing with possible instances of assault will now be considered.

By far the majority of such cases – thirteen – involve homicide, which can be considered the ultimate case of assault. Eight of these are rulings in which the defendant is found guilty; in all but one a written quitclaim

---

137 Hübner, *Gerichtsurkunden aus Deutschland und Frankreich*, #148.
138 Ibid., #155 through #159; originals in Zeumer, *Formulae Merowingici et Karolingi aevi*, 534–7, which contain the first seven chapters of the *Formulae Extravagantes* I.

(*securitas*) is given in exchange for the wergild.[139] Alamann law stipulates that no written document (including, and perhaps especially pertinent to, the quitclaim) was valid unless it clearly indicated the year and day of its recording.[140] The formulary of Angers provides a template for such a document (although the repeated use of *ille*, 'this man,' for both the victim and the perpetrator renders the interpretation somewhat confusing):

> As it is not unknown that *n*. days ago a certain man named A had a quarrel with B on a public road and dealt him some blows, this man thus agreed before the good men mediating [in this matter] that this man should make this deed of security regarding the blows and this quarrel which he had with me; and this he did. And if, as I do not think will happen, either myself or one of my heirs or any opposing person dares to oppose this deed of security, let him pay him *n. solidi*, and let him be unable to assert his claim, and let this deed of security remain firm for all time.[141]

An unusual case in Bavaria required the gift of a pig in lieu of the quitclaim.[142] Perhaps the successful litigant shrewdly negotiated this substitution of the animal itself in place of the skin of said animal on which the *securitas* would have been written.

Of the next four cases, the first concerns a – presumably unusually belligerent – accuser who was enjoined to adhere to the quitclaim or be subject to a fine. The second homicide action records the non-appearance of the defendant, who, in absentia, was declared liable for the wergild.[143] The third case, stemming from Angers at the beginning of the seventh century, concerns the killing of a relative that had taken place several years previously. The defendant was ordered to appear after a specific period with twelve neighbours who were his peers to swear in church that he was in no way guilty of the murder.[144] The fourth case demonstrates the single instance in which a quitclaim was not required: this suit involved the killing of a servant/slave, for whom both status and value was considerably dif-

---

139 Hübner, *Gerichtsurkunden aus Deutschland und Frankreich*, #51, 88, 96, 108, 147, 158, 160; the case without mention of quitclaim is #109.
140 *Lex Ala.* §43.
141 Rio, trans., *Formularies*, 53. This collection contains several formulae for quitclaims regarding the transfer of land; Marculf II, 18 presents a formula for a quitclaim in a case of homicide (see ibid., 203–4).
142 Brown, *Unjust Seizure*, 135–8.
143 Hübner, *Gerichtsurkunden aus Deutschland und Frankreich*, #5.
144 Ibid., #21.

ferent than for freemen – Anglo-Saxon law, for example, refers to *weorþ*, 'worth,' rather than wergild even in regard to *esnas*, 'servants,' whose rank was higher than that of *þeowas*, 'slaves.'[145]

The final three homicide actions all revolve around pleas of self-defence. In the 770s case from Sens, discussed above, the defendant was remanded to appear at the altar in forty-two days with three property-owners and twelve oath-helpers to support his contention that he acted in self-preservation.[146] In a second case from Sens, the defendant admitted to the killing but alleged self-defence; this claim appears not to have been successful, as he was required to pay compensation to the kin. Unfortunately, only the outcome, lacking any argumentation, is recorded. As in the cases previously discussed, the defendant was given a quitclaim.[147]

The third, a case from Tours in the middle of the eighth century, presents a particularly interesting set of circumstances. A *iudex* arrived in a location where a man had just been killed. Those who were there or who hurried to the place shortly thereafter supported the defendant's version of the facts. The dead man had intended to rob the defendant, coming against him with unsheathed sword, and causing mutilations and blows. The killer swore with upraised hand 'as is the custom' (*sicut mos est*) that he acted in self-defence; furthermore, he exhibited his bruises. He thus 'acted according to law' (*secundum legem fecit*) in killing his assailant (*ferrebattudo*). His swearing was accompanied by twelve men, with himself as the thirteenth. The *iudex* set in that place the requirement that the slayer appear in church forty days later with thirty-six oath-supporters, himself as thirty-seventh, to repeat his claim of self-defence. 'And if he is able to do so, [the case of] that death should remain at rest' (*Et si hoc facere potuerit, de ipsa morte quietus valeat requiescat*).[148] Three interesting points arise from this unsatisfactorily brief survey. First, the *iudex* did not – indeed, might not – rule independently, even though this case appears to be relatively clear-cut: there is no indication that anyone challenges the claim of self-defence, and the killer even demonstrated his bruises. The public hearing was necessary, however, to compel the slain man's kin to accept the judgment that the killer was not guilty of homicide in order to ward off later feud. Second, even though the *iudex* might not pronounce a

---

145 Oliver, *Beginnings of English Law*, 114–16.
146 Hübner, *Gerichtsurkunden aus Deutschland und Frankreich*, #97.
147 Ibid., #87; Zeumer, *Formulae Merowingici et Karolingi aevi*, 256–7.
148 Hübner *Gerichtsurkunden aus Deutschland und Frankreich*, #68; Zeumer, *Formulae Merowingici et Karolingi aevi*, #30.

verdict, he did set the evidentiary requirements for the case, thus effectively bypassing the preliminary hearing. Third, although twelve men supported the killer's contention of self-defence at the scene of the slaying, he was required to triple that number to thirty-six when he appeared at the altar. It might be tempting to hypothesize that a greater number of witnesses was required in cases of homicide, but this theory does not stand up in light of the earlier-mentioned Sens case, which only called for three land-holders and twelve oath-helpers. The Sens and Tours suits are fairly close both geographically and chronologically, so this discrepancy probably rests on particulars presented in evidence which has not come down to us. A purely speculative hypothesis is that the *iudex* stipulated a greater number of oath-supporters in lieu of the preliminary hearing.

Four and a half further records warrant mention here, of which the first two and a half seem more pertinent than the last two. The formula from Angers mentioned above involved an accusation of ambush, which was resolved by fine and quitclaim. There is no mention of whether or not injury resulted from the attack, and the amount of the fine is not notated.[149] From Ende in the later part of the seventh century a layman was accused of ambush with intent to steal; this attack caused heavy bruising (*graviter livorassetis*). The case was adjourned until *kalendas illas proximas* (the first day of the following month, thus less than forty days) to give the accused time to prepare his defence. The defendant did not appear at the hearing and was fined in absentia according to *lex loci vestri*, 'the law of your place.'[150]

What I define as the 'half case' stems from Sens around 770, and has already been discussed under homicide. A woman fell upon a man and his wife, wounding the man in the knees. Then she killed their daughter. The woman was little able to deny her guilt (*minime potuit denegare*), and was assessed the required *leod* (the Frankish term for wergild) to be paid to the husband and wife. Presumably this fine must have included payment both for the injury to the husband's knees and for the death of the daughter, although the document is silent as to the amount and constitution of these fines. Counterbalancing the misogyny prevalent in the Middle Ages, Zeumer footnotes this case with the disclaimer: 'I would have preferred in this outrage the accused to have been a man, but as the manuscript

---

149 Hübner, *Gerichtsurkunden aus Deutschland und Frankreich*, #2; Zeumer, *Formulae Merowingici et Karolingi aevi*, #61. Two similar formulae can be found in *Marculf* I, 29 and I, 37 (Rio, trans., *Formulae*, 162, 171–2).
150 Hübner, *Gerichtsurkunden aus Deutschland und Frankreich*, #48/49; Zeumer, *Formulae Merowingici et Karolingi aevi*, #29/37.

consistently uses the feminine gender in that role, we are not able but to accept a feminine villain for the crime.'[151]

The last two cases only speculatively involve assault. In the beginning of the seventh century in Angers a woman brought a claim against a cleric (*aput homine sancti*) for what might have been abduction and might have been rape – the actual wording is 'intencione abuit de illo rapto' (he had the intention towards her *rapto*), which does not clear up the ambiguity. He was ordered to pay in compensation *soledus tantus*, 'a *solidus* of such size.' Unfortunately this does not make any more sense in Latin than in English, but likely it means the full thirty-*solidi* fine required by *Lex Salica*.[152] Finally, under the broadest definition of assault, in Sens around 770 a defendant brought oath-supporters to swear that he never tried to poison his accuser, either with herbs or with poisoned drinks. The resultant harm, in any case, would have damaged the internal organs which (except in Frisia) were not protected by law.

In conclusion, in Hübner's collection for Francia we have seventeen cases – roughly 8 per cent of the total – which could be defined as involving assault. Of these, thirteen – roughly 6 per cent of the total – concerned homicide, which is outside the framework of the personal injury tariffs. Only four may have involved external physical harm: the Sens case involving bodily damage and death, the Angers and Ende cases concerning ambush, and the Angers *raptus* case – likely, but not definitely, involving rape. Due to the laconic nature of the court records, however, we have no indication of what specific damage was done, the amount of restitution required or how the judgment was reached.

Cases from Langobardia

The total number of cases up to 814 from Lombard Italy recorded by Hübner, 1893, is seventy-nine. Again, the majority of these cases involve property, theft, or immunities. No damage-to-vineyard claims are found

---

151 Hübner, *Gerichtsurkunden aus Deutschland und Frankreich*, #108; Zeumer, *Formulae Merowingici et Karolingi aevi*, #51. Zeumer's footnote reads: 'Quamquam ex ipso scelere virum accusatum interpretari maluerim, tamen, codice semper in hac parte genus femininum facinoris ream accipiamus.' Alice Rio delineates one difference between charters and formulae: 'Whereas charters only document single events, the decision of scribes to convert their documents into models shows that they expected what happened once to happen again' (Rio, *Legal Practice*, 172). One hopes that no scribe actually anticipated a repeat of this offense.
152 *Lex Sal.* §XIV.1.

here, but instead we have suits regarding loss of freedom, which do not appear in the Frankish listing.

No tabulation need be assembled for the Lombard records, as we have only one case each involving homicide and possible assault. The homicide case is the last listed within the boundaries of our reckoning, dated between 774 and 814. A man incited a servant/slave to kill his two underage masters, and then threw the killer himself into a grave. (Presumably he himself murdered the murderer, although this is never explicitly stated.) He was obliged to pay three times the wergild of the nine-year-old and twice the wergild of the eleven-year-old, to restitute three times the worth of the servant/slave, and to pay the court costs (presumably the king's ban).[153] This case is considerably more complex than any recorded suit from Francia. The accused not only instigated homicide but also performed it himself. This account leaves three questions open.

- What would have been the division of culpability had the unfree killer of the two boys survived?

  The probable answer to this question is more transparent than for those that follow: a master is always responsible for the actions of a slave if they were committed according to his commands.
- Why is the fine for the younger son a greater multiple of the wergild than for the older?

  This ruling remains impenetrable. Perhaps the wergild for the older son was higher than that for the younger, and the adjustment was made to equalize the fine for each. But if the older son as primary heir had been assigned a higher wergild, this assignment surely indicates greater value in the eyes of the law, and thus demands commensurate compensation. Even this desperate hypothesis fails on the basis of available legal evidence, which nowhere (as far as I know) assigns a greater wergild to an elder son.
- Finally, presumably the man stood to benefit by the death of the boys. But if he is next-in-line to inherit, he must be a close relation. Who, then, is responsible for paying wergild and to whom is it paid, when both slayer and slain belong to the same kin?

  The *Edictus Rothari* rules that in the event of kin-slaying, if the killer would have been the heir, the inheritance goes to the next in line. If none is living, it goes to the king's court. The uncle would have been wise to better conceal the traces of his crime!

---

153 Hübner, *Gerichtsurkunden aus Italien*, #698.

The single assault case stems from Spoleto in 798. The men of the local count were accused by the neighbouring monastery of attacks on the monks at the local fishing grounds. The count admitted the facts but denied prior personal knowledge or intent. (If he had instigated the attack by men in his service, he would himself have been liable.) The penalty was restoration of lost goods and payment of a fine. 'Restoration' seems to be used formulaically when 'replacement' is surely the intention: what would the monastery do with old, rotted fish? Again, it seems likely that at least bruising occurred during these attacks, but we are given no specifics. It is not unlikely that the fine was imposed as legal restitution for personal injuries sustained, although this, once again, is conjecture.

Speculative Reconstruction of Personal Injury Cases

The reconstruction of process and procedure set out above has been based on a variety of facts from a plurality of locations; it endeavours, however, to include only those elements which apply in some form to a majority of the barbarian territories. The examination of roughly contemporary hearings demonstrates how very little we actually know about how personal injury cases were resolved in court. However, the accumulated evidence gives us the possibility of creating an informed hypothesis as to how such litigation might have proceeded.

The present section, thus, moves to the realm of fiction, constructing two very different cases, and suggesting how they might have been resolved depending on circumstances. The amounts of restitution are based on those stipulated in the laws of Æthelberht, king of Kent, promulgated in approximately 600 CE.[154] Although the actual monetary fines may differ according to region, the underlying principles remain the same. The second study is more complex than the first, as it involves rulings on payment for medical fees and lost work which are specific, albeit not unique, to Æthelberht's laws.[155] These cases are hypothetical, and details of procedure would have varied both regionally and chronologically. Nonetheless, these fictional cases should be useful in attempting to recreate the possible routes that personal injury cases might have followed through contemporary legal systems. Both cases thus present a range of possible resolutions, and both move from least to most disputative.

---

154 See Oliver, *Beginnings of English Law*, 34–51, for discussion on dating of these laws, and in particular the personal injury tariffs.
155 Oliver, 'Sick-Maintenance in Anglo-Saxon Law,' discusses the appearance of similar stipulations elsewhere in barbarian and Northern Germanic territories.

The Case of the Missing Hand

The particulars of this case are as follows:

> Francis and Joseph, both right-handed lumberjacks, go into the woods to chop down trees. They carry their axes with them. When they emerge, Francis is missing his left hand: only a bloody stump remains at his wrist. Joseph is seen by several witnesses carrying his axe, the blade dripping with blood. Francis claims that Joseph struck off his hand in the woods.

POSSIBLE RESOLUTION
Back at home, Joseph admits to having struck off Francis's hand, whether intentionally or not. They decide mutually on an appropriate amount of restitution, which Joseph pays. There is thus no need to take this case to the *mæpel*.

Scenario #1. Joseph admits to the act, but claims that the common practice is to set a penalty for the right hand. In fact, none of the barbarian laws makes a distinction between the right and left hand (or for the predominant and non-predominant hand in the case of left-handers). Two possibilities present themselves. The simplest is that the two parties settle privately on a lesser restitution. If, however, they are unable to come to an agreement, they must take the case to the assembly.

Scenario #2. Joseph admits to the act, but claims it was an accident. However, Francis and Joseph cannot agree on a proper compensation. Two possibilities arise here: a) They agree that the injury was accidental, but differ on the appropriate amount of restitution, b) Francis insists that the blow was not accidental, but deliberately struck. Under either scenario, this dispute must go to the assembly.

Scenario #3. Joseph admits to the act, but asserts that he acted in self-defence. Joseph claims that Francis threatened him with a raised axe. Francis denies this allegation. This dispute must go to the assembly.

Scenario #4. Joseph claims that he did not, in fact, strike off Francis's hand. He left Francis in the woods and headed home. On the way, he was attacked by a wild boar, which he fended off with his axe, thereby causing his axe to become bloodied. He does not know how Francis's hand was severed from his wrist (although perhaps it was a further attack by the boar he had driven away). Francis insists that Joseph did indeed strike off his hand in the woods. This dispute must go to the assembly.

> ### Excursus on absolute liability
>
> Before pursuing these cases to court, it is worth considering the rulings on liability in barbarian law. Almost unanimously the texts preclude using accident as a defence.[156] Thuringian law generalizes this principle: whoever unintentionally kills or wounds a man pays the same fee as if it were intentional.[157] Ripuarian law states: 'If however someone maims another's arm, foot, eye, hearing, smelling, finger, or any other of the limbs, let him pay, as if he had wounded that same man with a sword.'[158] Other texts exemplify the same concept for particular incidents. For example, Saxon law rules that if a man is killed by a falling tree, the one who felled the tree must pay full wergild. Lombard law – perhaps more justly – holds the survivor liable for only a half wergild, assigning half the blame to the killed man (as he could have avoided injury had he been paying attention).
>
> Some of the stipulations on liability are so specific that they may be based on actual cases. An oft-cited example comes from Alfred's laws: 'If anyone has a spear over his shoulder, and a man is transfixed on it, the wergild is to be paid without the fine ... if the point is three fingers higher than the butt end of the shaft. If they are both level, the point and butt end, that is to be considered without risk.' A similar ruling regulates a different mishap in Saxon law: if a man drops an iron that pierces another man, he must pay restitution to the victim,

---

156 The salient difference is *Forum Iudicum* VI, 5, ii: 'If one man should kill another, either standing, coming, or passing by, not being aware of his presence at the time, where no cause of enmity had previously existed between them, and he who committed the homicide shall declare that he did it involuntarily, and shall be able to prove this in court, he shall depart in safety' (trans. Scott, *Visigothic Code*, s.v.).
157 *Lex Thur.* §5.49.
158 *Lex Rib.* § 5. 'Quod si quis absque effusione sanguinis alio brachium, pedem, oculum, auditum, muccatum, digitum vel quocumque libet membrorum mancaverit, sic eum conponat, ac si cum cladio ipsum debilitasset.'

but need not add the fine for disturbing public peace.[159] In both the Anglo-Saxon and Saxon clauses, the perpetrator need only pay the necessary restitution to the injured party; the accidental nature of the injury obviates the payment of fine for disturbing the public peace. Furthermore, although the Saxon ruling requires the payment of restitution, it does not specify that this be full restitution.[160] A later Lombard addition by Liutprand states that the kin of someone who was killed by a falling water-hoist deserved no recompense, as he should have looked where he was standing.[161] Visigothic law allows a plea of accidental homicide if the death occurred in public view and the accidental nature of the deed was substantiated by witnesses[162]

To some extent the purpose of these clauses must have been to prohibit a man who deliberately injures another to escape on the sham plea of lack of intention. However, in clear situations of accident, the fine for restitution was reduced – this applies unambiguously to the clumsy Lombard tree-feller. My hypothesis – and unfortunately we have no case studies which either support or refute this theory – is that the fines set by law are maximum penalties, which can be reduced if the circumstances indicate accidental rather than deliberate injury. Here I align myself with Sir Percy H. Winfield, who argued long ago that 'no sane human being, ancient or modern, needs any mental education beyond that of general experience to say "A did not mean to do this," and therefore to inflict a lighter penalty or possibly none at all. Mediaeval man is at least that much removed from a beast.'[163]

Process and Procedure in Disputed Claims

FIRST APPEARANCE: PRESENTATION OF THE CASE
Francis claims in the *mæþel* that Joseph struck off his hand, and that he is liable for full compensation – fifty shillings, which equals half a wergild – for the loss of his hand. The court consists of a gathering of local freemen

---

159 *Lex Sax.* §59.
160 *Lex Thur.* §49; *Lex Sax.* §54; *Edictus Rothari* §132; *Wessex* §36; *Lex Sax.* §59.
161 *Leges Liutprandi* §136. See Wormald, 'The *Leges Barbarorum*,' 39.
162 *Forum Iud.* §VI, 5, vii. Trans. Scott, *Visigothic Code*, s.v.
163 Winfield, 'The Myth of Absolute Liability,' 37.

versed in common law, with a presider whose job is to ensure that the judgment concurs with tradition or written law.

A. In the event that Joseph has admitted the act but is unwilling to pay the legally mandated restitution as it was the left hand which was struck off (Scenario #1), the assembly will rule as to whether or not a lesser penalty should be applied for the non-predominant hand. Similarly, if the two parties agree that the blow was accidental but Francis demands restitution (Scenario #2a), the assembly will determine the appropriate amount of the fine. Either party could presumably appeal this ruling, but as long as the penalty imposed by the assembled court is within fair parameters, it seems unlikely that a higher court would re-open the case.
B. If Joseph denies culpability, claiming that the blow was accidental, or that he acted in self-defence, or that he never struck Francis at all (Scenarios #2b, 3, 4), the court grants an adjournment – likely periods are forty or forty-two days – to give the contestants time to seek out witnesses. In both early and later laws, Joseph would be allowed to present supporters in his defence; some sources imply that this same possibility only came into being later for Francis, the accuser. The assembly will determine what supporting evidence should be brought to the next hearing.

This postponement allows the possibility that Francis and Joseph will still find a way to settle out of court. (Some regions, however, required that once a procedure was set in motion, it had to be carried to public conclusion.)[164]

SECOND APPEARANCE: PRESENTATION OF WITNESSES.
The witnesses are produced in front of the presider and the assembled group of local freemen who constitute the court. The nature of their presentations will depend on the details of our hypothetical case. If there are eye-witnesses, they can be called for sworn testimony, either on behalf of one of the parties in the suit, or, perhaps in personal injury cases that require medical testimony, as impartial witnesses of the court. If there are no eye-witnesses, each litigant swears an oath as to the veracity of his version of the events. His oath-supporters back up the oath, and furthermore serve as character-witnesses. Local politics undoubtedly played a large

---

164 See discussion above, p. 37.

role at this point in the proceedings, with each side striving to produce the most influential witnesses.

After the assembly arrives at a verdict, it is ratified by the presider. If the court rules against Francis, it seems harsh if any further payment were exacted: the loss of his own hand is penalty enough. Nonetheless, Francis may be assessed a fee for bringing a false accusation. This penalty would be rendered to the presider as payment for the expense of bringing the suit to judgment. If Joseph is found guilty, he will be assessed a fine payable to Francis. Since the legal penalty for the loss of a hand is half a wergild in almost all barbarian law, the fine would be fairly stiff if the court allowed no mitigation for the loss being that of the non-predominant hand. Joseph is given forty days to produce the money (or goods of equal value). He gives surety that he will pay.

THE CONCLUSION OF THE CASE.
Within forty days, Joseph pays Francis the stipulated penalty, and Francis gives him a quitclaim. This exchange would likely occur in the assembly; however, perhaps the trade could take place in private. As such transactions leave no permanent parchment trail, this latter speculation echoes in silence. The process is completed, and peace has been restored.

The Case of the Damaged Skull[165]

The circumstances of this case occur in two stages. The particulars of the first are fairly straightforward.

> Francis and Joseph, both right-handed lumberjacks, go into the woods to chop down trees. Each carries his axe with him. Over lunch, they get into a dispute. Joseph smacks Francis with the side of his axe blade, fracturing the outer layer of Francis's skull. Both are aghast, and the fight immediately comes to an end. Joseph offers to pay Francis for the damage, but they are uncertain how to settle on a suitable amount.

They amicably go to the assembly, where they are informed that the legal ruling is ten shillings for damage to the outer *tabulum* of the skull. (As

---

165 The outlines of this case were presented to me by my neighbour Ben Guelfo, whose career as a trial lawyer in Louisiana has encompassed cases even more unusual. For discussions of the ramifications of the evidence, see Oliver, 'Æthelberht and Alfred's Two Skulls.'

discussed in chapter 3, the human skull is tripartite, consisting of an outer *tabulum* [or bone structure], an intermediate layer of tissue, and an inner *tabulum*. Damage can be inflicted to the outer *tabulum* without breaking the inner which would still protect the brain and its surrounding membranes.) Joseph pays Francis, Francis gives Joseph a quitclaim, and the case seems to be closed.

The particulars of the second part demonstrate complex variations.

> Two months after the incident, Francis begins to be subject to painful headaches. Eventually he passes out at work one day, and has to be carried home. Here he is confined to his bed, but the headaches do not stop. Finally his wife summons a doctor. The surgeon performs a trepanation to release pressure on the brain. Francis claims that the swelling of the brain was a result of the earlier accident. Joseph replies that there is no proof of this: the headache is more likely the result of spiritual illness. In any event, he continues, Francis gave him a quitclaim. Francis counters that the quitclaim was only good for the visible damage to the skull, and did not include the hidden injury to the brain that resulted from the blow. They take the case to the *mæþel*.

This case presents a wide range of possible rulings upon which the assembly of men knowledgeable in law must deliberate. The pertinent clauses from Æthelberht's laws are as follows:[166]

> §36. If the outer layer of the skull becomes broken, let him pay with ten shillings.
> 36.1 If both [layers of the skull] should be [broken], let him pay with twenty shillings.
> §63. If a person becomes cured [after being wounded], let him [who caused the wound] pay with thirty shillings.
> 63.1 If a person should be wounded such that he becomes bedridden, let him [who caused the wound] pay with thirty shillings.

Clause 36 regulates against injury individually to the outer and inner *tabula* of the skull (as examined in chapter 3). Clause 63 requires the assaulter to pay medical fees, as well as a recompense of thirty shillings for lost work if the victim were confined to his bed.

---

166 I have emended the reading of both these clauses from Oliver, *Beginnings of English Law*. The update for §36 can be found in Oliver, 'Æthelberht and Alfred's Two Skulls'; for §63 in Oliver, 'Sick-Maintenance in Anglo-Saxon Law.'

Presumably Francis would bring to the next hearing among his witnesses his wife, who nursed him at home, and his doctor, who examined the injury. Joseph would be wise to include in his group of supporters others (at least claiming to be) versed in medical practice who could support his contention that the original injury and the headaches were not necessarily related. Although it might seem unlikely that rural Kent was teeming with doctors, it is important to remember that this society was used to coping with medical emergencies, both for livestock and for humans. Injuries which in our own more professionalized days are promptly concealed within ambulances and whisked off to sanitized hospitals were treated at home in full view of all members of the household.

The permutations of the possible rulings for this case are laid out below. In all instances, the fine is in addition to the ten shillings Joseph paid following the first hearing. (In calculating the size of these fines, keep in mind that Kentish wergild was 100 shillings.)

A Joseph must pay for damage to outer and inner *tabula* of the skull, since the trepanation of necessity pierced the inner *tabulum* as well. As he has already paid for the damage to the outer, he owes an additional ten shillings. (Total fine: 20 per cent wergild.)

B Joseph must pay the thirty shillings for Francis's cure. He need not pay additionally for the piercing of the inner *tabulum*, as this was part of the medical procedure, not of the injury. (Total fine: 40 per cent wergild.)

C Joseph must pay the thirty shillings for the time Francis was confined to his bed. (Total fine: 40 per cent wergild.)

D Combining A and B (or A and C, although this combination seems less likely), Joseph must pay ten shillings for piercing of the inner *tabulum* and thirty for the medical fee. (Total fine: 50 per cent wergild.)

E Combining B and C, Joseph must pay thirty shillings for the medical treatment and thirty for the work Francis missed while he was confined to his bed. (Total fine: 70 per cent wergild.)

F Combining A, B, and C, Joseph must pay ten shillings for the piercing of the inner *tabulum*, thirty shillings for the doctor's fee, and thirty shillings for the work Francis lost while confined to his bed. (Total fine: 80 per cent wergild.)

G An argument could even be made that since the trepanation caused a different break in the outer *tabulum* than the original blow, Joseph is responsible for ten shillings for the new piercing of the outer skull, and ten for the concomitant piercing of the inner. In addition, he owes

thirty shillings for the doctor's fee, and thirty for Francis's missed work: a total of eighty shillings. (Total fine: 90 per cent wergild for a man who may already be back at work.)
H Finally, it is also possible that the court could rule that there is insufficient evidence that Francis's headaches were caused by Joseph's original blow, and let Joseph off. Or it could present an alternate ruling that the quitclaim released Joseph from all responsibility not only for the original wound, but for any resulting damage.

The case is hypothetical and there is no correct answer. Were I part of the deliberating body (which would not, however, be possible as I am a woman), I would argue that Joseph should be assessed for the medical fee and at least part of the lost work (depending on how long Francis was actually incapacitated). My ruling would be a forty-five shilling fine for the second suit. The sum total amount Joseph would have to pay would be fifty-five shillings.

Yet even as I proclaim my judgment, I doubt its fairness on a wider scale. When Francis lost his hand, Joseph was fined a maximum of fifty shillings. But Francis's hand will never grow back, and his work will always be impeded. When Francis suffered a skull fracture and had to be trepanned as a result, I chose to fine Joseph fifty-five shillings. But the head wound should eventually heal, and it is perfectly possibly that Francis will suffer no lasting damage. The two injuries are not commensurate in terms of their permanent impact. Is it, then, fair for Francis to receive less restitution for a lasting than for a temporary incapacitation?

Conclusion

The desire to present a public alternative to bloodfeud by requiring compensation in money or in kind for inflicting personal injury can be seen throughout the Germanic laws. Some tariffs are extremely detailed: Frisia regulates damage to individual joints of the fingers, and Alamannia distinguishes between harming the upper and lower eyelid. Other territories concentrate only on more prominent limbs, such as hands and feet. No matter the degree of specificity, the laws present finite amounts of restitution for specific injuries. These clauses might erroneously leave the reader with the impression that compensation for personal injury was regulated unambiguously in the written codices of early Germanic Europe.

As the hypothetical cases above demonstrate, although the written laws provide precise amounts of restitution for physical injury, the process of arriving at a fair construal for any specific suit must always rest on individual interpretation, both then and now. Law in practice must have been far more complex than its representation in writing. Ian Wood provides an example of the need arising in a Merovingian case for the judges to display their knowledge of legal procedure beyond the pertinent written rulings committed:

> On one occasion, the *Pactus Lex Salicae* deals with those *rachinburgi*, or local law-men, who were unable to state the law in response to the demand, 'Tell us the Salic Law': *Dicite nobis legem Salicam*. This suggests that there was unwritten law, supposedly known by the *rachinburgi*, which was not contained in the *Pactus Legis Salicae*.[167]

This dependence on oral tradition to enhance written stipulations continues into the later Frankish Ripuarian law, which demanded the following ability of its judges:

> If anyone pursues his own complaint and the rachinburgii are to speak the Ripuarian law [correctly] to him, then let [the litigant] about whom they have rendered a false judgement say: 'I compel you to speak the law to me.'[168]

The verb employed is 'speak,' not 'read.' The written laws provided a blueprint for the adjudication of suits brought before the court. But, as the hypothetical cases presented above clearly demonstrate, the written statutes leave glaring lacunae in the ability to resolve complex cases.[169] In these instances, the presider would have been expected to draw upon the collective memory of legal proceedings to arrive at a judgment. His databank would include orally transmitted traditions (Isidore's *mos*), rulings committed to writing (Isidore's *lex*), and precedent-setting case law. Three crucial attributes, then, must have distinguished a good *iudex*: familiarity with

---

167 Wood, *The Merovingian Kingdoms*, 110.
168 *Lex Rib.* §55; translation from Rivers, *Laws of the Salian and Ripuarian Franks*, 192.
169 Marculf II, 12 presents a formula for a father wishing his daughter to share equally with his sons in his inheritance, in contradiction to the stipulations of written Salic law. Rio indicates that 'we can only speculate as to how successful this preemptive discarding of legal custom may have been, and as to whether A's daughter was really able to secure her inheritance in practice. Either way, this text does indicate that law, written or otherwise, was not understood as having to be observed rigidly, but rather as one possible source of authority among several.' Rio, trans., *Formularies*, 195–6; see also Rio, *Legal Practice*, 206–7.

the written law; knowledge of orally transmitted analogues; and the ability to choose wisely between conflicting options. A good judge knows the laws and the customs, and combines them with the exercise of reason in arriving at proper judgment.

3 The Head[1]

God the Creator of all things, in his arrangement of the human form, placed the head above the body, and caused all the different members of the latter to originate from it, and it is, therefore, called the head; there being formed the brightness of the eyes, by which all things that produce injury can be discerned; there being born also the power of intelligence, through which the members connected with, and subject to, the head may either be controlled or protected.

(*Forum Iudicum* II, 1, iv; Flavius Recesvintus, King)[2]

In his *Ecclesiastical History*, Bede repeats several stories told by Abbot Berhthun, deacon to Bishop John of Hexham, about miracle cures that John achieved primarily by prayer and blessing. Help from above did not always suffice, however, as evidenced in the following story (from Bede V.6) told by Abbot Herebald, formerly a clergyman under John. Young men of John's clergy are racing their horses, but Bishop John denies Herebald's request to be allowed to join them. Herebald, however, cannot resist: 'overcome by a spirit of wantonness,' he joins in the racing.

---

1 The clauses which will be considered in this chapter are presented in chronological order. *Lex Sal.* §§29.1, 12–16; *Liber Const.* §§11.2, 5.4; *Kent* §§33, 36, 38–49, 60–1; *Lex Rib.* §§5.1–3, 68; *Lex Ala.* §§59–60; *Edict Roth.* §§46–56, 377, 383; *Forum Iud.* §VI.4.iii; *Lex Baiu.* §§4.5–9, 13–16; *Lex Sax.* §§5, 7, 11–12; *Lex Fris.* §§22.1–1, 5–21, 45–6, 65; *Lex Thur.* §§I.13–14, 23–5; *Lex Cham.* §§18, 20; *Wessex* §§35.3–6, 44–52, 66.11, 71. For philological discussion of vernacular terms concerning the head, see Niederhellmann, *Arzt- und Heilkunde*, 241–99.
2 Trans. Scott, *Visigothic Code*, s.v.

Immediately, as my fiery horse took a great leap over a hollow in the road, I fell and at once lost all feeling and power of movement just as if I were dead. For in that place there was a stone, level with the ground and covered with a thin layer of turf, and no other stone was to be found over the whole plain. Thus it happened by chance, or rather by divine intervention in order to punish my disobedience, that I hit it with my head and with the hand which I had put under my head as I fell; so my thumb was broken and my skull fractured and, as I said, I lay like a corpse … [Bishop John] spent the whole night alone in vigil and prayer, imploring, as I suppose, God's mercy for my recovery. In the early morning he came in to me, said a prayer over me, and called me by name. I awoke as though from a heavy sleep and he asked me if I knew who it was who was talking to me. I opened my eyes and said, 'Yes, you are my beloved bishop.' He answered, 'Can you live?' I said, 'I can, with the help of your prayers, if it is the Lord's will.' Then, placing his hand on my head with words of blessing, he returned to his prayers; when he came back very soon afterwards, he found me sitting up and able to speak; and urged as it soon appeared by a divine instinct, he began to ask me whether I was perfectly certain that I had been baptized … I told him the name of the priest who had baptized me. The bishop answered, 'If you were baptized by that priest you were not perfectly baptized, for I know that, when he was ordained priest, he was so slow-witted that he was unable to learn the office of catechism or baptism; and for this reason I ordered him not to presume to exercise this ministry because he could not perform it properly.' Saying this, he made it his business to catechize me forthwith; as he did so and breathed upon my face, I immediately felt better. Then he called a doctor and ordered him to set and bind up my fractured skull.[3]

It seems that Herebald was fortunate not to have died, despite his botched baptism. Although prayer from a proper cleric was necessary to save his life, human intervention was still required to properly set his skull. (The broken thumb is never mentioned again, so it is unclear whether it was cured by prayer, physician, or perhaps even Time, the great healer.) This excerpt demonstrates the importance placed upon prayer in the healing process. Although disease was often viewed as divine retribution for sin, the same reasoning was unlikely to apply to injuries inflicted by mortals. Nonetheless, prayer for recovery was considered a crucial factor in the

---

3 *Bede's Ecclesiastical History of the English People*, 467–9. For medical analysis, see Bonser, *The Medical Background of Anglo-Saxon England*, 99–100.

healing process. Man could provide the technology for the cure, but God would determine its efficacy.

Injuries to the head such as those suffered by Herebald are unsurprisingly the most universally and extensively regulated wounds in early medieval law. Since the ancient studies of Herophilus and Erasistratus, medical scholars have identified the brain as the interpreter of sensation: sight, hearing, smell, and taste.[4] As the skull is the protector of this most vital of organs, it is here we begin our studies of the personal injury tariffs.[5]

Skull

Almost all early medieval personal injury tariffs list body parts from top to bottom, beginning with a cover term for 'head' or 'skull': most of the Latinate laws use Latin *caput*, 'head,' and the Old English clauses replace this term with the vernacular cognate *heafod*.

Many of the continental barbarian laws include variations on the wounding of the skull, given here in its most detailed version from the Lombard laws:

> If someone wounds another in the head, so that bones are broken, for one bone let him pay twelve shillings; if there are two, let him pay twenty-four shillings, if there are three bones, let him pay thirty-six shillings; if there are more, they are not reckoned. Thus as follows, that one bone must be found of such a sort, that it is able to make a sound in a shield at twelve paces across the road, and that measurement shall be truly taken by the foot of a medium-sized man, not by the hand.[6]

---

4 See Siraisi, 'Early Anatomy in Comparative Perspective: Introduction.' In the Middle Ages, the brain was also seen as the locus of demonic possession and related dementia (see Niederhellmann, *Arzt- und Heilkunde*, 44–53).

5 For an overview of skull wounds in the *Leges*, see Niederhellmann, *Arzt- und Heilkunde*, 77–81.

6 *Lex Lang.* §47. 'Si quis alium plaguauerit in caput, ut ossa rumpantur, pro uno osso conponat solidos duodicem; si duo fuerint, conponat solidos uiginti et quattuor; si tres ossas fuerint, conponat solidos trigenta et sex; si super fuerint, non numerentur. Sic ita, ut unus ossus tales inueniatur, qui ad pedes duodicem supra uiam sonum in scutum facere possit, et ipsa mensura de certo pede hominis mediocris mensuretur, nam non ad manum.' For discussion of the shields into which these bones would have been tossed, see Hüpper-Dröge, 'Schutz- und Angriffswaffen nach den Leges und verwandten fränkischen Rechtsquellen,' 121–2.

Salic law likely has a similar stipulation, although this depends crucially on the analysis of the Frankish *inanbina ambilicae* of *Lex Salica* §17.5. The vernacular terms included in the Salic laws can be difficult to interpret, as they are generally corrupt in transmission – the scribe who recorded the laws seems not to have been a native speaker of Frankish, and thus often garbled the unfamiliar Germanic terms. (Marianne Elsakkers refers to these words as being in 'phonological and orthographical disguise,' and correctly points out that many interpretations represent 'wishful thinking on the part of etymologists.' Edward Schröder concurs that '[famous philologers] have not exactly won their laurels here.')[7] Annette Niederhellmann (following previous analyses by Beyerle and Keil) breaks the Frankish phrase down as *in an/bina am/bilicae*. She takes *in* as a misreading for *iii*, a number echoing the three bones stipulated in the Lombard regulation, and goes on to postulate that *an* may be descended from Indo-European **an-*, 'onto' or 'high,' showing where the wound took place (on the high bone). The morphemes *bina* and *bilicae* she compares to §34 in the laws of Kent, which states:

Gif banes blice weorðeþ, III scillingum gebete

If exposure of a bone occurs, let him pay with three shillings.[8]

By this reasoning, Frankish *bina* = Old English *banes* and Frankish *bilicae* = Old English *blica*. This otherwise attractive hypothesis does not account for *am-*, the first element in the second compound, which finds no parallel in the Old English clause. Beyerle's earlier suggestion, interpreting the last compound as *antbillôe*, 'strike out,' with an aggregate sense of 'three high bones struck out,' seems more persuasive. Crucially, however, both assume that the copyist committed the error of 'minim confusion,' the misreading of small verticals in the graphic representation which could create *in* from *iii*. Given the Lombard parallel, the assumption that three bones are regulated in this clause seems to be a tenable hypothesis.[9]

---

7 Elsakkers, 'Abortion, Poisoning, Magic and Contraception in Eckhardt's *Pactus Legis Salicae*,' 249 and 263. Schröder cited in Niederhellmann, *Arzt- und Heilkunde*, 24–5; on p. 3, Niederhellmann lays out some of the difficulties for interpreters.
8 Oliver, *Beginnings of English Law*, 71–2.
9 See Niederhellmann, 'Heilkundliches in den Leges'; Beyerle, 'Die Malberg-Glossen der Lex Salica,' 23.

Other continental laws are less specific as to the number of splinters legislated: *Lex Alamannorum* §57.4 regulates the spall (bone splinters) from the skull regardless of how many might sound in a basin when lobbed across a street, while the earlier *Pactus* §I.4 distinguishes between spall which sounds and that which does not. It must be scant consolation to the wounded victim that his skull splinter is so small that it does not clang against a shield! He would probably be happier in Bavaria, which requires only that a bone splinter be separated from the skull, with no further requirement for aural proof.[10] *Lex Ribuaria* §71.1 requires a payment of thirty-six *solidi* for a bone from the skull (but also from any limb) that sounds across the street at twelve feet. This seems high, considering Salic law's fine of thirty *solidi* for the first three bones, but in Ripuaria any subsequent sounding bone is only fined at one *solidus*, so the penalty would balance out for more egregious wounds. However, the heading to *Lex Ribuaria* §71 stipulates that the rulings which follow concern 'a bone sounding across the road without shedding of blood' (De osse super viam sonante vel absque effusione sanguinis), which seems physiologically impossible, particularly in the case of a head wound. Finally, Alamann law provides us with a ruling which both demonstrates medical intervention and simultaneously warns against shady medical practitioners. If the doctor loses or does not produce the bone splinter from the skull, the victim has two legal recourses: either the doctor admits that the physical evidence was misplaced, or the victim brings two witnesses to swear to the outcome of the bone-toss. Annette Niederhellmann takes this to indicate the worth of the doctor's word: it is equal to the oath of two laymen.[11] An alternate possibility is that this clause was designed to protect a victim whose doctor was later bribed by his assailant.

The skull of a man between the ages of twenty and thirty from Hailfingen provides an apposite image for a splinter wound in the cranium (see Fig. 3.1). Alfred Czarnetzki et al. hypothesize that the hole was caused either by a falling stone (which could have been an unfortunate accident), or by a blow from a blunt instrument, such as a cudgel (in which case the perpetrator would have been liable). The edges of the wound demonstrate only incipient healing; the archaeologists conclude that the young man lived only a short while afterwards, probably dying from internal bleeding of the brain.[12] If this wound was deliberately inflicted, the perpetrator would have been assessed the wergild appropriate to the social status of the victim.

---

10 *Lex Baiu.* §3.6.
11 Niederhellmann, *Arzt- und Heilkunde*, 66–7.
12 Czarnetzki, Uhlig, and Wolf, *Menschen des Frühen Mittelalters im Spiegel der Anthropologie und Medizin*, 48.

Figure 3.1 Skull from Grave 506, Halifingen (Kreis Tübingen, Germany). Splinter wound resulting in death.[13] Photograph reproduced by permission of Carestream Health Germany GmBH.

The laws imply that most splinter wounds did not result in death (or the penalty would involve paying the person's wergild rather than a fine). Archaeological support for this implication can be seen in the skull of a twenty- to thirty-year old man from Kirchheim/Ries, which demonstrates a breach from a blow that fractured the outer skull at the margins and at its depth went right through to the brain (see Fig. 3.2).[14] The rounded edges of the lesion confirm that this man survived the wound, as the bone demonstrates healing at the parameters of the wound.

---

13 A map indicating locations of all grave finds discussed in this study can be found in Online Appendices, II.
14 Between 1962 and 1964, excavations were undertaken in the Alamann cemetery at Kirchheim. More than 500 graves were discovered, dating from the mid-sixth to eighth centuries. The fact that so many examples from this site are included in this study may simply be due to the number of graves excavated. I know of no study which specifically describes the Kirchheim archaeological finds, although such a study would certainly constitute a major contribution to the history of this region.

78 The Body Legal in Barbarian Law

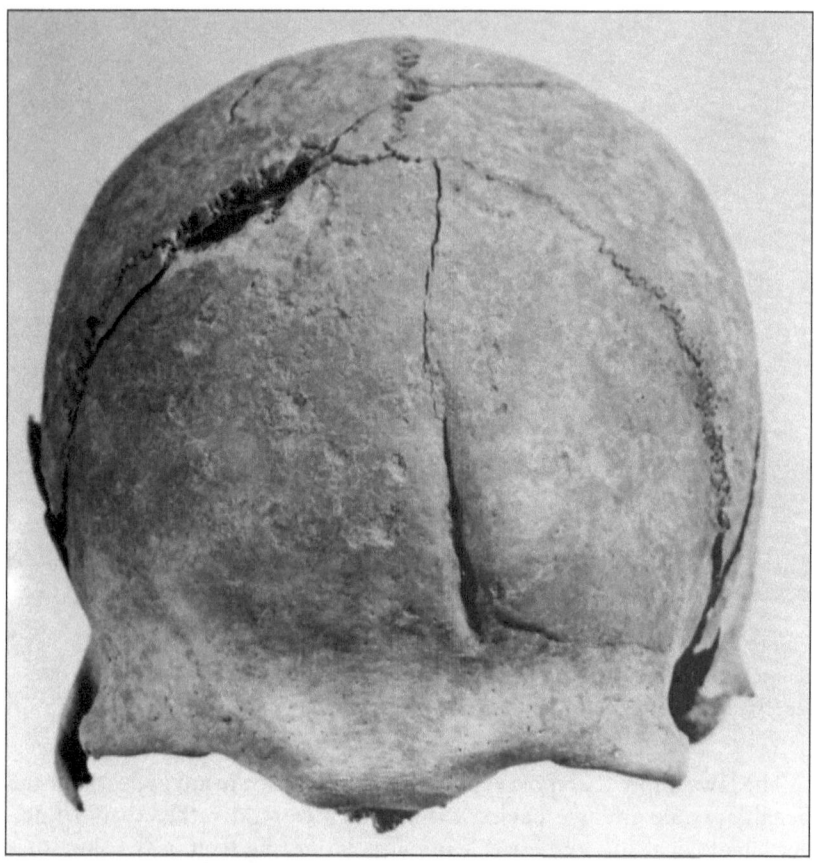

Figure 3.2 Skull from Grave 234, Kirchheim/Ries (Ostalpkreis, Germany). Splinter wound, healed. Photograph reproduced by permission of Carestream Health Germany GmBH.

Grave finds have produced at least one example of a sliver which remains in the excavated skull, albeit not in situ. From the Merovingian burial field at Wies-Oppenheim we have a skull with a bone fragment about 5 cm long x 2 cm wide that seems to have been displaced towards the middle and front in the healing process.[15] Two possibilities occur here:

---

15 Lehmann-Nitsche, *Beiträge zur Prähistorischen Chirugie nach Funden aus Deutscher Vorzeit*, 12.

either the spall remained where it had been displaced, or it was removed and replaced in a proximate position by a doctor. The first hypothesis implies that nature achieved the cure on its own; the second that medical intervention was efficacious, if not precise. At this remove in time, it is impossible to choose between these options.

The laws set by the Anglo-Saxons across the Channel demonstrate a significant differentiation in determining the regulation for skull wounds. The laws of Æthelberht demand a ten-shilling fine for breaking the *uterre hion*, 'outer *hion*' and twenty shillings for breaking both (presumably the outer and inner).[16] This regulation provides the basis for the fictive case discussed in chapter 2, which assumes the viability of the following analysis. The interpretative difficulty rests on the fact that *hion* is a *hapax legomenon* – it does not appear elsewhere in the Germanic corpus.[17] Thus we must consider the possibility that, like so many of the vernacular Frankish terms, it was produced by an error either in copying or in understanding the Old English original.

Since Æthelberht's schedule of personal injury tariffs follows the usual pattern of head to foot, and *hion* appears at the beginning of this section, logic dictates that it should refer to the head or skull.[18] The immediately obvious connection to Modern German *Hirn*, 'brain,' is very attractive, although unfortunately still problematic. The modern definition of 'brain' as opposed to 'skull' (which we would want for the medieval attestation) does not actually present any difficulty, as the two are often equated in other languages, such as Latin *cerebrum*, which can stand for either 'skull' or 'brain.'[19] However, the Old English demonstrative *sio* which precedes *hion* indicates that the noun must be feminine, which is not the case for

---

16 For full discussion of skull regulations in Anglo-Saxon law, see Oliver, 'Æthelberht's and Alfred's Two Skulls.'
17 Felix Liebermann suggested an association of the 'outer' and 'inner' *hion* with the *dura mater* and *pia mater* ('Kentische *hionne*: Hirnhaut'). This represents a revision of his analysis in *Gesetze der Angelsachsen*. In the later article he postulates that scribal omission left out an extension stroke, and that the word should actually read *hionne*, cognate to Suio-Gothic *hinna* and Old Danish *hinnæ*, which both mean 'any species of membrane.' For arguments against this interpretation, see Oliver, 'Æthelberht's and Alfred's Two Skulls,' and Rubin, 'Æthelbert 36: A Medico-Linguistic Discussion on the Word *hion*,' *Nottingham Medieval Studies* 39 (1995): 21–2.
18 For extensive analysis, see Oliver, 'Æthelberht's and Alfred's Two Skulls.'
19 Buck, *A Dictionary of Selected Synonyms in the Principal Indo-European Languages*, 212–15.

any Germanic cognates of *Hirn*, 'brain.'[20] If we accept an interpretation linking *hion* to *Hirn* – as I believe is almost surely the case – the problem of grammatical gender remains unresolved. A second, albeit more interpretable, conundrum is that if we are to translate *hion* as 'skull,' what are the inner and outer elements?

Additional clues towards answering this latter question can be found in the later laws of Alfred, which present a similar ruling regulating damage to an inner and outer *heafodban*, 'headbone.'[21] Here, as in the laws of Æthelberht, damage to the inner requires a payment of twice that for damage to the outer. In both Æthelberht and Alfred the same verb regulates damage to the outer and inner surfaces – *þirel*, 'pierced,' for Æthelberht and *gebrocen*, 'broken,' for Alfred – which implies identical substances. Furthermore, the nature of the verb, at least in Alfred, suggests a rigid material.

In fact, the human skull is tripartite: there is an outer bony layer (*tabulum*) surrounding soft tissue (the *diploe*) which itself rests upon an inner bony layer (*tabulum*). The distinctions become obvious upon examining the diagrams in Fig. 3.3 created by forensic anthropologists O.C. Smith, Elayne J. Pope, and Steven A. Symes, which display effects of bullet wounds to the skull.[22]

These diagrams illustrate clear differences between a direct strike and a tangential strike to the skull. A bullet (or battle-axe) in a direct blow will penetrate the outer skull bone, the spongy intermediate tissue, and the inner skull bone. There will be considerably more spall (bony splinters) into the skull from the inner than from the outer bone layer. A tangential blow, on the other hand, will cause spall outwards from the outer bone layer and inwards from the inner. Most crucially, however, a glancing – that is, superficially tangential – blow can cause the outer bone to be broken without actually damaging the inner.

Although this last instance may seem unlikely, an excellent example was broadcast in an interview on CNN Larry King Live, *Interview with Director,*

---

20 Schwyter, 'L1 Interference in the Editing Process,' suggests that the scribe could have been thinking of *hirnhaut*, which is indeed feminine in German. If my suggested analysis is correct, this implies that the scribe did not have access to the same anatomical knowledge as the compilers of the personal injury tariffs. The term *hirnschal* which appears in a later manuscript of *Lex Baiuariorum* (Niederhellmann, *Arzt- und Heilkunde*, 159–62) similarly would account for the feminine gender but not the duality of the anatomical substance.
21 *Wessex* §70, 70.1.
22 These diagrams are taken from a very useful introduction to bones and forensic anthropology: Smith, Pope, and Symes, 'Look until You See,' diagrams 141–2.

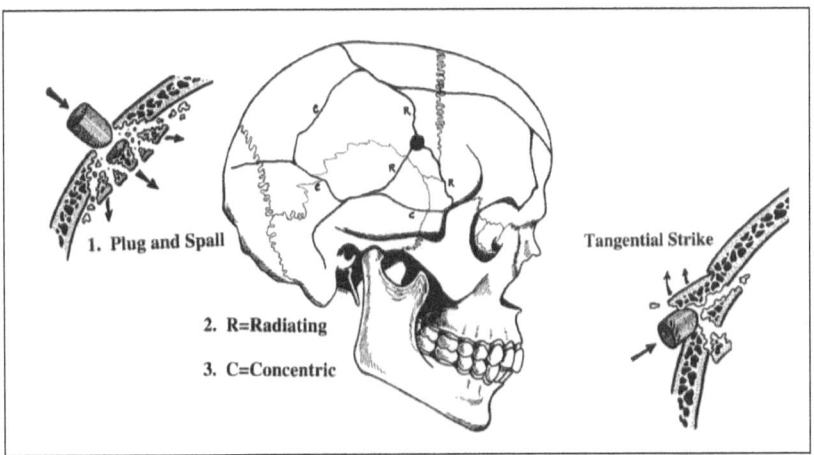

Figure 3.3 Difference in spall between direct and tangential wounds to skull. Diagrams used with permission from Pearson Education, Inc, a division of Prentice Hall.

Cast of Bobby (the film biography of Robert Kennedy), which aired 2 December 2006. In the excerpt below King is talking with Paul Schrade, who was one of two men besides RFK himself who were hit by bullets fired by Kennedy's assassin Sirhan Sirhan. Schrade's account provides us with a first-person description of the physiological reaction to the trauma of such a wound.

> SCHRADE: I was with Bob on the platform listening to his victory speech ... And as soon as he was through, I got off and went towards the pantry, because that's where I was directed to go ...
> KING: And then what?
> SCHRADE: And I turned to go, and all of a sudden I started shaking violently. I was going into shock. I didn't know what had happened. I thought it was – I thought I was being electrocuted.
> KING: Did you hear a gunshot?
> SCHRADE: I heard no gunshots at all. I just passed out completely ...
> KING: Where were you shot?
> SCHRADE: In the head ...
> KING: A scalp wound, or ...?
> SCHRADE: Well, no, it penetrated *the first layer of skull* [emphasis mine]. The doctor took out about a third of the bullet. Two thirds blew away.
> KING: When did you find out that Bobby was dead?
> SCHRADE: It must have been a day or two later, because I was out of it from then on.

'Out of it,' but not dead. Were this his only crime, Sirhan Sirhan would have been liable for ten shillings under Æthelberht's laws, and fifteen under Alfred's. The only offence which demands an equal fine in Æthelberht is striking off the great toe;[23] even today, injury to the outer *tabulum* of the skull and loss of the great toe do not seem to be vastly inequivalent injuries. Schrade recovered from his skull wound without any damage permanent enough to have warranted mention in the interview; he went on to become president of United Auto Workers. Had his great toe been cut off, he would have limped for the remainder of his life.

The archaeological record of the early medieval period demonstrates several instances of damage to the outer *tabulum* which either does not touch the inner, or leaves there a much smaller trace. The skull of a woman from Worms has a 2 cm diameter bone knot (presumably from a healed contusion) on the outer surface of the skull, with no mark at the corresponding spot on the inner surface.[24] Grave 31 from Allach, Upper Bavaria, produced a skull with a depression 4.5 cm x 2 cm on the outer surface that measures only 2 cm x 1 cm on the inner. A skull from the Merovingian burial field at Wies-Oppenheim has a long, oval pathological wound, almost 5.5 cm long and 2.9 cm wide, that generally reaches only into the central area which represents the *diploe* and just touches the inner surface in the middle.[25]

Visual confirmation of these written reports is provided by a skull of a man twenty to forty years old found in Weingarten (Fig. 3.4). The

---

23 Alfred's compensations are left out of consideration here, as his laws offer a bewilderingly inconsistent list (in terms of physiological value) which is difficult to take too seriously since the same fine is assigned, for example, to striking off the arm below the elbow and striking off the 'shooting finger' or forefinger. Fifteen shilling fines are due for (in order) an outer head wound; knocked-out canine tooth; slit cheek; arm cut off below elbow; forefinger off; 2nd (not great) toe off; piercing into scrotum; cut from shoulder-bone; cut from rib. (See Liebermann, *Gesetze*, 1:78–89.)

24 Not long after inhumation, the *diploe* disintegrates, and the two *tabula* become indistinct. Thus we must look to the surfaces of the bony material remaining to us for pre-mortem distinction between outer and inner *tabula*.

25 For European examples, see Lehmann-Nitsche, *Beiträge zur Prähistorischen Chirugie*, 23, 11, 12–13 respectively. For England, Hirst, *An Anglo-Saxon Inhumation Cemetery at Sewerby, East Yorkshire*. Further historical parallels are provided by several skulls from burials of the Chumash Indians in California which exhibit blunt trauma injuries that have caused depression fractures of the outer *tabulum* only. See Fagan, *Time Detectives*, 89. A modern example is provided by the corpse of Kathy Nishiyama, who was murdered in Tennessee in 1982. Among many wounds, she had two different blows to the skull that fractured the outer but not the inner *tabulum* of the skull. See Bass and Jefferson, *Beyond the Body Farm*, 61–2.

Figure 3.4 Skull from Grave 561, Weingarten (Kreis Ravensburg, Germany). Different damage to outer and inner *tabula* of skull. Photograph reproduced by permission of Carestream Health Germany GmBH.

depression certainly fractured the outer *tabulum*, and seems to have also broken the inner *tabulum* at the most egregious point of injury. It appears, however, that the back of the wound fractured the outer layer of the skull, but did not extend to the inner.[26]

Although the insular – that is, Anglo-Saxon – laws seem to demonstrate more precise anatomical knowledge of the structure of the skull, they do not indicate further interest in damage to the cranial region. Lombardy,

---

26 Czarnetzki et al., *Menschen des Frühen Mittelalters*, 45.

Alamannia, Bavaria, and Frisia all legislate against causing injuries to the scalp, with Lombardy demonstrating the distinction between visible wounds and those hidden by hair.[27] Visigothic Spain demonstrates a slightly different breakdown: causing a bruise on the head is fined by five *solidi*; if the skin (presumably of the scalp) is broken, ten; if the wound extends to the bone, twenty. The latter two rulings distinguish between lesser and greater damage to the scalp: in the former instance the skin is simply scratched, whereas in the latter it is peeled back so as to reveal the skull. That is, while Lombardy is concerned with degrees of visible damage, Visigothic Spain concentrates on the physical extent of the injury. The *Forum Iudicum* fines breaking a bone in the head at 100 *solidi*; this global ruling considers neither the spall of the continental stipulations nor the *tabula* of the skull discussed in the Anglo-Saxon clauses.

The *Forum Iudicum* additionally imposes a punishment of thirty lashes for a blow to the head which does not cause blood to flow. Salian Francia, Alamannia, Bavaria, and Frisia reverse this distinction by imposing a fine for a wound to the head which does produce blood.[28] All of these regions thus differentiate between contusion and intrusion. These same territories – with the exception of Spain – add an additional fine for exposure of the brain.[29] (Although Visigothic law regulates against breaking a bone in the head, such a wound would likely but not necessarily expose the cerebrum.) These contintental rulings may, in fact, provide a parallel to the insular clauses concerning skull wounds: splinters from the outer *tabulum* alone are fined according to their ability to sound, whereas if the inner *tabulum* is broken in such a manner that the brain is laid bare, the compensation is increased.

Although it seems unlikely that the inner *tabulum* could be broken without exposing the brain, a skull from Kirchheim/Reis belonging to a

---

27 Injuring the scalp: *Edict. Roth.* §46; *Lex Ala.* §57.3; *Lex Baiu.* §3.4; *Lex Fris.* §22.5.
28 *Forum Iud.* §VI.4.iii. Causing blood to flow: *Lex Sal.* §17.3; *Lex Ala.* §57.2; *Lex Baiu.* §3.2; *Lex Fris.* §22.4. (*Lex Rib.* §2 probably belongs in this group, but it does not specify that the blow need be to the head.) For discussion of 'dry' wounds, see Niederhellmann, *Arzt- und Heilkunde*, 218–28; for bleeding wounds see 229–35. A tenth-century Welsh legal triad from NLW Wynnstay §36 states: 'There are three stays of blood: blood from the head to the chest, blood from the chest to the belt, and blood from the belt to the floor. And if it is spilt from the head to the floor, it is called compete [shedding of blood]' (Roberts, *The Legal Triads of Medieval Wales*, 151). Similar reasoning may underline the reasoning on which rulings on the shedding of blood in barbarian laws are always connected to the head.
29 Exposing the brain: *Lex Sal.* §17.4; *Lex Ala.* §6; *Lex Baiu.* §3.6; *Lex Fris.* §22.8.

Figure 3.5 Skull from Grave 410, Kirchheim/Ries (Ostalbkreis, Germany). Skull break that does not expose brain. Photograph reproduced by permission of Carestream Health Germany GmBH.

man between the ages of forty and fifty demonstrates an injury of this precise nature (Fig. 3.5). Czarnetzki et al. suppose that this wound was caused by a sword blow from the side strong enough to displace the skull. As the lesion has been partly closed by regeneration of the bone, it is clear that the man survived this injury, perhaps after hearing part of his cranium resound in a nearby shield.[30]

The following table summarizes the regulations for injuries to the skull discussed above. The monetary amounts are in shillings for the insular kingdoms of Wessex and Kent, and in *solidi* for the continental regions. In determining actual value, it is crucial to keep in mind the various wergilds (listed in parentheses in the left column).

---

30 Czarnetzki et al., *Menschen des Frühen Mittelalters*, 45.

86 The Body Legal in Barbarian Law

Table 3.1
Skull injuries in barbarian laws
(Injury = Amount of Recompense in *Solidi* [Continental] or Shillings [England])

Territory (wergild)	Wound to Skull		Wound to Membrane	Wound reaches brain	Other
	Spall	Damage to tabula			
Lombardy (100)	1st 3 = 12				scalp covered by hair; 1st 3 wounds = 6
Visigothic Spain (200)				broken bone =100	head bruised = 5 scalp skin broken = 10 wound extending to bone = 20 stroke on the head where blood does not flow: 30 lashes
Francia Salian (200)	1st 3 = 30			brain shows = 15	blood spilt = 15
Ripuarian (200)	1st = 36; others =1				
Bavaria (160)	bones = 6			brain shows = 12	
Alamannia (Pactus) (160)	bone = 6 (not-sounding bone = 3)			brain shows = 12 medical attention required = 40	scalp injury = 3
Frisia (100)		skull-bone pierced = 12	membrane touched = 18	brain shows = 24	scalp injury = 2 blood spilt = 1 lump = 1/2
England Kent (100)		outer = 10 both = 20			
Wessex (200)		outer = 15 both = 30			

An interesting geographical question becomes apparent upon examining this chart: how to assign the Frisian stipulations? As a rule, there is a distinct division between the insular laws – regulating damage only to the two *tabula* – and the continental laws – distinguishing between spall and exposure of the brain. Frisia adds a third category: the laws differentiate between touching the 'membrane' (probably the *dura mater* – the tough, rubbery membrane immediately inside the skull – implying a break of both outer and inner *tabula*) and exposing the brain (which must then logically mean piercing the *dura* and probably also the *pia mater* – the finer membrane that directly surrounds the brain).[31] This suggests that the Frisian laws should be grouped with the insular laws, which distinguish between fracturing the outer *tabulum* or breaking both *tabula*. However, Frisia also aligns itself with several continental laws in fining injury to the scalp and spilling of blood, and alone with Visigothic Spain by ruling that compensation is due for a blow which raises a lump on the head. The evidence tabulated above indicates that Frisia represented a transitional territory between the continent and the British Isles. Frisian law recognizes the difference between the two bony layers of the skull, as is the case in Anglo-Saxon England, but extends legislative rulings to the scalp and the spilling of blood, evidenced only in continental law.

Another important observation to be drawn from this chart is that Visigothic Spain alone requires corporal punishment in addition to the payment of fine. This pattern is repeated throughout the Visigothic laws, and will be discussed in detail in chapter 6. Only *Lex Baiuariorum* §7.3 allows a freeman to be scourged: he receives fifty lashes if he sows, mows, or gathers hay on Sunday. While some other barbarian laws permit the scourging of slaves (see, for example, Wihtred §8.1, stipulating that a slave must pay 'with his hide' for working on Sunday), with the exception of this unique ruling in Bavaria, no other laws even suggest that a freeborn man might be whipped in public. Furthermore, the ruling requiring thirty lashes if blood does not flow from the head wound can only be associated with the five-*solidi* bruise. But in the case of skin broken down to the bone, which would surely cause an effusion of blood, is the monetary fine simply quadrupled to the requisite twenty *solidi* while the requirement for public scourging is removed? This reading seems unlikely. My hypothesis is that the clause should be interpreted that thirty lashes are added to the monetary fine for causing a head wound even if blood does not flow – that is, the attacker is scourged whether or not the wound produces blood.

The rather grisly data supplied by the various skulls depicted above demonstrates the reality of surviving (at least sometimes) head wounds in early medieval Europe. Survival is, of course, a necessary concomitant to bringing a case to court. Both contemporary medical records and

---

31 On the origin of the terms *dura mater* and *pia mater*, see Strohmaier, 'Dura Mater, Pia Mater. Die Geschichte zweier anatomischer Termini.'

archaeological finds provide confirmation of medical intervention in curing injury to the head.

Let us look first at medical evidence. James T. McIlwain's emendation to chapter 33 of Bald's *Leechbook* provides a dramatic image of the brain appearing through a skull wound.³² The text reads:

> Gif man sie ufan on heafod wund & sie ban gebrocen, nim sigel hweorfan, & hwite clæfran wisan, & wudurofan do on gode butran aseoh þurh clað & lacna siþþan. Gif seo eaxl upstige nim þa sealfe do hwon wearme med feþere him bið son sel.

McIlwain argues persuasively that the exemplar more likely read *ex* or *exe* 'brain' for *eaxl* 'shoulder,' which would then give the following translation:

> If a man be wounded from above in the head and the bone be broken, take heliotrope and white clover sprouts and woodruff, put into good butter, strain through a cloth, and then treat (the wound). If the brain [*per McIlwain's emendation*] mount up, take the salve, apply a little warm with a feather, it will soon be well with him.

Simply stated, the passage 'is concerned with a penetrating head wound that has caused the brain to swell and protrude through a defect in the skull and overlying tissue.' McIlwain's hypothesis is supported by a similar treatment described earlier in the *Leechbook*, which states that in the case of a 'broken head':

> If the brain protrude, take the yolk of an egg, and mix it with a little honey, and fill the wound, and bind up with tow and leave it thus: and again after about three days syringe the wound.³³

Lex Alamanorum provides financial restitution in the case of an almost identical treatment:

> §6. If, however, the head becomes laid open, so that the brain appears, so that the doctor must touch the brain with a feather or with a cloth, let him pay with twelve *solidi*.

---

32 McIlwain, 'Does OE *ex* for Brain Lie behind an Instance of *eaxl* in Leechbook III?' I have inserted the emendation into McIlwain's translation.
33 *Leechbook* I, i. 15. Cited in Bonser, *Medical Background of Anglo-Saxon England*, 381.

§7. If however from that same wound the brain mounts up so that it is able to be touched, so that the doctor covers it with medication or with a cloth and afterwards cures it and this is proved to be true, let him pay with forty *solidi*.³⁴

Indeed, *Lex Salica* claims that in the event of a constantly bleeding wound to the head, the perpetrator should pay 62.5 *solidi* to the victim, and another 9 to the doctor. This clearly indicates successful medical intervention: had the wounded man died, the ruling would address wergild rather than fine.³⁵

I know of only one surgical treatise, much of which concerns cranial operations, preserved into and from the early Middle Ages, albeit in two considerably variant versions and probably slightly post-dating our period. One edition is contained in a section in a ninth- or tenth-century manuscript whose heading reads *Incipit Cirugia Eliodori* (BN Paris Cod. 11219, ff. 36v to 38v), which Henry Sigerist entitles the *Cirugia Eliodori*.³⁶ The second is contemporary in manuscript date, found under the superscript *Codex medicinalis de leccionibus Heliodori* (Glasgow Codex Hunterian T. 4. 13, ff. 48r–52r) which Sigerist edits as the *Lecciones Heliodori*.³⁷ Heliodorus was an early surgeon about whom we know almost nothing but what

---

34 §6. 'Si autem testa trescapulata fuerit, ita ut cervella appareant, ut medicus cum pinna aut cum fanone cervella tetigit, cum XII solidis conponat.'

  §7. 'Si autem ex ipsa plaga cervella exierunt sicut solet contingere, ut medicus cum medicamento aut cum sirico stuppavit et postea sanavit et hoc probatum est, quod verum sit, cum XL solidis conponat.'

  For the translation of this phrase I essentially follow the interpretation of Keil, 'Roger Frugardi und die Tradition langobardischer Chirugie,' 23–4, contra Niederhellmann, 'Heilkundliches in den Leges,' 81–2.

35 *Lex Sal*. §22.4; see discussion in Niederhellmann, *Arzt- und Heilkunde*, 87–91.

36 Edited in [Helidor] Sigerist, 'Die "Chirugia Eliodori."' Beccaria notes a second surgical excerpt from the ninth century (Karlsruhe, Reichenauer Codex CXX). This section consists of four folios in a ninth-century manuscript in Karlsruhe, which Beccaria describes as 'a listing of names of maladies with their explanations, following which is another similar listing of operations.' This excerpt is headed by the (confusing) incipit: *Ciruge autem catholice et naturales duo sunt* (Surgery, however, is [of] two [parts], universal and natural). This unedited (and inaccessible to me) fragment is of approximately the same length as the Heliodorus excerpt, and, in light of Beccaria's description, it seems plausible that it is similar. The catalogue of Karlsruhe manuscripts assigns this codex a date of ninth or tenth century, and so it appears to postdate our period in any event (Holder, *Die Handscrhiften der Grossherzoglich Badischen Hof- und Landesbibliothek in Karlsruhe*, 304–7).

37 Sigerist, 'Die "Lecciones Heliodori."'

Juvenal tells us in a poem: that he was a skilled castrator. As a contemporary of Juvenal, he must have been active in the reign of Trajan, that is, 98–117 CE. The name Heliodorus implies African origins; Africa was the homeland for many physicians of late antiquity. The *cirugia* attributed to Heliodorus (almost surely in a legendary rather than actual sense) falls into the following categories: cutting, sewing, wounds, cauterization, and operations on bone. Unfortunately, most of the material consists of definitions in debased Latin rather than instructions – Sigerist assumes that the scribe almost surely had no personal knowledge of the subject matter. The enumeration of Greek terms for operations on bones, even if not elaborated on, implies a robust interest in surgical procedure, whether or not understood by the scribe: *ecprismus*, sawing-out bone splinters; *cataferismus*, filing rough places in the bone; *anatrisis*, boring through a bone from below; *catatrisis*, boring through a bone from above; *peritrisis*, creating a round hole in the skull; *extresis*, energetic boring (also performed with a knife); *paratrisis*, careful boring of the skull as preparation for cutting the bone; *eccope*, cutting a lightly broken bone, *ecprisis*, sawing through the bone; *xyssis*, smoothing a rough bone with the instrument named *xyster*, 'scraper'; *aporinisis*, filing rough places in the bone; *prisis*, cutting into a bone or limb with a saw.[38] The only place Heliodorus goes into detail which might help a practising physician is in how incisions should be made:

> We make a direct incision in the head, ears, in the neck or nearby regions of the femurs, hips, ears, breasts or chest and feet. We make an incision at the boundary of the head and ears. We make a limited, rounded vaulted incision in the forehead.[39]

This is the only early medieval text that includes a 'how-to' guide to surgery. The only other contemporary technical reference to surgery I know of immediately precedes the *Cirugia* in the Paris manuscript; the text consists of an unelaborated list of sixty-three medical instruments. Some of these terms are Latinate in origin, such as *acus*, 'needle,' or *auriscalpium*, 'ear scoop.' Far the majority, however, demonstrate Greek sources, such as *flebotomum*,

---

38 Sigerist, 'Die "Chirugia Eliodori,"' 6–7.
39 'Incisuram rectam facimus in caput . aures . in collum . vel convicina loca . femorum . coxarum . aurium . mammarum vel pectora et pedium ∫ Incisuram in decus facimus in caput et aures ∫ Incisionem absidatem in frontem ∫ Circumcisionem facimus in rotundo.' Sigerist, 'Die "Chirugia Eliodori,"' 4.

'phlebotomy instrument,' *odontoxyster*, 'tooth-scraper,' or *syringotomum*, '?tube.' As this inventory appears again in the contemporary Glasgow manuscript (Hunterian T.4.1) and – remarkably similar – in an eleventh-century Greek codex (Laurentianus gr. LXXIV 2), it seems to have been considered a standard catalogue.[40] No mention is made, however, of how these instruments are to be employed. Clearly surgical practice did not enjoy the same written guides to procedures as provided in medical texts such as Bald's *Leechbook*; setting of bones depended instead on experiential learning.

Archaeological finds confirm the data from legal and medical sources that practitioners were on call to help heal injuries to the head. A grave excavated in Aschersleben, Germany, revealed a variety of instruments of Germanic manufacture for operating on skull injuries, including a hook to open the wound, two instruments for lifting bones, and a combination bone-lifter and pincers with a serrated grip.[41] The results of medical intervention helping in the cure for skull injuries have been discussed in regard to some of the skulls depicted above.

The most convincing proof for early medieval skill in dealing with head injuries comes from the numerous examples of trepanation found in graves of this period. Head wounds could be aided in their cure by trepanation, as drilling or gouging a hole in the skull can relieve pressure on the brain. This art was known and practised throughout medieval Europe. Of the twenty-four trepanned skulls discovered in England which date from the fifth to the eleventh centuries, twenty belong to the first half of this period, and most of them come from the southeast of England.[42]

There are only eight cases of pre-mortem trepanation[43] in Britain up to and including the Middle Ages which actually demonstrate why the surgery had been performed: 'In all cases the evidence was a head injury and in all except one example the head injury had healed.'[44] A grave in Mädelhofen, Bavaria (Germany), dated between the sixth and seventh

---

40 Schoene, 'Zwei Listen Chirugischer Instrumente'; Sigerist, 'Die "Lecciones Heliodori."'
41 Keil, 'Roger Frugardi,' 23; Niederhellmann, *Arzt- und Heilkunde*, 79.
42 Roberts and McKinley, 'Review of Trepanation.'
43 The great early neuro-linguist Broca defined as 'posthumous trepanation' the procedure of sawing out a fragment from the skull after death, so that the living were left with a memento or an amulet. Posthumous trepanations are easily distinguished from pre-mortem – those performed on living humans: in the former case the edges of the hole will have remained sharp, whereas in the latter the bones around the incision will have begun to heal. (Lehmann-Nitsche, *Beiträge zur Prähistorischen Chirugie*, 26.)
44 Roberts and McKinley, 'Review of Trepanation,' 61.

century, demonstrates that this procedure was not limited to Anglo-Saxon England; here the purpose of the trepanation in the left parietal bone may have been to ease swelling caused by contusion. Likewise, Grave 40 from Bonaduz (Switzerland) produced the skull of an adult man whose three head injuries are augmented by a trepanation, presumably performed to relieve cerebral pressure caused by the other wounds. His survival is indicated by the healing of the bone around the trepanned hole.[45]

Despite the obvious skill displayed by these operations, not all were successful. Two skulls of this period demonstrate the arbitrary nature of survival. The skull of a man between thirty and forty years old from Kirchheim/Ries indicates that the operation was performed with a relatively dull boring tool, which may have saved his life. The instrument was apparently not sharp enough to pierce the membranes of the brain, and he survived the operation. Conversely, a skull of a man between the ages of twenty and thirty from Jungingen was trepanned by a much sharper tool, which may have made the procedure itself less painful. However, the sharp edges of the incision remaining in the bony matter demonstrate that the patient did not survive the operation, presumably because the sharper instrument pierced the brain, causing either internal bleeding or infection.[46]

As a final note, we might question the claim by Baldur Keil (in his entry 'Chirugie' in the LMA) that archaeological evidence indicates that operations on skull and brain seem to be more typical for the eastern regions, that is, Germany rather than France or Switzerland. The pervasive evidence for trepanation alone from Anglo-Saxon England, as well as individual grave finds noted above, imply that surgical procedures on the skull were widespread throughout the territories regulated by the barbarian laws. Furthermore, the incidence of success in these operations seems to have been quite high.

Sensory Organs

The sensory organs protected by the skull constitute the eyes, nose, ears, and the various elements that comprise the mouth. Only the first of these is regulated in all barbarian laws; as personal injury tariffs in Burgundian

---

45 Schneider-Schneckenburger, *Churrätien im Frühmittelalter auf Grund der archäologischen Funde*, 26; for more on this find, see also Baumgartner, 'Fussprothese aus einem frühmittelalterlichen Grab aus Bonaduz,' 160.
46 Czarnetzki et al., *Menschen des Frühen Mittelalters*, 99. See Online Appendix III.5 for photographic images of these skulls.

and Chamavan law are far more meagre than the others, it is unsurprising that it is the eye alone which is mentioned in these two texts.

The most usual pattern for compensation is that eye = nose = ear. This is the extent of regulation in Salic and Thuringian law, and I would be inclined to take such a ruling as implicit for Burgundian and Chamavan law also. Ripuarians, Alamanns, Bavarians, and Saxons all add to the equation a half fine either if the organ is struck off but the sensory perception remains, or if the sensory perception is damaged but the organ remains. For example, if the eye remains in situ, but has been blinded, the fine is half the amount it would be if the eye has been struck out. Saxon law extends this even further, charging one quarter of the total fine if the vision is merely impaired, as opposed to destroyed. The regulation of the ear presents the converse to that for the eye: if the ear has been struck off but hearing is not damaged, the fine is half what it would be for striking off the ear and causing deafness. These stipulations demonstrate the medieval understanding that the outer ear aids in, but is not integral to, the hearing process. Interestingly, none of the barbarian laws regulate against damage to the vestibular apparatus ('the inner ear structures that are associated with balance and position sense'), although the medieval acquaintance with vertigo is demonstrated by, for example, the Old English term *swinglung*.[47]

The pertinent function of the nose is assessed in Ripuaria and neighbouring Alamannia differently than in Saxony. The two more southern territories demand a half fine if enough of the nose remains so that it can contain mucus. If, however, a sufficient amount has been struck off so that mucus constantly dribbles from the stump, a fine equal to the full penalty for eye or ear is required. This legislation addresses the physical task of the nose to contain mucus; in contrast, Saxony regulates according to sensory function. If the nose remains in place but the sense of smell is destroyed, the fine is half that for a severed nose; if the sense of smell is merely damaged, the fine is one-quarter. This echoes the Saxon pattern established for the eye. None of these laws, however, address loss of taste which is concomitant with loss of smell. The danger rests in the fact that the victim cannot determine either by smell or by taste if he is consuming food so spoiled that it may cause illness or even, in extreme cases, death. Furthermore, a person who has lost the sense of smell will not be able to perceive subtle traces of smoke in the air, which may presage a life-threatening fire. Finally, striking off the nose

---

47 I owe this observation to Jim McIlwain. The definition is excerpted from *Mosby's Medical Encyclopedia*.

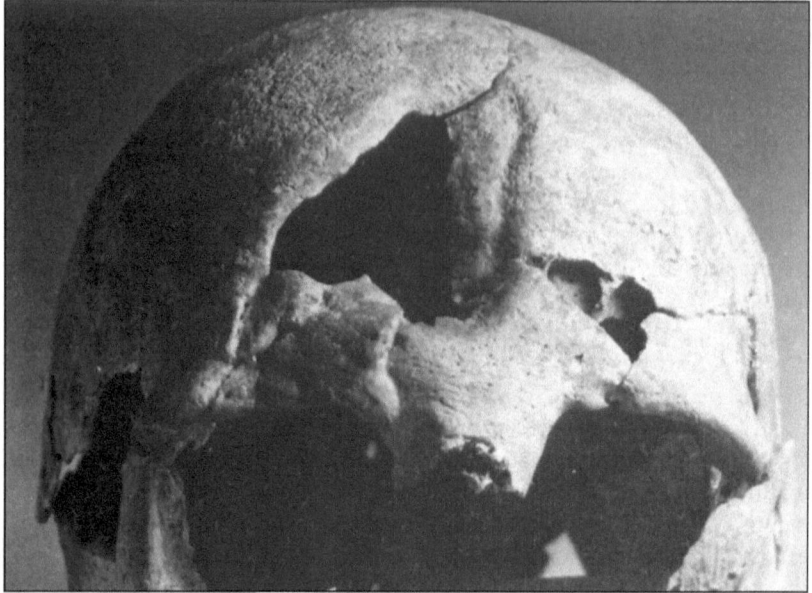

Figure 3.6 Skull from Horrheim, Germany. Regeneration of bone indicates that victim survived. Photograph reproduced by permission of Carestream Health Germany GmBH.

causes considerable cosmetic damage – perhaps even more so than the loss of an eye, which may be less obvious simply due to its more retracted position in the face. A somewhat later literary example can be found in Marie de France's lay of *Bisclavret*, in which the werewolf bites off the nose of his faithless wife, thereby destroying the beauty for which she is renowned.[48]

A fairly dramatic case of damage to the eye can be seen in the skull of a fifty- to sixty-year-old man from Horrheim (near Stuttgart, Germany), who was struck a mighty blow on the right side of the cranium (see Fig. 3.6). The eye-socket was fractured in several places, and the right eye was lost; both temples were breached. The large triangular hole indicates an open skull-brain injury, and demonstrates proof of operative care. The surgeon evidently removed several bone fragments, but left a finger-long break to heal on its own. Regeneration of the bone demonstrates that, despite the gruesome appearance of this skull, the victim survived his injuries.[49]

---

48 Burgess and Busby, trans., *The Lais of Marie de France*, 68–72.
49 Keil, *Roger Frugardi*, 22–3. For photograph, see Czarnetzki et al., *Menschen des Frühen Mittelalters*, 47.

Five territories have been excluded from the discussion so far: the insular kingdoms of Kent and Wessex, and the continental regions of Frisia, Lombardy, and Visigothic Spain. The Spanish rulings show considerable difference from all the others; they will thus be considered at the end of this section. The Lombard laws align themselves with those of Salic Francia and Thuringia in ignoring damage to the senses. The Anglo-Frisian grouping has no regulation against damage to smell. All four regions share two features unattested (except in one instance) by the other continental laws addressed above. First, although restitution for the eye (within a close approximation) equals that for the nose, only half this compensation is due for damage to the ear. If the ear is struck off without causing deafness, the compensation is halved again. This could conceivably be due to the fact the loss of an ear may not be immediately visible, as the site of the wound can be covered by hair or a hat. On the other hand, there is no disguising the loss of an eye or the nose.

The eye and nose are probably valued most often in the barbarian laws due to both their crucial physiological functions and to the obvious visible impact of their loss. The loss of a single eye, however, does not destroy all vision; indeed, often the sight in the remaining eye grows stronger in compensation. This fact is demonstrated in the draconian Visigothic ruling that a traitor shall have both his eyes put out 'so that he may not see the wrong in which he wickedly took delight.'[50] In a Frankish capitulary of 779, we find a regulation supporting the hypothesis that the visible damage to eye and nose can be a factor in recompense: a thief must lose an eye for his first theft, for the first repeat theft his nose, and for the second repeat theft his life.[51] Conversely, an argument for the equality of all facial organs could be adduced by the fact that when Gaiseric, king of the Vandals, wished to disembarrass himself of his Gothic wife so he could marry into the Empire, she was accused of plotting to poison him and was sent back to her father with her nose and ears mutilated.[52]

The second differentiation is that these territories (joined by Alamannia) contain rulings on damage to the mouth. The proposal above that the lesser fine for the ear might be attributable to a greater concern for the visual

---

50 *Forum Iud.* §VI.4.iii. Trans. Scott, *Visigothic Code*, s.v.
51 Schmidt-Wiegand, *Wörter und Sachen*, 38.
52 Bury, *The Invasion of Europe by the Barbarians*, 128.

nature of the damage receives some substantiation from the southern version of stipulations regarding the mouth. Both Lombardy and Alamannia regulate against a cut to the lip that reveals the teeth. Alamannia, however, distinguishes between upper and lower lip. Damage to the upper is adjudicated purely on the visual criterion of exposing the teeth. Damage to the lower is based on physiological function similar to the clause addressing the nose: a fine is assessed if the lower lip is damaged in such a fashion that it is unable to contain saliva.

The more northern territories of Frisia and Kent concentrate on the ability of the mouth or lips to speak rather than to cover the teeth or control the flow of saliva. The Frisian laws fine the infliction of a wound that renders the victim mute, and the Kentish laws similarly protect a person whose speech has been impaired. Although Wessex contains a clause against damage to the Adam's apple, two facts remove this ruling from inclusion in the grouping addressing speech impairment. First, Alfred's clause is gender-specific, since women lack Adam's apples; both sexes, however, are equally capable of talking. Second, although Frisia is the only territory to rule unambiguously against damage to the throat, Liebermann postulates that *þrot* has been inadvertently omitted in the copying of Æthelberht §46. This might, however, equally probably be restored as Adam's apple (*þrotbolla*) on the model of Alfred.[53] Neither Frisia nor Kent connects the inability to speak directly to an injury to the throat. The Wessex ruling is thus probably not related to the speech faculty.

Salian Francia and Thuringia, which do not join the majority of continental laws in regulating damage to vision, hearing, or smell, both contain clauses within the sections on teeth that address injury to the tongue. Although the Thuringian laws do not elaborate on this ruling, Salic law specifically associates the concomitant damage to the ability to speak. It seems a tenable conclusion that the same underlying association is intended in the laws of Thuringia. These two territories alone consider impairment of speech while ignoring sensory functions. In the laws of Wessex, the penalty for slander is to have the tongue cut out, although this can be redeemed with the appropriate wergild.[54]

---

[53] This hypothesis should have been included in the discussion of Æthelberht's §36 in Oliver, *Beginnings of English Law*, 70–1. For Liebermann's restoration, see *Gesetze*, 3:11.

[54] *Wessex* §32. See discussion in O'Brien O'Keeffe, 'Body and Law in Late Anglo-Saxon England,' 215.

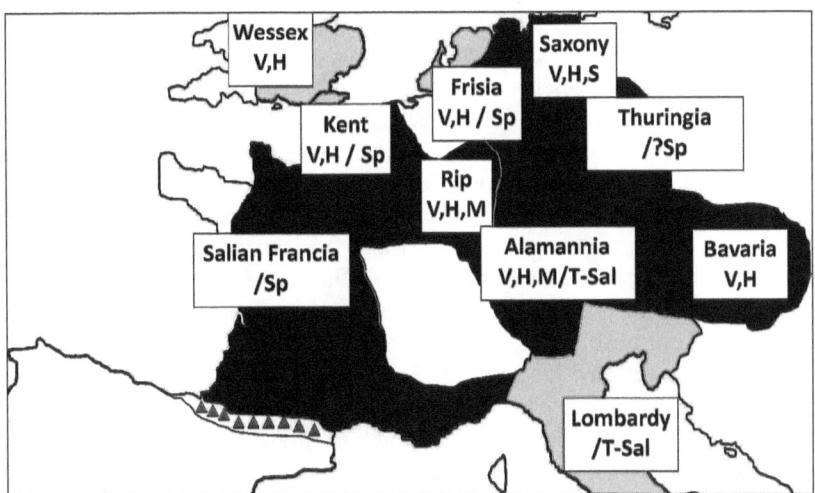

Map 3.1 Regulation of sensory organs.
Dark shading = equation between eye, ear, and nose
Light shading = ear is 50 per cent of eye and nose.

Damage to sensory capacities / Injuries to mouth:
  V (vision), **H** (hearing), **S** (smell and taste), **M** (mucus)
  T (exposure of teeth)
  Sal (inability to contain saliva)
  Sp (impairment of speech)

Finally, Visigothic law demands a pound of gold if the eye is maimed but can still see, but does not address the case of loss of sight. If the nose is entirely destroyed, the fine is 100 *solidi*. Unlike any other territory, the fine for damage to the nostrils, ears, or lips is assessed by the judge according to the deformity produced. While every other law regulates injury to the sensory organs with a finite amount (often keyed to the wergild), Visigothic law leaves the amount of compensation to the discretion of the presider. If we accept the hypothesis that this option was also available in other territories, then the salient difference is that no upper limit was set in Visigothic Spain. Or perhaps openness of the ruling permitted the addition of corporal punishment in particularly egregious cases.

Map 3.1 lays out the geographical distribution of clauses regulating sensory organs. Dark shading demonstrates an exact equation between eye, ear, and nose, while light shading means the ear is assigned half the value of the eye and nose. Rulings for damage to sensory capacities are indicated in the upper line of the text box by **V** (vision), **H** (hearing), and/or **S** (smell and taste). In the lower line of the text box, three different rubrics are provided for the mouth: **T** represents exposure of teeth, **Sal** the inability to contain saliva, and **Sp** impairment of the speech function. (Due to the unique nature of their rulings, the Visigothic laws are excluded from this map.)

This map presents several possible regional affiliations, although none are unproblematic. The northeastern Anglo-Frisian territories of Frisa, Kent, and Wessex all regulate vision and hearing while ignoring smell: however, the furthest-eastern kingdom of Bavaria shares this feature. The hypothesis of an Anglo-Frisian cluster is strengthened by the fact that Frisia and Kent both regulate against speech impairment, although Wessex does not contain any such ruling. A grouping which may have been in place before the setting of a unique code for Ripuaria unites the horizontally centrally located Salian Franks and Thuringians, who ignore all sensory functions but include penalties for damage to speech, shared by the northeastern block of Kent and Frisia. A vertical axis is provided by the territories that consider damage to the nose: northern Saxony concentrates on the sensory impairment of smell, while further southern Ripuaria and Alamannia address the more visual aspect of allowing mucus to flow uncontained. Finally, the southeast territories of Alamannia and Lombardy are the only two to regulate against exposing the teeth or releasing saliva.

We should not leave the rulings on sensory organs without considering terminology. Overall this provides us with little insight: all regions use terms directly inherited from Indo-European for eye/see (*ok^w-) and ear (*ous-). Almost all the barbarian laws similarly use the inherited Proto-Indo-European term *nas- for nose. One of the two exceptions is found in the Greek translation of the Lombard laws, which uses the standard Greek term *rhis*, derived from the PIE root *sreu-, 'flow,' a common if unattractive function of the nose. (This prefigures the regulation on the inability to contain mucus contained in the Alamann and Ripuarian laws.) The Latin original of the Lombard clause, like all the other Latin texts, employs the inherited *nas-.

The second, and slightly more interesting, exception is found in the laws of Alfred, which refer to the nose as *neb*. The inherent meaning of 'beak' is demonstrated by the Old English poem *Phoenix*, a verse translation of a Latin original, which provides the following description of the bird:

> Sindon þa fiþru hwit hindanweard, ond se hals grene nioðoweard ond ufeweard, ond þæt nebb lixeð swa glæs oððe gim.[55]

---

55 Krapp and Dobbie, *The Exeter Book*, 102, ll. 297–9.

The feathers are white in back, and the neck green below and above, and the <u>beak</u> shines like glass or gem.

This meaning persisted into the Renaissance, as demonstrated by a quote from the 1535 Coverdale Bible describing the dove returning to Noah's ark with proof of the re-emergence of land:

Gen. 8:11 She had broken of a leaf of an olyue tre, & bare it in hir <u>nebb</u>.[56]

She had broken off a leaf of an olive tree, and bore it in her <u>beak</u>.

At least by the time of Alfred's laws (871 x 901), the sense of 'beak' had been metaphorically extended from fowl to human. This transference exactly parallels the modern American usage: 'Would you look at the beak on that guy?' Just as the term 'beak' is employed in dialect or slang in the United States today, so is the word 'neb' in Britain, as illustrated by a use in modern British fiction to represent Yorkshire patois: 'This is *men's* work. You keep your little turned up neb out of it.'[57] (Interestingly, the dialect form 'neb' was the native term used by James Murray, the compiler of the first editon of the *Oxford English Dictionary*.)[58] Finally, this term has crossed the ocean to appear in Appalachian 'nibb' and 'nib-nosed,' the latter of which demonstrates a persisting awareness of the original meaning.[59]

Other Facial Features

Aside from the sensory organs, the most commonly regulated facial feature in barbarian law is hair, which will be discussed in its own section. The chart below indicates the other constituent elements for which fines are assessed, as well as the territories in which these rulings can be found.

The most immediately striking fact demonstrated by this chart is the close grouping between Bavaria and Alamannia on the one hand and the Anglo-Frisian territories (Kent, Wessex, Frisia) on the other. The two eastern-most regions differentiate between the two eyelids on the basis of their differing functions: destroying the lower so that the eye cannot contain tears draws a fine twice that for destroying the upper so that the eye

---

56 Cited in Bosworth and Toller, *An Anglo-Saxon Dictionary*, 713, at *neb*.
57 Allingham, *Mystery Mile*, 41.
58 Murray, *Caught in the Web of Words*, 17.
59 I owe this observation to Aurora Jurasinski.

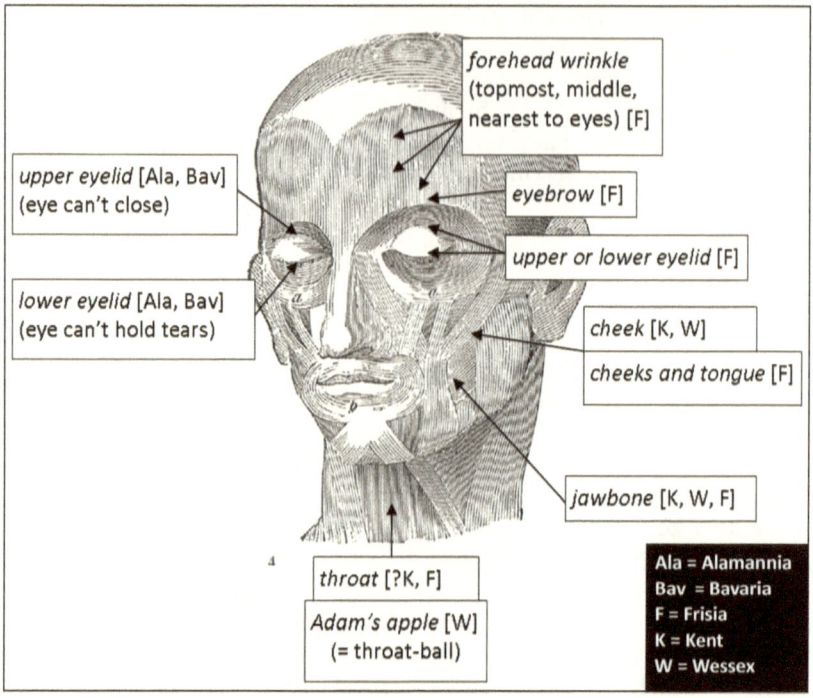

Figure 3.7 Non-sensory organs regulated in barbarian laws.

cannot close. These very specifically located injuries may well have been inflicted for the purposes of deliberate mutilation, perhaps a case of personal revenge. Actually the upper eyelid should be valued more highly for three reasons. First is the fact that it 'is the principal mover in blinking, which is important for distributing the tear film in a smooth layer over the cornea. This has important consequences for image formation as well as preventing dessication of the cornea.'[60] Second, if the eye cannot be covered, it remains unprotected from flying dust and debris. (No person suffering such an injury could ever, for example, ride a horse.) The third problem comes when the victim attempts to sleep with a permanently open eye. The only remedy for the loss of an upper eyelid is to wear an eyepatch. But then vision is impaired, if not inherently, at least by the inability to see through the patch

---

60 Dr James McIlwain, personal communication.

material; nor does a bandage provide the close contact to help the distribution of tear film. The primary reason to legislate against striking off the lower eyelid is that the eye cannot retain necessary moisture. There is no easy patch for this problem, which may explain the higher fine.[61]

The North Sea grouping is more thorough in what it regulates, but makes no mention of functionality. The Anglo-Saxon territories limit their interest to the lower part of the head: cheek, jawbone, and throat or Adam's apple. Frisia aligns itself with them, but goes on to legislate against mutilation of either eyelid, the eyebrow, and even (individually) the three wrinkles on the forehead. The assessment for slicing the forehead wrinkles increases the closer they are to the eye. Clearly these fines primarily consider cosmetic rather than physiological harm. The only other early medieval laws to give such prominence to visible damage to the face – that is, insult added to injury – are those of the Irish, who regulate injury to eyelash, eyebrow, cheek, chin, and jawbone.[62] The evidence from legal texts suggests that early medieval Frisia and Ireland placed a higher value on insultingly visible but only superficially harmful damage than did their contemporaneous neighbours, who legislated primarily for functional damage. Adding the evidence for cheek and jawbone from the Anglo-Saxon territories indicates a fairly strong Insular-Frisian areal connection.

Finally, many barbarian laws have a generic clause requiring a fine for damage to the face. Regions lacking such a ruling are the Frankish grouping of Salian, Ripuarian, and Chamavan Francia, as well as the Frankish-dominated Saxony; and Bavaria and Frisia, who perhaps felt that they had already dealt specifically with injuries of this nature in their more detailed rulings on facial features. Tellingly, the only Germanic term employed in the Thuringian personal injury tariffs is *wlitewam*, 'damage to the face,' exactly paralleling the terminology in Kent, thus demonstrating the importance of this concept to barbarian legislators. Stefan Jurasinski has recently pointed out that Old English *wamm* implies shame more than damage or disfigurement, citing the following parallel from *Maxims* I:

> Here we are told the consequences of [a woman's] not staying at home and minding one's own domestic duties: 'word gespringeð, oft hy mon <u>wommum</u> biliho // hæleð hy hospe mænað, oft hyre hleor abreoþeð' (Word spreads,

---

61 I am indebted to Dr Jennifer Szurgot and Dr James McIlwain for these observations. See also Bevin, *A Pictorial Handbook of Anatomy and Physiology*, 64–5; Memmler, Cohen, and Wood, *Structure and Function of the Human Body*, 130–4.
62 See Binchy, 'Bretha Déin Chécht.'

often they encompass one with *shameful [accusations]*, men speak of her insultingly, often her face becomes marred). It is perhaps relevant to the usage of wlitewamm in [Æthelberht] chapter 56 that public disgrace is linked in this passage, associatively, but perhaps causally, to embarrassing marks on one's face.[63] (emphasis in original)

Jurasinki's interpretation for Anglo-Saxon England parallels the fact that the Old Irish term *enech*, 'face,' takes on the legal meaning of honour; 'face-price' is equivalent to 'honour-price.'[64]

Burgundy, Alamannia, and Wessex all demand a higher restitution if the wound is not covered by clothing or hair. These clauses emphasize the concern for 'insult' wounding – that is, visible if not necessarily debilitating injury. It seems apposite to conclude this section with the ironic observation that in nineteenth-century Germany dueling scars came to be seen as a badge of honour.

Teeth[65]

In terms of physiological function, the most valuable teeth in the mouth are the canines. These are the teeth which keep the jaw from dislocating: the lower canines will strike against the upper to prevent the jaw either from lurching to the sides or launching itself pugnaciously out of the face. The second-most utile teeth are the molars, which grind and process food. Molars found in early medieval burials emphasize by their wear the importance of this function in a society where much food was coarse and gritty.[66] This group divides into two: the smaller pre-molars at the front of the mouth and the larger molars at the back. Molars and pre-molars function alike, although the molars have greater functional value due simply to the larger surface area. The least necessary teeth are the incisors, whose role is to tear or rip food – a task which can easily be performed by a *seax* or short knife. We can diagram the functional hierarchy as in Fig. 3.8: first the canines, second the molars, and last the incisors.[67]

---

63 Jurasinski, 'Germanism, Slapping and the Cultural Contexts of Æthelberht's Code,' 61.
64 Binchy, *Críth Gablach*, 84–6.
65 This is a revision of the analysis published in Oliver, 'Lex Talionis in Barbarian Law.'
66 See Bonser, *Medical Background of Anglo-Saxon England*, 387–92; Hedemann, 'Zahn- und Kieferbefunde,' 87–90.
67 I owe these observations to personal communication from Kenneth Wilkinson, DDS. His analysis is supported by Toby Charamie, Dean of Louisiana State University School of Dentistry (personal communication):

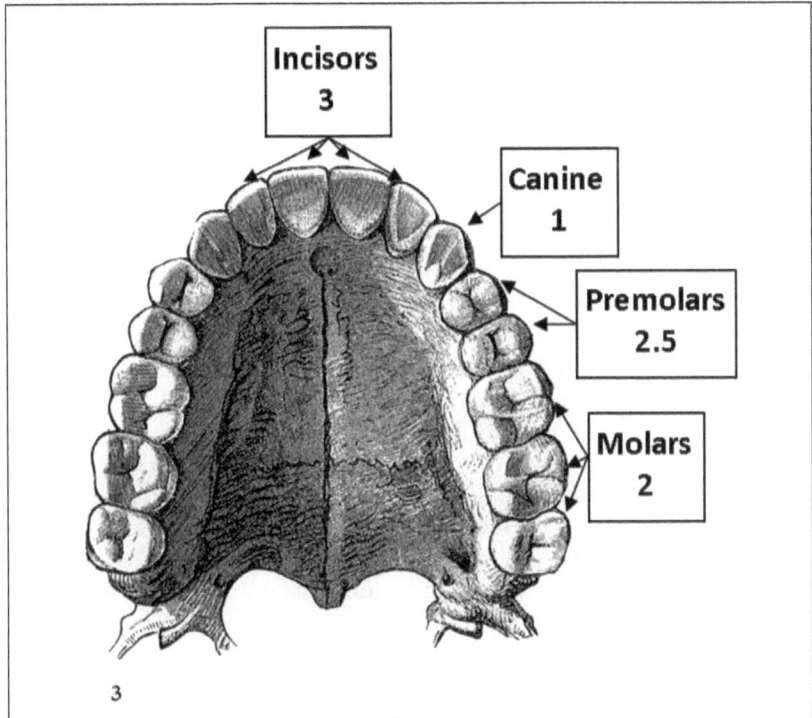

Figure 3.8 Relative functional value of teeth.

I never considered each tooth individually from a value perspective, but I certainly agree with Dr. Wilkinson that the canines would be the most valuable (we refer to them as the 'cornerstones' of the mouth), and our restorative treatment plans are extremely limited if we don't have the canines to work with – not to mention they are also the longest (and therefore strongest) rooted teeth in the mouth. It's more interesting, however, to divide the teeth values by two categories: function and esthetics. So, just for fun (and entirely in my opinion), I would weigh those two categories as follows.
FROM MOST VALUABLE TO LEAST VALUABLE
Function: Canines, 1st and 2nd molars, central and lateral incisors, premolars, 3rd molars.
Esthetics: Central and lateral incisors, canines, premolars, 1st, 2nd and 3rd molars.
Although Dr Charamie assigns certain molars a functional value lower than the incisors, he agrees with Dr Wilkinson in the assessment of the primary molars as more functionally utile than the incisors. See Kraus, Jordan, and Abrams, *Kraus's Dental Anatomy and Occlusion*, §§2–5; also Lucas, *Dental Functional Morphology*, 16–21, 97–132.

How do the distributions in barbarian laws match up against this? The numbers on the charts below indicate the relative amounts of fines assessed for striking out teeth in each region, descending from 1, which marks the teeth whose loss was most highly appraised. The individual charts are ordered in terms of how closely the territorial laws match the functional hierarchy displayed above (see Fig. 3.9). (Omitted territories have no rulings on teeth.) Almost inconceivably, only three regions agree in their valuations! This may be one of the factors that led Patrick Wormald to hypothesize that perhaps the personal injury tariffs were deliberately structured to distinguish regional identity.[68]

None of these breakdowns agrees exactly with functional value. The closest is that of the Bavarians, which gives priority to the canine, implying recognition of its role by assigning it the Germanic vernacular term *marchzand*, 'bordertooth' – its position at the corner of the perimeter allows it to contain the movements of the jaw.[69] (The valuation of teeth presents one of the few distinctions between Bavarian and Alamann law; the Alamanni employ the same terminology but end up in a dismal tie for last place with the Kentsmen in the race for functional accuracy.) I have ranked the Frisians second even though they don't assign the canine teeth their full worth, since they are the only ones who properly recognize the value of the molars.

This gives them priority over the legislators of Wessex. Although Alfred rates the canines highest, he gives second ranking to the incisors, which definitely should be third. The Frisians recognize the value of the molars, but rank them above the canines. The Salian Franks, Burgundians, and

---

68 Wormald, 'The *Leges Barbarorum*,' 41.
69 Annette Niederhellmann analyses *marchzan* differently, relating the first element to Modern German *Mark*, 'marrow,' and taking the compound to refer to molar(s). She bases her hypothesis on two facts: first, that the molars have considerably more pulp than the other teeth (which I find a somewhat weak argument), and second, that variations of a form *Marchzahnd* meaning 'molar' persisted in Austria into the twentieth century (which is certainly more persuasive). One manuscript of the *Lex Baiuariorum* presents the alternate *stockzan*, '?stick-tooth.' This seems to me again likely to refer to the longer canine. However, she points out that the *Deutsche Wortatlas* lists *Stockzahn* as a variant of *Backenzahn*, 'molar,' in areas of Bavaria, Switzerland, and Austria. In this instance, the first element must be associated with the common use of *Stock* as referring to a stump left in the ground. Interestingly, even if we accept Niederhellmann's argument that *marchzahn* in fact refers to the forward molars, the relative value hierarchy does not change, since, if the canines are left out of consideration, the most valuable teeth would, in fact, be the forward molars. See Niederhellmann, *Arzt- und Heilkunde*, 164–8.

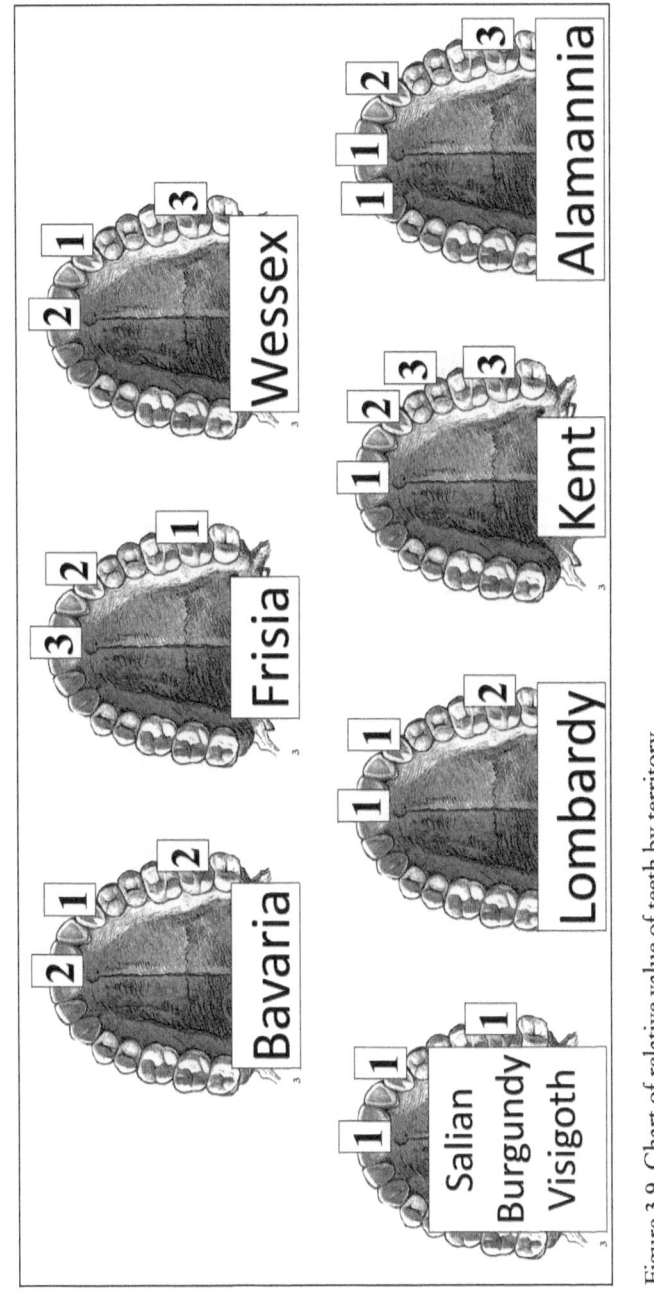

Figure 3.9 Chart of relative value of teeth by territory.

Visigoths categorize all teeth equally. The others all place the incisors highest in value, moving from front to back in stages, thus positioning the molars at the bottom of the hierarchy. The Lombards alone group incisors and canines. Both Alamanni and Kentsmen assign descending values to incisors > canines > molars, with Æthelberht distinguishing the incisors in prominence although not in valuation between the two front teeth and '*se toþ se þanne bi standeþ*' (the tooth that stands beside [them]).[70]

This analysis presents a clear distinction of purpose in these clauses. Whereas legislation in Bavaria, Frisia, and Wessex approximates physiological worth, that in Salic Francia, Burgundy, and Wessex ignores any differentiation. All other territories, however, place greater importance on aesthetic than functional worth. Although the incisors are replaceable in function, their loss is immediately visible any time you open your mouth to speak. Most of the Germanic territories, then, are more concerned with the observable evidence of lost teeth than the resulting inconvenience. Here we seem to have a payment for damage to honor taking precedence over physical loss: the insult outranks the injury.

Map 3.2 below lays out the regulations on teeth; shading goes from dark to light as the relative values of the fines correlate less and less with the functional value of the teeth. Darker shading thus represents a greater emphasis on physiological utility, whereas lighter indicates greater interest in recompense for visible damage. Another way of interpreting this map is that darker shading preferences function, while lighter stresses aesthetics.

The southwestern territories group together in assessing all teeth equally. The grouping of Frisia and Wessex, which we find elsewhere, adheres closely to functional verity, a point which lends itself to easy explanation. In later Frisian legal compilations, personal injury tariffs become increasingly detailed in respect to anatomical detail.[71] This later almost obsessive fascination with legislating the human body is predicted in the functional accuracy with which *Lex Frisionum* addresses fines for knocking out teeth. Furthermore, we have already seen evidence for the influence of Frisian law on the laws of Alfred; the difference in Wessex is to give the incisors increased value, thus bringing these rulings closer to those of Alfred's ancestor Æthelberht of Kent. The later laws of Alfred, then, drew upon both the cross-Channel influence of Frisian legislators, and the inherited rulings of previous Anglo-Saxon laws. With the exception of Bavaria, all other central

---

70 Kent §48, 48.1. See Oliver, *Beginnings of English Law*, 70–1.
71 See Buma, *De Eerste Riustringer Codex*, 107–14.

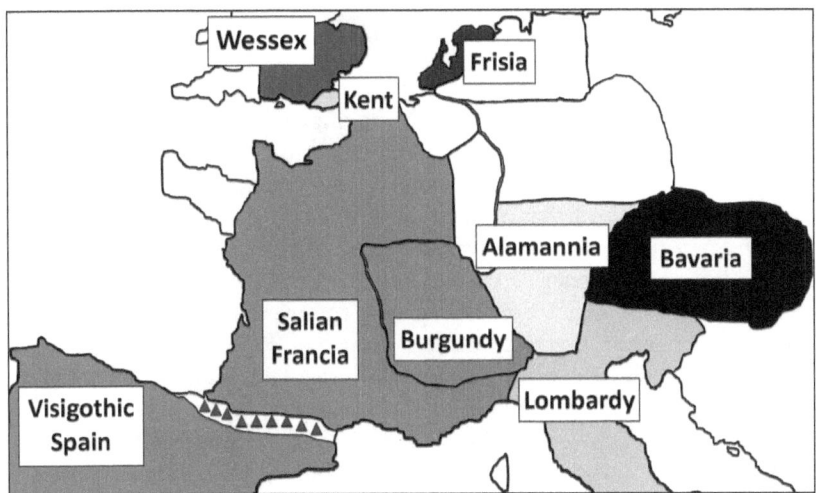

Map 3.2 Regulations of teeth according to physiological value.

Darker shading = emphasis on physiological utility
Lighter shading = greater interest in visible damage

regions place higher valuation on the more visible loss of the incisors, demonstrating a greater concern for appearance than for utility.

Archaeological finds provide us with (at least) one indication that an early medieval dentist was at work in the area of modern France, attempting to salvage the important molars. The Latin scholar Celsus (25 BCE to 50 ME) states in *De Medicina*: 'If teeth become loosened by a blow, or any other accident, they are to be tied by gold wire to firmly fixed teeth.'[72] In both Graves 247 and 249 in the Merovingian cemetery at Lavoye, a small piece of bronze was found between the molars on the left side.[73] These fragments are presumably to be explained as the remnants of wiring securing wobbly teeth to their more anchored neighbours. No evidence remains as to what caused the loosening, but a blow from a hostile fist certainly cannot be ruled out.

---

72 Shklar and Chernin, *A Sourcebook of Dental Medicine*, 100.
73 Joffrey, *Le Cimetière de Lavoye (Meuse)*, 126.

Hair

The only purely cosmetic feature to appear in the majority of the barbarian laws is hair.[74] Particularly for the Merovingian kings, wearing long hair was a badge of honour – other noblemen had to trim their locks shorter. These kings are so often referred to as the *reges crinati* (following the lead of Gregory of Tours) that Wallace Hadrill entitled his famous book on Merovingian rulers *The Long-Haired Kings*. The late Empire recognized the symbolic importance of these flowing locks, as the Theodesian Code in 416 introduced legislation 'forbidding the wearing of such barbarian garments as trousers or the sporting of long hair.'[75]

The laws of Wessex and Alamannia both regulate against cutting someone's hair – in the case of Alfred, the fine is tripled if you cut the hair like a priest's (which will be discussed below). Both of these territories also legislate against cutting someone's beard. These stipulations concentrate on the insult of shearing manly locks. In cremation burials in Anglo-Saxon England we find a large number of grooming tools for hair: tweezers, razors, shears, and combs, found in adult graves of both genders. These finds emphasize the significance of hair at least in the burial ritual.[76]

History provides us with a grisly example of insult wreaked by damage to long Merovingian hair, although here the locks belong to a woman rather than a man. Brunhild, queen of the Merovingians, was accused of plotting to kill the Mayor of the Palace. According to the Frankish historian Fredegar:

> Brunechildis was brought before Chlothar who was boiling with fury against her ... She was tormented for three days with a diversity of tortures, and then on his orders was led through the ranks on a camel. Finally she was tied by her hair, one arm and one leg to the tail of an unbroken horse, and she was cut to shreds by its hoofs at the pace it went.[77]

For a Frankish warrior of noble rank, sporting long hair could bring its own dangers, demonstrated by the following historical anecdote:

---

74 For a discussion of the importance of facial hair in Early Irish law, see Sayers, 'Early Irish Attitudes toward Hair and Beards, Baldness and Tonsure.'
75 Collins, *Early Medieval Europe 300–1000*, 57.
76 Williams, 'Artefacts in Early Medieval Graves,' 96–7 and *Death and Memory in Early Medieval Britain*, 91–6.
77 Cited in Geary, *Before France and Germany*, 151.

[T]he Byzantine historian Agathias noted that when the Burgundians in a battle against the Franks caught sight of the long-flowing hair of a slain enemy they realized that they had killed the Frankish chief himself ... The Burgundians cut off and displayed King Choldomer's head with its long flowing hair in order to sow fear among the Franks.[78]

The Burgundians may not have placed the same import on flowing locks as the Merovingians: in Burgundian law the regulation concerning hair is not for shearing, but for seizing: grabbing with two hands incurs twice the penalty of grasping with one. Kent, Saxony, and Chamavan Francia all have clauses concerning clutching someone's hair, while Frisia more explicitly rules against grabbing hair in anger. The legislation in these territories recognizes that pulling on hair can serve as the precursor to a fight. Early Irish law considers the degree of provocation in judging on such assaults: William Sayers points out that 'foltgál, "seizing by the hair" in a fight between a wife and a new concubine was serious yet understandable under the circumstances and was not a punishable offense.'[79] The Germanic clauses similarly consider the physical commencement of a struggle, which may lead to further injuries requiring additional reimbursement. For example, Beowulf begins his attack on Grendel's mother by seizing her hair and dragging her to the ground.[80]

We should thus probably consider these clauses twofold in intention: they regulate against a deliberate affront in which the hair is jeeringly (and probably publicly) pulled, and they also fine the person who makes the first physical attack in a fight. The public nature of the offence is emphasized by the Burgundian, Chamavan, and Frisian rulings that require additional payment to the king's coffer for disturbance of the peace. The importance attached to this particular legislation is demonstrated by the fact that the Chamavans include this as the only ruling on the head other than that for damage to the eye.

One final examination of the rulings against cutting hair must concentrate on the clause in Alfred mentioned above, in which the fine for cutting hair is tripled if the victim is tonsured like a priest. This stipulation may seem odd to the modern reader – why would the Christianization of hairstyle be impugned? Several historical examples from Francia provide the answer to this question. When Pippin seized the throne of Francia from

---

78 Dutton, *Charlemagne's Mustache*, 12.
79 Sayers, 'Early Irish Attitudes toward Hair and Beards, Baldness and Tonsure,' 175.
80 As per an emendment by E.G. Stanley; see Oliver, *Beginnings of English Law*, 105.

Carloman in 754, he had Carloman's sons forcibly tonsured as monks to exclude them from the possibility of succession. Charlemagne had his own rebellious son, Pippin, shorn and committed to a monastery. But in order to secure the line of succession to his more favoured offspring, in 806 Charlemagne commanded that his grandchildren 'under no circumstances … be killed, mutilated, blinded, or shorn against his will without a legal investigation and trial.'[81]

Tonsure was obviously a fraught issue in the early Middle Ages. Indeed, it was one of the contentious issues raised at the Synod of Whitby, in which the Irish and Catholic parties argued for their respective styles of tonsuring. The overarching ramifications are legal rather than cosmetic. Tonsured hair would cause a number of problems for the layman:

1 Tonsure originated as a haircut given to Greek and Roman slaves in order to visually distinguish them from freepersons. It was adopted by the church as both a symbol of the monk's submission to divine service and as a deliberately humbling or humiliating fashion choice. For a layperson, tonsure was both a symbol of servitude and an embarrassment.
2 Forcible tonsure was a part of the strategy used to compel individuals [especially political adversaries] to enter a monastery.
3 As a sign of monastic profession, tonsure enabled its wearer to certain legal privileges and subjected him to certain religio-legal obligations. To tonsure someone was to blur the social and hierarchical distinctions the laws (and the injury statutes) were designed to maintain.[82]

To be tonsured against one's will visually removed the victim from the rank of lay freeman, with its concomitant rights and responsibilities. The laws of Alfred are unique in adjudicating this violation.

Somewhat ironically, many of these barbarian laws with their concentration on hair are recorded or reworked in the Carolingian period. Charlemagne and his successors followed a tonsorial model popular among earlier Roman emperors: hair cut short and beard shaved, leaving the mustache prominent.[83] Is it only coincidence that the only barbarian ruling specifically addressing mustaches is presented in the Frisian laws, formulated in a Reichstag under Charlemagne 802 or 803?[84] Perhaps we

---

81 Becher, *Charlemagne*, 38, 122, 129.
82 Personal communication from an anonymous reader of this manuscript.
83 Dutton, *Charlemagne's Mustache*, 20–42.
84 Eckhardt, *Die Gesetze des Karolingerreiches*, 714–911, 19–20.

are seeing here the legal echoes of the shift from the older Germanic style of hair favoured by the once-dominant Merovingians to the new Carolingian fashion sported by Charlemagne deliberately channeling the tonsorial style of the Roman Empire. No matter what the reason, this shift in tonsorial concentration in the laws presented its own difficulties, as Dutton points out: 'Latin ... has no perfectly satisfactory word for "mustache" since the uneconomical *labri superioris capilli* [hairs of the upper lip] seems a definition rather than a simple signifier.'[85] The compilers of the Frisian laws circumvented this problem by using a Latinized form of an older Germanic term: *granones* (compare ON *grön*), derived from PIE *ghers-, 'to stick out.' The enduring popularity of this fashion is demonstrated by an idiom lasting at least into early nineteenth-century Italy, according to Andrea de Jorio:

> When we say that something or some person or some operation is *coi baffi* ('with mustaches'), we mean that it is perfect of its kind. This saying, while it is in very frequent use today, used to be used even more often.[86]

---

85 Dutton, *Charlemagne's Mustache*, 25.
86 De Jorio, 1832. *Gesture in Naples and Gesture in Classical Antiquity*, 322.

4 Torso, Arms, and Legs[1]

This chapter addresses wounds to the torso and the extending limbs of arms and legs. The details of hands and feet will be addressed in chapter 5, as the specific anatomical functions of individual fingers (and less so, toes) influence the value placed upon these digits. Curiously, regulation of wounds to the torso in barbarian law generally do not receive the detailed attention given to the head or the fingers. The breakdown of how damage to the trunk is assessed divides the barbarian territories into what I will term the 'major four' and 'the rest.' The major four – consisting of Frisia, Alamannia, Wessex, and Kent – demonstrate considerably more interest in legislating injury to the torso than the rest. Frisian law specifies thirty-two wounds against the core, inflicted on eighteen different body parts (compared to thirty-three wounds for hands and feet).[2] The Alamanni specify fines for nineteen wounds on twelve parts of the torso; Wessex twenty-one on ten, and Kent seventeen on seven. All other territories come in with a scant reckoning of a maximum of five rulings (Lombardy) on a maximum of four parts of the torso (Visigothic Spain, Saxony, Thuringia, and Bavaria). Barely in consideration are the Burgundians, who only name wounds to the arm and the tibia; and completely out of the picture are the Chamavan Franks, who ignore the torso altogether. (Likely rulings in Chamavan Francia were

---

1 The clauses discussed in this chapter are presented here in chronological order: *Lex Sal.* §§17.1, 3, 6, 10, 17–18, 32, 71; *Liber Const.* §§11.2, 48; *Kent* §§34–4, 50–2, 61–8; *Lex Rib.* §§1–4, 5.6, 6, 68; *Lex Ala.* §§61, 63–6, 92; *Edict Roth.* §§41–5, 57–61, 74, 384; *Forum Iud.* §VI.4.iii; *Lex Baiu* §§4.1–5, 7–8, 19, 12, 27; *Lex Sax.* §§1–5; *Lex Fris.* §§5.3–4, 22–6, 38–40, 43–4, 47–61, 66–75, 77–6; *Lex Thur.* §§I.5–11, 17–18; *Wessex* §§53–5, 61–3, 65–8, 70–7. Included in these enumerations of clauses are general regulations against causing bruises or unspecified wounds, including those causing blood to flow.
2 This will play out later in Frisian laws, which become exceedingly baroque as time goes on in detail regarding the wounding of all body parts.

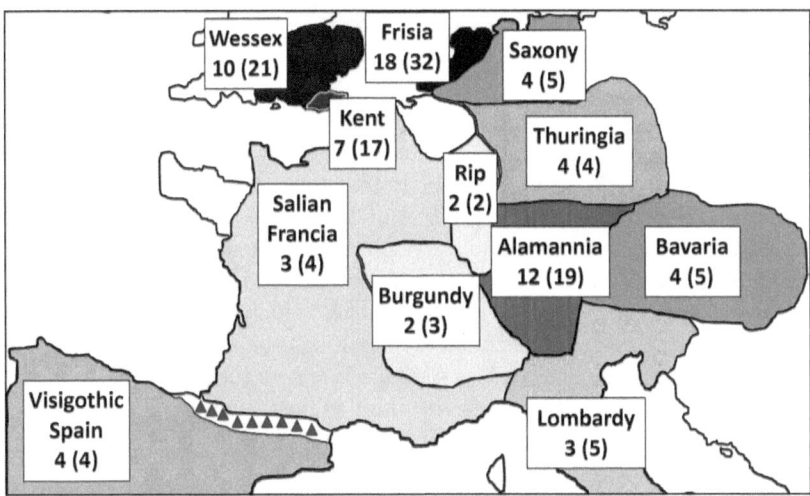

Map 4.1 Regulations on injury to torso.

1st number: # of body parts identified.   Darkest shading = greatest specificity.
(Number) = total # of regulations.   Lightest shading = least specificity.

based on those extant in Salic Law.) Map 4.1 illustrates the geographical distribution of numbers of clauses addressing wounds to body parts, with the first number representing the number of body parts identified, and the figure in brackets the number of regulations. Darkest shading indicates greatest specificity and lightest indicates least.

This map clearly connects the Anglo-Frisian kingdoms in their emphasis on legislating against wounds to the body core. Separated geographically, but showing a similar interest in injury to the torso, is Alamannia. Next in order of specificity (although considerably lower than the major four) are the eastern regions of Saxony, Thuringia, and Bavaria (four body parts each); equal consideration is provided in the farthest western territory of Visigothic Spain. Weighing in lowest on the scale are the western/central continental territories of Salic Francia and Lombardy (three body parts each), and Ripuarian Francia and Burgundy (a scant two apiece). A comparison of regulation of damage to the torso to injuries inflicted elsewhere in randomly selected territories reveals that Saxon law contains twenty-five clauses considering injury to hands and feet and thirteen for wounds to the head, as opposed to five for the torso. Bavarian law legislates twelve times against injury to hands and feet, fifteen times against wounds to the head, but only five times against damage to the torso.

Three possible explanations spring to mind to account for this comparative legislative paucity regarding wounds to the body core. First, the personal injury tariffs are not relevant to wounds the victim received while fighting on the side of an army of the king or overlord. Instead, these clauses address injuries arising in the course of private conflicts. Perhaps it is simply more frequent or more likely that such altercations will result in damage to the face (as in a blow from the fist), or to the hand (which itself might be a weapon in a private skirmish, thus exposing the fingers to injury). Second, a wound to the torso may be covered by clothing, thus not as visible as those to face or hands. Injuries which can be concealed are often assigned less value than those which cannot. (Chapter 6 discusses this differentiation.) Finally, and perhaps incorporating the two previous considerations, some laws contain rulings against generic injury: the laws of both Kent and Thuringia have clauses addressing damage to any bones, and Salian Francia and Lombardia stipulate recompense for unspecified wounds. These more general rulings may subsume fines against injuries to the torso not detailed in the laws themselves.

Figure 4.1 provides a summary overview of the frequency with which individual body parts are specified in the Germanic law codes. In this layout, I have grouped together injuries to the major parts of the torso from top to bottom: shoulder, arm, ribcage or chest, hand, abdomen, genitals, leg, and foot. These meta-categories are shaded in black, with the attached boxes giving local variations.[3] (The sum of the numbers in the grey boxes may not add up to the number in the black box, as individual territories may legislate several different wounds for a single body part – for example, the Alamann stipulations against cutting off an arm at the shoulder or the elbow; maiming the arm or elbow; or piercing or breaking the arm above or below the elbow. In the meta-analysis, these injuries are all subsumed under 'arm.')

Wounds against major body parts in descending order of frequency are:

- 12: Foot
- 10: Leg
- 9: Arm; Hand
- 8: Ribcage; Genitals
- 7: Abdomen
- 4: Shoulder

---

3 These variations can be found in the charts for individual regions in the online appendices.

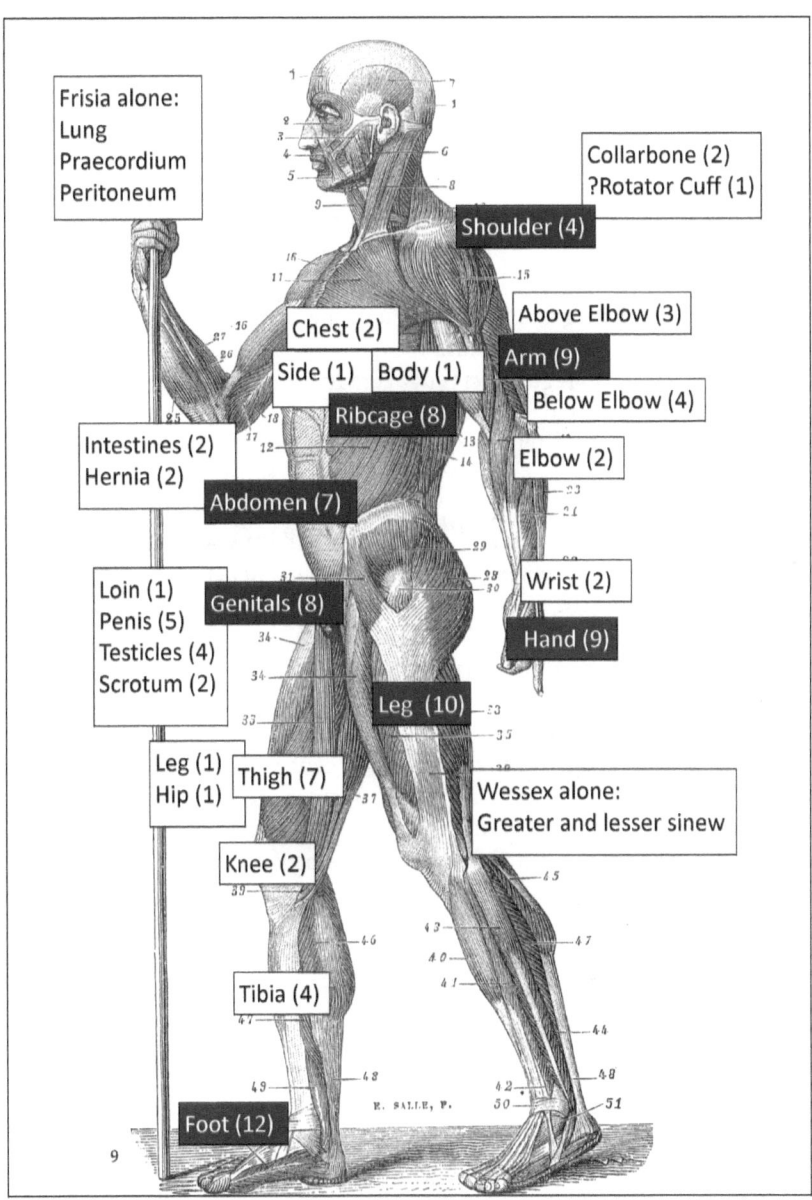

Figure 4.1 Regulations on injury to torso.

| Most commonly regulated body parts | Territorial variations |

The order of the following discussion adheres to the outline of comparative value presented above, beginning with leg and foot, moving then to arm (including shoulder) and hand, and finishing with the torso proper, including ribcage, genitals, and abdomen.

The leg and its appended foot receives the greatest attention in respect to physical damage. Although the capacity to complete a day's work may rely more upon the proper functioning of the arm or hand, the ability to actually arrive at the work place depends upon the potential of ambulation. This distinction may dictate the increased number of clauses dealing with damage to the leg and foot, although the actual numerical difference is not statistically very significant.

The most common regulation is damage to the foot, which is also one of the most highly assessed wounds – usually half a wergild. Injuries to the leg are regulated in ten territories. The cover term is most often 'thigh' (Latin *coxa*, Old English *þeoh*). Where the only regulation against damage to the leg concerns the thigh, this designation can be taken as standing in for the leg as a whole.[4] Three of the major four have separate rulings for the lower leg (Frisia,[5] Wessex [a disproportionate 40 per cent wergild] and Alamannia [6 per cent wergild]);[6] in these regions the stipulations for wounds to the thigh mean exactly that. Furthermore, these assessments must address breaking rather than striking off the limb, unless we assume that in the case of cutting off the lower leg, the fine for the concomitant loss of the foot is added. Surprisingly, Burgundy is the only other region to rule against damage to the tibia [10 per cent wergild]. The only other core body part represented in Burgundian law is the arm [10 per cent wergild]; furthermore Burgundy has no stipulation regarding the leg or thigh.[7] It thus seems likely that Burgundy here is using the lower leg as a *pars pro toto*, just as most other regions use the thigh – this hypothesis is substantiated by the equality of the assessed fines.

The various wounds to the legs mentioned in the laws descend in gravity from striking off the leg at the hip (Alamannia [40 per cent wergild] and Frisia);[8] maiming the leg (Frisia and Kent [12 per cent wergild]);[9] piercing

---

4 See discussion under *huf* in Niederhellmann, *Arzt- und Heilkunde*, 85, 169–70.
5 The wergild structure in *Lex Frisionum* is peculiar, and will thus not be included here; see Appendix for details.
6 *Lex Fris.* §22.61; *Wessex* §63; *Lex Ala.* §57.63.
7 *Liber Const.* §48.1, 2.
8 *Lex Ala.* §57.68; *Lex Fris.* §79 based on §77.
9 *Lex Fris.* §79 based on §78; *Kent* §65.

through the thigh (most common [Alamannia 6 per cent wergild]); and stabbing into the thigh [Kent from 1 per cent to 6 per cent wergild depending on the depth of the wound]). The texts do not make it clear whether the designation 'thigh' means the bone or the fleshy matter. However, in both Saxon and Lombard law piercing the thigh is equivalent to cutting off the little finger, and in Lombard law also to striking out a molar.[10] For these territories we must reverse the assumption made earlier that the designation of thigh represents incapacitating damage to the leg; here the injuries more likely are inflicted on flesh rather than bone.

The only possible rulings on damage to the knee or ankle occur in Alamann and Bavarian law, both containing clauses setting compensation in the event that the foot becomes *taudragil*, 'dragging in the dew.'[11] Certainly this ruling could refer to any damage to the leg that incapacitates the foot. However, such injuries subsume those to the foot and ankle, which are specified nowhere else in the laws. As one who is walked by her dogs in the early morning, being pulled through dew means that your shoes and socks are uncomfortably damp throughout the rest of the day. This annoyance does not apply to the Germanic territories, which regarded dew as a healing medium. The process of dragging the foot through damp grass, necessitated by the damage somewhere in the leg – likely in the hip, knee, or ankle joints – was seen in the barbarian territories as restorative due to the healing powers inherent in dew.[12]

Alfred alone legislates for a wound to the *geweald* (literally 'power') resulting in laming: Liebermann assumes this refers to the top of the spinal column.[13] The 100-shilling fine represents 50 per cent of a Wessex freeman's wergild; the total fine of sixty shillings in Kent [60 per cent wergild] for causing a person to become bed-ridden [30 per cent] and to require medical attention [30 per cent] might subsume regulation for a similar

---

10 *Lex Sax.* §5.5, 5.13; *Edict Roth.* §§62, 57; 52.
11 *Lex Ala.* §§57.62, 57.29.
12 'Germanisch ist auch eine Sitte, die uns an manche Kneippdur in modernen Wörrishofen erinnert, in den frühen Morgenstunden des Mai auf den Wiesen durch den Tau zu streichen, um durch den fruchtbaren, gesundheitbringenden Maitau das gelähmte Bein gesund zu machen. Gerade in den indikationen verrät sich der empirische Kern der kultischen Handlung. Die warmen Quellen wendete man, wie noch heute in unseren Rheumatismusbädern an, um steife und gelähmte Glieder in Ordnung zu bringen' (Diepgen, *Deutsche Volksmedizin*, 19–20.) See also Vorwahl, *Deutsche Volksmedizin in Vergangenheit und Gegenwart*, 8, and Niederhellmann, 'Heilkundliches in den Leges,' 78.
13 *Wessex* §43; Liebermann, *Gesetze der Angelsachsen*, 3:63.

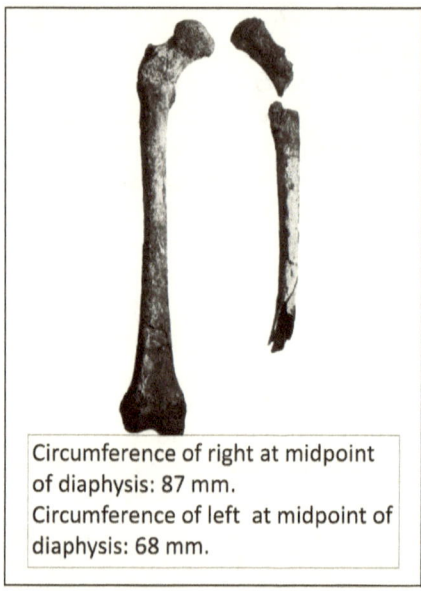

Circumference of right at midpoint of diaphysis: 87 mm.
Circumference of left at midpoint of diaphysis: 68 mm.

Figure 4.2 Femurs from Greisheim Grave 226. Photograph reproduced by permission of *Fundberichte aus Hessen*; Landesamt für Denkmalpflege Hessen.

wound, although the Kentish clauses apply to any injury causing temporary incapacitation.[14]

The archaeological record is rich in evidence for medical intervention in the case of injuries to the leg. A particularly dramatic example is provided by the remains of an artificial limb created to replace a missing lower leg.[15] Between 1975 and 1977, 470 graves were excavated in the old Frankish cemetery south of Greisheim, near Darmstadt, Germany. Grave #226, like many others, had been robbed long ago. Except for the skull, nothing remained of the upper body; the lower body, however, was fairly well preserved. That this skeleton was male can be inferred by the damascened sword placed at the left side;

---

14 See Oliver, 'Sick-Maintenance in Anglo-Saxon Law.'
15 This material is primarily drawn from Keil, 'Eine Prosthese aus einem fränkischen Grab von Greisheim.' See also Baumgartner, 'Fussprothese aus einem frühmittelalterlichen Grab aus Bonaduz.'

Torso, Arms, and Legs 119

Figure 4.3 Fragment of mosaic from Cathedral of Lescar in southern France showing prosthetic leg. Reproduced by permission of *Fundberichte aus Hessen*; Landesamt für Denkmalpflege Hessen.

abrasion on the teeth implies an age at death of 57–63 (see Fig. 4.2). Strikingly, the left leg ended at the knee, and in place of the foot was the remains of a prosthesis for the lower leg. The base consisted of a rectangular, slightly conical bronze fastener about 9 cm long; the bottom measured 6.5 x 5 cm, and the top 7 x 3.5 cm. This seems to have served as the protection for the lower end of a pegleg, as bits of wood and a number of nails for attaching the bronze tube to the stilt were also found.[16] The reason for the surgery remains buried in the past; for whatever reason, the patient suffered exarticulation (that is, severing the limb at the joint) rather than an amputation (cutting off the limb itself). The difference in diameter between the two femurs is significant.[17]

Generally a leg with a prosthesis cannot bear the same amount of weight as a healthy leg. Favouring the leg with the artificial limb causes a

---

16 A schematic of this prosthesis can be seen in Online Appendices III.5.
17 Keil, 'Prosthese,' 201.

weakening of the muscle with concomitant atrophy of the bone. This degeneration takes a considerable period of time, which allows us to deduce that the patient lived for many years after the operation. The prosthetic limb was attached to the upper leg, although the grave presents no evidence as to the means employed. Baldur Keil offers a possible comparison for how this attachment might have appeared.[18]

This depiction (see Fig 4.3) shows an upper fork to the wood leg in which the knee rests: the remainder of the lower leg (the operation pictured here was an amputation rather than an exarticulation) sticks out behind. Presumably the fork was somehow strapped to the upper leg, or perhaps even reached high enough to be secured around the waist; unfortunately the fragmentary nature of the mosaic makes the precise method impossible to determine. The man is shown in the process of shooting a bow, which provides excellent evidence that although the man lost his leg, he could still fulfil the functions of warrior or hunter.

A rash of injuries of this nature seems to have broken out in Norway not long after our period. Oenund Ofeiggson lost his leg below the knee at the battle of Hafrsfjord in 872. His saga relates that 'Oenund was later healed and went with a pegleg his whole life. Therefore he was named Oenund Tree-foot [Trēfōtr].'[19] In 981, Thorir Arnason lost a leg in battle; after having it replaced by a wooden prosthesis he became known as Viðleggr 'Wooden-leg.'[20] Literature echoes the evidence from history: in the *Eyrbyggjasaga* the warriors Thorolf and Thorleif both lost their legs and afterwards wore wooden prostheses.[21]

The *Pactus Alamannorum* §11.3 lessens the fine for a leg wound if the victim can go about on *stelzia*. B. Keil and Annette Niederhellmann both suggest that this refers to a prosthesis like that found in Greisheim.[22] I believe a better comparison comes from Exodus 21:19 where the fine is lessened 'si surrexit et et ambulaverit foris super baculum suum' (if he rises and walks about on his staff).[23] The Alamann ruling seems more likely to refer to a cane or crutch than an actual prosthesis. The photograph below, from Grave 57 in Kirchenheim, provides visual evidence of damage to the hip which might have resulted in just such a wound.

---

18 Ibid., 207.
19 Ibid., 204.
20 Bonser, *The Medical Background of Anglo-Saxon England*, 101.
21 Keil, 'Prosthese,' 204.
22 Keil, 'Chirugie,' 1846; Niederhellmann, *Arzt- und Heilkunde*, 83–5.
23 The relevant clause in the Vulgate Bible can be found at *Biblia Sacra*, 106.

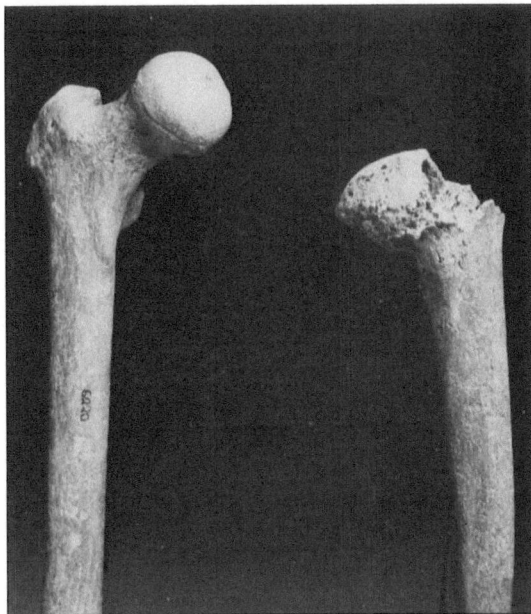

Figure 4.4 Femurs from Grave 57, Kirchheim/Ries (Ostalbkreis, Germany). Adult male demonstrating damage to hip. Photograph reproduced by permission of Carestream Health Germany GmBH.

The left hip-bone (on right side of Fig. 4.4) of this adult male is considerably shortened, presumably due to a violent fall; the archaeological record does not reveal whether this injury was accidental or deliberately inflicted by a hostile push. Although healing stabilized the break, Czarnetzki et al. assume a concomitant lessening of the load-bearing strength of the upper thigh-bone. Furthermore, the approximately 3 cm shortening of the bone would have resulted in a considerable limp; it is certainly possible that the wounded man had to use a cane or crutch – that is, rely on the support of *stelzia*.[24]

A transition from the discussion of injury to the upper leg to consideration of wounds to the lower leg is provided by the leg bones of a thirty- to

---

24 Czarnetzki et al., *Menschen des Frühen Mittelalters*, 53.

forty-year-old man found in Grave 71 in Pleidelsheim.[25] The head of the right femur is bent downwards, with concomitant broadening of the neck. Furthermore, both the right fibula and tibia are grotesquely distended, with pocked holes and wax-like formations disfiguring the bones. While the upper injury seems to have healed without much damage, Czarnetzki et al. suppose that the swelling of the lower bones indicate that the patient suffered from osteomyelitis:

> an infection of bone and bone marrow. It is most often caused by germs that enter the bone during an injury or surgery. The germs may also reach the bone directly from a nearby infection or through the bloodstream ... Continuing and increasing bone pain, tenderness, local muscle spasm, and fever are symptoms of the disease. [Modern t]reatment includes bed rest and anti infection drugs by injection for several weeks. Surgery may be necessary to take out dead bone and tissue, to fill holes, and to use artificial devices to keep the diseased bones and joints from moving. Long-term osteomyelitis may go on for years with periods of many or fewer symptoms in spite of treatment.[26]

This kind of deformity presents an interesting legal question. If the wounds to the leg were deliberately inflicted, should the perpetrator later be responsible for the onset and continuation of the osteomyelitis? Is there any statute of limitations, and if so, how long does it last? Unfortunately, we have no answers to these questions in the written texts, and no access to oral rulings which may have addressed them.

Only four regions specifically address damage to the lower leg. Furthermore, the term 'tibia' in Burgundian law simply substitutes for 'leg,' serving as a counterpart to the only other member of the torso regulated in Burgundy, namely, the arm. We can, however, again draw upon the archaeological record for evidence as to how such wounds were treated.

Medical attention was almost surely given to the damage to the lower leg found in a grave excavated in the Schwabian-Alemann cemetery in Memmingen, Bavaria (fifth to seventh century). The left tibia has a fracture which has healed without dislocation; the fibula has a corresponding diagonal fracture which has also healed. Only the application of a strong bandage could have allowed this double fracture to knit without lasting

---

25 A picture of this find can be seen in Online Appendices, III.6.
26 Mosby, *Mosby's Medical Encyclopedia*, s.v. *osteomyelitis*.

damage.[27] This patient was more fortunate than the one found in Grave 157 in the Merovingian cemetery at Lavoye, who similarly suffered a double fracture of tibia and fibula which Joffroy believes to have been intentional; the break must have caused great pain, and the sharp edges on the broken bones indicate that the victim probably died soon afterwards.[28] If indeed this wound was deliberately inflicted, the perpetrator must have paid restitution. The laws of the Salian Franks do not specify the amount of recompense due for fracturing the lower leg: the closest equivalent is the 50 per cent wergild for striking off the foot. However, if the victim died shortly after the wound was inflicted, the man who struck the blow may have been liable for the full wergild of 200 *solidi*. Once again, we are faced with the unanswerable question of limits of liability.

Next most frequently addressed are injuries to the arm and hand. Striking off the hand, mentioned in nine territories, is fined by half a wergild – the identical assessment for striking off a foot. None of the territories inhabited primarily by Franks provide specific brachial legislation, although, as stated above, these wounds may be subsumed under the rubric *vulnus*, 'wound,' in *Lex Salica* (33⅓ per cent wergild).[29] Conversely, damage to the arm is one of only two injuries regulated in Burgundy (10 per cent wergild; same assessment as damage to the tibia, representing the leg as a whole). Most regions use the cover term 'arm' (Latin *brachium*, Old English *earm*) as a generic designation. Four territories additionally distinguish the arm below the elbow: Wessex (40 per cent wergild for striking off), Frisia, Bavaria, and Alamannia (each 1.5 per cent wergild for break).[30] The equality of these fines in Alamannia and Bavaria, coupled with the ruling on the lamed knee discussed earlier, provide two important connections between the personal injury tariffs of these geographically contiguous regions. Frisia and Alamannia regulate on damage to the complete

---

27 Lehmann-Nitsche, *Beiträge zur Prähistorischen Chirugie nach Funden aus Deutscher Vorzeit*, 14. Medical treatment is not, of course, ubiquitous. The skeleton of a grown man found in Grave 280 in Kirchenheim produced a right shin-bone with the lower half bent towards the front. After a break, the lower part of the bone seems to have become displaced during the healing process. A splint or strong bandage would have prevented this from happening, so it appears that no doctor attended to this wound. (Czarnetzki et al., *Menschen des Frühen Mittelalters*, 54.)
28 Joffrey, *Le Cimetière de Lavoye (Meuse)*, 116.
29 *Lex Sal.* §17.1–10.
30 Wessex §55; *Lex Fris.* §22.25; *Lex Baiu.* §3.12; *Lex Ala.* §57.39.

trio of arm, upper arm, and lower arm:[31] Alamannia extends these rulings in the most detailed breakdown of fines for injury on the arm:

- striking arm off at the shoulder (40 per cent wergild);
- striking arm off at elbow (20 per cent wergild);
- maiming the arm so it is useless (10 per cent wergild);
- maiming elbow so victim cannot lift hand or carry (6 per cent wergild);[32]
- piercing arm above elbow; breaking arm above elbow with skin intact (3 per cent wergild);
- piercing arm below elbow; breaking arm below elbow with skin intact (1.5 per cent wergild).

Archaeological finds provide us with evidence that such breaks occurred and were survived. The excavation of Grave 24 in Kirchenheim produced the skeleton of a male between the ages of twenty and thirty whose left upper arm had been broken in two places. The left humerus was shortened by the setting of these two fractures.[33] We have no indication as to whether this injury was inflicted deliberately or simply occurred in the course of everyday work. If the former were the case, this wound might provide a complex legal problem. Czarnetzki et al. suggest that a wound of this nature often causes nerve damage, with concomitant loss of the use of the hand. Should the perpetrator then be fined for both the break to the arm and the maiming of the hand? Once again, the laws provide us with only a suggestion as to how to interpret the legal responsibility for the wound demonstrated by the grave find.

Less ambiguous is the archaeological evidence in the case of breaks of the lower arm. The left-hand side of Figure 4.5 represents the forearm bones from a skeleton of a thirty- to forty-year-old male found in Grave 363 in Weingarten. Czarnetzki et al. hypothesize that this injury occurred when the living man raised his arm to ward off a hostile blow, as reconstructed in the drawing on the right. The break to the right elbow, with the concomitant misalignment of the bone, is clearly demonstrated in the

---

31 *Lex Fris.* §22.24–6; *Lex Ala.* §57.38–40.
32 *Lex Ala.* §61.7. The ruling is that the arm cannot lift anything; nor can it move the hand to the mouth. The latter ruling seems to indicate that the victim could not feed himself, although presumably he would eventually be able to compensate with his non-predominant hand.
33 Czarnetzki, Uhlig, and Wolf, *Menschen des Frühen Mittelalters*, 55.

Figure 4.5 Ulnae from Grave 363, Weingarten, Kreis Ravensburg. Artistic reconstruction of cause of injury. Photograph of bones reproduced by permission of Carestream Health Germany GmBH. Photograph of illustration reproduced by permission of P. Frankenstein, H. Zwietasch; Landesmuseum Württemberg.

photograph. Although the elbow itself seems to have healed successfully, the subsequent mobility of the wrist may well have been impaired.

The skeletal remains of a sixty- to seventy-year-old male from a grave found in Eichstätten display a similar injury to the lower arm, with a break of both the ulna and radius (see Fig. 4.6). During the healing process, both arm bones have twisted towards the inside by about 30 degrees. Czarnetski et al. comment that the wrist would have been virtually immobilized; the placement fixed in the healing process would not have inhibited the ability to grasp and hold, so the victim should have considered himself fortunate.[34]

---

34 Czarnetzki et al., *Menschen des Frühen Mittelalters*, from left to right 58, 56, 57.

126 The Body Legal in Barbarian Law

Figure 4.6 Ulna and radius from grave in
Eichstätten, Kreis Breisgau-Hochschwartzwald.
Photograph reproduced by permission of
Carestream Health Germany GmBH.

Again, the question arises as to which injury would have been brought before a court of law. In the cases above, the elbow healed without apparent consequence to the joint itself. But both injuries would have prevented the victim from subsequently enjoying full use of his right wrist and hand. This echoes the first legal docu-fiction presented in chapter 2: if these men were right-handed, the injury would be more damaging than if they occurred on the left sides. The very fact that instinctively (at least in the pictorial reconstruction) the victim raised his right hand to ward off the blow suggests a right-handed bias. But the laws never differentiate between the predominant and non-predominant hand or arm in considering restitution.

There is no evidence one way or the other to determine whether the bones above were set by a doctor, or healed on their own (although historical and archaeological evidence would both weigh on the side of the

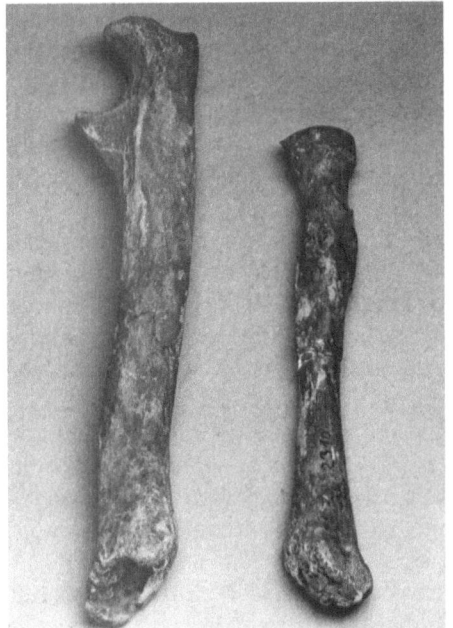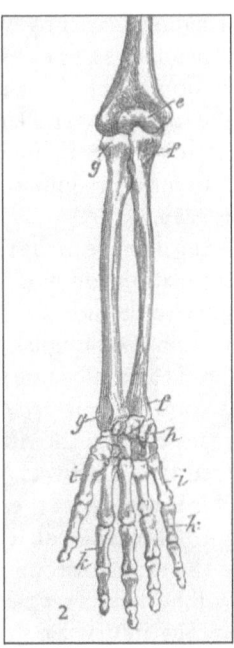

Figure 4.7 Forearm bones from grave in Balingen, Zollernalbkreis, showing successful amputation of lower arm. Photograph reproduced by permission of Carestream Health Germany GmBH.

former). Unambiguous, however, is the evidence of medical intervention provided by the remains pictured in Fig. 4.7 of an adult of indeterminate sex found in a grave in Balingen, Zollernalbkreis.[35]

Here we see the results of the amputation of the left lower arm shortly above the wrist. Both lower arm bones (the radius and the ulna) have been sharply cut through. Knobby scars on the bones and the almost hoof-like thickening at the place of amputation indicate that the wound had healed well at the time of death, despite the original inflammation indicated by the overlay of bone scars. Czarnetzki et al. hypothesize that the arm was damaged by a sword blow or by accidental crushing. This find demonstrates

---

35 Ibid., 96. Diagram of arm-bones from *Mosley's Medical Encyclopedia*, s.v. forearm.

precisely the ruling shared by Wessex and Frisia, in which breaking both lower arm bones draws a fine of sixty shillings (30 per cent of the wergild).[36]

This discussion concludes with an examination of the assessments for wounds to the torso proper. Damage to the leg is regulated in ten territories, and injury to the arm in nine. Consideration of such wounds is closely followed by attention to injury of the ribcage and genitals, weighing in at eight regions each.

In considering damage to the ribs or ribcage, I assume that the Thuringian and Saxon stipulations on wounds to the body (*corpus*) and the Alamann ruling on injury to the side (*latus*) are the equivalent of the more common terminology of rib (Old English *rib*) or ribcage (Latin *costa*).[37] Conceivably this rubric should also subsume the designation of chest used by Lombards and Frisians (*capsum* and *pectus* respectively). But the Frisians impose fines for damage both to the ribs and to the chest.[38] On the one hand, the Frisian differentiation between chest and ribcage may indicate a division of upper and lower areas of the trunk. On the other hand, the ribcage extends to right below the collarbone, so the Frisian overlap may simply demonstrate the same anatomical legislative exuberance noted earlier. A broken rib will heal in its own given time; furthermore, it is a painful, but not incapacitating injury. Sarah Caldwell, the first woman to conduct at the Metropolitan Opera, managed to conduct a performance at her home company in Boston, despite the fact that she had two broken ribs, which must have made lifting her hands to cue musicians fairly tortuous.[39]

The genitals show more variation in the specifics of the damage: most common are rulings against damage to the penis (Latin *virilia*, *viricula*, *vectis*, *veretrum*, Old English *gekyndlice lim*), followed by testicles (*testicula*, Old English *herðas*), scrotum (Latin *folliculo testium*), and loins (Old English *lendenbræde*). The laws generally do not distinguish between castration and amputation of the penis: the crucial disability is the loss of the ability to create offspring.[40] However, with their typical anatomical fascination, the Frisians include clauses on all but the loins, although oddly the ruling on the scrotum requires piercing of both the scrotum and the hip.[41] Literary evidence suggests that this may not be as

---

36 *Wessex* §55; *Lex Fris.* §22.26.
37 *Lex Thur.* §10; *Lex Sax.* §5.5; *Lex Ala.* §57.54.
38 *Edict Roth.* §59; *Lex Fris.* §§22.47, 22.23.
39 I was present at that performance, having served many years as assistant director to Miss Caldwell at the Opera Company of Boston.
40 See discussion on 'Kastration' in Niederhellmann, *Arzt- und Heilkunde*, 149–54.
41 *Lex Fris.* §22.57–9.

peculiar as it appears. Charlemagne's biographer Einhard describes a nobleman who had 'the lower part of his chest crushed, the right side of his ear torn and his right thigh next to his loins crushed. But ... the perseverance of the doctors who attended him resulted in a most speedy recovery: twenty days afterwards he went hunting.'[42] Frisia continues the pattern of greatest specificity by regulating recompense for cutting off both testicles, one testicle, or causing one testicle to emerge which can later be set in place. Only the first of these would destroy reproductive functionality.

The abdomen is the body part most often referred to in Germanic vernacular terminology. Bavaria and Alamannia demonstrate another connection by using the compound *hrevavunt*, and the Anglo-Saxon territories of Kent and Wessex employ the cognate *hrifwund* (in all cases 'wounded in the abdomen').[43] This designation probably incorporates all the area between the lower ribcage and the genitals. Frisia, Alamannia, and (likely) Salian Francia also rule on damage to the intestines.[44] Frisia includes a fine for causing the intestines to spill out such that they have to be replaced. Early medieval literature provides several examples of intestines extruding from a gash to the abdomen, as evidenced by the following incident in the Irish tale *Fingal Ronain*, in which Mael Fothertaig chides his jester for letting his intestines spill forth from his abdomen which is gashed open during a family brawl.

O Mac Glass,
Gather your bowels in,
Though you know it no shame,
Churls are laughing at you.[45]

Alamannia and Visigothic Spain both legislate against injuries leading to hernias, which I have subsumed under the rubric of abdominal wounds.[46] The extrusion of a hernia could perhaps have been equated with damage to the bowels. As far as I know, no contemporary written sources discuss hernia operations, and physical evidence of such procedures would not

---

42 Einhard *Annales* anno 817, cited and translated in. McKinney, *Early Medieval Medicine*, 91–2.
43 *Lex Baiu.* §3.6; *Lex Ala.* §57.55; *Kent* §62; *Wessex* §61. The Alamannian form is *hrevovunt*. See discussion in Niederhellmann, *Arzt- und Heilkunde*, 170–5.
44 *Lex Fris.* §§22.53, 22.56; *Lex Ala.* §57.57; *Lex Sal.* §17.8.
45 *Ancient Irish Tales*, ed. and trans. Cross and Slover, 542.
46 *Lex Ala.* §57.69; *Forum Iud.* §VI.4.iii.

survive. However, bandages designed to contain hernias have been found in graves containing remains both male and female. Generally these are iron bands terminating in a spoon-shaped disk. To mitigate chafing, these bands would be wrapped in cloth or leather.[47] G. Keil claims that iron bands for hernia retention occur mostly in the left-Rhine territories of Switzerland and France; this assertion is substantiated by extant grave finds.[48]

The shoulder area receives about the same amount of attention as the tibia, although the latter has been subsumed under wounds to the leg. This category most clearly distinguishes the 'major four' from 'the rest.' Anglo-Frisian territories all regulate against injuries to the shoulder. The Anglo-Saxon territories each add an additional stipulation: in Kent the collarbone, and in Wessex the rotator cuff. The only inland continental law to consider this area of the body is Alamannia, which agrees with Kent in legislating against a fracture of the collarbone.[49]

Grave 45 from Nusplingen (Fig. 4.8) produced both collarbones from an adult male, the left of which demonstrates a break that shortened the bone. Czarnetski et al. assume that this was the result of a fall; we have, however, no evidence that the fracture might not have been caused by a blow to the shoulder.[50]

The only consequence of the break is minimal shortening of the upper (left) bone. An injury of this nature would normally heal within four weeks with a bandage immobilizing the fracture. Even without immediate rest, the bone will eventually reknit. American cyclist Tyler Hamilton, caught in a crash in the early stages of the 2003 Tour de France, fractured his collarbone. Wearing a tight bandage around his shoulder, he managed not only to complete the grueling, weeks-long race, but to finish in fourth place.[51]

Except for the attention given to the shoulder by the major four, connecting joints are virtually overlooked in barbarian law. Although many of the laws have stipulations against maiming the hand or foot, with one exception these do not specifically mention the wrist or ankle. Lacking other regulations, it seems a fair assumption that damage to the wrist or ankle must tacitly have been viewed as a type of mutilation of hand or foot.

---

47 See image in Online Appendices III.7.
48 Keil, 'Chirugie.'
49 *Kent* §§37, 50; *Wessex* §53; *Lex Fris.* §§22.40, 22.44; *Lex Ala.* §57.28.
50 Czarnetzki et al., *Menschen des Frühen Mittelalters*, 56.
51 As this book goes to press, Tyler's legacy has been tainted by allegations of blood doping. Although this technique may have increased his stamina, it would not have lessened the achievement of riding through the pain of a broken collarbone.

Torso, Arms, and Legs 131

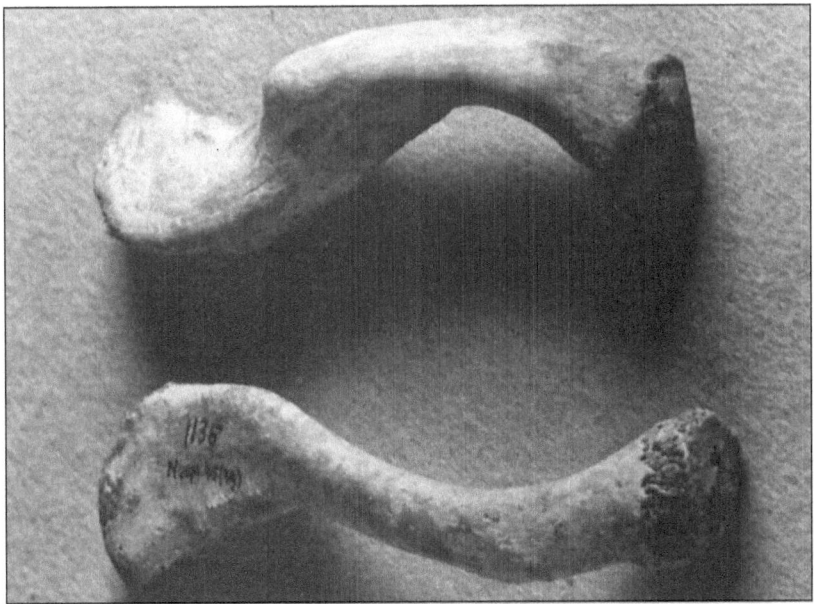

Figure 4.8 Collarbones of adult male showing break on left (upper). Grave 45, Nusplingen, Zollernalbkreis.

Similarly, the Alamann reference to an arm rendered useless probably implies damage to the shoulder.[52]

The single territory that specifies injury to the wrist is ruled by those indefatigable legislators, the Frisians. They consider wounds to *iunctura manus et brachii*, 'joints of hands and arms'; *cubitum*, 'elbow'; and *iunctura scalpulae*, 'shoulder joints.'[53] For these major joints, as well as the individual joints of the fingers, the law requires for recompense that

> humor ex vulnere decurrat, quod lidu uuagi dicunt
>
> liquid runs from the wound, which they call *lidu uuagi*

This liquid is almost surely the synovial fluid that cushions and protects joints such as the elbow and knee. A synovial membrane is 'the inner layer

---

52 *Lex Ala.* §57.38.
53 *Lex Fris.* §22.35–44; citation from §22.35.

of a capsule surrounding a freely movable joint. The synovial membrane secretes into the joint a thick fluid that normally oils the joint but that may collect in painful amounts when the joint is injured.'[54] Alfred similarly describes a wound to the shoulder in which *liðseaw*, 'synovia,' flows out, providing yet another connection between the laws of Frisia and Wessex.[55] What we might term the 'synovial sequence' in Frisian law moves from the fingers to the wrist to the shoulder, considering each joint in sequence. Curiously, no like consideration is given to the knee, or indeed, any joints of the leg.

The *Pactus Alamannorum* is the only text to address damage to both elbow and knee.[56] For both joints, the clauses stipulate that recompense is due if

nervora tetegerit ut ibi wasilus intrat.

the nerve is touched so that *wasilus* gets in.[57]

It seems likely that Alamann *wasilus* also refers to synovial fluid. Certainly, the root seems to be associated with Indo-European *wes-, which gives various Germanic words for 'water, fluid' such as Modern German *Wasser*, 'water,' or Old High German *wazerīn*, 'watery.' The root survives in Modern English *ooze* from Old English *wōs*, 'juice.'[58] Modern readers may recognize the Alamann complaint better as 'water on the knee,' which is not at all water, but synovial fluid, a mixture of mucin, albumin, fat, and

---

54 *Mosby's Medical Encyclopedia*, s.v. synovial membrane. See also Memmler, Cohen, and Wood, *Structure and Function of the Human Body*, 74–7; for discussion of the vernacular term, see Niederhellmann, *Arzt- und Heilkunde*, 195–200.
55 Wessex §53.
56 *Pactus Ala.* §7.5. The slightly different wording for the clause concerning the elbow in *Pactus Ala* §8.9 reads: 'Si nervora tangit et wasilus intrat ...' The difference in verb choice is trivial. For discussion of the vernacular term, see Niederhellmann, *Arzt- und Heilkunde*, 203–6.
57 Whether the mention of *nervora* indicates knowledge of anatomical function of the nerve is unclear in this reading; I am unaware of any other contemporary treatise addressing damage to the nerves, and thus assume that it simply refers to pain caused by swelling of the joint.
58 Pokorny, *Indogermanisches Etymologisches Wörterbuch*, 1172, *wes-³; Watkins, *American Heritage Dictionary of Indo-European Roots*, 101, wes²-; Schützeichel, *Althochdeutsches Wörterbuch*; Köbler, *Neuenglisch-Althochdeutsches Wörterbuch* (www.koeblergerhard.de/germanistischewoerterbuecher/, 2006) gives *wasilus* as the gloss for Modern English *dampness*.

mineral salts.[59] The oozing of this concoction into the linkage between upper and lower leg is precisely what gives the sensation of an infusion of water. This Alamann regulation probably describes excess synovial fluid leaking into the joint, where the Frisian and West-Saxon clauses reverse this by depicting synovial fluid leaking out of the membrane. The resulting pain in the joint, however, is the same.

Finally, there is almost no legislation regarding internal organs, with the exception of the scanty instances of clauses concerning hernia or intestines discussed above. Salian Francia indicates that wounds to ribcage and stomach incur fines if they touch the internal organs (assuming this is the correct interpretation of the *mallberg* term *gisifrit*).[60] *Lex Alamannorum* has the excessively vivid ruling that forty *solidi* are due if the intestine is damaged so that excrement comes out.[61] But the only laws to show more than cursory interest in internal organs are those of the Frisians, which include rulings against damage to the *praecordium* (the area around the heart), the lung, the *peritoneum* (the membrane lining the abdominal cavity), as well as rulings either for having the bowels spill out but be put back (as described in the Irish tale above), or for having fat emerge and have to be cut off.[62]

The final consideration is how these members of the torso were valued. I will consider first the relative values assigned by the 'primary four,' then compare the results obtained for the remaining territories. Table 4.1 lays out for the primary four the fines assessed for damage to the major limbs which were presented in black boxes on the chart at the beginning of this chapter. The darker the shading, the higher the particular body part ranks in the assessment scheme. In the event that one part of the torso is accorded multiple values according to the severity of the wound, I have taken the largest fine as representative of the meta-category. Each individual cell contains the percentage of wergild required for reparation, and (in parentheses) a hierarchy number. The latter merely assigns a mathematical value to the shading in order to aid comparison: from six for darkest down to one for lightest.

I have included two methods of assessment in the columns on the left. The first is an average of percentage of wergild. The second is the sum of the hierarchy points: the higher the figure, the more value is assigned cross-territorially to that particular body part. That is, a body part that

---

59 See *Mosby's Medical Encyclopedia*, s.v. synovial.
60 *Lex Sal.* §17.8.
61 *Lex Ala.* §57.57.
62 *Lex Fris.* §22.48–56.

Table 4.1
Relative assessment of damage to major limbs for 'major four' territories

Average % of Wergild	Hierarchy Points	Body Part	Kent	Wessex	Frisia	Alamannia
18.5	14	Shoulder/Collarbone	30 (5)	30 (4)	4 (2)	10 (3)
30	19	Arm	6 (3)	40 (5)	53 (5)	20 (6)
8.5	12	Rib/Side	3 (2)	7.5 (3)	12 (3)	12 (4)
21.5	17	Stomach/Internal Organs	12 (4)	30 (4)	24 (4)	20 (5)
112.5	20	Genitals	300 (6)	40 (5)	100 (6)	10 (3)
36	21	Leg	12 (4)	50 (6)	53 (5)	20 (6)

For individual cells:
  1st number = % of wergild for fine.
  (2nd number) = number of clauses naming body part.
Darker Shading = higher valuation of body part.
Lighter Shading = lower valuation of body part.

draws the lowest fine is assigned a hierarchy rating of 1, and further points accrue systematically according to how great the fine is in comparison to other assessments.

Surprisingly, the leg surpasses the genitals in hierarchy points. The highest fine assessed in Alfred's laws is for permanent laming. Similarly, the highest fines in Alamannia are for cutting an arm off at the shoulder or a leg at the hip. Alfred immediately thereafter rules on damage to the testicles resulting in an inability to create children. Alamannia, on the other hand, only considers a fine for the penis being unable to have an erection, and this is assessed less steeply than damaging the intestine so that excrement comes out. The small degree of interest accorded the penis in Alamannia is more than balanced out in Æthelberht's Kent, where damage to the *gekyndlice lim* (literally 'child-creating member') is fined at three times the wergild, to compensate for the inability to generate future offspring.

The arm is roughly equivalent to the leg in value. Kent puts it lower in the hierarchy than the others. Note, however, the higher fine assessed for the shoulder in Kent. Where most territories focus on damage to the arm, Æthelberht appears to locate the source of injury at the shoulder. Both Anglo-Saxon territories assign this joint more importance than their continental cousins. However, Æthelberht regulates against damage to both the shoulder and the collarbone, whereas the Alamann ruling refers to only the latter. Furthermore, the Frisian ruling specifically mentions synovial

Table 4.2
Relative assessment of damage to major limbs for secondary territories

Av. % Wergild	Hierarchy Points	Body Part	Bav	Thur	Sax	Lomb	Sal	Burg	Rib	Visi
0	0	Shoulder/Collarbone								
16	26 (av. 5.1)	Arm	3 (5)	15 (5)	16⅔ (5)	16 (5)		50 (6)		
15	25 (av. 5)	Rib/Side		5 (4)	16⅔ (5)	20 (6)	15 (5)		18 (5)	
24	12 (av. 4)	Stomach/Int. Organs	6 (6)				15 (5)			50 (1)
62 ½	24 (av. 6)	Genitals		50 (6)	100 (6)		50 (6)		50 (6)	
8⅔	25 (av. 5)	Leg	6 (6) (knee)	5 (4)	16⅔ (5)	16 (5)		10 (5) (tibia)		

For individual cells:
1st number = per cent of wergild for fine.
(2nd number) = number of clauses naming body part.
Darker Shading = higher valuation of body part.
Lighter Shading = lower valuation of body part.

excretion; the wound may be painful, but it is not completely incapacitating. The amount of reparation demanded by the Anglo-Saxon regulations implies a more comprehensive injury.

Ranked higher than the collarbone but lower than the shoulder are the stomach and internal organs. Alamannia leads the pack with their concern about that pesky excrement-leaking intestine. Finally, lowest in all rankings except Alamannia (due to their seeming insouciance about damage to the penis) is the side or rib.

What can we deduce from this hierarchy? Unsurprisingly, wounds that may cause permanent incapacitation or disability are fined higher than those which may eventually heal. A maimed arm or leg will impair the ability to work. Damaged genitals will prevent the creation of future labourers to share the work and provide support in old age. But a fractured collarbone can knit itself back together, and a rib will heal without intervention given time. If wounds to internal organs do not prove fatal (in which case the assessment would be for a full wergild rather than some percentage), then these organs, too, are likely to regenerate.

Table 4.2 presents the same comparisons for the rest of the barbarian territories, excluding only the Chamavans, who have no rulings on the torso. The regions are listed in the order of most to fewest regulations concerning the torso.

The paucity of evidence in the legal stipulations of these regions renders statistical analysis less accurate. Any single assessment which is considerably higher or lower than general will skew the percentages either of average wergild or of hierarchy points. However, we can still draw some conclusions from these data.

Those territories that rule against damage to the genitals all assess this most highly, and the average fine is considerably more than for any other body part. Arm and leg are roughly equal in the hierarchy structure, particularly if we take out of consideration the two rather oddly calculated Burgundian rulings. What is striking in this grouping as opposed to the major four is the importance assigned to reparable bones (such as the rib) and curable organs. In Saxony, a broken rib is valued equally to a broken arm or leg, and in Lombardy even higher. Similarly, in Bavaria damage to the stomach overshadows a broken arm.

Finally, we can conclude this chapter with an edifying story illustrating the efficacy of medical practice in barbarian Europe without the need to depict bones. Eddius Stephanus, in his early eighth-century *Life of Bishop Wilfred*, tells how a young man fell from a pinnacle during the building of Hexham Priory: 'his arms and legs were broken, all his limbs were out of joint and he lay breathing his last ... [After the bishop prayed] the physicians bound the broken limbs with bandages and he grew better gradually from day to day.'[63] This provides us with a salutary reminder that religious intervention was regarded as an essential component of any cure.

---

63 Bonser, *Medical Background of Anglo-Saxon England*, 100.

5 Hands and Feet[1]

Offending Limbs: Hands, Feet, Eyes

This chapter begins with a look at what I have elsewhere called the 'Matthew limbs.'[2] The Gospel of Matthew 18:8–9 quotes Christ as saying:

> If your hand or your foot causes you to stumble, cut it off and throw it away; it is better for you to enter life maimed or lame than to have two hands or two feet and to be thrown into the eternal fire. And if your eye causes you to stumble, tear it out and throw it away; it is better for you to enter life with one eye than to have two eyes and to be thrown into the hell of fire.[3]

Although I use the rubric 'Matthew limbs' for the sake of convenience, it would be a mistake to connect the biblical association with the laws for two reasons. First, the eye/hand/foot connection is not unique to the Bible. Aristotle in *Nichomachean Ethics*, Bk. 7 asks:

---

1 The clauses under consideration in this chapter are presented in chronological order: *Lex Sal.* §29.1–11; *Kent* §§53–9, 60–71; *Lex Rib.* §§4–9, 68; *Lex Ala.* §§62, 65; *Edict Roth.* §§62–73; *Forum Iud.* §VI.4.iii; *Lex Baiu.* §11; *Lex Sax.* §13; *Lex Fris.* §22.27–38, 41–3, 62–4, 76; *Lex Thur.* §I.15, 19–22; *Lex Cham.* §20; *Wessex* §§56–60, 64, 69, 71.
2 I have elsewhere also called these the *Lex Talionis* members (Oliver, '*Lex Talionis* in Barbarian Law'). *Lex Talionis* refers to the stipulation set out in Exodus 12:23–4: 'Life for life, eye for eye, tooth for tooth, hand for hand, foot for foot.' However, I now believe the Matthew citation is more likely, given the inclusion of the tooth in the *Lex Talionis* enumeration.
3 *The New Oxford Annotated Bible*, ed. Metzger and Murphy, New Testament, 27.

Table 5.1
Assessment of 'Matthew limbs'

Region↓ Limb→	Wergild	Eye	Hand	Foot
Salian Francia	200	50%	50%	50%
Ripuaria	200	50%	50%	50%
Thuringia	200	50%	50%	50%
Burgundy	100	50%		
Visigothic Spain	200	50(+)%	50%	50%
Saxony	1440	50%	50%	50%
Kent	100	50%	(50%)	50%
Lombardy	150	50%		50%
Wessex	200	33%	33%	33%
Chamavan Francia		25%	25%	25%
Frisia	100	25%	25%	25%
Bavaria	200	20%	20%	20%
Alamannia	200	20%		

Eye/Hand/Foot as Percentage of Wergild
Lighter Shading = Higher Percentage

> Have the carpenter, then, and the tanner certain functions or activities, and has man none? Is he born without a function? Or as eye, hand, foot, and in general each of the parts evidently has a function, may one lay it down that man similarly has a function apart from all these? What then can this be? Life seems to be common even to plants, but we are seeking what is peculiar to man.[4]

Second, as discussed in chapter 3, the Germanic laws variously equate the values of nose and ear with that of the eye. Thus 'eye' should be interpreted here as a cover term for sensory organs. Most of the barbarian laws tied the reparation for eye, hand, and foot to a proportion of the wergild (given in *solidi* for the continent and shillings for England), as indicated in Table 5.1.[5]

---

4 *Aristotle's Ethica Nicomachea*, trans. Ross, s.v.
5 In actuality, only the neighbouring Chamavans and Frisians explicitly express restitution for the 'Matthew limbs' as a percentage of wergild, but elsewhere the numbers themselves unambiguously reflect the relationship (in particular, the odd 66 shillings, 6 1/3 pence demanded by Alfred, whose math is, however, slightly off). Bavaria and Alamannia both require that 160 *solidi* be paid as wergild (with another 40 shillings to the public coffer).

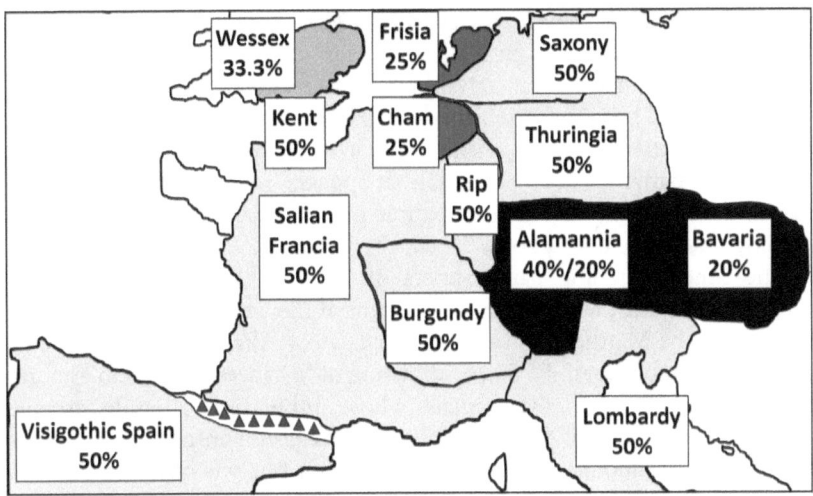

Map 5.1 Assessment of 'Matthew limbs.'

Eye/Hand/Foot as Percentage of Wergild
Lighter Shading = Higher Percentage

Map 5.1 represents Table 5.1 in geographical format, with the shading, as in the preceding chart, moving from highest percentage/lightest colouring to lowest percentage/darkest colouring.

This map allows us to draw several conclusions. Most obviously, the overwhelming regulation against damage to the Matthew limbs is 50 per cent of the wergild. It is only in the farthest eastern and northern regions that differences appear.

We find again the close connection we have seen before between Alamannia and Bavaria in regulation against damage to the eye; both textual and geographic connections render this parallel unsurprising. Nonetheless, an unexpected anomaly arises in the laws of Alamannia, which contain the only clauses not equating the Matthew limbs: the foot is valued at 40 per cent of the wergild, the eye at 20 per cent, and the hand not considered. Interpretation of other evidence presented in the map will eventually provide a hypothesis for this incongruity. Before leaving these regions, it is important to note that the percentages depend crucially on how we define wergild for these two territories. Both codes set the fine for homicide at 160 *solidi* to the family and an additional forty to the public coffer, a total of 200 *solidi*. No other regions employ such a division. Taking 160 *solidi* as the wergild proper gives percentages of 25 per cent for the eye (and 50 per cent for the Alamann foot); the former figure would align these territories with the northeastern regions of Frisia and Chamavan Francia. Although this reckoning is attractive for the Matthew limbs, assuming a 160-*solidi* wergild makes the percentages of fines assessed for other injuries mathematically irregular,[6] which is atypical of the style of the barbarian laws as a whole. It appears, rather, that these calculations were based on the full assessed fine of 200 *solidi*; I have thus opted to employ this figure throughout.

The other matching pair consists of the neighbouring Frisians and Chamavan Franks, who require 25 per cent of the wergild as restitution for damage to the Matthew limbs. The later laws of Alfred strike an approximate medium between the 50 per cent fine of his ancestor Æthelberht and the 25 per cent fine of the Frisians (whose influence is often discernable elsewhere in the laws of Wessex). These three regions constitute a geographical cluster (excluding the kingdom of Kent), but we nowhere else see Chamavan Francia aligned with the Anglo-Frisian grouping. Perhaps more pertinent is the fact that the territories whose wergild percentages are lower than the norm – Frisia, Chamavan Francia, and Wessex – are three of the last four to commit their laws to writing. Apparently, the legal amount of compensation for damage to the Matthew limbs tended to drop over time.

Peculiar as this fact seems, it may help explain the surprising differences in the laws of Alamannia and Bavaria. My tentative scenario is that the Alamann laws originally required a payment of 40 per cent wergild for all the Matthew limbs. In the laws of Bavaria, the tendency for lowering the required percentage of wergild had begun; thus the 40 per cent model taken from Alamannia was reduced to 20 per cent. As this trend continued in the latter half of the century, the Alamann 40 per cent was halved for the foot; restitution for the eye was overlooked in the revision and thus remained at its previous level. This (tentatively offered) speculation explains the numbers, but unfortunately no evidence exists to corroborate or refute it. Although the fact of the lessening of wergild for the Matthew limbs in the later laws is actual, the reason for such an odd shift is impenetrable.

Hand

Only the laws of Kent, Alamannia, and Lombardy lack any specific recompense for damage to the hands. In the case of Kent, the sum of the fines for fingers equals 50 per cent of the wergild. Logically then, the palm

---

6 See chart for *Lex Baiuariorum* in the appendix, p. 255.

itself must have no intrinsic value, as the hand is considered a compendium of the individual digits. Then again, if the palm were crushed, all the fingers would likely be rendered inutile; Æthelberht's legislators may have been following this reasoning. Conversely, the sum of fines for fingers in Frisian law is forty-one *solidi*, leaving an implicit fine of nine *solidi* for the palm. However, Frisia also includes a fine specifically for striking off (*abscisus*) the palm, which seems to me a fairly bizarre injury.

Lombardy extends compensation as percentage to the 25 per cent wergild fine for injury to the thumb: that is, thirty-seven and a half *solidi*. Thus the total of all Lombard fines for cutting off fingers is eighty-two and a half *solidi* (55 per cent wergild rather than the expected 50 per cent). Conversely, in Alamannia, the sum of fines for fingers in the *Pactus* is forty-two *solidi* (21 per cent wergild) and in the *Lex* forty-nine (25½ per cent wergild); these fines are lower than the eighty *solidi* (40 per cent wergild) for the foot. Although a Saxon mutilator would be well advised to amputate the entire hand after striking off the individual fingers, as he could plead the Matthew equation and save himself money, an Alamann attacker would be better to quit while the hand still remains.

Two remarkable points arise in connection with the rulings on hands. First, there is nowhere a differentiation between the predominant and non-predominant hand. Alamann law does indeed regulate against damage to the elbow so that the victim cannot raise his hand to his mouth, presumably to feed himself, and I suppose that this must be a covert reference to the predominant hand.[7] I myself am right-handed, but when I temporarily lost the use of my right hand due to a bicycling accident, I managed to keep from starving by using my left hand. (The result was messy, but still life-sustaining.) More crucial would be the impairment of such occupations as the shooting of a bow, or the yoking of oxen. Yet both hands are valued equally in barbarian law. Frisia is the only territory to regulate injury to the hand according to profession: maiming the hand of a harpist or a goldsmith requires fourfold compensation.[8]

The second surprising feature of these tariffs is the invariable equation of the hand with the foot and the eye/nose(/ear). Intuitively, it would seem that the hand should be valued more highly, as overwhelmingly it is the only limb in barbarian law which can be struck off as punishment. For example, both Saxon and Chamavan laws demand the loss of the right

---

7 *Lex Ala.* §61.7.
8 *Lex Fris, Iudicia Wulemari* §10.

hand for perjury: the hand which swore the false oath is struck off.[9] The laws of Alfred stipulate that for stealing in church, the thief must pay fine and fee, and have the hand with which he did the deed severed.[10] The laws of Burgundy demand that a freeman who forges papers (*litteras fecerit*) for an escaping slave lose his right hand, as does a Jew who raises a hand against a Christian or seizes him by the hair. The Jew can redeem his hand with a fine of seventy-five shillings and a payment of twelve to the public coffer. The laws are not clear as to whether the same option is open to the forger, but since seventy-five shillings is the usual half-wergild fine for the hand, I think this is a fair assumption.[11] Both Chamavan law and that of Alfred permit the hand to be redeemed by payment of the appropriate fine, and likely the same held for Saxony. In Frisia, a thief who is proven guilty by ordeal must redeem his hand with sixty *solidi*; conversely, if someone accuses another of theft but ordeal demonstrates that the purported thief is innocent, the accuser is liable for the sixty-*solidi* fine in lieu of losing his own hand. Only in the West Saxon laws of Ine is the punishment for a commoner found guilty of theft the loss of his hand or his foot.[12] (These two limbs have equal recompense assigned in law, but can you actually steal with your foot? Perhaps the reasoning was that the thief could not escape with his ill-gotten gains.)

Historical example substantiates the legal rulings. When Witteric in 603 deposed the nineteen-year-old Liuva, king of the Visigoths, he had his right hand struck off to prevent him from retaking the throne. As Visigothic tradition required the king to be able-bodied, the mutilation would render him ineligible. This punishment may have served to add insult to injury: not only was Liuva maimed, but the choice of the right hand might imply that he was guilty of legal transgressions while he held the kingship.

Given the propensity elsewhere in the laws to fine visible damage at a higher rate than hidden, one might intuitively expect the hand to have a greater compensation value than the foot. A man without a foot has clearly been wounded. A man without a hand may have suffered injury, but may conversely have been found guilty of perjury or theft. There is, rather surprisingly, no punitive surcharge for this more ambiguous amputation.

---

9 *Lex Sax.* §21; *Lex Cham.* §23.
10 *Wessex* §6.
11 *Liber Const.* §6.10 and §102.1, 2.
12 Ine §§18 and 37. See discussion in Liebermann *Die Gesetze der Angelsachsen*, vol. 1, 96; also O'Brien O'Keeffe, 'Body and Law in Late Anglo-Saxon England,' 215.

Finally, we find in the laws of Alamannia and Bavaria evidence for medical intervention on wounds to the hand. These two territories, once again in agreement, require that if a hand was pierced so that a hot iron had to be inserted to close the veins in order to still the blood, the perpetrator was fined three *solidi*.[13]

Fingers

Although the names of many body parts originally derive etymologically from function, these connections are generally deeply buried in the past. The early seventh-century *Etymolgies* of Isidore of Seville often demonstrate the practice of 'folk etymology' – hence many of the fanciful associations made by Isidore. For example, *oculus*, 'eye,' simply derives from the Indo-European root *okʷ- – 'to see'; Isidore's conjecture that the name comes from either the fact that membranes of eyes cover (*occulere*) them or that they have hidden light (*occultum lumen*) has no basis. Even more fanciful is his connection of *tempus*, 'temple of the head,' to *tempus*, 'season,' since the temples move and change like seasons.[14] Although the origin of the term *temple* is uncertain – possibly connected to Indo-European *temp-, 'to stretch,' as here the skin is stretched from behind the eye to the ear[15] – certainly Isidore's speculation smacks of etymological desperation. In any event, long before we reach the recordings of the Germanic laws, the functional derivations have simply been converted to nomenclature.

The barbarian laws generally avoid this etymological trap in regard to fingers, whose names often relate directly to their use, although with some interesting variations. In order to better understand the specifics of terminology and how they relate to compensation value, we must first examine the functional uses of the fingers.[16]

The most important unit on the hand is the thumb – the digit which allows a human to grasp and use a tool effectively. This ability distinguishes humans from most other mammals.

---

13 *Lex Ala.* §61.3, 4; *Lex Baiu.* §4.4.
14 For Isidore, see *The Etymologies of Isidore of Seville*, ed. Barney, Lewis, Beach, and Berghof, 233.
15 Watkins, *American Heritage Dictionary of Indo-European Roots*, s.v.
16 For functions of fingers, I consulted practising professionals in various fields: orthopaedic surgeon Riccardo Rodriguez; former Canadian junior archery champion Peter Clayton; former Olympic decathlete 'Coach Hat' Bachar, currently throws coach for Episcopal Academy in Baton Rouge, LA; and javelin coaches at the same school, Amanda Harmata and John Woosley. See Behnke, *Kinetic Anatomy*, 91–7.

Figure 5.1 Warriors wielding spears and swords. Franks Casket, 8th century. Photograph reproduced by permission of British Museum Publications Ltd.

The second most important finger physiologically is the little finger, which allows the hand to cup and hold water. This digit thus provides the hand with its fullest extension of functionality.[17] The little finger is also crucial for wielding thrusting weapons. The most common grave goods found in male burials both on the continent and in Britain are spears and swords.[18] When these were held in position to thrust or stab, most of the weight was cantilevered out front, as demonstrated in Fig. 5.1.

---

17 Friends of mine who have waited tables – Anglo-Saxonists Janet Erikson and Tom Hall – both agree that the extended little finger is crucial in the ability to balance a loaded tray above the shoulder.

18 For examples, open to virtually any page in Joffrey, *Le Cimetière de Lavoye (Meuse)*, or Meaney, *A Gazatteer of Early Anglo-Saxon Burial Sites*. Also commonly found are shield bosses; the shield, of course, is another weapon for which good grasping ability is a great advantage but not an absolute necessity. In the third century BC the Roman

Germanic swords were heavy, and the weight of an iron-tipped spear was not inconsiderable. The little finger functions as a crucial pivot for keeping the point of the weapon up. A spear-fighter or sword-man who loses his little finger will be at a considerable disadvantage in time of battle, as he will find it extremely difficult to control his weapon. The same is true to a lesser degree for the shield, which is also a heavy piece of battle equipment. The physical prowess required to handle a sword/spear and shield is demonstrated in the burial goods in the Edix Hill Cemetery. Men buried with shield and spear all died in the prime of life – between eighteen and thirty-five years old; this symbolized their ability to wield both weapons simultaneously. The graves of older and young males in contradistinction had only one weapon.[19]

The functional importance of the little finger may be augmented by compensation for visible damage: in a world in which the handspan serves as a measuring device, the loss of the little finger becomes obvious whenever a measurement must be made. This important consideration is actually fairly arbitrary. The distance between the tip of the thumb and that of the extended little finger varies greatly according to the size of the individual's hand. For my hand, the span measured with the ring finger is almost identical to that determined by the little finger. However, as convention dictates that the little finger is the unmarked digit for measuring a handspan, any deviation becomes instantly noticeable.

Next in order of physiological worth is the forefinger, with which (in conjunction with the thumb) one can perform activities requiring finer grasp, such as delousing, using tweezers (not uncommonly found in grave goods),[20] or spinning – all activities commonly performed by women. The forefinger is also more important than the little finger for a spear thrower as opposed to a warrior who used his spear as a thrusting weapon. The spear is balanced at its midpoint on the first three fingers, with the forefinger or the forefinger and mid-finger (depending on the grasp) providing the propulsion.

---

    warrior Marcus Sergius was said to have a prosthetic hand made of iron to help wield his sword, but modern scholars believe that this was used to hold the shield (Keil, 'Eine Prosthese aus einem fränkischen Grab von Greisheim,' 204).
19 Hines, 'Lies, Damned Lies, and a Curriculum Vitae,' 95. For further on status of weapons burial, see also Stoodley, 'Multiple Burials, Multiple Meanings?' 118.
20 For example, in burial finds in Girton or Little Wilbraham; see Meaney, *Gazatteer*, 66 and 71 respectively.

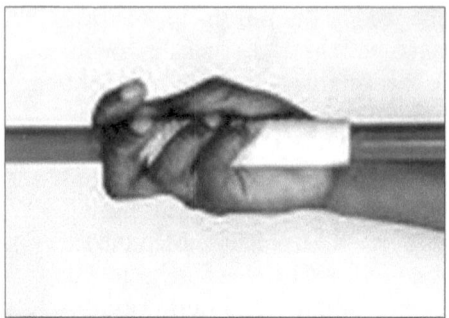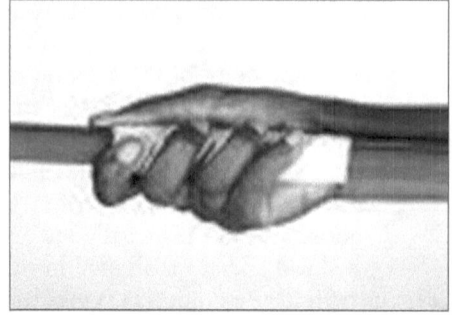

Figure 5.2 Configurations of throwing hand for spear warriors. Photographs reproduced by permission of DK Images.

The diagrams above demonstrate the importance of the forefinger in throwing, regardless of the specific grip. As a final note, the forefinger is the default digit used for pointing for both men and women (see discussion of 'index' below). A person with a missing forefinger will be required to improvise, thus drawing attention to the loss every time he or she wishes to draw attention to something else.

On a purely physiological basis, there's not much to choose between the middle and ring fingers. One might give slight preference to the ring finger for its assistance in the cupping and gripping process. A man using a spear to thrust or stab will miss his fourth finger more than his third; however, the converse is true for a man using a spear as a throwing weapon, as demonstrated by Fig. 5.2. Bavarian law requires that for any finger, if it cannot bend so as to hold a weapon, an additional 1/3 is added to the fine; a similar stipulation in Ripuarian law adds a surcharge of twelve *solidi*.[21]

Turning to what terminology may tell us, the thumb is almost universally and uninterestingly referred to in Latin as *pollex* and in Old English as *þuma*. In every body of law it is – anatomically correctly – valued most highly of the digits on the hand. (The thumb has thus not been numbered in the charts which follow to avoid redundancy.) Only the *mallberg* glosses in the laws of the Salian Franks give us variation, and then more than we might want. Annette Niederhellmann correctly advises that

---

21 *Lex Baiu.* §IV.11; *Lex Rib.* §LVII.53.

die salfränkische Fingerbezeichnungen offensichtlich einen Sprachstand wiedergeben, der sich nur zu einem Teil in Bezeichnungen späterer Sprachschichten erhalten hat, zu einem anderen Teil anscheinend schon von den Schreibern der Lex Salica nicht mehr verstanden wurden.[22]

For the vernacular designation for the thumb, manuscript variants in Salic law provide *alathamo*; *alachtamo*; *athlatam*; *ablatam*. Franz Beyerle postulates an original **allatamo*, 'useful in all places.' Ruth Schmidt-Wiegand suggests that the ur-form was **alathumo*, 'the complete strength.'[23] Neither of these etymologies seems impossible for this important digit. (It is superficially attractive to break Schmidt-Wiegand's protoform into a compound **ala-thumo* with the prefix as an intensifier similar to Old Norse *all-* or Old English *eal-*, and a compound meaning of 'great thumb.' However, the Second Germanic Sound Shift predicates Frankish **d** in place of Old English þ if the stem is bi-morphemic.)

When not otherwise identified, the forefinger is referred to as the *secundus digitus*, 'second finger,' or *proximus a police*, 'closest to the thumb.' Frisian, Saxon, and Thuringian create a northern isogloss here by calling the forefinger the *index*. This term dates back to classical antiquity, as Quintilian explains: 'When three fingers are doubled under the thumb, the finger, which Cicero says that Crassus used to such effect, is extended. It is used in denunciation and indication – whence its name as index finger.'[24] This is the primary name assigned it by Isidore.

The southernmost and westernmost regions – Salian and Ripuarian Francia, Kent, and Wessex – refer to the forefinger by its use in archery: the *sagittur* or *scytefinger* respectively.[25] A layman might well assume (wrongly) that this refers to the forefinger of the right hand, which helps to draw

---

22 'The Salic-Frankish designations for fingers apparently reflect a linguistic stage that has, on the one hand, been only partially maintained in the designations of a later stage of the language, and, on the other hand, seem to have been no longer understood by the scribes of the Lex Salica' (Niederhellmann, *Arzt- und Heilkunde*, 189).
23 Beyerle, 'Die Malberg-Glossen der Lex Salica,' 24; see also Schmidt-Wiegand, in Niederhellmann, *Arzt- und Heilkunde*, 186–9.
24 Quintilian XI, 3: 'At cum tres contracti pollice premuntur, tum digitus ille, quo usum optime Crassum Cicero dicit, explicari solet. Is in exprobrando et indicando (unde et nomen est) valet.' Trans. H.E. Butler, cited in De Jorio, *Gesture in Naples and Gesture in Classical Antiquity*, 204.
25 Hüpper-Dröge, 'Schutz- und Angriffswaffen nach den Leges und verwandten fränkischen Rechtsquellen,' 118–19, discusses various evidence for the use of bow as weapon or in the hunt. Even in the hunt, there was the possibility that arrows would be poisoned.

back the bowstring. In fact, the fingers used for this purpose depend both on the material used for the bow, which determines the concomitant strength required to bend it, and on local custom. In 1845, G.A. Hansard reported that 'modern English bowmen generally draw with three fingers. The Flemings use the first and second only ... The Indians of Demerara use only the thumb and forefinger.'[26] He goes on to relate this anecdote about an aged Welsh archer:

> [When] Rhys Wyn, a gentleman advanced in years, came with William Cynwal on a visit to Edmund Prys, archdeacon of Merioneth, they found him engaged in archery ... Rhys Wyn spoke thus: 'Had I a bow weak enough, old as I am, you should not shoot alone.' Then William said he had a bow that would reach thirty yards, which Rhys could draw with *his little finger* [emphasis Hansard's].[27]

Hansard speculates that the strength of military bows would probably have required a three-fingered draw, despite the fact that early illustrations almost invariably depict only two fingers on the string. (One of the origin legends for the 'victory' symbol made popular by Winston Churchill is that the gesture was used by English archers after the battle of Agincourt in 1415 to demonstrate that their bowstring fingers were still intact.)[28]

A more precise linguistic interpretation of *sagittur*, 'arrow finger,' makes it obvious that the term relates to the arrow rather than the bow. The name refers to the first finger on the left hand, whose knuckle, aligned with that of the thumb, provides a level platform from which to launch the arrow shaft; this function is demonstrated in Fig. 5.3. This same purport is presented less specifically in the Old English term *scytefinge*, 'shooting finger.'

Counterintuitively, then, the 'shooting finger' takes its name from the use in the non-predominant hand. Although most right-handed people will point with the index finger on their right hand, all (who are archers) must invariably support an arrow with their arrow (or shooting) finger on the left. While the loss of the forefinger on the string hand can be compensated for by replacing its use with any of the other fingers on that hand, the loss of the forefinger on the bow hand creates an uneven surface, impairing the ability both to gauge the necessary arc for distance and to guide the shaft straight. As we will see, this dichotomy in naming between predominant and non-predominant hand is not unique to the forefinger.

---

26 Hansard, *The Book of Archery*, 82–3.
27 Ibid., 169.
28 Barker, *Agincourt*, 284.

Figure 5.3 Anglo-Saxon archer. Franks Casket, 8th century. Photograph reproduced by permission of British Museum Publications Ltd.

A final note on terminology for the forefinger: Salic laws incorporate in the *mallberg* glosses the Frankish term *briorotero* in various scribal variations (see Fig. 5.4). Franz Beyerle rejects previous scholarly interpretations linking *brio-* with German *Brei* (English *brew*), which assume it means something like 'the finger that stirs the brew.' I am sympathetic to Beyerle's query 'gab's keine Kochlöchel?' (were there no cooking spoons?). Given the instantiations in other Germanic laws, far more appealing is his own hypothesis that this term could go back to an original **bigrôtaro*, 'threatener, warner,' which would link it to the classical definition of 'index' cited above, namely, 'used in denunciation and indication.' I have thus assumed Beyerle's interpretation in the following discussion.[29]

---

29 Beyerle, 'Malberg Glossen,' 24. Jacob Grimm connected the first element to OE *briord*, 'point, border,' or *brord*, 'point, lance, throwing spear,' and defined the compound as the finger 'der die pfeile von des bogens spitze sendet' (the one that sends the arrow from the point of the bow). If one accepts this etymology (which I find a bit of a

The middle finger invokes no such inventiveness in naming. With only one exception, the scribes refer to it by position as the *medianus/medius/* OE *middel* 'middle,' *tertius*, 'third,' or *longissimus*, 'longest.' The Thuringians revert to a time-honoured custom in calling this finger *inpudicus*, 'obscene.'[30] Isidore says the term arises from the fact that 'often an accusation of a shameful action is expressed by it.'[31] (The stem is a negation of *pudicus* 'chaste' – it is termed the 'unchaste finger' for reasons I decline to discuss.) Again, we find precedence for this in classical antiquity: Martial says of a rascal: 'Ostendit digitum, set impudicum' (he points his finger – and the insulting one).[32] Similar gesticulation with this finger continues into our own day. In what will appear to be a leitmotif, the Frankish term *taphano*, with various scribal alternatives, has spawned equally variant interpretations. Relying on both early Germanic and cross-cultural comparative evidence, I would favour Kern's association with Saxon *derbhi* 'expressing disapproval,'[33] and have thus linked the Frankish term to Thuringian *inpudicus*.

The fourth finger is usually referred to simply as *quartus*, 'fourth.' Once again, however, the two more descriptive choices come one each from the predominant and non-predominant hand. The first to be considered is the reference more familiar to modern readers to the fourth finger as the bearer of a ring: the *digitus anullaris*, 'ring finger,' of the Alamann *Lex* and Frisian laws and the *goldfinger*, 'gold finger,' of both Anglo-Saxon texts. In the cemetery at Bonaduz, ten graves contained rings, only one of which was on the right hand; in the Merovingian necropolis at Lavoye, for all nine graves in which bodies were buried wearing rings, these were on the left hand – unfortunately the archaeologists are not specific as to which finger.[34]

Rings are customarily worn on the left hand because it is considered more intimately connected to the heart – for a similar reason, in ancient

---

stretch), the term would be related to the arrow-finger rather than the index. See Niederhellmann, *Arzt- und Heilkunde*, 178–81.

30 More usually, the coronal **n** will have assimilated to the labial **p**, giving *impudicus*; this is likely just morphemic spelling.
31 *Etymologies of Isidore*, ed. Barney et al., 235.
32 Martial VI 70, trans. Walter Ker, who adds in a footnote: 'The middle finger was called *infamis* and was used to point in scorn.' De Jorio, *Gesture*, 193–4.
33 Cited in Beyerle, 'Malberg-Glossen,' 24; for other analyses, see Niederhellmann, *Arzt- und Heilkunde*, 181–3.
34 For the cemetery at Lavoye, see Joffrey, *Le Cimetière de Lavoye (Meuse)*. For the grave finds at Bonaduz, see Schneider-Schneckenburger, *Churrätien im Frühmittelalter auf Grund der archäologischen Funde*, 26; for rings, 34.

Egypt statues were carved with the left foot forward, or in nineteenth-century Italy the back of the left hand was kissed as a sign of respect (while kissing the back of the right hand signified disdain).[35] The (mistaken) assumption that a vein leads from the gold finger directly to the heart is one of the reasons the wedding ring is commonly worn on that finger. The designation of the ring as gold in the Anglo-Saxon laws might refer specifically to a wedding band, although the wearing of gold may have also indicated high status. Of the ten rings found on fingers in Lavoye, five were bronze, four were silver, and only one was gold; nine of the ten rings of Bonaduz are bronze, the tenth is iron. Of the rings found in early Kentish cemeteries, the most common material is similarly bronze, with silver and iron about equal. Only one gold ring was found in Kent: a male inhumation burial at Milton-next-Sittingbourne contained a Roman gold finger-ring of the second century.[36] A grave in Chur, St Regula, contained two thin gold rings, one open and one decorated with two small, dice-like cubes. This grave also produced a pair of elaborate armbands; it seems that this burial was very high-status.[37] Certainly the inclusion of gold rings in grave goods must have served as a signal of unusual wealth.

The Salic laws again present us with the problem of scribal transmission: Beyerle chooses from the options *malachano*, connecting this term (hypothesizing a syllable lost in the cutting of the margins of the manuscript) to Middle High German *mahelvingerlîn*, 'the engagement finger.'[38] This hypothesis seems acceptable, as it links it to the ring/gold finger found elsewhere.

We find a slightly tighter northern isogloss than for the *index* finger in the second choice: the Saxon and Thuringian use of *medicus* for the fourth finger. This was a fairly common medieval designation; in later Anglo-Saxon glosses we find the vernacular equivalent *læce-finger*, 'leech-finger.' According to Isidore, this designation stems from the fact that 'physicians

---

35 De Jorio, *Gesture*, 107.
36 Meaney, *Gazatteer*, 108–42.
37 Schneider-Schneckenburger, *Churrätien im Frühmittelalter*, 56. The value placed on rings is substantiated by a template for a will in Angers #54, which includes a ring among the items left to the inheritor (Rio, trans. *The Formularies of Angers and Marculf*, 95–6).
38 Beyerle, 'Malberg-Glossen,' 24; for other etymological views, see Niederhellmann, *Arzt- und Heilkunde*, 183–5. Jacob Grimm took *ma-* as an abbreviation for *mallberg*, and connected *lechano* to OHD *lahhi* 'doctor.' Following this analysis, one would assign the Malberg gloss to the *medicus* group. The ring finger is not necessarily restricted to the left hand; Maren Wagner, master's candidate at Heidelberg University, informs me that in modern Germany, the engagement ring is worn on the fourth finger of the left hand, while the wedding ring is worn on the same finger on the right hand.

(*medic[i]*) use it to scoop up ground eye-salves.'³⁹ A poem from an English fifteenth-century manuscript demonstrates the persistence of this custom:

> Like a fyngir has a name, als men thaire fingers calle,
> The lest fyngir hat litye man, for hit is lest of alle;
> The next finger hat leche man, for qwen a leche dos ozt
> With that finger he tastes all thynge howe that hit is wrozt.⁴⁰

This practice may not be unrelated to the finger's purported connection to the heart: 'according to Levinus Lemnius ... the old physicians would stir up their medicaments and potions with it, because no venom could stick upon the very outmost part of it but it will offend a man and communicate itself to the heart.'⁴¹ Nomenclature of the fourth finger leaves us thus with two possible isoglosses: western territories (and the Alamanns) use gold finger/ring finger while northern territories use *medicus*.

Finally, the little finger inspires even less nomenclatural creativity than the middle finger. The Frankish-inspired texts uniformly refer to it as *minimus*, 'smallest,' and the Anglo-Saxon texts as *lytel*, 'little.' The Lombards and Visigoths opt for sequence rather than size in *quintus*, 'fifth.' The first element of Frankish *minecleno* looks to be related to *minimus*; the second element is unclear, although Beyerle may be correct in relating it to Old High German *hlinôn*, 'support.' This interpretation would give a compound meaning of 'the small support,' which seems apposite for this digit

---

39 *Etymologies of Isidore*, ed Barney et al., 235. The ninth- or tenth-century medical compendium *Lecciones Heliodori* contains the phrase: 'Qui vero his subiacient cubiti, manum V, qui nominantur pollex, quem greci antichir (before the hand) vocant, secundum autem greci lacanon (forefinger {lichanon}) dicunt, medium, et circa medium minorem quem diatricon (medical {iatricon}) appellant, id est medicinalem' (Sigerist, 'Die "Lecciones Heliodori,"' 150). The almost identical text appears in an eleventh-century manuscript edited by Rudolf Laux in 'Ars medicinae: Ein frühmittelalterliches Kompendium der Medizin,' *Kyklos* 3 (1930), 422. The variant but better readings from the Greek from this later manuscript are given in {curly brackets}. My translation of this text reads: 'Indeed here lie the digits, five of the hand, which are called thumb, which the Greeks call *antichir* [before the hand], the second however the Greeks name *lichanon* [forefinger], medium, and around the medium the lesser which they call *iatricon*, that is, *medicinalem* [medica].' Unless I am mistranslating, there are only three fingers listed here in addition to the thumb; comparative evidence would imply that the exemplar omitted the little finger.
40 Bosworth and Toller, *An Anglo-Saxon Dictionary*, 667, which contains similar citations under *laecefinger*, 'leechfinger.'
41 Kent, 'The Number and Location of Rings Worn in Different Cultures.' http://www.jjkent.com/articles/number-location-rings-worn.htm. 2004.

when used to help grasp.⁴² (Despite the modern caricature of the uncouth barbarian, none of these scribes are crude enough to use Isidore's recommended *auricularis*, 'ear finger,' thus called 'because we use it to scrape out the ear [*auris*].'⁴³ Burial finds on both sides of the Channel include the occasional ear-scoop, demonstrating the importance of personal cleanliness in the afterlife,⁴⁴ but this role did not translate to legal terminology.)

The charts which follow lay out the fingers as regulated in each territory, showing the names as discussed above, and indicating the order of compensation value. (Alamanns, Bavarians, Saxons, and Frisians all give a more precise breakdown, indicating differing fines for different joints struck off or for maiming versus striking off. This information is included in the appendix, but has been omitted here for the sake of readability. For the same reason, the actual amount of the fines is omitted.) The charts are presented in descending order of physiological accuracy.

Half of the territories properly give the little finger the highest value, although two of these five equate it with the forefinger. Among these latter are the Bavarians, who, in a separate clause, require an extra 1/3 recompense if the fingers are unable to bend sufficiently to hold a weapon. It may not be coincidental, then, that the arrow finger and spear-grasping finger were considered of equal value, and of greater worth than the interior digits. The Salian Franks put the forefinger first, and emphasize this by calling it the 'arrow finger' – terminology and assessment act in unison. (The Salic *mallberg* gloss aligns instead with the *index* group.) Ripuaria echoes the Salic ruling for the *sagittur*, but does not address compensation for any other fingers. A similar unity between valuation and nomenclature can be seen for the Frisians and Alfred, who both give precedence to the ring finger and also call it respectively *anullaris* or *goldfinger*. This order of compensation has no basis in physiological value, and can only be explained as a punitive surcharge for the loss of the finger which can show marital or economic status by the wearing of the ring. There is neither a physiological nor a social explanation for the Thuringian equation of all fingers, including the thumb. Striking off any digit requires payment of 1/6 wergild, which is ridiculously high for the ring and middle finger. The Visigoths regulate according to sequence, with the forefinger most highly

---

42 Here I find Beyerle's interpretation ('Malberg-Glossen,' 25) of 'memory prop' (from *mine*, 'memory,' and *hlinon*, 'support') unsubstantiated by comparative evidence.
43 *Etymologies of Isidore*, ed. Barney et al., 235.
44 Williams, *Death and Memory in Early Medieval Britain*, 43.

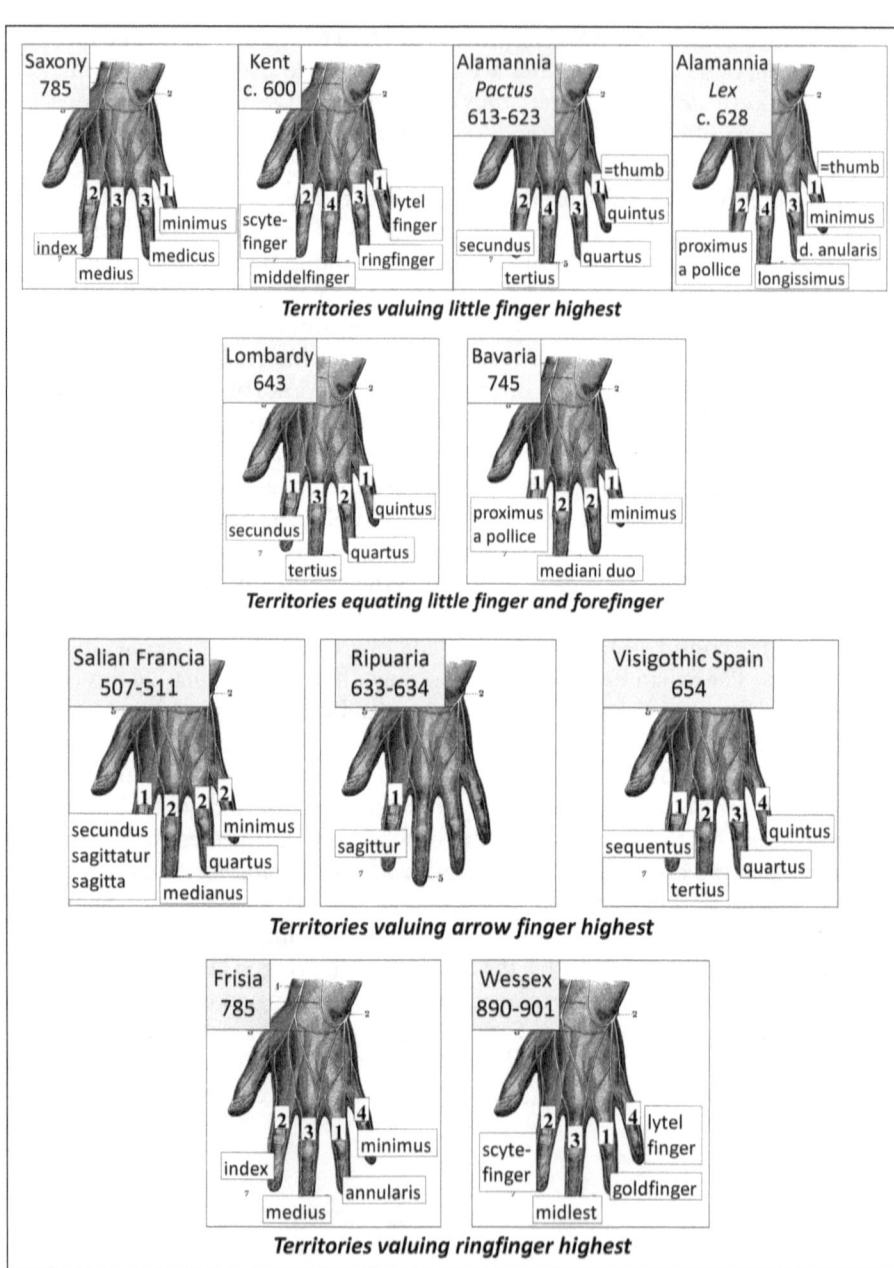

Figure 5.4 Charts of finger values in descending order of functional accuracy.

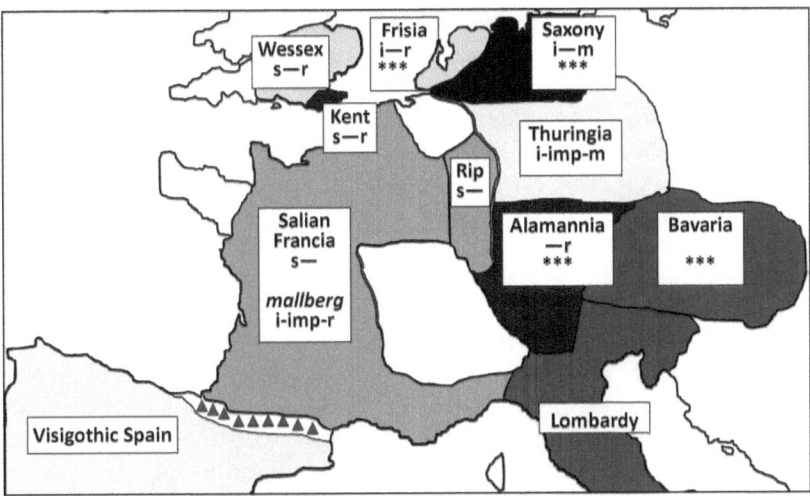

Map 5.2 Distribution of terminology and functional approximation for fingers.

Darker shading = closer to physiological accuracy.
s = *sagittur* or *scytefinger* for forefinger; i = *index*.
r = *anullaris* or *goldfinger* for ringfinger; m = *medicus*.
imp = impudent/immoral for middle finger.
*** indicates more detailed anatomical breakdown.

valued and the little finger least. These last two regions employ bad anatomy and bad social analysis, and their rulings thus represent bad law.

Map 5.2 summarizes the evidence we can glean from the compensations for fingers in barbarian law. Shading on the map goes from darkest, meaning closest to physiological value, to lightest, meaning furthest. An **s** designates the use of the term *sagittur* or *scytefinger* for the forefinger, and an **i** indicates that the territory in question uses *index*. Similarly, an **r** designates the ring finger – *anullaris* in Latin and *goldfinger* in Old English – and an **m** indicates the use of *medicus*. The designation **imp** stands for some variant of impudent/immoral for the middle finger. The lack of any label indicates that the fingers are simply enumerated according to position. Finally, *** indicates more detailed anatomical breakdown.

An adherence to functional import is predominantly demonstrated in the eastern regions (with the exception of the early Kentish laws of Æthelberht). As to terminology, Salic Francia presents something of a problem, as the *mallberg* glosses are inconsistent with the Latin designations. As a rule, the westernmost (cross-Channel) regions employ a term connected with archery for the forefinger. However, connecting the *mallberg 'index'* with those of Frisia, Saxony, and Thuringia might imply instead a western continental grouping. There is a clear northern connection in the use of *medicus* for the ring finger. A cross-Channel littoral group is presented by the use of some form of ring finger, although this designation also appears in the more eastern Alamannia. In the northeast, all territories except Thuringia regulate damage to individual finger joints. Coupled with the fact that these are the territories that most closely approach physiological utility, we might tentatively hypothesize that for the west, the compensation schemes in the laws stood more as legislative monuments, while in the east they were more likely to be put to practical use. This hypothesis is highly speculative. Finally, only the Old English laws regulate damage to fingernails, although the loss of a nail, particularly on the thumb or forefinger, can substantially reduce the ability to do fine work.

A final consideration in the nomenclature assigned to fingers concerns the terminological preference for male over female occupations. The names for fingers used in the laws indicate that – at least in this regard – the importance of a woman's work was viewed as less than a man's. The forefinger is sometimes called an arrow-finger (*saggitarius*) or the virtually synonymous shooting finger (*scytefinger*), but is never named, for example, a spinning finger, although the presence of spindle whorls in women's graves demonstrates that this was a common female activity.[45] The use of the term *inpudicus* or 'unchaste' for the middle finger would seem to be associated with men (although women are not necessarily precluded). The appellation of *goldfinger* or ring finger could belong to either male or female – rings are found in graves of both sexes, although more commonly in women's. (Thuringian law stipulates that threefold restitution must be paid for the theft of *ornamenta muliebria*, 'women's decorations,' although does not specify what these might be.)[46]

The variant term for the fourth finger of *medicus*, 'doctor, fourth finger,' is masculine in gender, although grammatical and sexual gender need not be related. The *Life of Corbianus* mentions healing women, as does Tacitus in chapter 7 of the *Germania*.[47] Furthermore, Gregory of Tours describes a woman who heals sores using saliva, fruit leaves, and (characteristically for Gregory) the sign of the cross. Katherine Park points out that Gregory's account confirms that 'women worked as healers and certainly as midwives,

---

45 See, for example, ibid., 46–62.
46 *Lex Thur.* §III.35.
47 Niederhellmann, 'Heilkundliches in den *Leges*,' 79.

even though, obscure and illiterate, they do not appear by name in the surviving records.'⁴⁸ The issue here is not whether women could work as healers, but whether they would then be designated with the term *medicus* (used for the fourth finger in the legal anatomical breakdowns). The sixth-century *Rule of St Benedict* only uses the term *medicus* once, and then to refer metaphorically to the abbot.⁴⁹ Elsewhere the designation of *medicus* is almost always restricted to males.⁵⁰ The *Pactus Alamannorum* suggests that there may be a terminological difference between male and female healers: a woman skilled in medical practice is known as *herbaria*, a woman who knows the medicinal properties of herbs.⁵¹ The laws of the Visigoths indicate that the difference may be more than terminological. If a doctor must bleed a woman, the law requires that a woman's family (*propinquis*) must be present.⁵² Loren McKinney interprets this as implying that the medical profession, at least in the Visigothic territories, included 'a rather low type of personnel.'⁵³ In contradiction, Clare Pilsworth has demonstrated that *medici*, at least in the southern territories, were often of high enough rank that they could append their names to charters. She qualifies this statement by the assertion that 'the snapshot provided by charters, however, is like a family photo in which several key (discredited) members have been carefully edited out.'⁵⁴ The crucial fact in the usual relegation of

---

48 The Gregory citation is *Liber in gloria confessorum*, chap. 24. Cited in Park, 'Medicine and Society in Medieval Europe,' 69.
49 Siraisi, *Medieval and Early Renaissance Medicine*, 9.
50 For *medicus*, see McKinney, *Early Medieval Medicine*, 69; and Langslow, *Medical Latin in the Roman Empire*, 28–48. In slightly later medieval Naples we find a woman named Anna referred to as *medica de Balusano*, and the same area produced Trota (putative), author of the medical treatise known as the *Trotula*; see Skinner, *Health and Medicine in Early Medieval Southern Italy*, 88–91. Some near-contemporary male *medici* of the same region are discussed in Pilsworth, 'Could you just sign this for me, John?' Green, 'Documenting Medieval Women's Medical Practice,' suggests that female medical practitioners in later medieval Europe may be underrepresented due to the nature of the documentation. Many references to *medici* appear in legal documents, but a woman's lack of legal standing would subordinate her mention to that of her husband, under whose name such legal references would be documented.
51 Niederhellmann, 'Heilkundliches,' 79.
52 *Leges Visigothorum* §Xi.i.
53 McKinney, *Early Medieval Medicine*, 71–2; see also Niederhellmann, *Arzt- und Heilkunde*, 72–3.
54 Pilsworth, 'Could you just sign this for me, John?' Pilsworth's assertion that only the names of successful doctors survive in the written records is substantiated by the prosopography of medieval French doctors compiled by Ernest Wickersheimer: entries for this period concentrate on medical practitioners serving rulers or bishops (such as

158 The Body Legal in Barbarian Law

the term *medicus* to male practicioners may imply that men were responsible for major surgical procedures and the medical treatment of high-ranking individuals, while women were active in more local practices of childbirth and herbal healing of systemic illnesses.

Foot

We have already examined rulings against striking off a foot. Furthermore, the discussion of the importance of the handspan in measurement has also been addressed above. A ruling in Lombard law replaces the hand as a measuring device by the foot:

> Thus as follows, that one bone must be found of such a sort, that it is able to make a sound in a shield at twelve paces across the road, and that measurement shall be truly taken by the foot of a medium-sized man, not by the hand.[55]

The requirement is quite specific that the measurement shall be based on the footspan and not the handspan. This augments the burden of proof, since the length of the foot from heel to tip of great toe is greater for most people than that of the handspan from extremity of thumb to the tip of the little finger. Like the handspan, the actual measurement of the footspan varied according to the individual. Twelfth-century London used the foot of the first prebendary of Islington, from his image carved on the base of one of the main pillars of St Paul's Cathedral.[56] The current standard was

---

Christophe le Chastellain or Barthélemy le Flemeng, also described as a surgeon), and categorize doctors as versed both in medicine and astrology (such as Galearius or Dalmadion de Bourgoigne), demonstrating the importance placed on prognostics in medieval medical practice; or record the healing capabilities of saints (such as St Germain or St Bernard de Tiron) (Wickersheimer, *Dictionannaire Biographique des Médecins en France au Moyen Age*, respectively 61, 99, 163, 112, 188, 80). On the social position of the doctor as delineated in the laws, see Niederhellmann, *Arzt- und Heilkunde*, 66–70.

55 *Lex Lang.* §47. 'Si quis alium plaguauerit in caput, ut ossa rumpantur, pro uno osso conponat solidos duodicem; si duo fuerint, conponat solidos uiginti et quattuor; si tres ossas fuerint, conponat solidos trigenta et sex; si super fuerint, non numerentur. Sic ita, ut unus ossus tales inueniatur, qui ad pedes duodicem supra uiam sonum in scutum facere possit, et ipsa mensura de certo pede hominis mediocris mensuretur, nam non ad manum.' For discussion of the shields into which these bones would have been tossed, see Hüpper-Dröge, 'Schutz- und Angriffswaffen nach den Leges und verwandten fränkischen Rechtsquellen,' 121–2.

56 Boyle, *The Troubadour's Song*, 220–1.

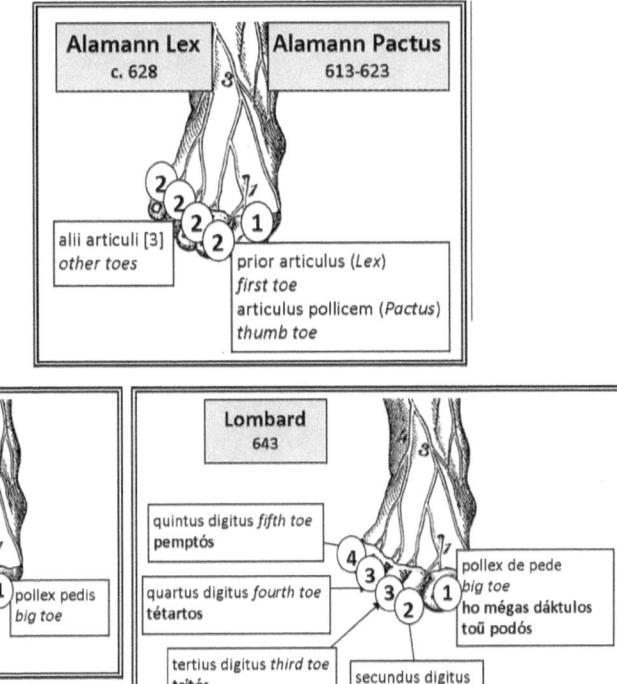

Figure 5.5a Charts of toe values in descending order of functional accuracy.

set in 1305 in England, when the foot was defined as twelve inches, 'where one inch equaled the length of "three grains of barley dry and round."'[57]

Toes[58]

We now turn to the less interesting patterning of toes (see Fig. 5.5a, Fig. 5.5b). The great toe is not only largest, but also most valuable: it carries half the weight borne by the front part of the foot. Furthermore, it keeps the

---

57 Field, 'Foot,' *World Book* Online Reference Center, 2009, s.v.
58 The analysis of functional importance of toes and medical intervention is based on an interview with professional orthotist, Susan Postell. See Behnke, *Kinetic Anatomy*, 234–6; 246–8; Memmler, Cohen, and Wood, *Structure and Function of the Human Body*, 78.

160 The Body Legal in Barbarian Law

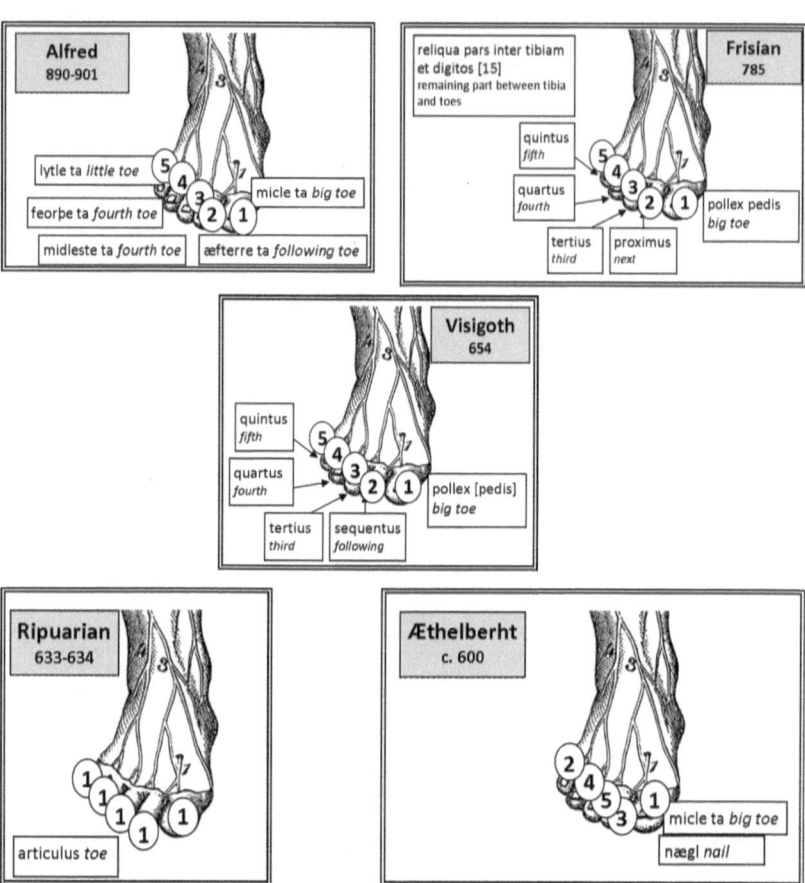

Figure 5.5b Charts of toe values in descending order of functional accuracy.

foot from pronating inwards and stablizes the walk. Years of such pronation may cause damage to the ligaments, which can result in permanent lameness. (Modern orthotical practice puts a plate under the entire foot of a person who has lost a great toe, in order to distribute the weight and preserve the balance.)[59] Next in worth to the great toe are the two on the other side, particularly the little toe. Both these toes can aid balance. Furthermore, the loss of the little toe leaves the foot thinner, which can cause uncomfortable

---

59 Personal communication, Susan Prostell, professional orthotist.

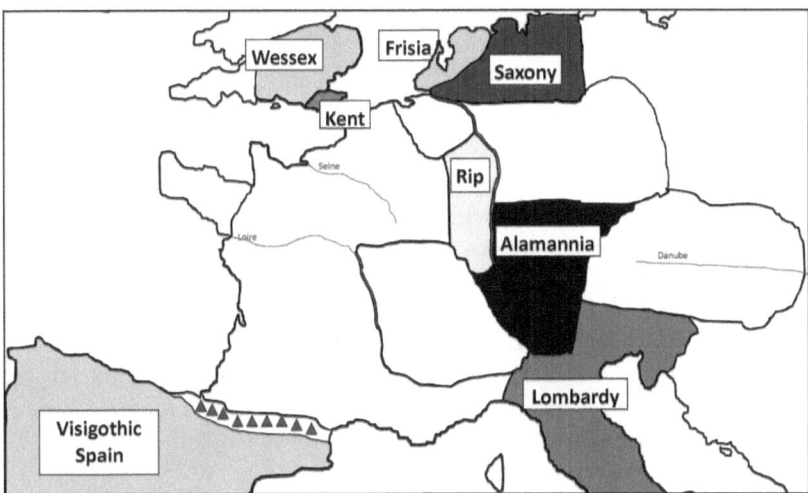

Map 5.3 Distribution of functional approximation for toes.

Darker shading = closer to physiological accuracy.

chafing when shoes or boots are worn, and may consequently impair the ability to work. There is not much to choose between the three interior toes in terms of function. Figs 5.5a and 5.5b lay out order of value and nomenclature for toes in the territories which regulate them, in descending order of functional accuracy.

None of these territories except Kent give the small toe the consideration it deserves. The Alamanns come closest: they do not value it less than any of the other toes. Saxons, Lombards, Alfred, and Frisians all decrease the fines in various gradations from the great toe to the small toe, which makes visual if not physiological sense. Virtually out of consideration in any anatomical sense are the Ripuarians. They value all toes – including the important great toe – equally: recall that this is the group that only regulates the thumb and shooting finger, so they consistently gave scant attention to compensation for digits. Visigothic law demonstrates the same cavalier attitude towards valuation of the toes as it did for the fingers; the digits of the feet are reckoned at half those for the hand, once again thus simply decreasing in value from great to small toe. This makes no anatomical sense at all. Æthelberht's ruling on the toes seems to demonstrate legislative exhaustion. While he did pretty well in valuing the fingers, like the Visigoths, he simply reckons the toes at half the value of the

162 The Body Legal in Barbarian Law

corresponding fingers. Relating the toes to the fingers leaves Kent as the only territory to value the small toe second to the great toe, but this seems to be a lucky mathematical fluke rather than anatomical sagacity. On the other hand, Kent and Wessex are the only regions to regulate against striking off a toenail, the loss of which leaves a pulpy nub which can make wearing shoes painful and impair the ability to work. This parallel provides a crucial piece of evidence that, despite the differences in both amount and terminology between the personal injury clauses of Kent and Wessex, Alfred's legislators seem to have had access to the text of Æthelberht's laws.

Map 5.3 lays out the valuation of toes in terms of functional utility, again shading from darkest for those which are most accurate to lightest for those who stray furthest from anatomical reality. Even more strikingly than for the fingers, we find the shading darker towards the east, indicating a tendency for greater anatomical awareness in the eastern territories.

Evidence for Medical Intervention on Damage to Feet

To conclude this discussion on legal rulings on damage to feet, I present the only example I know of medical intervention.[60] This case probably did not involve physical assault, but the evidence allows us to extrapolate the possibility of medical assistance had the damage been deliberately inflicted. In 1962, a large fourth- to seventh-century cemetery was discovered in the small town of Bonaduz in Switzerland. Among the 710 graves, #248 contained the skeleton of a man, between the ages of forty-one and fifty at the time of death (Fig. 5.6). The right foot – like the lower leg discussed in chapter 4 – had been surgically removed by exarticulation at the upper ankle joint. No signs of injury appear elsewhere, and forensic anthropologists have suggested that the operation was necessitated either by an accident followed by gangrene, or by diabetes. Following the surgery the patient seems to have been subject to chronic osteomyelitis, causing a constant seeping of pus from the wound.

To help protect the injured foot, a prosthesis was made consisting of a leather pouch with a wooden block inserted in the bottom, enforced on the outside by an iron plate rather like a sled runner – the result looks in schematic remarkably like a dog's paw (Fig. 5.7).

---

60 This discussion is based on Baumgartner, 'Fussprothese aus einem frühmittelalterlichen Grab aus Bonaduz.' The find was discussed in the popular press by Schmidt, 'Prothese aus dem frühen Mittelalter,' and 'Steinzeitmensch im Merovingergrab.'

Hands and Feet 163

Figure 5.6 Prosthesis in situ, Grave 248, Bonaduz, Switzerland. Photograph reproduced by permission of *Fundberichte aus Hessen*; Landesamt für Denkmalpflege Hessen.

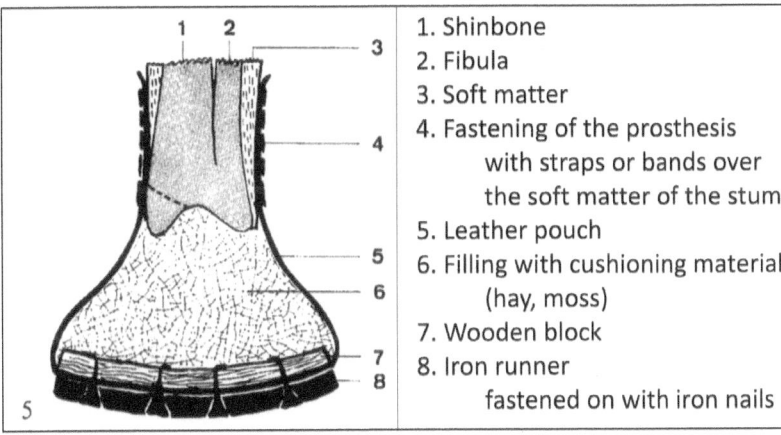

1. Shinbone
2. Fibula
3. Soft matter
4. Fastening of the prosthesis with straps or bands over the soft matter of the stump.
5. Leather pouch
6. Filling with cushioning material (hay, moss)
7. Wooden block
8. Iron runner fastened on with iron nails

Figure 5.7 Schematic of stump and prosthesis from Bonaduz,[61] Switzerland. Reproduced by permission of Rene Baumgartner, Zürich.

---

61 From Baumgartner, 'Fussprothese,' 159.

The interior of the prosthesis was filled with hay and moss to cushion the impact on the stump of the leg, and perhaps also to soak up the pus. René Baumgartner indicates that the bag could also have held herbs or other medicaments, but it is impossible to tell from the remains we have. The prosthesis was presumably strapped around the stump of the leg – traces appear on the bone to a height of 10 cm. A prosthetic foot meant for extended use would have to have a considerably more substantial attachment, and so this appears to have been intended more for the period of the cure than for permanent use.

The end of the stump never knitted together. Baumgartner proposes two explanations for this. First, the patient may have died soon after the operation, before time and rest allowed the healing process to take place. Second, the patient may have been using the leg, which would have impeded the cure. But this could only be possible if his sense of pain had been impaired, as would be the case for a diabetic, a leper, or a person with nerve damage. In any event, the state of the bone stump indicates that the man lived no longer than two years after the operation; this procedure was considerably less successful than the exarticulation of the lower leg discussed in chapter 4.

6 Insult and Injury

Punitive vs Compensatory Damages

The preceding three chapters have examined how individual body parts are regulated in barbarian personal injury tariffs. These analyses have concentrated on the value assigned according to function, but have occasionally noted instances in which the fine is higher than might be expected on a purely physiological basis. The discussion in this chapter recapitulates and expands on how wounds with greater visibility may be fined higher than those which are less immediately apparent. In legal terms, these excessive fines represent punitive reparation – either overt or covert – added to the compensatory charges assigned for actual injury. Overt rulings clearly differentiate between visible wounds and those hidden by hair or clothing. Hidden charges may be more difficult to distinguish. However, if the fine for damage to a given body part is considerably greater than one might expect on the basis of functional worth, the additional fee is likely to be a surcharge for the embarrassment caused by visible disfigurement.

Obviously, all wounds are not equal, nor do all carry an additional punitive charge, even if this might seem appropriate. The loss of a hand in a fight is always going to be immediately obvious to any observer, but the functional value of the hand is so great that the fine for the loss is high enough to obviate any further assessment. It is in more minor impairments that we find punitive supplements added to the fine.

The most obvious of insult surcharges is found in the laws of Kent, which rule that a bruise outside clothing should be fined by one and a half shillings, as opposed to a single-shilling fine for one which can be discretely covered by tunic or britches.[1] Wessex ups the ante by charging

---

1 *Kent* §61.

twofold for causing a bruise below the sleeve or knee (where the hemline of the tunic ends).² The laws of Frisia, Saxony, and Lombardy also include clauses dealing with bruising.³ None of these last, however, distinguish between covered and obvious bruises, so it seems likely that these stipulations are primarily compensatory in nature: that is, the fine is awarded to reimburse the pain – and perhaps the temporary embarrassment – caused by the contusion.

Parallel to his rulings on bruises, Alfred requires twofold compensation for a facial wound below the hairline.⁴ This judgment finds a counterpart in Alamann law, which sets a twofold fine for causing a bruise to the face not covered by hair or beard.⁵ The Burgundian legislators seem to have been a little confused when they set out the corresponding stipulation:⁶

> If someone inflicts a wound on someone else's face, we order to be paid for the wound threefold what those wounds would have been assessed if they were covered by clothing (*vestibus*).

Three possible interpretations can be presented for this odd ruling. First, the Burgundian *vestibus*, 'by clothing,' may stand in for the 'hair and beard' we find elsewhere in the barbarian laws in regard to facial wounds. I am uncomfortable with this hypothesis, lacking any comparative evidence elsewhere in the Germanic territories. Second, perhaps covering the visible damage with clothing actually refers to donning caps and scarves to cover the damage (although the wearing, at least of the latter, would have aroused some suspicion while harvesting grapes in hot Burgundian summers). Finally, the last phrase might conceivably differentiate any wound which could be concealed (either by facial hair or by clothing) from a wound which cannot be hidden from public view. Given the terse formulations in the personal injury section in Burgundian law, this last hypothesis seems to be the most plausible interpretation of this clause.

We might well consider all the rulings involving shearing facial hair to be insult rather than injury payment. True that Samson's strength fails when his hair is shorn, and Pushkin's evil magician Tschernamor loses his magic powers once his beard is cut. But in everyday life, no victim suffers

---

2 *Wessex* §§45, 66.1.
3 *Lex Fris.* §22.42; *Lex Sax.* §V.2; *Edict Roth.* §43.
4 *Wessex* §41.
5 *Lex Ala.* §64.2.
6 *Liber Const.* §11.2.

disability from the cutting of his hair or beard, or the removal of his mustache.[7] Nonetheless, as we have seen in chapter 3, stipulations of this nature are extremely common throughout the barbarian territories. The most bizarre occurs in the laws of Alfred, who rules twice against cutting someone's hair like a priest: the fine is sixty shillings if the victim is bound, and thirty if the victim is unbound.[8] Violent tonsuring visually removes a man from the status of free layman, with the legal rights and privileges accruing to that rank.

Hair plays a role in the Lombard ruling that injuries above the hairline are fined less than those below, demonstrating again the distinction between visible wounds and those able to be concealed.[9] Visigothic Spain demonstrates a slightly different breakdown: causing a bruise on the head is fined by five *solidi*; if the skin (presumably of the scalp) is broken, ten; if the wound extends to the bone, twenty. The latter two rulings distinguish between lesser and greater damage to the scalp: in the former instance the skin is simply scratched, whereas in the latter it is peeled back so as to reveal the skull. While Lombardy is concerned with degrees of visible damage, Visigothic Spain concentrates on the physical extent of the injury.

Æthelberht of Kent assigns two fines for disfigurement of the countenance (*wlitewamme*); that for a greater defacement six shillings, and for a lesser, three.[10] That damage to the face is customarily abhorred by the Germanic peoples is demonstrated by the fact that this identical linguistic compound can be found in the laws of Thuringia and Saxony (*wlitewam* and *wlitivam* respectively).[11] Lombardy similarly requires compensation for any wound to the face, but expresses the concept in Latin (*plaga in facie*) and Greek (*prosōpōi*).[12] Recall also that Frisian law levies different fines for injuries to each of the three wrinkles on the forehead individually: the further from the hair and closer to the eye, the higher the fine.[13] The more obvious the injury, the greater the assessed compensation.

Most of the barbarian territories assign a larger fine for striking out a front tooth than one further back in the mouth, despite the fact that the

---

7 Unless this refers to the plucking-out of his mustache hair by hair, which would certainly be painful, although not debilitating. None of the laws, however, contain such an implication.
8 *Wessex* §§34.5–6.
9 Injuring the scalp: *Edict. Roth.* §46; *Lex Ala.* §57.3; *Lex Baiu.* §3.4; *Lex Fris.* §22.5.
10 *Kent* §60.
11 *Lex Thur.* §26; *Lex Sax.* §V.5.
12 *Edict. Roth.* §54.
13 *Lex Fris.* §§22.11–13.

molars are far more crucial for processing food than the incisors. This supplement is a clear instance of a covert punitive charge assessed on top of compensatory damage: the greater visibility of the front teeth makes their loss an insult, while only the victim will be aware of the loss of a back tooth. The rationale behind this differentiation is actually expressed in the Lombard laws, which assign a higher value to a tooth that appears in the smile (*qui in risu apparit*) than to the molars (in Greek, *odoùs mulítes*, 'chewing teeth'). Alamann laws share with Lombardy an increased fine if a cut lip allows the teeth to show, thereby making the wound more obvious.[14] This analysis presents a clear distinction of purpose in those clauses regulating damage to teeth. Whereas the Bavarians, Frisians, and the legislators of Wessex approximate physiological worth, the others all place greater importance on appearance. For example, although the incisors are replaceable in function, their loss is immediately visible any time you open your mouth to speak. Most of the Germanic territories, then, are more concerned with the observable evidence of loss of teeth than the resulting physiological inconvenience. Here we have a payment for visible damage to honour taking precedence over physical loss: the insult outranks the injury.

In Ripuarian law, a damaged nose that can still contain mucus must be compensated for with fifty *solidi*, but if the stump cannot hold mucus (*muccare non possit*), the penalty is doubled to 100 *solidi* – 50 per cent of a freeman's wergild.[15] Certainly these rulings consider the greater degree of injury to the dribbling nose; however, it seems at least possible that in setting the assessment for the perpetual drip, the Ripuarian legislators may have also taken into account the visual embarrassment. If this hypothesis is true, the punitive surcharge would not seem to have been assessed in Alamann law, in which restitution for slicing off a sufficient portion of the nose so that mucus flows freely is a mere twelve *solidi*, or 6 per cent of the wergild.[16]

One of the most obvious examples of payment for insult can be found in the Bavarian clause regarding damage to the ear. Piercing the ear draws a fine of three *solidi*; cutting it off, twenty; causing deafness, forty. This list ends with the stipulation that if someone maims the ear so that it is disgusting to the sight (*turpis appareat*), the fine is six *solidi*.[17] Appearance is equally stressed in the phraseology of the Lombard clause which requires that if someone wounds another in the nose, let him pay him sixteen *solidi* if it

---

14 *Edict. Roth.* §§50–2; *Lex Ala.* §57.18.
15 *Lex Rib.* §5.2.
16 *Lex Ala.* §57.16. This stipulation is not in the *Pactus*.
17 *Lex Baiu.* §3.14.

heals so that only a scar appears (*cechatrix appareat*). If it does not heal, the perpetrator is responsible for one quarter of the wergild.[18] The important consideration is that in either case, the scar provides permanent evidence of the injury. Æthelberht's ruling in the case of causing a *waeltwund* (wound that causes a welt) seems to add a surcharge of three shillings to a wound leaving a permanent scar inflicted on any part of the body.[19]

The importance of lasting visible evidence may underlie the regulations concerning the torso in Burgundian law. If an arm or tibia is broken but heals without evident disability (*sine certa debilitate*), the recompense is set at 10 per cent of the victim's wergild. The following clause addresses the fine if the impairment is evident.[20]

> If further however the arm of someone or the tibia according to the act described above becomes disabled with a visible disability (*evidenti fuerint debilitate damnatae*), it must be held thus with the compensation as it was decreed to be read in the previous laws.

It is not clear, however, that the damning circumstance is necessarily purely visual witness. These clauses may simply distinguish between a wound that heals without lasting damage and one which leaves the limb maimed for life. Unfortunately, it is neither clear what is meant by 'the previous laws' nor stated how much greater would be the fine for causing permanent impairment. (Franz Beyerle, following Saupp, thinks this refers to §11.2, which stipulates that striking off an arm or gouging out an eye requires payment of one half of the wergild. I find this analysis unlikely: in the clause as it stands, the arm seems to be maimed, which surely should require less compensation than if the arm is struck off).[21]

A ruling that clearly includes covert punitive damage in the amount of the fine is the stipulation in both Wessex and Frisia that cutting off the ring finger incurs a higher fine than a similar injury to any other finger on the hand. Arguments can be made for the greater functional value of either the little finger or forefinger, thus dictating higher assessments for those digits. But the only possible motivation for valuing the fourth finger at the top of

---

18 *Edict. Roth.* §55.
19 *Kent* §68.
20 *Liber Const.* §§XLVIII.1–3. §3 reads: 'Ceterum si aut brachium cuiuscumque aut tibia supradicto ordine fractae et evidenti fuerint debilitate damnatae, ea compositionis forma servabitur, quae antedatis legibus legitur fuisse decreta.'
21 Beyerle, *Die Gesetze der Burgunden*, 73.

this hierarchy is the visible offence of losing the finger that bears the ring (in Old English, *goldfinger*, in the Latin of the Frisian laws, *digit annularis*).[22] Punitive damage for the visible insult must thus have been added to the purely compensatory damage for the anatomical loss.

An interesting historical example of mutilation to the fingers is provided by the fate of Pope Formosus, who had incurred the enmity of his successor, John VIII. After the death of Formosus in 896, John had his body exhumed.

> In an extra-ordinarily macabre scene, it was propped on a throne to stand trial for the charges that John had originally brought against him. The dead pope was, not surprisingly, found guilty. After he was declared unfit to have been pope, his papal vestments were torn away, and the three fingers of his right hand (which he had used in consecration) were hacked off. Finally his body was dumped in the Tiber.[23]

The final insult to be considered here is binding. Almost all the laws include this assault within the structure of the personal injury tariffs. Although binding is, of course, not an injury, it appears among these clauses due to its nature as a personal offence. In fact, Lombardy ranks binding higher than any wound, equivalent only to (the somewhat unlikely) striking out an eye from a one-eyed man.[24] (One wonders, indeed, whether the latter clause, which occurs outside and much later than the personal injury schedule, stems from an actual case rather than from juridical invention.) Both *Lex Salica* and *Lex Ribuaria* legislate against both binding a freeman and taking him to another place, thus adding abduction to the offence.[25] The legal transgression targeted in all these binding clauses is that of falsely accusing an innocent freeman of a crime. *Lex Ribuaria* plays a variation on this theme by requiring that if a freeman has bound a thief and frees him before the appearance at the judicial hearing, the normal fine of thirty *solidi* for binding is doubled to sixty.[26] That is, binding an innocent man and bringing him to court draws half the fine for letting a guilty man escape. The bribe offered by the thief for his release would have to be substantial to offset the sixty *solidi* his captor would be liable for if caught.

---

22 *Wessex* §59; *Lex Fris* §22.31.
23 Pollard, *Alfred the Great*, 237.
24 *Edict. Roth.* §42, 377.
25 *Lex Sal.* §32; *Lex Rib.* §45.
26 *Lex Rib.* §76.

Although restitution for the eye (within a close approximation) equals that for the nose, generally – although not always – half this compensation is due for damage to the ear. If the ear is struck off without causing deafness, the compensation is halved again. This could conceivably be due to the fact the loss of an ear may not be immediately visible, as the site of the wound can be covered by hair or a hat. On the other hand, there is no disguising the loss of an eye or the nose. In a Frankish capitulary of 779, we find a regulation supporting the hypothesis that the visible damage to eye and nose can be a factor in recompense: a thief must lose an eye for his first theft, for the first repeat theft his nose, and for the second repeat theft his life.

The preceding discussion demonstrates that no territory in barbarian Germania overlooks the importance of physical appearance. In some instances, reparation for the insult of a lasting scar or an obvious bruise is clearly delineated in the tariff structure. In others, an additional assessment of punitive damage can be inferred by the (relatively) excessive amount of the fine. Although the concept of honour-price is never directly addressed, the barbarian laws imply that shaming an opponent with deliberate disfigurement must be suitably recompensed. The best summation for this section is provided in §41 of the Lombard *Edictus Rothari*:

> Of beating of a free man. If someone ambushes a free man with force or with assistance, seeing him standing or walking utterly unprepared, [and] immediately falling on him, and he shamefully holds him and beats him without order of the king, let him pay half of his wergild, which he would have paid if he killed him, because he handled him so badly as to cause him shame and ridicule.[27]

Mutilation as Punishment[28]

The previous section addressed surcharges assessed to the perpetrator in the case of a wound leaving obvious traces, thus causing the 'shame and ridicule' mentioned in the Lombard ruling cited above. Some territories

---

27 *Edict. Roth.* §41. The Latin reads: 'De homine libero battuto. Si quis homine libero insidiatus fuerit cum virtute aut solatio, vedens eum inparatum simpliciter ambolantem aut stantem, subito super eum adveniens, et turpiter eum tenuerit et battuerit sine iussione regis, medietatem pretii ipsius, ac si eum occidisset, ei conponat, eo quod in turpe et in derisculum ipsius eum male tractauit.'
28 For differing views on the infliction of insult by legal mutilation in Anglo-Saxon England, see O'Brien O'Keeffe, 'Body and Law in Late Anglo-Saxon England'; and Richards, 'The Body as Text in Early Anglo-Saxon Law.'

reverse this concept by requiring that the perpetrator of a crime lose the limb which allowed him to transgress the law.[29] Here, legal mutilation provides a lasting visible witness of the offense committed.

Amputation

The body parts most commonly subjected to judicial amputation are the 'Matthew limbs' of eye and hand; the foot is less generally included in these judgments. The hand is often subject to the legal penalty of amputation. As discussed earlier, both Saxony and Chamavan Francia require that a perjurer have his (presumably right) hand struck off; in Chamavan Francia the same mutilation is assigned to a freeman who commits theft aided by a freeman.[30] Wessex requires amputation of the hand for a thief who stole property from a church.[31] Theft in Frisia similarly demands the loss of the hand, although the thief can buy off the judgment with the appropriate wergild of sixty *solidi*. Burgundy requires the loss of the hand for a freeman who forged papers for an escaping slave; Visigothic Spain demands the same punishment for a freeman who inserts a false statement into a royal decree.[32] In all these cases, the hand is punished for the illegal deed which it performed, respectively, perjury, theft, or forgery. A grave from Switzerland produces a skeleton that had the lower ends of both arms amputated, which could possibly be the result of judicial mutilation. The regeneration of bone indicates that the amputee survived for many years.[33]

The next body part most frequently subjected to legal amputation is the eye. A transitional clause between regulations for hand and eye found in Bavarian law stipulates that a master who orders a slave to sell a freeman must lose his hands or his eyes.[34] No convincing explanation springs to

---

29 Much later, this same precept is expressed by the Mikado in Gilbert and Sullivan's operetta, who states that his legislative object is to 'let the punishment fit the crime.'
30 *Lex Sax.* §21; *Lex Cham.* §§23 and 45. Karl Eckhardt translates the *raptus* of §45 as referring to abduction of a woman, but Marianne Elsakkers convincingly argues that the term in this context simply means theft. Certainly the hand would be an odd limb to cut off in case of rape. Elsakkers interprets the phrase *cum uno wadio et una manu emendare* to mean 'that the wadium [security] must be accompanied by an oath.' If she is correct, this clause is inapplicable to a discussion on mutilation; I have chosen to align this with the parallels elsewhere for the amputation of a hand which committed theft. See Elsakkers, 'Raptus ultra Rhenum,' 45–6.
31 *Wessex* §6.
32 *Liber Const.* §6.10; *Forum Iud.* VII, 5, i.
33 See Niederhellmann, *Arzt- und Heilkunde*, 85.
34 *Lex Baiu.* §9.4

mind for this duo; perhaps the owner suffers either the loss of the hand with which he gave the command or the eyes with which he watched his slave go out to fulfil his order?

A clear rationale is provided by a clause supplied in the *Forum Iudicum* by Flavius Recesvintus requiring that a traitor shall have both his eyes put out 'so that he may not see the wrong in which he wickedly took delight.'[35] No clear reasoning, however, arises from the Visigothic ruling that a person who has sought sanctuary in a church and has been evicted will be blinded in both eyes or be delivered to the relatives of his victim.[36] This clause is particularly unusual in the denial of sanctuary; one longs for a greater understanding of the circumstances under which it was formulated.

Let us return to a clause discussed above: in Francia, a ruling from 779 states that for a first theft the thief should lose an eye, for the first repeat theft his nose, and for the second repeat theft his life.[37] The striking-out of the eye might be justified as retribution for greed, but the subsequent loss of the nose cannot be associated with thievery. Although the first mutilation arguably fits the crime, the second simply provides visible proof of a repeat offender.

Multiple mutilation can be seen in a clause added to Frisian law, which requires for a person living in the area across the Laubach River who robs or damages a temple to have his ears slashed, be castrated, and finally buried in that temple that he violated (*templa violavit*). Annette Niederhellman suggests that these draconian regulations were designed to concentrate on the evil-doer the ill will of the gods, which might otherwise be loosed upon the community. This clause is particularly odd, as the designated region of Frisia was Christian at the time. Is this paragraph meant to provide an example to be followed in the case of desecration of a church, or was it seen even by its scribe as an historical remnant?[38]

Only one other territory allows castration for a freeman.[39] In Visigothic Spain, the punishment for pederasty or for (self-)circumcision after the fashion of the Jews is emasculation.[40] In the laws of Wessex, the penalty for slander is to have the tongue cut out, although this can be redeemed with

---

35 *Forum Iud.* §II, 1, vi. Trans. Scott, *Visigothic Code*, s.v.
36 *Forum Iud.* §VI, 5, xvii.
37 Schmidt-Wiegand, *Wörter und Sachen*, 38.
38 *Lex Fris.*, *Additio Sapiendum* §XI; see discussion in Niederhellmann, *Arzt- und Heilkunde*, 146–7.
39 Slaves, on the other hand, could be castrated for a variety of offences.
40 For pederasty, *Forum Iud.* §III, 5, v; *Forum Iud.* §II, 5, vi; for circumcision, *Forum Iud.* §XII, 3, 4; see discussion in Niederhellmann, *Arzt- und Heilkunde*, 144–5.

the appropriate wergild.⁴¹ For both rulings, the connection between transgression and punishment is obvious. It is worth reconsidering Christ's exhortation quoted earlier from the Gospel of Matthew:

> If your hand or your foot causes you to stumble, cut it off and throw it away; it is better for you to enter life maimed or lame than to have two hands or two feet and to be thrown into the eternal fire. And if your eye causes you to stumble, tear it out and throw it away; it is better for you to enter life with one eye than to have two eyes and to be thrown into the hell of fire.⁴²

For an offender who is unable to control his sinful impulses, the temporal law fulfils the command of Christ. The limb which committed the offence is cut off. Whether indeed this saves the wrong-doer from the eternal fire is never addressed in the written statutes. Certainly the offender has paid his legal due to mankind, but it is very possible that he also must undergo penance to pay his spiritual due to God. The human laws themselves are silent on this issue. Lastly, the Visigoths protect slaves against extra-legal mutilation:

> If any master or mistress, without a preliminary investigation in court, should openly and wickedly deprive their slave of his nose, lip, tongue, ear, or foot, or should tear out his eye, or should mutilate any other part of his body ... he or she shall be sentenced ... to three years in exile.⁴³

The implication is that these mutilations were legal if mandated by the court. A slave, then, faced a far greater range of possible judicial mutilations than a freeman, but was protected against violent outbreaks on the part of his owners that would leave him permanently incapacitated. Furthermore, if a person mutilates someone else's slave, the perpetrator must restitute with a slave of equal value. In addition, he receives two hundred lashes in public – a typical Visigoth ruling discussed below. The law recognized and protected the full functional value of the working slave.

---

41 *Wessex* §32. See discussion in O'Brien O'Keeffe, 'Body and Law,' 215.
42 *The New Oxford Annotated Bible*, ed. Metzger and Murphy, New Testament, 27. Matt 18:8.
43 *Forum Iud.* §VI, 5, xiii. Trans. Scott, *Visigothic Code*, s.v.

Scourging and Scalping

Another physical punishment employed in barbarian law, certainly painful and debilitating, but not with the lasting of impact of amputation, is scourging. This penalty likely left permanent scars, but these could be hidden by clothing. Thus the damage inflicted on both body and honour was temporary. Many territories allow slaves to be beaten for a variety of delicts. However, only two regions permit a free man to be publicly beaten. I have already discussed the sole ruling in Bavaria requiring the scourging of a free man.[44] If he sows, mows, or gathers hay on a Sunday, he receives warnings for the first two instances. At the third disobedience, he receives fifty lashes. If he continues to ignore the Sabbath prohibition on work, he is made a slave because he did not wish to be free on the holy day. Perhaps the lashing required by the third violation is meant to give him a feeling for what life as a slave might be, thus deterring him from toiling once again on the Sabbath.

Public beating is so often legally mandated in Visigothic Spain as to discourage complete enumeration.[45] One interesting example arises where slander against the living requires the payment of a fine in property, while slander against the dead is punished instead by fifty lashes, 'for the reason that he is evidently insane who heaps detraction upon one who cannot comprehend it.'[46] This clause draws an interesting distinction between judgment of the sane versus the insane; distinct from modern law in the United States, in early medieval Europe insanity seems to have been a plea which brought with it a harsher rather than lighter sentence.[47] I know of no ruling in Visigothic law that allows an insane man to hold property, but we might plausibly infer that the ruling cited above implies that control over the property would devolve upon the man's heirs (as he is no longer allowed to dispose of it to expiate his offence). The advantage to the charge of insanity thus lies with the kin of the slanderer. The property remains in the family, but the transgressor is subjected to physical pain and public

---

44 *Lex Baiu.* §7.3.
45 Curiously, we also find more references to medical practitioners in the south. The preponderance of both corporeal punishment and medical training in Visigothic law may perhaps be traced to the extended connection with Roman law. See Niederhellmann, *Arzt- und Heilkunde*, 85–7.
46 *Forum Iud.* §II, 1, vii. Trans. Scott, *Visigothic Code*, s.v.
47 For comparative discussion, see Jurasinski, 'Madness and Responsibility in Anglo-Saxon England.'

humiliation. Marianne Elsakkers cites clauses which equate a twenty-*solidi* fine with two hundred lashes; it is possible that elsewhere – although never directly stated – the scourging could be paid off at the rate of one *solidus* per ten lashes.[48]

Somewhat surprisingly, whipping could even be assessed for a judge in the event that he delivered a false judgment. The *Forum Iudicum* requires him to compensate with an equal amount of property (presumably to that under contestation); if he is not sufficiently wealthy he must be deprived of all he does own, and either submit himself to the unfairly judged litigant as a slave or receive fifty lashes in public.[49]

Even more draconian, Visigothic law often adds scalping to the humiliation of public beating. The following offences all draw a penalty of two hundred lashes and a scalping:

- Falsely writing a royal order.[50]
- Abetting a homicide.[51]
- Delaying to join the army, failing to march, or withdrawing from military service.[52]
- Inciting a man's mind with demonic possession.[53]
- For a husband who extorts writing from his wife to obtain a divorce.[54]

The addition of scalping (*Forum Iudicum* uses the term *decalvare*, thus clearly distinguishing it from simply shearing the hair discussed above for the laws of Wessex) attaches evident disfigurement to the scars from the lashing, which might be covered by clothing. If a portion of the scalp is removed, it takes with it the embedded hair follicles. Hair cannot grow back on the scalped portion of the head.[55] Not only is the transgressor publicly humiliated and physically tortured, but he is branded for life.

---

48 Elsakkers, 'Inflicting Serious Bodily Harm,' 60.
49 *Forum Iud.* §II, 1, xix.
50 Ibid., §VII, 5, ix.
51 Ibid., §VI, 5, xii.
52 Ibid., §IX ii.
53 Ibid., §VI, 2, iii.
54 Ibid., §III, 6, civ.
55 See online appendices for photograph of Robert McGee, scalped by the Sioux chief Little Turtle in 1864.

Literary Examples of Mutilation

Two interesting literary depictions of legal mutilation stem from early medieval Bavaria. First, in 834 a cleric from Freising wrote a poem called *The Song of Count Timo*, describing court appearances ruled over by Timo in Weihenstephan:

> Therefore, when the count arrives, he orders that thieves be hanged,
> and that the cheeks of robbers be forever branded.
> That criminals be disgracefully maimed by having their noses cut off;
> this one loses a foot, and that one loses a hand.[56]

This poem provides us with a very different look at judicial mutilation than that presented in the laws. Apparently Timo used his position as presider to hand down judgments not precisely stipulated in the written rulings. Recall that the Visigothic *Forum Iudicum* allows the judge to decide the penalty in cases of damage to the nose, ear, or mouth. Timo seems to have invoked a similar flexibility, although his judgments are not specifically mandated in the recorded laws. This comparison implies a possible conjunction between the laws of the Visigoths and those of the Bavarians. The Visigoths began their journey to the Iberian peninsula in the far east of Europe, and the Bavarian confederation was always located in that region. We may be seeing in these clauses on legal mutilation a pre-literate tradition stemming from the eastern regions of Europe. However, Theodulf, the Carolingian judge whose poetry was presented in chapter 2, provides evidence that such practices were also found in Francia, even if not stipulated in the Frankish *leges*:

> Modern law takes away eyes, the source of begetting beautiful offspring, a leg and a hand at the same time. They order that backs be cut with brands, lead be poured into the mouth, that ears, noses, and all that is beautiful be cut off. They order that swift feet be amputated and that with a rope around it, the neck, suspended from a high pole, should bear the weight of a thief.[57]

Clearly the codified laws provide only a partial view of legal practice. Patrick Geary suggests that Theodulf's account may be 'a critique not

---

56 Brown, *Unjust Seizure*, 2–3; see also 206–9.
57 From MGH *Poetae Latini aevi Carolini* 1: ll. 517, 518, cited and translated in Geary, 'Judicial Violence,' 84.

only of torture as punishment but also of the torture of individuals intended to coerce confession to the accusations of the powerful.'[58]

Another literary description of mutilation is contained in the Bavarian *Life of St Emmeran*, written c. 772. This hagiography describes the saint's martyrdom by dismemberment.[59] Ota, the young daughter of Duke Theodo, had been willingly seduced by the son of one of the duke's judges. Bishop Emmeran assigned them penance and instructed them to let him assume the accusation of seduction, so that the young couple might escape execution. Ota's uncle 'had the bishop stripped and tied to a ladder. [His] men then began to cut off Emmeran's extremities and limbs piece by piece while the bishop praised God and asked for their salvation. They finished by ripping off Emmeran's genitals and tearing out his tongue; leaving the mutilated torso to die.' Warren Brown cites Bernhard Bischoff's hypothesis that this may be the impetus for *Lex Baiuariorum* C I/10, which

> forbids the murder of a bishop on suspicion of guilt for a range of crimes (including unchastity); the clause mandates instead recourse to a court and, if the bishop is found guilty, condemnation according to canon law. Bischoff suggests that the clause reflects an actual event, and that Arbeo [authour of the *Life of St Emmeran*], with only a dim memory of the violent death of his subject, reached for it to give structure to his story.

If Bischoff is correct, this provides us with a fascinating example of literature – preserving communal memory of the outrage – regulating the laws.

Finally, the laws seem to imply that judicial mutilation – or at least public scourging – was a punishment more commonly assessed for men than for women (although in this analysis, we are faced by the common conundrum of distinguishing sexual from grammatical gender). Lashing a woman in public would expose her breasts, an action frequently legislated against in barbarian law.

However, the lives of female saints recorded from the fifth to the twelfth century provide us with numerous examples of self-mutilation. These stories involve nuns who, most frequently, cut off their noses to make themselves less appealing to potential rapists: the theme is common enough

---

58 Geary, 'Judicial Violence,' 86.
59 See Brown, *Unjust Seizure*, 36–40; he cites 'Nachwort' to *Vita et passio Sancti Haimhrammi Martyris*, ed. Bernhard Bischoff (Munich, 1953), 90–2; text given in Brown, *Unjust Seizure*, 33, n. 19. The translation of Bischoff's analysis is Brown's.

in hagiography to warrant its own reflexive verb: *se exnaseverunt*, 'they de-nosed themselves.'[60] A nun, as the bride of Christ, could not allow herself to be defiled by a mortal man, since this would be the earthly equivalent of adultery. *The Lessons of the Office of Saint Eusebia* recount that when infidels attacked Eusebia's monastery near Marseilles in 738, she 'urged the holy virgins, caring more for preserving their virginity than their life, to cut off their noses in order to irritate by this bloody spectacle the rage of the barbarians and to extinguish their passions. With incredible zeal, she and all her companions accomplished this act; the barbarians massacred them in the number of forty, while they confessed Christ with an admirable constancy.'[61] Their revolting appearance seems to have allowed this band of nuns to immediately enter the heavenly kingdom as brides of Christ with their virginity intact.[62]

A similar, but more extreme, stratagem was employed by St Ebba, abbess of Coldingham. When her monastery was attacked by Vikings around 870,

> the abbess, with an heroic spirit ... took a razor, and with it cut off her nose, together with her upper lip unto the teeth, presenting herself a horrible spectacle to those who stood by. Filled with admiration at this admirable deed, the whole assembly followed her maternal example, and severally did the like to themselves ... [When the pagan attackers came,] on beholding the abbess and the sisters so outrageously mutilated, and stained with their own blood from the sole of their foot unto their head, they retired in haste from the place.[63]

Like Eusebia's followers, those of Ebba could go as virgin brides to the next life. Unlike them, they also were able to enjoy earthly existence until old age naturally called them (noseless) to ascend to heaven.

---

60 Schulenberg, *Forgetful of Their Sex*, 148.
61 Cited and translated in ibid., 145.
62 Disappointingly, this does not seem to be the direct origin of the Modern English phrase 'cut off your nose to spite your face,' although certainly the medieval act and the modern idiom must be thematically related.
63 Roger of Wendover, cited and translated in Schulenberg, *Forgetful of Their Sex*, 146.

7 Assaults against Women[1]

One of my friends in graduate school complained about her in-laws that 'they regard me only as the receptacle of my husband's sperm.' This view of woman as primarily the incubator of future humans is hardly unique to present times, and is repeatedly addressed in Germanic legal regulations. However, these laws also consider the inherent physical weakness of the female sex compared to the male, with the concomitant lesser ability for self-protection.

The previous chapters have considered laws concerning injury inflicted on those of the rank of freeman, as this is the focus of most of the injury schedules. (A few territories address differentiation in compensation according to rank, which will be discussed in the next chapter.) The term 'freeman,' commonly used in scholarship, is somewhat misleading, as the appellation subsumes both males and females of free status.[2] Thus as a whole, the discussion on maiming of various sorts pertains to both men and women. Assaults applying specifically to women, such as rape or forced abortion, are considered as offences distinct from the group of clauses addressing injury or laming which could affect either sex. This chapter extends our knowledge about restitution due for damage to free women, adding to the non-gendered rulings of the injury tables stipulations addressing assault against free women contained elsewhere in the legal texts.

---

1 As the clauses addressing assault against women are generally scattered throughout the individual bodies of law, the notes for this chapter provide specific reference to the regulations under discussion.
2 The same inherent gender difficulty applies to the alternative term 'freeborn'; this latter choice, however, suffers further from the exclusion of manumitted slaves, who can rise to free status during the course of their lives.

Injury

The Kentish laws specify that for damages laid out in the personal injury schedule, *mægþbot sy swa friges mannes*, 'let compensation for a maid be the same as for a free man.'[3] The term *mægþ* generally refers to a maiden or unmarried woman; however, as there is no other clause concerning non-sexually related assaults against women, I assume that *mægþ* is simply used here as a cover-term for any female: namely, injuries inflicted on a free woman require the same compensation as those inflicted on a free man. The laws of Alamannia double for women the fines due to freemen,[4] presumably recognizing that a woman would be physically less able to defend herself against assault than a man. Substantiation for this hypothesis is provided in Bavarian law, in which the fine for injuring a woman is twice the fine as for a free man because she cannot bear weapons, unless she decides to fight with weapons like a man.[5] Although Alamann law does not include the clause on women warriors, given the similarities elsewhere between Alamann and Bavarian law this differentiation between peaceful and belligerent women might have been tacitly understood in Alamannia. Burgundian law provides a more specific, although less drastic, parallel. A freeman who cuts off a woman's hair in her house must pay her thirty *solidi* for the insult and a further ten for the disturbance of public peace. However, if she runs from her house to take part in a fight and her hair is cut off in the process, the hair-cutter is not liable for the penalty, as she has lost her status as a non-combatant.[6] Even more drastic is the example provided by Lombard law, in which 'where certain men get together a band of women, arm them, and set them upon their men under the assumption that the women would be protected by the heavy nine-hundred-solidi-violence composition, it is reaffirmed that such women … may not claim this composition.'[7]

I believe that the Kentish regulations equating fines for injuring women to those for injuring men likely reflect the norm (at least for women who preserve their essential, non-combatant femininity) in regions which do

---

3 *Kent* §73. Hough, 'Two Kentish Laws Concerning Women,' suggests that this clause refers to violence perpetrated by (rather than against) women. Although there is nothing grammatically to preference either reading, I find Hough's reasoning somewhat forced, and thus align myself here rather with the *communis opinio*.
4 *Lex Ala.* §49.2.
5 *Lex Baiu.* §4.29.
6 *Liber Const.* §92.2.
7 Drew, *Law and Society in Early Medieval Europe*, 4:37.

not address gender distinction. This speculation is based on the assumption that if the usual fine were doubled for assault against a woman elsewhere, that stipulation would have been committed to writing.

Rape

Unsurprisingly, the offence against free women most commonly addressed in barbarian laws is rape. The earliest code, that of the Salian Franks, demands a fine of 200 *solidi* for the rape of a man's wife:[8] this is equivalent to her wergild – that is, rape incurs the same penalty as murder. This stipulation is echoed by Thuringian law, which further states that if the rapist is a slave, his owner is liable for the fine.[9]

Several territories distinguish between married and unmarried women in the fines for rape, although hardly consistently. *Lex Salica* demands only sixty-two and a half *solidi* for the rape of a free girl:[10] the fine otherwise assessed for what Marianne Elsakkers defines as 'serious, debilitating injuries.'[11] The fee is equal to that for striking out an eye or off a foot. Presumably the greater fine of 200 *solidi* for raping a wife takes into account not only the insult to the husband, but also the possibility of a bastard being conceived outside the family bloodline. Alamann law similarly requires only half as much (forty vs. eighty *solidi*) for raping a maiden as for raping a (presumably married) woman.[12]

In Wessex, the fine for raping a girl is identical to that for raping an older woman, presumably beyond childbearing years; we will later see this doublet appearing elsewhere in cases of homicide.[13] In the case of the postmenopausal woman, the fine is split between the husband and the king, implying that in Wessex the institution of marriage belonged under regal protection.[14] Carole Hough argues convincingly that, at least in the case of §§11.2 and 11.3, which address a woman thrown to the ground and subsequently raped, we can extrapolate from the phrase *hire gebete* 'pay her compensation' that the compensation is meant to go to the violated woman

---

8 *Lex Sal.* §15.1. If the rapist is a freedman or slave, he pays with his life.
9 *Lex Thur.* §IV.56.
10 *Lex Sal.* §§13.4; 15.2.
11 Elsakkers, 'Abortion, Poisoning, Magic and Contraception in Eckhardt's *Pactus Legis Salicae*,' 239, n. 15.
12 *Lex Ala.* §58.1.
13 *Wessex* §26. This interpretation is taken from the surely correct re-analysis of this clause in Hough, 'A New Reading of Alfred, ch. 26.'
14 *Wessex* §29.

herself. The sixty-shilling fine due the woman is augmented by an additional payment of 120 shillings for disturbance of the peace.[15] If the woman had previously been accused of sexual misconduct, the fine is halved.

As in Wessex, Frisian law considers raping a virgin to some degree a public offense: the rapist must pay her wergild, an additional one third of her wergild to her protector, and a further one third of her wergild to the king, under whose protection stands the entire realm.[16] Both Frisia and Wessex demonstrate in their rulings on rape an interruption in the pattern of parallel compensation for injury – that is, kin to kin – with an echo of the Roman system of additional payment to the authority responsible for maintaining the laws, and concomitantly the peace.

The case of rape against a married woman presents an odd feature of the West Saxon ranking system. A husband is to be recompensed for the rape of his wife: for a 1200-wergild wife, 120 to her husband; for a 600-wergild wife, 100 to her husband; and for a *ceorl's* wife, 40 to her husband.[17] (Throughout the Germanic territories, the recompense for injury to a woman is almost invariably paid to the man under whose protection she lives. Although the damage physically affects the woman, the assault is legally regarded as an affront to the kin, and thus the fine is paid to the presiding male. A husband will receive the recompense for his wife, and a father for his daughter.) Curiously, the percentage of wergild is not only inconsistent in these rulings, but increases as the rank of the victim decreases. The rape of a noblewoman of highest rank demands 10 per cent restitution to her husband, while the percentage rises to 17 per cent for a noblewoman of lower rank, and to 20 per cent for a free woman. I can only speculate that this odd fine structure represents the greater ability of a wealthier man to pay the bride-price for a new wife. These fines for rape are considerably lower than all earlier barbarian laws, although they are likely also augmented by a payment for disturbance of the peace.

The laws of Wessex allow a man to fight without incurring a vendetta if he finds another man with his wedded wife within closed doors or under the same blanket, or with his mother who was given as a lawful wife to his father, or with his legitimate sister or his legitimate daughter.[18] It almost seems as if the laws of Alfred encourage a man to take private action if a woman under his protection is raped. Once again, we find a parallel to the

---

15 Analysis taken from Hough, 'Alfred's *Domboc* and the Language of Rape.'
16 *Lex Fris.* §9.8, 9, 10–11.
17 *Wessex* §10.
18 Ibid., §42.7.

laws of Wessex in Frisia, which permit an adulterer to be killed without penalty.[19]

The Visigoths similarly rule that if any rapist is killed the killing should not count as criminal homicide, because 'the act was committed in the defense of chastity.'[20] The stigma of the rapist does not, however, seem to extend to his kin. If a man rapes another's wife, he shall be delivered to the husband of the woman (presumably either to be put to death or to be subject to penal servitude). However, the rapist's property devolves on his legal heirs; in the event that he has no heirs, the property is given to the injured husband.[21] If a man rapes a virgin, he receives 100 lashes and must serve her as a slave forever.[22] In both cases, the rapist must make atonement directly to his victim (and her spouse) with lifetime servitude.

Lex Ribuaria presents a vivid picture of the immunity for a man taking revenge upon the rapist of his wife or daughter.[23]

> [If the father or husband] is unable to tie him up, and strikes him a blow and kills him, he should raise him up in a hurdle at the crossroads in the presence of witnesses and safeguard [the corpse] forty or fourteen nights. And then let him swear at the sanctuary [*harapus*] before the judge that the man he killed had forfeited his life. But if he does not do this, let him be held guilty of homicide.

Before leaving the legal stipulations against rape, it is worth reiterating that these clauses apply only to free women. A female slave raped by her owner had no such protection under the laws.

Abduction[24]

From the earliest laws on, we find clauses that address the abduction (often with implied rape) of a woman engaged to marry another man. I will present these in chronological order of the setting of the laws. *Lex Salica* states that:

---

19 *Lex Fris.* §5.1
20 *Forum Iud.* §III, 3, vi. Trans. Scott, *Visigothic Code*, s.v.
21 Ibid., §III, 4, i.
22 Ibid., §III, 4, xiv.
23 *Lex Rib.* §77; trans. Rivers, *Laws of the Salian and Ripuarian Franks*, 209.
24 For further discussion of issues addressed in the following section, see the comparative analysis in Elsakkers, 'Raptus ultra Rhenum.'

If anyone follows a betrothed girl in a wedding procession who is on her way to be married and assaults her on the road and forces her to engage in sex (known in the *mallberg* as *gangichaldo*), let him be liable for ... 200 solidi.[25]

This is a situation peculiar enough to warrant a suspicion that it was inserted to address a specific occurrence: that is, the regulation represents case law rather than judicial theory. This hypothesis is undercut by the fact that a similar stipulation is included in Burgundian law, close in time but far in legal or political influence from Salian Francia. The Burgundian *Liber Constitutionem* presents the following sequence:[26]

1 Abducting a betrothed girl requires a payment of ninefold bride-price and twelve *solidi* for disturbance of the peace.
2 If she is returned still a virgin (*incorrupta*), the repayment of bride-price is only sixfold, but the payment for disturbance to the peace remains the same.

   Although a romantic view might interpret this as a bride, betrothed against her will, rescued at the last moment by her true love, this scenario more likely represents abduction and rape, the latter in the first case fulfilled and in the second thwarted. Burgundian law goes on to state that:
3 If the abductor cannot pay the price, he is turned over to the kin of the bride. Here the financially challenged man who longed for the bride promised to another – or, probably more realistically, attempted to force a marriage to ally himself to an economically or politically powerful kin – could not afford the necessary penalty when his plan failed. What happens then? He becomes the property of her paternal kin, who could legally put him to death. However, this seems to be a waste of financial resources: more likely, the bride's family would put him to work as a slave. Burgundian law finishes with an unambiguously romantic flourish:
4 If she runs after him of her own volition, he must pay a threefold bride-price unless she returns still a virgin (*incorrupta*), in which case he owes no fine.

Both lovers are complicit in this scenario; thus the thwarted lover need pay no penalty as long as the frustrated affair was never

---

25 *Lex Sal.* §13.14; translation from Rivers, *Laws of Salian and Ripuarian Franks*, 57.
26 *Liber Const.* §12.1–4.

consumma-ted.²⁷ An even more complex stipulation is based on an actual case, presented later in the Burgundian *leges*:

> Since the facts of a criminal case which is pending between Fredegisil, our sword-bearer on the one side, and Balthamodus together with Aunegild on the other, have been heard and considered, we give an opinion which punished this recent crime and imposes a method of restraint for the future.
>
> Since Aunegild, after the death of her first husband, retaining her own legal competence, promised herself, not only with the consent of her relatives, but also with her own desire and will, to the above mentioned Fredegisil, and since she had received the greater part of the wedding price which her betrothed had paid, she broke her pledged faith, having been aroused by the ardor of her desire for Balthamodus. Furthermore, she not only violated her vows, but repeated her customary shameful union, and

---

27 Patrick Geary describes a typological parallel from the life of Judith of Flanders, although her noble position probably renders her exempt from these legal rulings. Judith was the daughter of Charles the Bald, ruler of the large territory of Western Francia (incorporating the old Neustria and Aquitaine). In 856 Æthelwulf of Wessex stopped at the court of Charles on his way back from a pilgrimage to Rome (having taken with him his youngest son, the future English king Alfred the Great). The two kings contracted an alliance which was sealed by the marriage of the twelve-year-old Judith to Æthelwulf, who had been subking of Kent for twenty-six years and king of Wessex for seventeen. The advantage to Charles was to gain an ally against his troublesome brother Louis, who was attempting to wrest Aquitaine from him. In addition, Danish ships were making incursions up the Loire and Seine rivers, and Charles may have hoped for martial aide from the island nation. The advantage to Æthelwulf was to bring back a substantial dowry with which he could buy off the rebellion of his son Æthelbald, who had overstepped the position of regent during his father's absence in Rome. The advantage to Judith is indiscernible.

Upon Æthelwulf's death two years later, Æthelbald took the throne of Wessex and, in a time-honoured Germanic tradition, consolidated power by marrying his former stepmother. Two years later Æthelbald died. Judith was now fourteen and a widow twice-over. She returned to her father's kingdom, presumably to await her next marriage. From here, she ran off as a sixteen-year-old with Baldwin, a count from the northern seashore. The *Annals of St Bertin* tell us that 'Charles now learned that she had changed her widow's clothing and gone off with Count Baldwin, at his instigation.' The instigator may well have been Baldwin, hoping to gain political and economic advantage by presenting the new marriage as a fait accompli. But the annals portray Judith as a willing party to this elopement (probably gratefully) exchanging her widow's weeds for clothing more appropriate to her young years. Although Baldwin never returned her, neither was he fined. In fact, his gamble paid off: Charles eventually granted him the county of Flanders, and it is from this alliance that the counts of Flanders trace their roots. This account is drawn from Geary, *Women in the Beginning*, 51–4. See also Abels, *Alfred the Great*, 78–91.

on account of this, she ought to atone for such a crime and such a violation of her free status not otherwise than with the pouring forth of her own blood. Nevertheless we command, placing reverence for these holy days before public punishment, that Aunegild, deprived of honor by human and divine judgment, should pay her wergild, that is three hundred solidi, to Fredegisil under compulsion.

Nor do we remove merited condemnation from Balthamodus who presumed to receive a woman due in marriage to another man, for his case deserves death. But in consideration of the holy days, we recall our sentence for his execution, under the condition that he should be compelled to pay his wergild of one hundred fifty solidi to that Fredegisil unless he can offer public oath with eleven oathhelpers in which he affirms that at that time in which he was united with the abovementioned Aunegild as by the right of marriage, he was unaware that she was pledged to Fredegisil. If he shall so swear, let him suffer neither loss nor punishment.

In truth we command that the judgment set forth in this case be established to remain the law forever ...[28]

Note that the wergild for the woman, Fredegisil, was twice that for the man, Balthamodus.

The laws of Kent require for the abduction of a maiden a payment of 50 shillings plus a bride-price to be determined by the owner of the stolen maiden's protection. Presumably this abduction resulted in a marriage contractually settled by a greatly increased bride-price demanded by the father. If the maiden was betrothed and the bride-price had been paid, the abductor must pay an additional twenty shillings to the bereft bridegroom. The next stipulation reads 'Gif gængan geweorðeþ, XXXV scill 7 cyninge XV' (if *gængan* occurs, thirty-five shillings and fifteen to the king). The difficulty here lies with the term *gængan*, which appears nowhere else in the corpus of Old English. Earlier, I followed the *communis opinio*, and interpreted it as 'return.' In other words, if the maiden is returned (and here we must assume, although the laws do not explicitly say so, that she is still a virgin), the abductor must pay thirty-five shillings (perhaps to the owner of her protection or perhaps split between him and the bridegroom) and fifteen to the king for disturbance of the peace. The fifty shillings would then represent the total fine for returning a virgin unharmed (like the Burgundian *incorrupta*), as opposed to the seventy shillings for

---

28 *Liber Const.* §LII, 2–5; from Drew, *Law and Society*, II, 19–20.

abduction and bride-price if the maiden had been violated. However, the resemblance in first elements of the Kentish compound *gængan* and the *mallberg* gloss *gangichaldo* (meaning to assault and rape a woman on the road) suggests the possibility that these two uncertain terms may be related. In this case, the Kentish fine for assaulting a betrothed woman on the road would be thirty-five shillings (presumably to her kin-group) and fifteen for disturbance of the peace. The former interpretation is modelled on Burgundian law and the latter on Salic; I tend now to favour the latter due to the linguistic similarity, although a superficial resemblance between two uninterpretable words hardly represents decisive evidence.[29] The laws of Kent are the first to discuss the distribution of the fine; the kin and bridegroom are both recompensed, and an additional fee goes to the public coffer.

Like the Kentish rulings, Alamann law augments the fines for abduction if the maiden were already betrothed.[30] Alamann laws require a fine of eighty *solidi* for abduction of a man's wife if she is returned, but 400 if she is not.[31] The implication is surely that the returned wife has not been violated; interestingly, however, the letter of the law would allow a husband devoted to his wife to take her back, no matter what happened while she was out of his protection.

Lex Ribuaria demands a much greater payment than the laws of Kent both for violating the kin's protection and for disturbing the peace: the fine is 900 *solidi*, half to the kin and half to the king. (Recall that the Ripuarian wergild was 200 *solidi* compared to Kent's 100; thus the Ripuarian fine represents 450 per cent of a wergild, while the Kentish total is a mere 70 per cent.) In addition, the abductor must repay twice the amount of the bride-price that the bridegroom had invested in the disrupted marriage.[32] *Lex Saxonum* similarly demands a payment of 900 *solidi*, but the restitution is differently divided: 300 *solidi* as fine to her father;

---

29 Kent §77.1, 2. See also discussion in Oliver, *The Beginnings of English Law*, 108–9. Hough, 'A Reappraisal of Æthelberht,' 84, argues that the term *gængang* refers to an attack on the open road rather than the return of the abducted maiden. Upon first reading, I found her argument unpersuasive, as the adduced parallels from Burgundian law did not seem particularly relevant. Curiously, she does not include the *mallberg* term of *Lex Salica* §13.14 in her discussion; when this is added to the other evidence, the argument takes on much more force. See also Hough, 'Alfred's *Domboc*,' 15–16.
30 *Lex Ala.* §50.
31 Ibid. §50.
32 *Lex Rib.* §191.

300 to the intended bridegroom; and a further 300 for her purchase price.³³ Marianne Elsakkers analyses this breakdown as follows:

> The abduction of an engaged woman described in article 49 must have been voluntary on the part of the woman, because, although the abductor is penalized for abducting a woman who is spoken for – he must pay her father and her finacé 300 solidi each – he does not have to return the bride-to-be, nor does he have to give her a compensation – on the contrary, he is allowed to 'buy' her for 300 *solidi*, the normal price for a bride.³⁴

Thus the total payment in Ripuarian Francia is, unusually, higher than in Saxony: the former requires 900 *solidi* plus twice the bride-price, while the latter subsumes the repayment of the bride-price in the fine itself. The total in either territory, however, represents a huge amount. In a modern setting such an enormous assessment might be intended to act as a deterrent; for our period, however, this interpretation would presuppose a greater common knowledge of written law than was likely to have existed.

In the only potential touch of sentimentality shown in all the barbarian laws, Saxony requires that if the woman was abducted while she was with her mother in the street, 300 *solidi* is also due to her mother. Marianne Elsakkers suggests two possible interpretations for this ruling: 'is it because of the shock or shame of seeing her daughter abducted in a public place, or is the money a reward for being in cahoots with her daughter?'³⁵ Under the second theory, the payment would be due the mother for abetting an abduction in which her daughter was a willing party. I find this reading unconvincing: although I think it perfectly possible that a bribe could be given by the abductor to the mother, it seems very odd that the mother would be openly and legally rewarded for being an accomplice in breaking a marriage contract. A more likely explanation is that the vulnerability is higher since the mother (being female, and perhaps old as well) would be unable to protect her as her father, husband, or brothers would if they were her escorts.³⁶

Legal restitution for abducting a maiden against her will does not always depend on her having been previously betrothed. The formulary of Marculf II, 16 presents a template by which the abductor could subse-

---

33 *Lex Sax.* §49.
34 Elsakers, 'Raptus ultra Rhenum,' 38.
35 Ibid.
36 I owe this insight and the wording to Maria Mahoney.

quently legalize the union by providing a suitable dowry, if the parents agree:

> To my sweetest wife, A, B. Since you were [not] betrothed to me by the will of your parents, and I married you through the crime of abduction against your will and that of your parents ... [I will now give] what I should have given to you as a gift before the day of the wedding ... I therefore give you the small place called C, situated in the *pagus* of D, with houses fit for habitation and all the useful necessary things inside them, with lands, tenants, *n.* unfree servants, vineyards, forests, meadows, pastures and every other benefit, *n.* horses, *n.* oxen, a herd of horses, a herd of cows, a herd of pigs, a flock of sheep, with gold and silver, jewels [and] carpets worth *n. solidi*.[37]

Does this represent a standard dowry? The total worth seems high; perhaps the parents extracted a greater payment due to the extra-legal abduction.

Ripuarian Francia provides us with a scenario by which a maiden – whether previously betrothed or not – could be stolen from her home, namely, abduction by a gang. If a group breaks in and seizes her, the first man pays the wergild (200 *solidi*), the next three men pay sixty *solidi* each, and each man after that pays forty-five. This fine is halved if the perpetrators are king's men or churchmen.[38] Although this seems a somewhat odd prerogative of rank, perhaps the assumption is that these potentially more reputable citizens might have a better excuse for their extra-legal behaviour. A slave, if he is unfortunately impressed into this service, must pay with his life.[39] The *Forum Iudicum* makes the deterrent greater for a freeman: each one assisting at the carrying off of a woman by force is fined six ounces of gold and receives fifty lashes in public view.[40]

The laws of Visigothic Spain set no finite limit on the restitution owed by a man who has abducted a virgin or widow and returned her still chaste: the kidnapper is liable for half his property. As in the rulings on rape, this property is assigned directly to her. If, however, rape has been committed

---

37 Rio, *The Formularies of Angers and Marculf*, 199–200. On the dower in early Anglo-Saxon law, see also Oliver, *Beginnings of English Law*, 106–7; and Fell, *Women in Anglo-Saxon England and the Impact of 1066*, 55ff.
38 *Lex Rib.* §34. The Angers formulary provides in #26 a template for a woman abducted against her will by a churchman, which certainly sheds a shady light on the clerical profession. See Rio, *The Formularies of Angers and Marculf*, 69–70.
39 *Lex Rib.* §38. *Lex Sal.* §13.1–2 presents a similar clause regulating the responsibilities of gang members abducting a female slave.
40 *Forum Iud.* §III, 3, 12.

during the time of abduction, he is given as a slave to the injured party with all his possessions, and receives two hundred lashes in addition.[41] Note that this is almost double the fine for rape without abduction discussed earlier; once again, however, the damages are awarded directly to the violated woman. If the abducted woman is betrothed yet returned intact, half the property of the rapist is given to the girl, and half to her betrothed. If the abductor does not have property sufficient for recompense in the eyes of the law, he is sold as a slave and the price is split between bride and ex-groom. If the rape has been consummated, he is punished as previously discussed.

A sequence of rulings in the *Forum Iudicum* demonstrate that the economic value of a potential wife might put a girl at risk even within her own family.[42]

- If parents abet an abductor taking off a daughter already betrothed, the jilted groom receives four times the dowry, and the abductor is given to him as a slave.
- If brothers commit the same deed while their father is alive, they receive the same sentence as rapists, except for death.
- If brothers after the death of their father permit their sister to be carried off by an abductor, 'for the reason that they have disposed of her in marriage to a person of vile character, or against her own will, when they should have protected her honor, they shall lose the half of their property, which shall be given to their sister, and, in addition, they shall each receive fifty lashes in public.'[43]

The first two stipulations are clearly put in place to protect the investment of the bridegroom. One phrase in the last that springs out is that the brothers are reprimanded for disposing of her in marriage 'against her own will.' We see few other legal indications that a woman might have been allowed input as to whom she might marry.[44] Visigothic law furthermore presents us with one of the few statutes of limitations in all barbarian law: a rapist can only be prosecuted within thirty years after the commission of the

---

41 Ibid. §III, 3, 1.
42 Ibid. §III, 3, iii and iv.
43 Ibid. §III, 3, iv; trans. Scott, *Visigothic Code*, s.v.
44 Marianne Elsakkers suggests that *Lex Saxonum* §40 also implies that a woman had some say in choosing her marriage partner. See Elsakkers, 'Raptus ultra Rhenum,' 36–7.

offence.⁴⁵ This ruling allows for (at least) two interpretations. First, at the time of a much later death, when property would be transmitted to heirs, no accusation of rape with concomitant legal loss of possessions could be raised to attempt to take over (either legitimately or fraudulently) the alleged rapist's land or goods. Second, the charge would have to be raised during a period of time when eye-witnesses could still be alive to testify.

Finally, the law of Wessex demands that if someone abducts a nun from a cloister, he shall pay 120 shillings, half to the king and half to the head of the religious house. Her sisters in the order have now become her kin. An interesting contradiction exists for the next generation. If she has children by the man, and one of them is killed, the paternal kin receives the fine due them, but the restitution due to the maternal kin goes to the king. Apparently substitution of the religious order for the woman's kin does not extend to her offspring: compensation is now given to the king rather than the abbot or abbess. In some sense, her children must have been considered wards of the king.⁴⁶

Although barbarian laws indicate that rape was considered a serious offence, archaeological records may contradict this view, at least in certain regions. Some evidence is provided by the bodies found in prone-burial graves, that is, graves in which the body is buried face down. Susan M. Hirst's research on the *Anglo-Saxon Inhumation Cemetery at Sewerby, East Yorkshire* indicates that

> there is an amalgam of two ideas about prone burial: a sense that to be buried face down is to be linked with the Devil in Hell where evil-doers belong; and the idea of making the corpse safe for the living – in a nineteenth century Devon farmer's words about the prone burial of a suspected witch, 'Her on't be troublesome then, 'cause if her do being to diggy her can on'y diggy downwards'... The pathology report for the skeleton from G78 at Kingsworthy suggests that traces of injury on the thighs are typical of injuries found in rape victims, and the authors have cited a number of late Saxon and other references suggesting that in cases of adultery the woman was often outcast and/or severely punished. They suggest that this treatment may have been extended to rape victims in dubious circumstances and stress the coincidence of prone burial with the absence of grave goods (rare at Kingsworthy) and suggest it may imply naked burial.⁴⁷

---

45 *Forum Iud.* §III, 3, vii.
46 *Wessex* §8.
47 Hirst, *An Anglo-Saxon Inhumation Cemetery at Sewerby, East Yorkshire*, 37.

Might this be a parallel to the misogyny so characteristic of clerical writing throughout the Middle Ages? Examples in literature abound. (Did Chaucer see the Wife of Bath as a character or a caricature?)[48] Hirst's hypothesis on the humiliating burial of raped women both adds another facet to this misogynist bias, and also predicts an unfortunate conclusion which has lasted to the present day, namely, that a victim of rape somehow brought it upon herself, and can never be fully cleared of guilt.

Drawing an example from slightly after our period, the tenth-century German female author Hrotswitha of Gandersheim describes the sexual harassment of her heroine Druisiana, who successfully prays to be allowed to die before having to submit to sexual intercourse. M.R. Spergerg-McQueen argues that Druisiana 'offers no defense of the woman whose chastity is violated against her will. Instead, her example suggests that the unchaste woman may always be indicted on two counts: losing one's chastity is a sin regardless of circumstances, and women are responsible for men's reactions to them.'[49] I am not convinced of this analysis, however, given the statement expressed by the much-revered St Augustine in *The City of God*:

> While the will remains firm and unshaken, nothing that another person does with the body, or upon the body, is any fault of the person who suffers it, so long as he cannot escape it without sin.[50]

This statement comes in response to those proposing that Christian women ought to commit suicide if they thought there was a possibility of being raped, say, during the sack of a city by the barbarian armies. Augustine responds that suicide is a sin no matter what the circumstances; further, if a woman is certain in her own mind that she did not consent with her will to what was done to her body, there is no cause for her to feel such shame that she would destroy herself. He goes on to state that it is a pagan idea that any sin attached to an unwilling rape victim. The tenth-century German tale may be trying to reconcile the pagan ideals and the Christian one, as Drusiana does not actually commit suicide, but still fulfils the pagan requirement of 'death before dishonour.' The burial discussed above could be the same compromise situation. The victim was given a burial (?in consecrated ground) in accordance with the Christian insistence that

---

48 A fine collection of examples can be found in Barmires, *Woman Defamed and Woman Defended*.
49 Cited in Schulenberg, *Forgetful of Their Sex*, 137.
50 Augustin, *City of God and Christian Doctrine*, Book I, chaps 16–18; citation from 16.

sin was only attached to consent of the will, but the old pagan ideals caused the prone burial.[51]

Killing and Degrees of Pregnancy[52]

Clauses that address killing women generally focus on their child-bearing ability. In Salic law, a female has a 200-*solidi* wergild until the age of twelve, when she was legally considered of child-bearing age. Once a free woman has begun to have children, her wergild is tripled to 600 *solidi*, but falls back to 200 when she reaches the age of sixty, legally considered past child-bearing age.[53] (A remarkable statistic that arises from these clauses is that if a woman gave birth once a year throughout all her legal child-bearing years, she would have given birth to forty-seven children, assuming she had no twins.) Like Salic Francia, Thuringia and Ripuarian Francia both triple the wergild for a woman when she is of child-bearing age, with Thuringia specifically stipulating that this is equally true for a noble woman, whose 600-*solidi* wergild becomes 1800 during her fertile years.[54] Thuringia does not specify what the boundaries of the child-bearing years might be, but Ripuarian Francia, more realistically than Salic Francia, sets an upper limit of forty.[55] (Ripuarian wives then could only maximally have given birth to twenty-seven children during their legally assessed child-bearing years). The 600-*solidi* fine for killing a potential child-bearer is three times the normal wergild for a freeman, and represents a huge amount of money. The Ripuarian laws recognize this financial burden by stipulating that the fine can be paid over the next generations. (As discussed above, Wessex draws the same distinction between prepubescent or post-menopausal and fertile women in regard to rape.)

Lex Saxonum reverses the values that other territories assign to virginity and fertility. Killing a virgin requires double compensation, but her wergild sinks to single after she has given birth.[56] These regulations would appear to stress a woman's value as a marriage commodity rather than as a producer of children: an unmarried virgin might bring a substantial bride-price into her father's family. Once this sum has been paid to the paternal kin and she has

---

51 I am indebted for both the inspiration and the wording of this passage to Maria Mahoney.
52 A good overview is presented in 'Schwangerschaft, Abtreibung und Empfängnisverhütung,' in Niederhellmann, *Arzt- und Heilkunde*, 120–41.
53 *Lex Sal.* §24.8–9, §65e.
54 *Lex Thur.* §V.46–7; *Lex Rib.* §§12, 13.
55 *Lex Rib.* §41.17.
56 *Lex Sax.* §15.

passed into the protection of her husband's family, she is no longer worth the enhanced fine, at least in regard to her ancestral family. Another, not necessarily competing, analysis, is that this increased fine is also intended to protect nuns and consecrated women. These do not have the protection of a husband or interested suitor, and since their connection to the paternal home is much looser than other women's, they would be particularly vulnerable. This reading of an increased fine being assessed for taking advantage of a woman without male protection echoes the clause regarding a maiden abducted in her mother's presence discussed above.[57]

Most barbarian laws further address the issue of attacking a pregnant woman, killing either the woman or the fetus, or both.[58] The clauses on abortion I will discuss here are not those considering intentional abortion, but those addressing miscarriage caused by assault against the mother. Clear abhorrence for the former is strikingly addressed in the *Forum Iudicum* in a clause added by Flavius Chintasvintus:

> No depravity is greater than that which characterized those who, unmindful of their parental duties willfully deprive their children of life, and as this crime is said to be increasing throughout the provinces of our kingdom and as men as well as women are said to be guilty of it ... we hereby decree that if either a freewoman or a slave should kill her child before or after its birth, or should take any potion for the purpose of producing abortion, or should use any other means of putting an end to the life of her child, the judge of the province or district, as soon as he is advised of the fact, shall at once condemn the author of the crime to execution in public, or should he desire to spare her life, he shall at once cause her eyesight to be completely destroyed; and if it be proved that her husband either ordered or permitted the commission of this crime, he shall suffer the same penalty.[59]

Heinous as this crime may be, it represents violence by rather than against the mother and is thus not relevant to this study.

Chronologically, the first laws on abortion occur in Salian Francia. *Lex Salica* requires the same fine for killing a woman of child-bearing age as for killing a woman who is actually with child: striking or killing a pregnant woman results in a 600-*solidi* fine. However, an extra 600 *solidi* is added if

---

57 I am indebted for this insight (and much of its wording) to Maria Mahoney.
58 Many laws also include penalties for intentional abortion, but as this does not strictly fit this study's topic of assault, these laws are not considered here.
59 *Forum Iud.* §VI, 3, vii; trans. Scott, *Visigothic Code*, s.v.

the unborn fetus was male.⁶⁰ As Elsakkers points out, if the sex of the fetus was recognizable, then this ruling 'punishes causing a late term abortion – and implicitly condones early-term abortion.'⁶¹ Another stipulation calls for a 100-*solidi* fine if the baby is killed in the womb or in the first nine days, before it has a name (thus before baptism).⁶² These two rulings are difficult to reconcile: perhaps the two clauses were added at different times leaving a contradiction in the collation. In Elsakker's analysis:

> The fine of 100 solidi indicates that abortion and infanticide were regarded as serious injuries or attempted murder, but not as homicide. This means that the fine for causing a miscarriage is for injuries to the mother, not for killing an unborn child, and that child murder was apparently not considered to be homicide until the child had a name, that is, after the child had been acknowledged as a separate individual ... [The 600-*solidi* fine] reflects a different attitude towards abortion, and must therefore have been added at a time when the Salians' views on abortion were changing, and when injuring or killing an unborn child was not only considered dangerous to the mother's health, but was also regarded as a separate crime, a crime against the fetus.⁶³

Lex Ribuaria calls for a 100-*solidi* fine for killing a late-period fetus or a child before baptism; it also requires the attacker to pay 700 *solidi* if the mother is killed. This fine is 100 *solidi* higher than for the similar offence in Salian Francia, but may represent the sum of 600 *solidi* for the death of the mother and 100 for the death of the fetus.⁶⁴

Visigothic law likewise gives consideration to the degree of development of an aborted fetus. The relevant clauses are defined as part of the old or customary law (*antiqua*), in distinction to the newer stipulations added to the original core.

> *Lex Vis* 6.3.2. Old law (*Antiqua*). If a free man causes a free woman to abort. If anyone strikes a pregnant woman by any blow whatever or through any circumstance causes a free woman to abort, and from this she dies, let him be punished for homicide.

---

60 *Lex Sal.* §24.5.
61 Elsakkers, 'Abortion, Poisoning, Magic and Contraception,' 245.
62 *Lex Sal.* §24.6. The nine-day stipulation is absent in some manuscripts; see Elsakkers, 'Abortion, Poisoning, Magic and Contraception,' 239 and 241–2.
63 Elsakkers, 'Abortion, Poisoning, Magic and Contraception,' 246.
64 *Lex Rib.* §36.10.

If, however, only the *partus* is expelled, and the woman is in no way debilitated, and a free man is recognized as having inflicted this on a free woman, if he has killed a formed fetus, let him pay 150 *solidi*; if it is actually an unformed fetus, let him pay 100 *solidi* in restitution for the deed.[65]

The crux of this clause is that a differentiation is made between a formed and an unformed fetus: that is, between early and late-term abortion. Elsakkers points out that this distinction is an innovation in Germanic law: 'late Roman law does not punish abortion and early medieval Church law condemns abortion as homicide without any regard for the stage of development of the fetus.'[66] She speculates that this ruling may have been based on the Septuagint Bible version of Exodus 21:22–3:

If two men fight and strike a woman who is pregnant, and her child comes out while not formed, he will be forced to pay a fine; according as the woman's husband lays upon [him] he shall give according to that which is thought fit. But if it is formed, he shall give life for life.[67]

Elsakkers goes on to explain that '"[f]ormed" means that features, form and sex of the child are recognizable, and that the fetus has started moving about in the mother's womb; the fetus is then approximately three months old (according to modern standards).'[68]

Fetuses seem to have been valued far less in Alamannia than elsewhere. In the *Pactus*, causing a still-born child is fined by forty *solidi*. In the later *Lex*, fines for destroying children in the womb drop even further. Killing a male child or a fetus in which the sex is not yet determinable draws a mere twelve *solidi*. Interestingly, the fine for killing a female fetus is doubled to twenty-four *solidi*, presumably to compensate for the loss of her future ability to bear offspring.[69] Clearly it was considered more advantageous to bear a girl child in Alamannia than it was in Salian Francia.

---

65 Elsakkers, 'Gothic Bible, Vetus Latina and Visigothic Law,' 39; translation based on Amundsen, 'Visigothic Medical Legislation,' 567.
66 Elsakkers, 'Gothic Bible, Vetus Latina and Visigothic Law,' 38. Later Frisian law uses the criterion that the fetus displays hair and nails to define late-term abortion. See Elsakkers, '*Her anda neylar*: An intriguing criterion for abortion in Old Frisian law.'
67 Elsakkers, 'Gothic Bible, Vetus Latina and Visigothic Law,' 40.
68 Elsakkers, 'Genre Hopping,' 76; see also discussion in Niederhellmann, *Arzt- und Heilkunde*, 133–8.
69 *Lex Ala.* §§78, 94; *Pactus Ala.* §31.

In Lombardy, unintentionally causing abortion requires a payment of half the woman's wergild if the mother survives. If the mother dies, the fine is raised to her wergild and a half wergild for the aborted child.[70] Lombard law further states that killing a maiden or woman must be recompensed by 1200 *solidi*: that is, 1/3 higher than the 900-*solidi* wergild for a man.[71] Thus presumably if you kill a pregnant woman and the child *in utero*, the fine is 1200 *solidi* for the woman and 600 for the fetus, making a total of twice the fine due for killing a freeman. Interestingly, a husband who kills his own wife is only fined 1200 *solidi*.[72] Perhaps uxoricide draws no heavier penalty than killing an unknown woman, unless we interpret the 1200-*solidi* fine as an additional surcharge, thus doubling the normal penalty because of the familial nature of the crime. Certainly this hypothesis seems plausible, particularly when considering the law stipulates that a woman who murders her husband is executed.[73] Kinship ties were taken very seriously throughout medieval Europe. Thuringian law requires a woman who pleads not guilty of poisoning her husband to be cleared by judicial duel or by nine hot irons.[74] That is, either she finds a champion to fight on her behalf, or she must walk barefoot and unscathed over nine hot irons. Better, perhaps, to have avoided serving him those questionable mushrooms!

The early laws of Lombardy and the late laws of Wessex share the feature that the unborn child is assigned its own wergild. The laws of Alfred present a slightly different reckoning of compensation: killing a pregnant woman must be recompensed by her wergild and half the father's wergild for the child.[75] The implication is that if the man and woman are of different rank, the rank of the unborn child is assumed to be that of the father. Thus a fetus carried by a free woman married to a noble man is of more value than that of a noble woman married to a free man. This is paralleled by the rulings in many regions that a wife takes on the rank of her husband at marriage.[76]

The laws of Frisia provide an interesting distinction between aborting one's own child or causing the abortion of another. *Lex Frisionum* does

---

70 *Edict. Roth.* §75.
71 Ibid. §201.
72 Ibid. §200, §213.
73 Ibid. §203.
74 *Lex Thur.* §6.52.
75 *Wessex* §9.
76 An interesting legal case in which the wife discovers only after the marriage that her husband is not freeborn, and sues to retain her inherited property, is discussed in Brown, *Unjust Seizure*, 160–2.

not fine a mother whose own child *ab utero sublato est enectus*, 'has been killed from the hidden womb.'[77] The use of *sublato* is interesting here; generally it indicates a furtive action. The wording implies that even if intentional abortion was not punishable under law, it still carried a stigma. If another woman, however, commits the similar offence against a baby not her own, she must pay the mother's wergild. That is, if the abortion were inflicted by a draught prepared by another woman, that woman is liable. The fact that she must pay the mother's wergild certainly implies that the mother was not complicit in the action.

Finally, I would like to return to some distinctive features in the laws on abortion in Visigothic Spain, as explicated by Elsakkers.[78] First, Visigothic law states that either a man or a woman could be capable of this offence. Although no other barbarian law rules out women as perpetrators, none specifically includes the possibility that a woman could have committed the assault.[79] Furthermore, the Visigothic laws

> demand a differentiated compensation for causing a woman to miscarry (LV 6.3.2), and damages for any other injuries the pregnant woman may have suffered as a result of the violence done to her (LV 6.3.2–6.3.3) ... If the woman had also incurred other injuries, (e.g., head injuries, bruising, internal injuries), she would have suffered two 'debilitating' injuries, thus doubly impairing her health.[80]

No other barbarian law explicitly considers the physical damage to a woman who aborts due to violent assault but survives the attack.

Improper Touching

The final offences against women deal with improper touching. *Lex Salica* provides an escalating scale depending on the inherent sexual nature of the contact. The fine for touching a woman's hand or finger is fifteen *solidi*; her arm thirty; her elbow thirty-five; and her breast forty-five. Cutting her breast so that blood flows draws an equal fine of forty-five *solidi*. The

---

77 *Lex Fris.* §5.
78 Elsakkers, 'Inflicting Serious Bodily Harm.'
79 Elsakkers suggests that this ruling might also subsume midwives, who 'were considered dangerous, because they were especially knowledgeable about matters such as abortion and contraception.' See 'Inflicting Serious Bodily Harm,' 57–8.
80 Ibid., 61–2.

financial equation of touching and cutting seems grossly unfair to the woman, unless we read the fine for cutting the breast as added to the fine for touching, since one cannot cut the breast without simultaneously touching it.[81] Burgundian law demands twelve *solidi* for grabbing a woman or revealing her flesh, unless the aggressor is a slave, in which case he receives 200 lashes.[82] *Lex Ribuaria* echoes two of these stipulations, demanding fifteen *solidi* for a touch of the hand and thirty for touching the arm above the elbow.[83] *Lex Alamannorum* restricts the fines for improper touching to those who assault virgins: revealing the skin or lifting the garment to the knee is fined by six *solidi*, while lifting the garment to reveal the genitals doubles that amount to twelve *solidi*. Frisian law seems to place less importance on sexual contact: a man who touches a woman's breast must pay two *solidi*, and four if he touches her pudendum. However, *Lex Frisionum* adds to each of these fees a two-*solidi* payment to the public coffer.[84] So while molesting a woman is a private, albeit legally fineable, transgression in Salian and Ripuarian Francia, it is also regarded as an offence against public decency in Frisia. The laws of Alfred demonstrate again the protection that Wessex offered to women in religious orders: seizing a nun in lewd fashion by her clothes or her breast requires twofold payment of the five-shilling fine set for lay women.[85]

In Burgundy, either uncovering a woman's hair or slandering her also draws a fine of twelve *solidi*.[86] These may be somehow equated: showing a woman's loose hair reveals her loose character. Far worse, however, is the offence of cutting off her hair, which requires not only a payment to the shorn woman of thirty *solidi*, but an additional twelve to the public coffer. (Recall, however, as discussed above, these fines are inapplicable if she has run from the house to fight like a man.) When the fourth-century bishop Donatus describes nuns shearing their hair before taking the veil, he explains that this practice was devised 'for use against ravishers or unwanted suitors.'[87] As the future nun had planned, her shorn locks rendered her unattractive to worldly men. The shearing of locks thus echoes, although

---

81 *Lex Sal.* §20. For comparative analysis of the clauses considered below, see Hough, 'Alfred's *Domboc*,' 16–18; Niederhellmann, *Arzt- und Heilkunde*, 189–91.
82 *Liber Const.* §331.
83 *Lex Rib.* §39.
84 *Lex Fris.* §22.88–9.
85 Wessex §§18; 11.2. See discussion in Hough, 'Alfred's *Domboc*,' 15–16.
86 *Liber Const.* §92.1.
87 See Schulenberg, *Forgetful of Their Sex*, 157.

less dramatically, the self-mutilation by nuns who cut off their noses described in chapter 6. The motivation for the nuns is to preserve themselves chaste as brides of Christ. When the same desecrations are performed on secular women against their will, they have the effect of removing them from the potentially lucrative marriage market.

Summary

1 For the personal injury tariffs themselves, fines against damage to free women are probably equal to those for the equivalent injury to free men in most territories. Only Burgundy, Alamannia, and Bavaria require a double compensation for women; the latter two regions specify that women are less able to defend themselves than men. However, clauses in Bavaria and Burgundy indicate that if a woman casts off her essential feminine nature and fights like a man, she should be treated as a man in the eyes of the law.
2 The most common assault against women addressed in the laws is rape. This is often assessed at the same amount as murder. In a sense, once the sexual purity of a woman has been violated, she ceases to have a full life in the family structure. The import of this violation differs according to region. Most laws (such as those of the Salian Franks) require a greater payment for raping a man's wife, implying that the legitimacy of his offspring may thereby be brought into question. However, Frisia and Saxony both focus on the rape of a virgin; as damaged goods, she can no longer bring the valuable bride-price into the family coffers. These two regions seem to give legal preference to the father's kin, who would lose a potentially economically valuable marriage alliance, rather than to the husband, the affront to whom results not only in the defiling of his wife, but also in the possibility of illegitimate offspring.

Almost all regions legislate against the abduction of a promised bride: the abductor (and presumably rapist) must pay not only the fine, but also the bride-price that the chosen groom had paid. Many territories demand an additional payment for disturbance of the public peace; the marriage contract is there protected by governmental authority. In Visigothic Spain, the fine is paid directly to the violated woman, and the rapist must serve as her slave for the rest of his life; although there is no possible restitution for the psychological effects of rape, the *Forum Iudicum* does its best. The laws of Wessex similarly require that the wergild be paid to the victim herself; there is no penal servitude, although the rapist must pay a further fine to the public coffer.

3 Homicide is the next most frequently cited offence against women. Overwhelmingly, the killing of a woman of child-bearing age is assessed more highly than the same offence against girls or post-menopausal women. As a rule, when the laws legislate specifically against the killing of the fetus, the male is valued more highly than the female. The only territory in which this does not hold is Saxony, which gives twice the value of a male fetus to the female, presumably because she would have been able to bear further offspring for the kin-group. Visigothic Spain implicitly distinguishes between early- and late-term abortion: the death of a fetus is subject to fine only if it has recognizable features and sexual organs. Furthermore, Visigothic law is the only code to consider the injuries incurred by a woman concomitant with an attack violent enough to cause her to abort.
4 Fines against inappropriate sexual contact, such as loosing the hair in Burgundy or touching a nun's breast in Wessex, appear only sporadically. These offences can be seen as lesser degrees of the assaults against femininity discussed above.

The last word on assaults against women belongs to the Bavarians and to Patrick Wormald:

> The provision in Bavarian law on striking a woman 'ictu quolibet' [any type of blow] appears in some manuscripts as 'coitu quolibet' (!) [any type of intercourse], or even coitu ictu quolibet (!!) [any type of intercourse blow]. This is obviously the blunder of a scribe, though it casts a lurid light on general knowledge of the law.[88]

---

88 Wormald, '*Lex Scripta* and *Verbum Regis*,' #1, 14.

8 Assaults According to Rank (Nobles and King's Servants, Freedmen, Slaves, Clerics, Foreigners)

Like gender, rank and status are of secondary interest in the personal injury schedules, which concentrate on establishing injury payments to free men and women. Some regional laws, such as those of the Bavarians and the Lombards, intersperse among the injury clauses varying values for nobles, freedmen, or slaves, but this is the exception rather than the rule. There are many problems inherent in determining fines for injury to various ranks, not the least of which is the fact that the determination of status differed greatly across territories. For example, while most regions only define one rank of manumitted slave, Kent establishes three: the penalties for killing a person in those positions are correspondingly varied. Furthermore, the relative social positions of noble, freedman, or slave differ from region to region. The discussion until now has compared apples to apples, evaluating fines for wounding freemen (and free women) across geographical and political boundaries. Within these borders, however, legal definitions of social classes are diverse enough to warrant a monograph of their own. A complete picture cannot be drawn by considering only wergild and injury fines, but must also take into account other rights and privileges that define each position within each individual territory.[1]

This chapter, then, provides an overview of general tendencies regarding wergild and recompense for personal damage, providing some specific examples. It does not pretend to give a complete picture of compensation for injuries inflicted according to rank in Germanic law, but rather seeks to identify considerations which must be taken into account when a (much-needed) full study of rank in the barbarian laws is undertaken. The notes

---

1 An introductory study for Lombardy can be found in Drew, 'Class Distinction in Eighth Century Italy,' chap. 4 in *Law and Society in Early Medieval Europe.*

to the headers on each section refer the reader to the clauses on injury specific to the category under discussion, providing guidelines for the direction of further study on rank and status.

Nobles and King's Servants[2]

Patrick Geary speculates that the reason noblemen are not included in the compensation tables for the earliest of the barbarian laws, the *Lex Salica*, is that

> a free noble could not be forced to accept compensation, which would offend the honor of his family, and thus could not be listed alongside simple freemen and royal agents.[3]

Although this code supplies only the appropriate wergilds due for killing men in various social and occupational positions, we might, however, extrapolate from these fines the equivalent difference in percentage for lesser injuries. If Geary's hypothesis is correct, we are left with the question of what happens if a free Frank should injure a nobleman. Surely this did not go unpunished. Unfortunately, however, both the legal and historical records are silent as to how such a case might proceed. It seems reasonable to assume that the freeman was assessed a fine greater than that for an identical wound to another freeman by the same multiple that he would have been assessed had he killed a nobleman. Compensation in *Lex Salica* for killing a *grafio*, 'count,' is 600 *solidi*, three times the 200-*solidi* recompense required for killing a freeman. Striking off the hand of a freeman draws a fine of 100 *solidi*; following the proportionality model, this fee might be amplified to 300 *solidi* for a *grafio*. The wergild of a *sacebaron* or *obgrafio*, 'viscount,' is only half this amount: 300 *solidi*, thus one and a half times the wergild for a regular freeman; striking off his hand might then be compensated by 150 *solidi*.[4] This hypothesis is bolstered by the fact that Burgundian law only recognizes one rank of noble, whose wergild, like that of the

---

2   Nobles and king's servants: *Lex Sal.* §§41, 42.4, 54, 63; *Liber Const.* §§2.2, 26.1; *Kent* §§13, 19; *Lex Rib.* §§11, 53; *Forum Iud.* §II, 4, iv; *Lex Sax.* §14, *2nd Sächische Königsgesetz* §7; *Lex Fris.* §§I.1–5, 8.10–16, 9.12, 17.1–2, 22.90; *Lex Thur.* §I.1,5.48; *Lex Cham.* §§7–8.
3   Geary, *Before France and Germany*, 111.
4   *Lex Thuringorum* lists the differing amounts of compensation for each body part due to a noble as opposed to a freeman. This legislative specificity seems redundant, as in all

Frankish *obgrafio*, is 50 per cent again that of a freeman. A person who strikes out the tooth of a freeman must pay recompense of ten *solidi*, while if the victim is a noble, the perpetrator is fined fifteen *solidi*. In Burgundy, the 150 per cent multiple for a noble's wergild exactly matches that for other compensations. (*Lex Ribuaria* adds the stipulation that a count might also serve as a judge, emphasizing his position in the legal system.)[5]

An example of the difficulty in assessing wounds to nobles is provided by the laws of Æthelberht of Kent, which contain only two rulings dealing with noblemen (*eorlas*). These clauses allot twelve shillings to an *eorl* if a person kills someone in his house or lies with his cupbearer (*birele*). The succeeding two clauses allot six shillings to a freeman for approximately equivalent transgressions: violating his *mund*, 'protection' (and there can be no greater violation of *mund* than the killing of a person within your house), and lying with his cupbearer.[6] From these parallels we might hypothesize that wergild and fines for noblemen were twice those of freemen. But the later Kentish laws of Hlothere and Eadric (c. 679–85) establish the wergild of a nobleman at 300 shillings – like the Frankish *grafio*, triple that of a freeman. Either the amount of wergild changed in the intervening eight decades, or there was a differentiation between the multiple for property violation (twofold) versus personal assault (threefold).

One consideration in assessing compensation for nobles is that they were expected to administer either the court hearings or the extraction and dispersal of fines. In a sense, then, they are judicial servants of the realm. This sense of royal service is extended by the Frankish conglomerate of *Lex Salica*, *Lex Ribuaria*, and *Lex Chamavorum*, which assigns a man serving in the king's service the same wergild as a *grafio*. That is, the normal 200-wergild for a freeman is tripled to 600 if he is directly under the command of the king. The Formulary of Marculf I, 18, provides a template by which this contract is legally established:

> It is right that he who promises undying fidelity to us should be protected by our help. And because our faithful follower A, with God's favour, having come here to our palace along with his weapons, was seen to swear into our hands military service and fidelity to us, we therefore decide and order by the

---

instances the fine for a noble is three times that for a freeman; perhaps the scribe was being paid by the word.

5 *Lex Rib.* §53.
6 *Kent* §§ 18–21.

present order that from now on the said A will be counted among the number of [our] antitrustions. And should someone perhaps dare to kill him, let him know that he will be liable [to pay] 600 *solidi* for his wergild.[7]

Saxon law applies this security from the time a man leaves his home, extending threefold protection to anyone going to or coming from military service. Considering the long record of Saxon rebellion and insurgency, the Franks setting the Saxon laws must have taken special care to protect those who were in place to preserve the peace.

Several territories (the Frankish group and Thuringia) demand the same threefold reparation for killing a man in his own house. These stipulations extend the concept of the king's *mund* – the protection legally offered to all under his rule. The modern British idiom that 'a man's home is his castle' seems apposite in early Germania: all the small, individual castles ruled by the heads of households are considered under the direct protection of the king. Every man is a lord in his own house. The laws of Wessex extend this protection to those who have sought sanctuary in the church: if an intruder breaks in and kills the man sheltering under the protection of God and his servants, he must pay the dead man's wergild, a fine to the community for breach of sanctuary, and forfeit any legal claim against the killed man.

Although Visigothic law prohibits any slave from accusing a freeborn, even his master, of offence, an exception is made for those raised to the king's service. These include 'the chiefs of the grooms, of the fowlers, of the silversmiths, and of the cooks; or any besides these who are superior to them in rank or position.' The *Forum Iudicum* extends this exemption to 'any slaves who are well and favorably known to the king, and who have never been guilty of depravity or crime.'[8] The concept that non-regal slaves may have come under the special protection of the king is unique in Visigothic law.[9]

---

7 Rio, trans., *The Formularies of Angers and Marculf*, 151–2.
8 *Forum Iud.* §II, 4, iv. Trans. Scott, *Visigothic Code*, s.v.
9 Conceivably *Kent* §13, ruling that a medium person price was to be paid by someone who killed a king's official [?] smith or herald/guide also refers to regal slaves. I interpreted this clause in *Beginnings of English Law* as referring to nobles of the court, who would receive an additional wergild for their service (87–8).

Freedmen and Freedwomen[10]

Our modern understanding of the differences in rank between a noble, free man, and slave is fairly straightforward. However, throughout the Germanic territories, we find another category, that of freedman. This refers to an emancipated slave; his actual rank varies according to regional manumission practice. For example, in the laws of Kent, we find three levels of *laet*, each with their own manprice. The wergild for a freeborn man is 100 shillings: killing the top rank of *laet* is fined by eighty shillings, the second rank by sixty shillings, and the third rank by forty shillings. I have argued elsewhere that this differentiation is based on a generational approach for the manumitted person from slave to freeman.[11] In the first generation he is pronounced free, but does not yet have the full status of a man born to freedom: the fine for killing a newly manumitted slave is forty shillings, the death of the manumitted slave's son is assessed at a fine of sixty shillings, and his grandson's at eighty shillings. By the fourth generation, the kin has achieved the same status as any other family born to freedom. This differentiation is unique in the barbarian laws to the kingdom of Kent (although we find similar breakdowns in Icelandic and Irish law).[12] In general, the barbarian territories recognize only one category of freedman.

Bavarian law provides us with one of the most extensive considerations of wounds to freedmen. *Lex Baiuariorum* stipulates that a man who kills a freedman must pay forty *solidi* to his (former) lord. Furthermore, it demands payments ranging from one half to one and a half *solidi* for spilling a freedman's blood to the ground; for laying on of hand, with a surcharge if the blow is struck in anger; for causing a wound which requires a doctor; and for tearing a vein. This *Lex* also stipulates payments for damage to specific body parts. Table 8.1 provides the respective tariffs and compensation rates for injuries adjudicated for both freemen and freedmen, omitting those tariffs assigned only for freemen.

---

10 Freedmen: *Liber Const.* §§5.2,4, 26.3, 32.3,5; *Kent* §27; *Lex Ala.* §77; *Edict Roth.* §§77–102, 126–9, 205–6; *Forum Iud.* §VI, 4, i, iii; *Lex Baiu.* §5; *Lex Sax.* §16; *Lex Fris.* §§I.4,7–15, 18, 21, 9.10, 12, 22.90; *Lex Cham.* §5,22.
11 See Oliver, 'Who Was Æthelberht's *laet*?' and 'Towards Freeing a Slave in Germanic Law.'
12 See Oliver, 'Who Was Æthelberht's *laet*?'

Table 8.1

Compensations for Bavarian freeman compared to Bavarian freedman

Category	Freeman	Freedman

Head	Skull
	  a. Bones from head [6]
	  b. Brain appears [12]
	Eye
	  a. Struck out [40]
	  b. Maimed [20]
		Skull
		  a. Bone from head [3]
		  b. Brain appears [6]
		
		Eye struck out [10]

Torso	Internal organs damaged [12]
	Arm
	  a. Pierced above elbow [6]
	  b. Bones from arm above elbow [6]
	  c. Pierced below elbow [3]
	Hand
	  a. Struck off [40]
	  b. Maimed [20]
	Lamed so foot drags in dew [12]
	Foot
	  a. Struck off [40]
	  b. Maimed [20]
		Internal organs damaged [6]
		
		Bone from upper arm [3]
		
		Hand struck off [10]
		
		Lamed so foot drags in dew [6]
		
		Foot struck off [10]

Fingers	Thumb
	  a. Struck off [12]
	  b. Maimed so cannot hold weapon [16]
	Forefinger
	  a. Struck off [9]
	  b. Maimed so cannot hold weapon [12]
	Either of two middle fingers
	  a. Struck off [5]
	  b. Maimed so cannot hold weapon [7.5]
	Little finger
	  a. Struck off [9]
	  b. Maimed so cannot hold weapon [12]
		Thumb struck off [6]
		
		Forefinger struck off [1.5]
		
		Either of two middle fingers off [1]
		
		Little finger struck off [1.5]

In Bavaria, the fine assessed for damage to a freedman is usually half the recompense that the perpetrator must pay if he inflicts a like wound on a freeman; the same ratio applies in Frisia and Alamannia. As shown above, the six shillings for laying open a freeman's brain is reduced to three for the same injury to a freedman, and likewise the twelve shillings for a wound causing a freeman 'to drag his foot through the dew' is halved to six for a freedman. We might thus assume that any wound to a freedman is assessed at half that assigned for the same damage to a freeborn man. However, the above chart also shows an unexpected discrepancy: gouging out the eye of a freedman or striking off his foot is fined by ten *solidi*. For a freeman, the equivalent fine is forty *solidi* for striking off; maiming the limb in question is fined at twenty. Lombard law expressly states that a maimed limb is recompensed at the same value as a limb struck off. Peculiar as this ruling may seem, it helps make sense of the apparent financial discrepancy in *Lex Baiuariorum*. Either maiming or striking off a freedman's foot is fined at ten *solidi*, half the value for maiming a freeman's foot. The laws perhaps imply that for a freedman, the catastrophe is restricted to the loss of functionality, whereas for a freeman, the visible fact of the amputation additionally represents a loss of honour in the sight of his fellow freemen. Crucially, only a freeman is assessed damages if his fingers are damaged so that he cannot wield a weapon; bearing arms was a right restricted to freemen.

The question of who should receive the fine for injuring a freedman varies from region to region. No resolution to this question is provided in Kentish law. Both Bavarian and Lombard law require the payment to go to the former master. This stipulation actually strengthens rather than weakens the status of freedman: while he may have a liminal position in the legal structure, he can still rely on his former master to represent him in a legal dispute. The laws of Alamannia, which so often mirror the laws of Bavaria, stipulate instead that the payment go to the children of the injured man or woman. Chamavan Francia and Burgundy both allow the manumitted slave his own recompense for injury. Both also require a surcharge for disturbance of the public peace. Thus, the laws of Chamavan Francia stipulate a fine for killing a freedman of 100 *solidi*, and add a payment of thirty-three and a third *solidi* to the public coffer. The total of the fine is half a freeman's wergild to the master and an extra one sixth for disturbing the peace; hardly an inconsiderable sum. Not only do Burgundy and Chamavan Francia grant the manumitted slave his own recompense for injury, they also protect his status in the public forum. Wounding a freedman in some sense wounds the very institution of manumission, and is thus fineable by payment to the public coffer.

Lombardy is unusual in equating the fines for wounds to a freedman to those for injuring a household slave, even though their wergilds differ according to position. The death of a freedman must be recompensed by sixty *solidi*; that of the best house slave by fifty *solidi*, and that of the second rank of house slave by twenty-five. Injury to top-ranking slaves is assigned an equivalent fine to that of freedmen. Other barbarian laws distinguish all freedmen from all slaves. Table 8.2 presents the respective fines for injury to Lombard freemen and Lombard freedmen or top-ranking slaves, omitting tariffs which apply only to freemen.

The respective fines for freeman and freedman indicate that in Lombardy the position of manumitted slave may have been somewhat more tenuous than in other Germanic territories. True, the most important working limbs receive major consideration: an eye, a hand, or a foot is valued at half the worth of the injured party, as for a freeborn man.[13] But elsewhere the compensation is considerably lower than the 50 per cent required for injury to freedmen in other regions. Nor is the percentage consistent: for the loss of the big toe, for example, a freeman is recompensed at sixteen *solidi*, whereas a freedman or household slave draws only a 25 per cent recompense to the (former) master of four *solidi*. The more egregious wound of breaking the leg is valued even lower for a freedman or manumitted slave: three *solidi* (i.e., less than 25 per cent) of the sixteen *solidi* assessed for merely piercing a freeborn man's thigh. However, Lombard law adds to many of these fines a crucial stipulation: if the injured party is unable to work due to the nature of the injury, the perpetrator of the wound must also pay the doctor's fee and a further amount for the work the victim was unable to perform during recovery.[14] This surcharge suggests that in Lombardy a freedman retains the obligation to perform some amount of labour for his former master.

Freedwomen

The barbarian laws do not devote much space to wounds inflicted on freedwomen. Lombardy equates their compensation schedule with that of freedmen, which seems a fair assumption for the other territories as well. Burgundian law states that uncovering a freedwoman's hair or slandering her is fined at six *solidi*. These non-maiming affronts on her virtue parallel

---

13 This ruling may provide us with insight as to the otherwise undefined intermediate position of the *esne* in Kentish law, whose eye or foot is valued at full worth. Could the *esne* represent, in other terminology, the first generation of manumitted *laet*? This hypothesis is not considered in Oliver, *Beginnings of English Law*, 114–15.
14 See Oliver, 'Sick-Maintenance in Anglo-Saxon Law.'

Table 8.2
Compensations for Lombard freeman vs freedman and house-slave

Category	Freeman	Freedman/Top Rank of Slave
Head	Scalp covered by hair a. 1st three wounds each [6] b. Bones from skull; 1st three each [6]	Head a. No bone appears: for first 2 wounds [1] b. Bone appears [4]
	Wound to face [16]	Wound to face [2]
	Eye a. Struck out [½ wergild] b. Eye struck out from one-eyed man [⅔ wergild]	Eye a. Struck out [½ worth] b. Eye struck out from one-eyed man [full worth]
	Nose a. Struck off [½ wergild] b. Wound leaving scar [16]	Nose Struck off [8]
	Ear a. Struck off [¼ wergild] b. Healed wound [16]	Ear Struck off [2]
	Lip a. Sliced [16] b. Cut so teeth appear [20]	Lip Cut so teeth appear [4]
	Teeth a. That appear in smile [16] b. Molars [8]	Teeth a. Front [4] b. Molars [2]
Torso	Chest pierced [20]	Chest pierced [8]
	Arm a. Pierced through [16] b. Pierced, not through [8]	Arm a. Broken [6] b. Pierced through [3] c. Pierced, not through [1]
	Hand a. Struck off [½ wergild] b. Maimed, not off [¼ wergild]	Hand Struck off [½ worth]
	Thigh a. Pierced through [16] b. Pierced, not through [8]	Thigh a. Broken [3] b. Pierced through [3] c. Pierced, not through [1]
	Foot a. Struck off [½ wergild] b. Maimed, not off [¼ wergild]	Foot Struck off [½ worth]

Table 8.2 (*Continued*)
Compensations for Lombard freeman vs freedman and house-slave

Fingers and Toes	Thumb off [¼ wergild]	Thumb off [8]
	Forefinger off [16]	Forefinger off [6]
	Middle finger off [5]	Middle finger off [2]
	Ring finger off [8]	Ring finger off [2]
	Little finger off [16]	Little finger off [4]
	Great toe off [16]	Great toe off [4]
	2nd toe off [6]	2nd toe off [2]
	3rd toe off [3]	3rd toe off [2]
	4th toe off [3]	4th toe off [1]
	Little toe off [2]	Little toe off [1]

those discussed in chapter 7 for similar attacks on a free-born woman; just as with wounds, these offences against freedwomen are to be compensated at half the amount required for similar transgressions against women born free. Finally, in Chamavan Francia, if a freedwoman is raped, she is due her own wergild, and an additional ten *solidi* must be paid to her former owner. As seen in the fines for damage to freedmen, Chamavan Francia took especial care to protect those who had been manumitted. This may recognize their intermediate legal status: they have more rights than slaves but have not yet attained the personal legal position of those born free.

Slaves[15]

Although Chamavan Francia is the only territory to equate freedmen with any rank of slave, several Germanic territories establish a hierarchical wergild structure according to the occupational position of the slave. Indeed, it is far more common for the barbarian laws to consider the worth of slaves than the worth of freedmen. In all laws which address the payment of recompense, reparation is due to the master, and it is a fair assumption that this held for all barbarian territories.

---

15 Slaves: *Lex Sal.* §§25.1–2, 5–6, 35.1, 7-9, 65f; *Liber Const.* §§5.3,5, 10, 26.4, 30, 32.3,5: Kent §16, 19, 21, 26, 79-81; *Lex Rib.* §§8–10, 14, 19–28; *Lex Ala.* §81; *Edict. Roth.* §§77–128, 130–7, 207; *Forum Iud.* §VI, 4, i, iii; *Lex Baiu.* §6; *Lex Sax.* §17; *Lex Fris.* §§I.11–22, 4.1, 13; *Lex Thur.* §§I.3–25, IV.56; *Lex Cham.* §6,23; *Wessex* §25. On Frankish formulae concerning slavery, see Rio, *Legal Practice*, 212–28.

Table 8.3
Values of Slaves

Worth	Lombardy	Salic Francia	Burgundy
150			*minora persona* goldsmith
100			silversmith
30 + 45 to public peace		(special status slaves) a. male household slave b. female household slave c. ironsmith d. goldsmith e. swineherd f. vintner g. stablehand	
60 + 12 to public peace			house slave
50	a. top rank house slave b. pig man supervising 3 boys		ironworker
25	a. 2nd rank house slave b. lesser pig man		
40			carpenter
30			field slave
20	a. shepherd b. goatherd c. plowman		
16	apprentice		

A slave is valued according to worth (=property value) as opposed to wergild (=man-price); the latter could only be assigned to a person who controlled his own legal status. Although the actual amounts vary, certain salient facts emerge in these valuations. All three of these regions differentiate between house slaves and field slaves. Both Francia and Burgundy assign greater worth to artisans: goldsmiths, silversmiths, and (in the case of Burgundy) carpenters. Despite the later reputation of Burgundy as the premier producer of French wines, it is western Francia that includes vintners in this group. Lombardy concentrates rather on agricultural functions. Interestingly pig men are equated with house slaves, while shepherds, goatherds, and plowmen are valued less highly. Perhaps the proximity of the pigsty to the household requires that the supervisor be a man of greater trustworthiness than the more remote shepherd or plowman.

Table 8.4
Compensations for Lombard freedmen/house slaves vs. field slaves

Category	Freedmen/House Slaves	Field Slaves
Head	Head a. No bone appears: for first 2 wounds [1] b. Bone appears [4]	Head a. Scalp torn; first 3 wounds [1] b. Bone(s) broken [3]
	Wound to face [2]	Wound to face [1]
	Eye a. Struck out [½ worth] b. Eye struck out from one-eyed man [full worth]	Eye a. Struck out [½ worth] b. Eye struck out from one-eyed man [full worth]
	Nose Struck off [8]	Nose Struck off [4]
	Ear Struck off [2]	Ear Struck off [1]
	Lip Cut so teeth appear [4]	Lip Cut so teeth appear [3]
	Teeth a. Front [4] b. Molars [2]	Teeth a. Front [2] b. Molars [1]
Torso	Chest pierced [8]	Chest pierced [3]
	Arm a. Broken [6] b. Pierced through [3] c. Pierced, not through [1]	Arm a. Broken [3] b. Pierced through [2] c. Pierced, not through [1]
	Hand Struck off [½ worth]	Hand Struck off [½ worth]
	Thigh a. Broken [3] b. Pierced through [3] c. Pierced, not through [1]	Thigh a. Broken [3] b. Pierced through [2] c. Pierced, not through [1]
		If arm, thigh, or tibia does not heal [¼ worth]
	Foot Struck off [½ worth]	Foot Struck off [½ worth]

Table 8.4 (Continued)
Compensations for Lombard freedmen/house slaves vs. field slaves

Category	Freedmen/House Slaves	Field Slaves
Fingers and Toes	Thumb off [8] Forefinger off [6] Middle finger off [2] Ring finger off [2] Little finger off [4] Great toe off [4] 2nd or 3rd toe off [2] 4th or little toe off [1]	Thumb off [4] Forefinger off [3] Middle finger off [1] Ring finger off [1] Little finger off [2] Great toe off [2] 2nd or 3rd toe off [1] 4th or little toe off [½]

Frisian law allows the master to set the worth for a slave who is killed: this must surely have produced many hotly contested discussions in legal proceedings. One other note of interest is that the fines assessed in *Lex Salica* apply not only to killing, but also to stealing a slave of special status. Both offences rob the master of the work of his slave.

Although the Lombard pig man may have a greater total worth than his less-smelly livestock-handling competition, his wounds seem to be equated with theirs rather than those of his equally valued house slave companions. Table 8.4 presents the relative values of wounding for freedmen and house slaves compared to field slaves.

In most instances, a wound to a field slave is valued at half the amount for the same injury to a freedman or house slave. The exceptions are for the major limbs of eye, hand, and foot, which are valued as half the worth of the slave. Thus, striking out the eye of a freedman or top-rank house slave is fined at twenty-five *solidi*, whereas the identical injuries to a shepherd or plowman are assessed at a mere ten *solidi*. These stipulations seem based on social theory rather than occupational logic: surely it is easier to prepare or serve dinner with one hand than to steer a plow. But a freeman's damaged house slave will likely be seen by more of his neighbours, who might be tempted to gossip about the visible affront inflicted upon his property. In Lombardy an injured slave's master must be recompensed both for medical fees and for any work lost by his slave while the slave is incapacitated, just as he would for his injured manumitted slave.

Clauses regarding damage to slaves include injuries which are not necessarily debilitating. In Lombardy, fines are assigned for striking blows against slaves which raise bruises. Bavarian law echoes the regulations addressing injury to freedmen, requiring recompense for laying on a hand; a

Table 8.5
Compensations for slaves in Lombardy, Ripuaria, Bavaria

Category	Lombard Field Slave	Ripuarian Slave	Bavarian Slave
Head	Head a. Scalp torn; first 3 wounds [1] b. Bone(s) broken [3] Wound to face [1]		Head Brain appears [4]
	Eye a. Struck out [½ worth] b. Eye struck out from one-eyed man [full worth]	Eye Struck out [18]	Eye Struck out [6] Upper eyelid [1] Lower eyelid [½]
	Nose Struck off [4]	Nose Struck off [18]	Nose Gashed [6]
	Ear Struck off [1]	Ear Struck off [18]	Ear a. Struck off [1½] b. Gashed [1] c. Deafened [4]
	Lip Cut so teeth appear [3]		Upper lip [1] Lower lip [½]
	Teeth a. Front [2] b. Molars [1]		Teeth a. Canine tooth [3] b. Other teeth [1½]
Torso	Chest pierced [3] Arm a. Broken [3] b. Pierced through [2] c. Pierced, not through [1]		Internal organ damaged [4]
	Hand Struck off [½ worth]	Hand Struck off [18]	
	Thigh a. Broken [3] b. Pierced through [2] c. Pierced, not through [1]		
	If arm, thigh, or tibia does not heal [¼ worth]		Lamed so foot drags in dew [4]
	Foot Struck off [½ worth]	Foot Struck off [18]	
		Castrated [36]	

Assaults According to Rank 217

Table 8.5 (*Continued*)
Compensations for slaves in Lombardy, Ripuaria, Bavaria

Category	Lombard Field Slave	Ripuarian Slave	Bavarian Slave
Fingers and Toes	Thumb off [4] Forefinger off [3] Middle finger off [1] Ring finger off [1] Little finger off [2] Great toe off [2] 2nd or 3rd toe off [1] 4th or little toe off [½]		Thumb off [4] Forefinger off [2] Middle finger off [1½] Ring finger off [1½] Little finger off [2]

blow struck in anger; (probably additionally) a wound in which blood is spilled to the ground or there is swelling from the wound; a vein torn; or a bone driven out. All these regulations may be in part motivated by the consideration that such damage to an owner's slave is a visible affront to his *mund*. These regulations may thus address insult to the master as much as injury to his slave. (This analysis assumes that an owner could legally physically punish his slave without paying damages.) Burgundy addresses similar assaults: a man who attacks a slave can be assessed for bruising him with whip, stick, kick, or punch, pulling his hair with either one or both hands (with a higher fine assessed for the latter), striking out a tooth, or binding him. However, only in Burgundian law is a surcharge to the public coffer added to the fine due to the slave's master. These additional payments seem to protect the position of slave beyond the simple happenstance of ownership. All slaves are to some extent protected by the state.

Table 8.5 provides an overview of the recompense required for damage to slaves in those regions which specify anatomical injury.

This table unsurprisingly demonstrates that anatomical consideration given to slaves in each region is a subset of that given to free men under the same territorial law. Ripuaria concentrates only on the most major of limbs. Lombardy and Bavaria retain much more of the detail ascribed to injuries against free men. This retention includes the primarily cosmetic ruling in Lombardy against slicing a lip so the front teeth appear. In Bavaria, damage to a slave's upper or lower eyelid is regulated individually. This is also true for Bavarian free men, but not for Bavarian freedmen. Apparently Bavarian legislators were more interested in protecting the property value inherent in slaves than providing security for freedmen, that is, the sequence of composition of these tariffs (no matter in what

Table 8.6
Relative compensations for Bavarian freeman, freedman, slave

Category	Freeman	Freedman	Slave
Head	Skull a. Bones from head [6] b. Brain appears [12]	Skull a. Bone from head [3] b. Brain appears [6]	Skull Brain appears [4]
	Eye a. Struck out [40] b. Maimed [20]	Eye Struck out [10]	Eye Struck out [6]
	Upper eyelid maimed [3] Lower eyelid maimed [6]		Upper eyelid maimed [1] Lower eyelid maimed [½]
	Ear a. Pierced [6] b. Struck off, no deafness [20] c. Wounded, deafness [40] d. Visibly maimed [6]		Ear a. Struck off [1½] b. Deafness [4] c. Maimed [1]
	Nose Pierced [6]		Nose Struck off [6]
	Upper lip maimed [3] Lower lip maimed [6]		Upper lip maimed [1] Lower lip maimed [½]
	Teeth a. Canine [12] b. Other [6]		Teeth a. Canine [6] b. Other [3]
Torso	Internal organs damaged [12]	Internal organs damaged [6]	Internal organs damaged [4]
	Arm a. Pierced above elbow [6] b. Bones from arm above elbow [6] c. Pierced below elbow [3]	Bone from upper arm [3]	
	Hand a. Struck off [40] b. Maimed [20]	Hand Struck off [10]	Hand Struck off [6]
	Lamed so foot drags in dew [12]	Lamed so foot drags in dew [6]	Lamed so foot drags in dew [4]
	Foot a. Struck off [40] b. Maimed [20]	Foot Struck off [10]	Foot Struck off [6]

Table 8.6 (*Continued*)
Relative compensations for Bavarian freeman, freedman, slave

Category	Freeman	Freedman	Slave
Fingers	Thumb a. Struck off [12] b. Maimed so cannot hold weapon [16]	Thumb Struck off [6]	Thumb Struck off [4]
	Forefinger a. Struck off [9] b. Maimed; cannot hold weapon [12]	Forefinger Struck off [1.5]	Forefinger Struck off [2]
	Either two middle fingers a. Struck off [5] b. Maimed; cannot hold weapon [7.5]	Either two middle fingers Struck off [1]	Either two middle fingers Struck off [1½]
	Little finger a. Struck off [9] b. Maimed; cannot hold weapon [12]	Little finger Struck off [1.5]	Little finger Struck off [2]

order they appear in the manuscripts) must have addressed 1) injuries to free-born men, including damage to eyelids; 2) injuries to slaves, including (lesser-valued) damage to eyelids; 3) injuries to freedmen, in which damage to eyelids is not considered.

Finally, as for a free man, the fine for killing a slave rises if he is in the king's service or in the service of the church. Exactly as for a freeman, the multiple is (at least approximately) three. In Ripuarian Francia, killing a slave is fined by thirty-six *solidi*, whereas killing a king's man or the church's man draws a penalty of 100 *solidi*. If this slave is injured, the normal assessment rises to half the fine assigned for freemen: both rank (=slave) and position (=servant of church or king) are taken into account when assessing these penalties.

As an intermediate summation of the sections on injuries to freedmen and slaves, Table 8.6 provides a schematic of the Bavarian assessments of damage to freemen, freedmen, and slaves.

The first, and obvious, conclusion to be drawn from Table 8.6 is that the law was far more concerned with regulating damage to freemen than to those with lesser status. Thirty clauses address injury to free-born men; only eleven to freedmen, and seventeen to slaves. But, at least in Bavaria, the value of a slave as property received greater consideration in the law than that of a freedman with his intermediate status. As a general rule, the compensations to freedmen and slaves represent a ratio of those assigned for equal injury to a free-born man: the freedman is assessed at 50 per cent, and the slave at roughly (but not always) 25 per cent. We might be tempted to generically extend assessment for all freemen's wounds to the lesser ranks by an equivalent percentage. This conclusion is, however, somewhat facile, as consideration for injury may in some instances have been extended to address the functionality of slaves.

Some curious statistics demonstrated in Table 8.6 support this hypothesis. One might expect damages to a freedman to be assessed more stringently than those to slaves, but this is only true in part. Injury to a slave's major limbs of eye, hand, or foot are fined 60 per cent of the assessment for the same fine to a freedman. Similarly, causing a slave's brain to appear, gouging out his eye, laming his knee, or damaging an internal organ is fined 66 2/3 per cent of the assessment for similar damage to a freedman. The same is true for maiming the thumb. But curiously, the fingers are assessed higher for the slave than for the freedman. The only explanation I can offer for this is that the value of a slave's fingers in terms of the work they help the hand perform is more crucial to the master than the value of the fingers of a man who does work (at least a portion of) on his own behalf. This hypothesis receives support from the fact that in Visigothic law, damage to a slave was valued at half that of a free-born, while an injury to a freedman was assessed at one-third that of a free-born. We see here again, as we did in the legal statutes prohibiting mutilation of a slave, the value that Visigoths placed upon their non-free workers.

Women Slaves

Barbarian legislators were far more interested in women slaves than they were in freedwomen, and the patterns of offences regulated against them generally match those for free women discussed in the previous chapter. A slave woman can produce both work and offspring for her master, while a manumitted female slave has been released from these obligations. The former thus finds more secure protection in the laws than the latter, who has been released (at least partially) from the protection of her master. *Lex Salica* provides a penalty of thirty-five *solidi* for a man who kills or steals a female slave;[16] in either instance, the owner will be deprived of her child-bearing ability as well as her work. *Lex Chamavorum* demands fifty *solidi*

---

16 This fine applies when the perpetrator is a freeman; if he is a slave, the owners divide his work.

for killing a female slave belonging to the church, and an extra sixteen and two thirds to the public coffer. The attack against the property of the church represents a breach of public security.

As for free-born women, rape is the offence most commonly legislated against in regard to female slaves (although crucially not applicable to the owner, who can do with his property as he likes). The laws of Kent are particularly prolific in regard to consideration of rape of non-free women. First, they address position, requiring twice the fine for raping a nobleman's cupbearer (*birele*) as a freeman's (twelve shillings to the nobleman, but six to the freeman). For a king's slave, the rape of a maid (presumably first rank of house-slave) draws a fifty shilling fine; that of a 'grinding slave,' responsible for food preparation, twenty-five shillings, and that of a slave of the lowest rank twelve shillings. Both household and cooking slaves are valued more highly, as they must be the most highly trusted. Since either would have the best opportunity to introduce poison into their master's drink, their character and loyalty must be beyond question. They are also difficult to replace (as an unwise choice could prove fatal), and this may account for an extra payment required by law. A woman working throughout the household would have the further opportunity to, for example, introduce a poisonous snake into the regal bed; thus she is worth even more than the woman relegated to the kitchen. Finally, Æthelberht §78 states: 'If a person lies with an *esne's* wife while the husband is alive, let him pay 2x what he would have paid were she unmarried.'[17] An *esne* seems to have had an intermediate status between freedman and slave (unless, perhaps, he represented the lowest rank of freedmen).[18] It is not clear who receives the fine for her rape, although the implication is that it goes to her husband.

Regulations in most other territories are more straightforward. *Lex Alamannorum* requires a six *solidi* fine for raping a house-slave, and a three-*solidi* fine for any other slave. The laws of Wessex set a penalty of five shillings (presumably paid to the owner), but add a whopping sixty shillings to the public coffer. Even an enslaved woman was due royal and public protection against rape.

Lex Ribuaria is the only text to specifically address the child-bearing capabilities of female slaves, although only in regard to the elevated slaves of the king or of the church. Killing a woman slave of child-bearing age draws a fine of 300 *solidi*; killing a girl or a woman over forty (thus no

---

17 Translation from Oliver, *Beginnings of English Law*, 79.
18 See ibid., 114–15.

longer able to produce offspring) is fined by 200. As for free women, the penalty for killing is increased during a slave woman's fertile years.

Finally, Burgundy provides fines for non-maiming offences to women slaves similar to those laid down for freewomen. Any violence (although presumably this means violence such as bruising rather than maiming) draws a fine of twelve *solidi*. The fine for cutting the hair of a female slave is six *solidi* plus two to the public coffer. Uncovering hair or slandering her is assessed at three *solidi*. It is interesting that the importance of curly locks pertains to slave women as well as free women: perhaps the shearing of hair renders a female slave a less valuable commodity on the open market.

Male and Female Religious[19]

Several regions address the special position of members of the clergy in cases of assault, as shown by Table 8.7.

All these laws agree in assigning an enhanced value to members of the church, although there appears to be no uniform system for determining this enhancement. Ripuaria classifies only the wergild due to various ranks of churchmen: a subdeacon's is twice that of a freeman, a deacon's two and a half times, a priest's three times, and a bishop's nine times. Ninefold recompense for injury to a freeman is the degree of compensation for a Visigoth king, so perhaps the Ripuarian laws equate the position of bishop and king: one guards the spiritual flock and the other the temporal folk.[20] *Lex Ribuaria* further assigns a threefold compensation for injury done to those under the protection of the church, identical to the ruling for those under the protection of the king.

Alamannia takes a different approach, multiplying the fine for any offence against a churchman according to his ecclesiastical position, and perhaps his status as well. Certainly both are true for the position of bishop, who is compensated for offences at thrice the amount due to a layman of the same rank. Thus a freeman who becomes a bishop, would have a wergild of 600 *solidi*.[21] Neither Alamannia nor Bavaria specify the wergild of

---

19 Clerics: *Lex Rib.* §§10, 36.5–9; *Lex Ala.* §§7–17; *Lex Baiu.* §1.5, 8, 9; *Lex Sax.* §5.
20 See Wallace-Hadrill, *Early Germanic Kingship in England and on the Continent*, 41. Against this, set the laws of Kent, which demand a greater recompense for stealing from a bishop than for stealing from a king. As these clauses address theft and not assault, I have not included them in the analysis here. For further discussion, see Oliver, *Beginnings of English Law*, 44–6.
21 Pope Gregory VII, for example, was the son of a man of low degree – his father is described variously as a peasant or a carpenter. Other bishops who rose from the rank of

Table 8.7
Compensations for male religious

Rank↓ Region→ Freeman's Wergild→	Ripuaria 200 solidi	Alamannia 200 solidi	Bavaria 160 solidi
Bishop	900 *solidi*	3x fine for rank	
Free Presbyter (Bavaria = parish priest)	600 *solidi*	3x fine	Wergild 300 *solidi* Fine 3x
Deacon	500 *solidi*	2x fine	Wergild 200 *solidi* Fine 2x
Monk		2x fine	2x fine for rank
Subdeacon (Bavaria adds lector, exorcist, acolyte, doorkeeper)	400 *solidi*		2x fine for free man
Cleric	According to blood rank	Add 1/3 to fine if he is performing service	

nobles. If, however, this man-price were to equal threefold that of a freeman, as is true in the Frankish territories, the wergild of a noble bishop would rise to a whopping 1800 *solidi*. In essence, an unpayable amount. *Lex Saxonum* recognizes this financial impossibility by assigning a death sentence to the killer of a bishop, priest, or deacon. A presbyter is also fined at thrice the value for his rank, but in this case the laws imply that this cleric was free-born. If he is in the act of performing the service, a 1/3 surcharge is added to the fine; not only is he God's servant, but he is actively engaged in God's work. An added amount is thus assigned for the additional offence against the Lord.

Finally, Bavaria draws on both conventions, specifying both wergild and rank. Interestingly, the clause requiring twofold fine due a monk adds the defining factor of *sicut parentes*, 'according to (the rank of) his relatives.' Perhaps this means that nobles might humble themselves to become monks (and indeed, we find many examples of this in the literature), as every monk in some sense is an individual worshipper. He might, however, be less likely to join the ecclesiastical hierarchy in the subordinate

---

freeman are Robert Grosseteste and Fulbert of Chartres. See *Catholic Encyclopedia Online*, http://catholic.org/encyclopedia, s.v. Gregory VII, Grosseteste, Fulbert.

position of subdeacon.²² Conversely, perhaps the phrase *sicut parentes* was simply omitted as redundant from the subsequent clause. Bavaria's listing of clerics seems to hark back to the tradition of Isidore, who defines *clerici* as including the *ostiarius, psalmist, lector, exoricista, acolythus, subdiaconus, diaconus, presbyter, episcopus*, 'doorkeeper, psalmist, reader, exorcist, acolyte, subdeadon, deacon, priest, bishop,' in reverse order of status.²³

Regarding the women in the church, the laws of Wessex demand twofold compensation for seizing a nun in lewd fashion by her clothes or by her breast. Bavarian law requires a twofold compensation for assaulting any servant of the church. The fact that Anglo-Saxon laws single out women in this respect is ominously echoed in later English history:

> In a denunciatory letter directed to King Ethelbald of Mercia, Boniface and other bishops condemned the king for his sacrilege of adulterous behavior 'committed in convents with holy nuns and virgins consecrated to God.' King Edgar (959–75) was also severely reprimanded by the Church for his abduction and violation of nuns.²⁴

Violation of nuns was not unique, however, to Anglo-Saxon England. An addition to the Lombard laws, probably by the highly Christian Liutprand, calls for a surcharge for abducting (and presumably raping) a nun. And Bavaria requires twice the fine for abducting a nun as for abducting a betrothed woman, on the premise that

> we know that the abduction of another's betrothed is a punishable crime; how much more punishable is a crime which usurps the betrothed of Christ.²⁵

Foreigners²⁶

The most difficult clauses to subsume under any generalization are those against attacking foreigners. This fact is unsurprising, as foreigners may

---

22 The position of subdeacon could actually be a pretty high rank depending on what diocese it was in. Furthermore, the subdeaconate could also be a preliminary position held for a number of years before higher ordinations were conferred. The office could thus be seen as subordinate, but not necessarily lowly.
23 See Du Cange, *Glossarium Mediæ et Infimæ Latinitatis*, 2:367–8.
24 Schulenberg, *Forgetful of Their Sex*, 140.
25 For Lombard and Bavarian rulings, see Schulenberg, *Forgetful of Their Sex*, 142.
26 Foreigners: *Lex Sal.* §41; *Lex Rib.* §36.1–4; *Lex Cham.* §3.

include others from Germanic territories, subject to their own laws in their homeland. Thus I provide here only two selected instances. *Lex Chamavorum* requires a wergild of 600 *solidi* for killing a foreigner (*wargengum*), but adds an additional surcharge of 200 to the public peace if the victim was a Frank, thus more closely politically connected to the native territory. *Lex Ribuaria* requires a compensation of 200 *solidi* for killing a Frankish man, but the fine is reduced to 160 if he came from the Germanic territories of Burgundy, Alamannia, Frisia, Bavaria, or Saxony. If he was a Roman, the fine sinks to 100 *solidi*. Thus these two legal collocations present opposing views of the worth of foreigners. The more hospitable Chamavan Francia accords them a higher protection than its own citizens, with possible echoes of an ancient tradition of honouring one's guest. Conversely, Ripuarian Francia preferences its own citizens.

Conclusion

What does this brief survey of relative assessments tell us about rank and status in the early Germanic territories? The fundamental value of a person is determined at birth: a baby enters the world with the rank of noble (with possible gradations), free-born, or slave. But none of these positions are necessarily permanent throughout the person's life span.

A man or woman may rise in legal value by the choice of profession. All entering the service of the church are assessed for damages more highly by virtue of their position as God's servant. The same is true for servants of the king, although this enhancement may be only temporary depending on whether the assignment itself is permanent (such as a position in the king's retinue) or temporary (such as participation in the king's army in time of war). A locational enhancement is also due to free-born men and nobles if they are injured within their homesteads, as they have the right to assume security under their own roofs. This surcharge would not apply to slaves, as they are housed by their masters.

Conversely, a man may have to deliberately lower his legal status if he performs a delict and is unable to pay the assessed fine. One option open to him is to indenture himself to the kin of the victim, serving as a penal slave until he has performed sufficient labour to pay off the fine. An example of this was mentioned in chapter 7, in which a man who abducts a betrothed woman and is subsequently captured must submit himself to the will of her family. (Such downward mobility is, of course, only open to nobles or free-born men, as slaves are already at the lowest end of the hierarchy. For equivalent offences, slaves are usually put to death.) I know of no evidence that disambiguates whether a man in the position of temporary servitude is recompensed for injury under the law according to his birth rank or to his current, lower status.

The children of women who marry outside their rank assume the birth status of the husband. Thus a free-born woman could ensure noble status for her children by marrying up: this is the scenario provided by the popular medieval story of Griselda, recounted by Chaucer in the Clerk's Tale. If, however, a free-born woman marries a slave, her children will also be considered slaves. I see no reason not to assume that a slave woman born to a cowherd who subsequently marries a pig man would not be able to claim enhanced slave status for her children. Furthermore, a female slave with a particular knack for cooking might raise her position within the household from daughter of a shepherd to cook for the master, with an enhanced concomitant worth.

Outside all of these considerations are slaves who have been manumitted. Occupying a liminal territory where they are neither enslaved, nor completely free, freedmen present the most complex and understudied rank in early medieval society. Barbarian laws present conflicting evidence as to how they were treated. In Bavaria and Lombardy, for example, a freedman was still obligated to work for his former master, who also continued to receive payment for injuries to his former slave. In contrast, Chamavan Francia took especial care to protect freedmen in their intermediate status; for example, not only does a manumitted slave receive his own compensation for inflicted injury, but the perpetrator is also fined for disturbance of the peace.

9 Summary: A Review of What Personal Injury Tariffs Have Told Us about Transmission of Law

This discussion gathers the evidence from the preceding chapters to summarize what these examinations have demonstrated about how law was transmitted throughout the Germanic regions. The personal injury tariffs were chosen as the focus of this investigation precisely because they are new within the written legal collocations. Retention of clauses from previous Roman legislation tells us nothing about transmission, as the incorporation of any such rulings could be independently borrowed from existing Roman law. Conversely, personal injury clauses are specific to the Germanic laws. They are free from the historical authority of Rome, and are the best indicators of geographical, political, or literary influences on the setting of laws within the Germanic territories. Keeping in mind the possible associations laid out in Table 1.1, we will now revisit some of the connections laid out in the previous chapters. Earlier discussions indicated possible interrelationships between various regions in respect to individual fines. What we are looking for now is repeated matching patterns.

First, let us re-examine the rulings on the 'Matthew limbs' (see Fig. 9.1). The dominant pattern follows that of Salian Francia which demands a half wergild for striking off hand, foot, or eye; nonetheless, a 50 per cent ratio is obvious enough to be trivial, and I do not believe much emphasis can be placed upon regions connected by this feature. Of greater interest are those territories that vary from the norm. Here we see a parallel between Alamannia and Bavaria; a connection echoed by textual similarities elsewhere in the laws. We also see a possible geographic link between Frisia and neighbouring Chamavan Francia.

In the case of clauses relating to the sensory organs of eye, nose, and ear (see also Fig. 9.1), some regions equate the three, whereas others assign the ear only half the value of the eye and nose. As in the Matthew limbs tabulation,

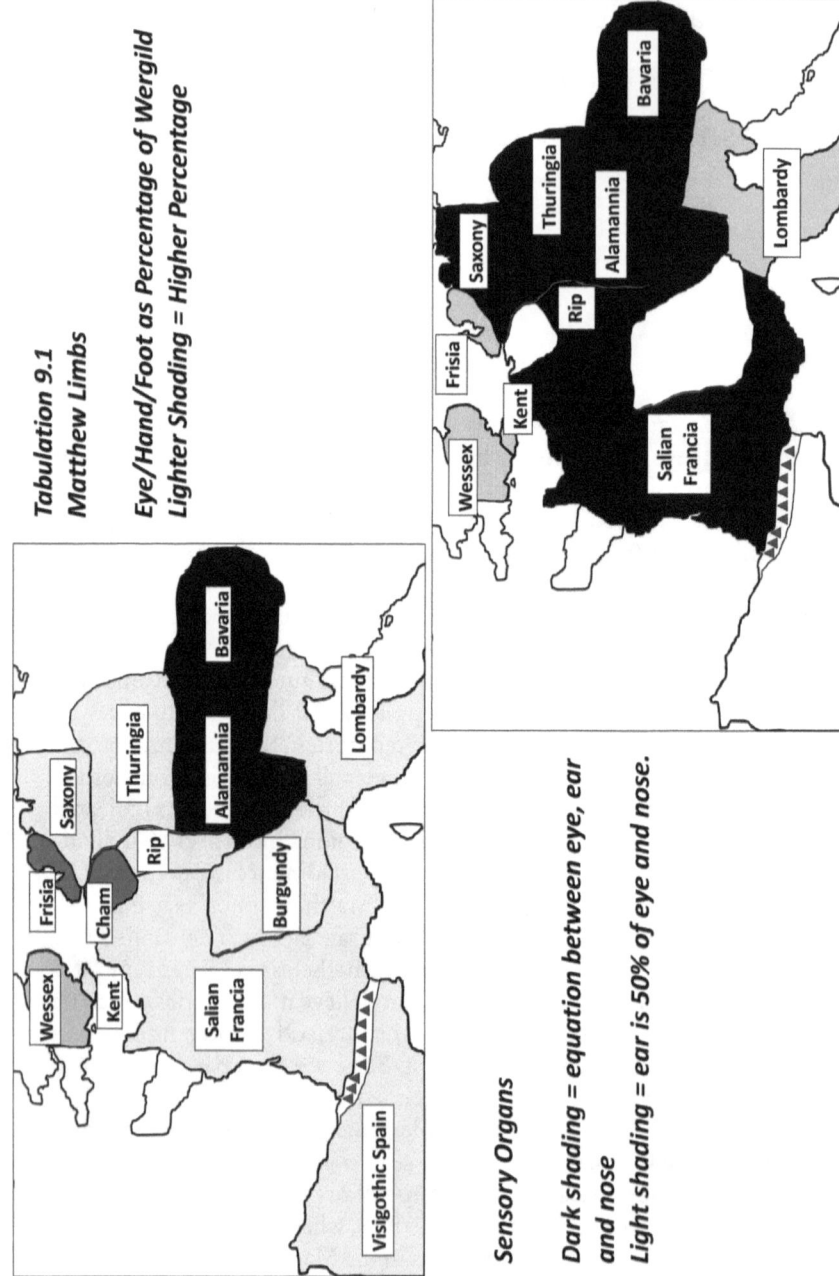

Figure 9.1 Tabulations for 'Matthew limbs' and sensory organs.

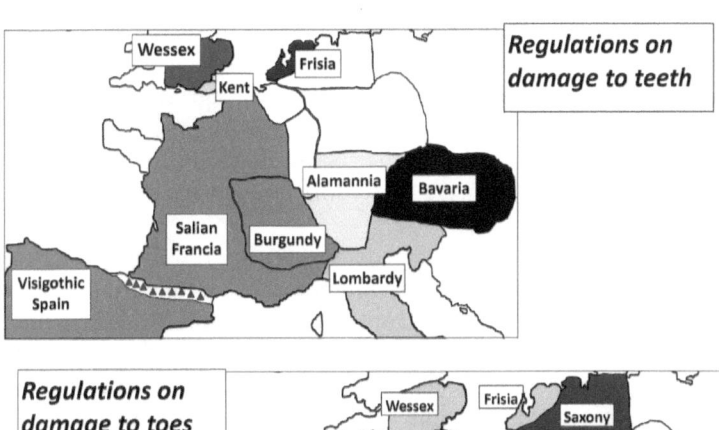
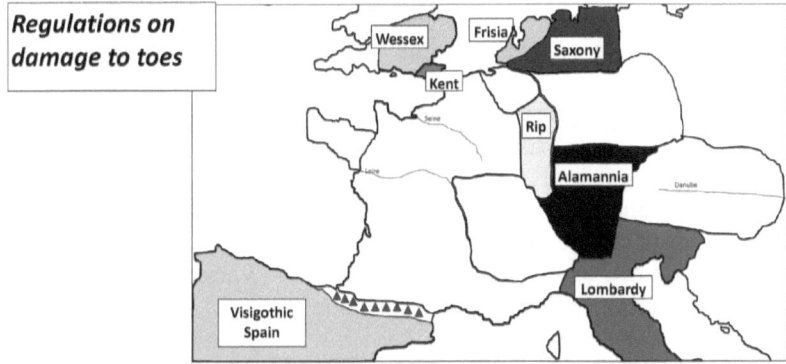
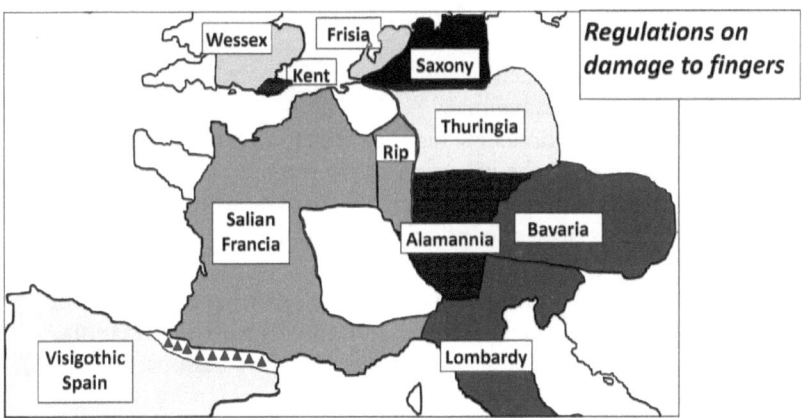

Figure 9.2 Tabulations of valuation of teeth, toes, fingers according to functional worth.

we see general agreement with Salian Francia. Once again, the exact equation of eye, ear, and nose does not represent a startling legislative position. However, we might postulate a weak tendency for agreement with the Frankish centre. Striking is the agreement within the Anglo-Frisian grouping of Kent, Frisia, and Wessex (in order of composition). In the case of Visigothic Spain, fines for damage to sensory organs are determined in each case by the presiding judge.

Next, I would like to collate maps demonstrating the distribution of how closely regional regulations match functional value for various limbs. Reproduced below are three maps from previous chapters, all of which shade the assessment of wounds based on approximation of worth according to physiological function. In all cases, darker indicates a closer agreement with anatomical worth, while lighter indicates greater interest in visible damage.

The most striking phenomenon demonstrated by the juxtaposed maps in Fig. 9.2 is almost total disjunction between all regions. The important exception is provided by Frisia and Wessex, who agree in every instance. The maps for toes and fingers tend to be shaded more darkly in the east, which may suggest that the eastern kingdoms took greater interest in anatomical function. But this tendency is not strongly pronounced. Figure 9.3, presenting number of body parts represented in the laws, appears to provide some support for this hypothesis. Certainly the western Frankish kingdoms, Visigothic Spain, and Burgundy show the least interest in detailed anatomical breakdown. But although the eastern territories demonstrate slightly more specificity than the Frankish regions, the greatest attention to anatomical detail is supplied in the Anglo-Frisian grouping (with the exceptional addition of Alamannia).

I would like to add three new maps to the tabulations above, providing geographic schemata of the valuation of the testicles, the equation of arm and leg, and the consideration of internal organs (see Fig. 9.4).

These three maps present conflicting geographic connections.

1 The genitals are not considered at all in the southeastern regions of Burgundy, Lombardy, and Bavaria, and only barely in Alamannia. Salian authority might be seen in the Ripuarian valuations, as the two are the same (while the laws of Chamavan Francia ignore the torso altogether). The similarly equal Thuringian ruling may also show Salian influence. The Anglo-Frisian group divides here. The highest fine for damage to the genitals is found in the laws of Kent; the laws of Wessex, however, contain close to the lowest. Frisia and neighbouring

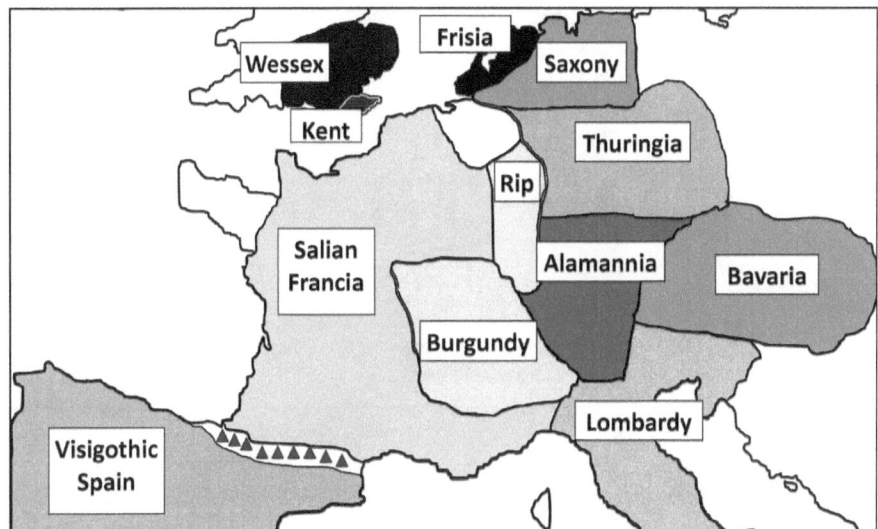

Figure 9.3 Tabulation of valuation of torso.

Saxony are also high, but neither approach Kent. With the exception of Wessex, the differentiation here is north/south, rather than the east/west tendencies we have seen earlier.

2 None of the Frankish territories contain rulings considering damage to arms and legs, which might be seen as an influence stemming from Salian Francia. The Anglo-Frisian alliance is fractured in a different combination. Kent, Wessex (and far-off Bavaria and Visigothic Spain) all assess damage to the arm more highly than the leg. Frisia is once again allied with its neighbour Saxony, as Alamannia is allied with its neighbour Lombardy, all of which assign a greater value to the leg than the arm. Thuringia and Burgundy both ascribe higher fines to wounding the arm than the leg.

3 The territories which consider damage to internal organs are those in the west (subsuming the Anglo-Frisian unit), and the doublet of Alamannia/Bavaria. Salic Francia alone of the remaining regions addresses such damage.

I would like to present one final group of data before pulling together the final results: the sparse linguistic evidence we can glean from word use. The most obvious connection is provided by the Germanic term *taudragil*,

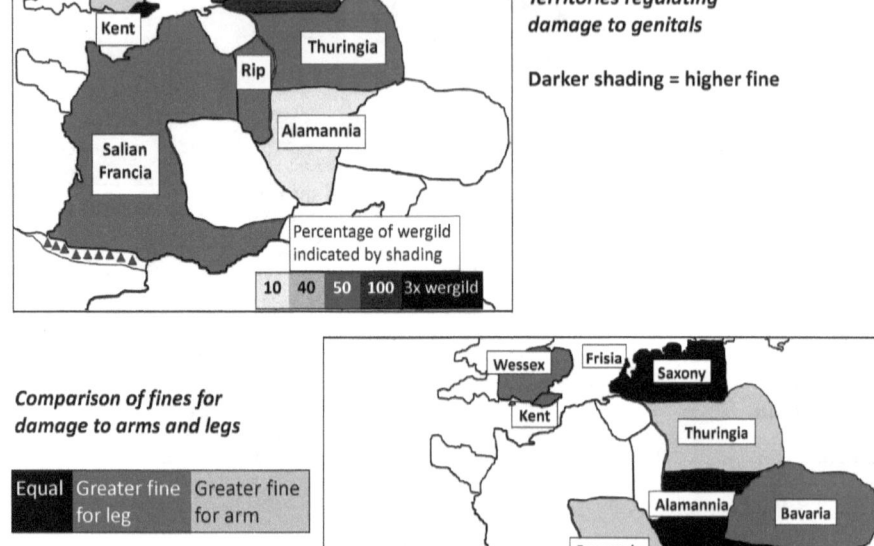

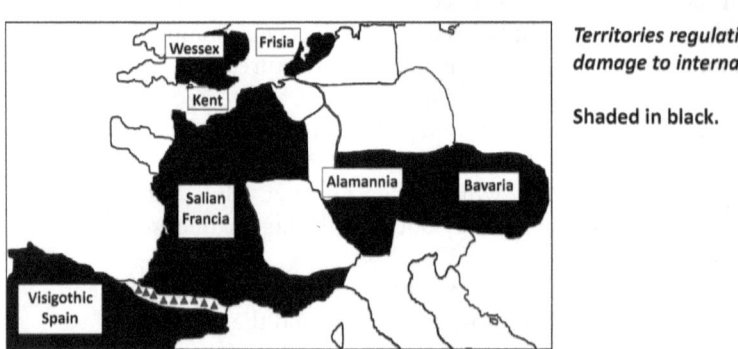

Figure 9.4 Tabulations of regulations for damage to genitals, arms and legs, internal organs.

'dragging in the dew,' which links the Alamann and Bavarian laws to the exclusion of any others: not only are they the only regions to use the compound, but they are also the only territories to include the concept of laming so that the foot is left dragging. This connection is strengthened by their shared use of Germanic *scardi/scarti* to describe a sliced ear. Another Germanic term used by both is Bavarian *hrevavunt*, Alamann *hrevovunt* or *reveunt*, 'wounded in the abdomen.' The compound itself does not really help much in an argument about influence from Alamannia on Bavaria, as it simply represents the Germanic way of saying 'abdominal wound'; we find the identical collocation in Kent's *hrifwund*. What could be adduced as evidence, however, is the fact that only these two territories choose to insert this native term into the Latin context of their laws.

I place little importance on Kent and Thuringia's parallel use of Germanic *wlitewam*, 'disfigurement of countenance.' Several laws have similar rulings in which the damage is described in Latin, such as Lombardy's *plaga in facie*. I would see Thuringia's incorporation of the Germanic term not as an echo of Kentish law, but as an indication of Thuringian lawmakers' understanding of the native and historical importance Germanic peoples put on wounds to the face, with the concomitant damage to honour.

Finally, let us return to the distribution of names for fingers, as illustrated in the Fig. 9.5. In regard to forefinger names, the Anglo-Saxon territories align with the Latin of the Salian and Ripuarian Franks. Frisia joins its northern continental neighbours, Saxony and Thuringia. Interestingly, the *mallberg* gloss in *Lex Salica* contradicts the association made by the Latin text; while the Latin word matches the usage in the Anglo-Saxon regions, the native term agrees with the northeast continental grouping. It is crucial to remember here that we are not considering an isogloss that represents the speech patterns of an entire community, but simply the instantiations used by the compilers of the laws. In the case of legal terminology to describe the forefinger, the scribes of the Latin laws followed a different custom than indicated by the native language practice.

In regard to the ring finger, we see some interesting divergence from the groupings for the forefinger. Saxony and Thuringia are still united in terminological choice, as are the Anglo-Saxon territories. But the Frisian term and the *mallberg* gloss now both parallel forms used in Anglo-Saxon legislation, whereas before they aligned with the continental regions of the northeast.

Finally, although not indicated in these maps, the neighbouring territories of Frisia and Saxony and of Bavaria and Alamannia all have extensive breakdowns of fines for damage to individual joints of the fingers.

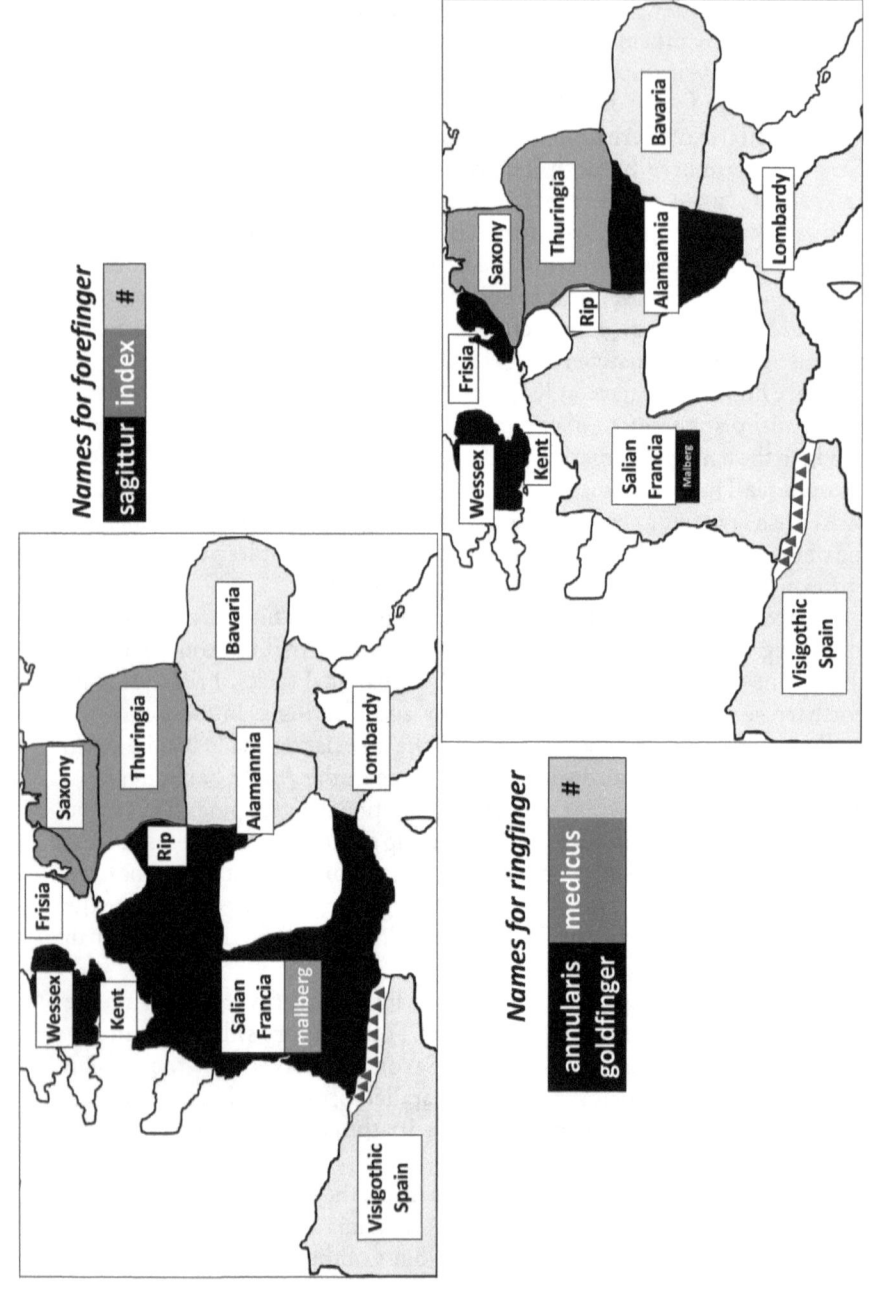

Figure 9.5 Terms for fingers.

Summary of Connections

1 *Francia*. Unsurprisingly, we may centre the locus of the connections in continental Europe in Salian Francia, with the exception of the laws of the Lombards and of the Burgundians. This holds particularly true for the valuations of major limbs and sensory organs (Fig. 9.1; 9.2). Most other considerations show more differentiation, although Ripuarian Francia and Chamavan Francia only separate themselves from Salian Francia once each when rulings are actually expressed (Fig. 9.3; 9.1 respectively). The injury tariffs then provide us with further evidence – as if more were needed – of the domination of the Salian Franks over their neighbours the Ripuarians and the Chamavans.
2 *Alamannia/Bavaria*. Again, the personal injury tariffs mirror what we know about the connections between these territories. Although they do not always agree, the overlap is significant. They differ together from the Frankish group on valuation of major limbs (Fig. 9.1); they assess sensory organs the same; they both include detailed anatomical breakdown of fingers; and they are the only eastern territories to address damage to internal organs. Furthermore, they insert identical Germanic terms into their Latin texts: *taudragil*, 'dragging in dew'; *scarti*, 'sliced,' and *hrevavunt*, 'wounded in the abdomen.'
3 *Anglo-Frisia*. The territories of Kent, Frisia, and Wessex often work in unison: regulations of sensory organs (Fig. 9.2), specificity of anatomical breakdown (Fig. 9.3); consideration for damage to internal organs (Fig. 9.4); and name of the ring-finger (Fig. 9.5). These territories share both a linguistic subgroup and geographical proximity to the North Sea. Even closer is the connection between Wessex and Frisia, which add to the similarities listed above the comparative valuations of teeth, toes and fingers (Fig. 9.2); furthermore, they are the only two regions to regulate against loss of synovial fluid. In fact, Frisia and Wessex are in agreement more than any other territories outside the Frankish regions. Clearly Frisians knowledgeable in their own law had a much greater influence on the compilation of Alfred's laws than has been recognized to date.
4 We find sporadic parallels between adjacent territories, which may show areal influence and may simply be coincidence. For example, Frisia and Saxony share the valuation of the genitals and the equation of fines for arm and leg (Fig. 9.4). Saxony and Thuringia both use identical terminology for both forefingers and ringfingers, and neither consider damage

to teeth – although as an argument from silence, not much weight should be attached to this shared omission (Fig. 9.5; 9.2).

5 Discussed earlier, although not yet mentioned in this chapter, are some curious connections between the laws of Bavaria and those of Visigothic Spain. The Visigoths specifically require a judge to determine the fine for wounds to the face according to severity; the Bavarian song of Count Timo seems to allow the judge the same flexibility. Outside of Visigothic Spain, only the Bavarian laws allow a freeman to be lashed in public; furthermore both permit the legal striking out of an eye. These two regions also share the feature of valuing damage to slaves higher than that of freedmen. The Visigoths began their trek to settle in Spain from an area near where the Bavarian confederation was formed. We may be seeing ancient legal traditions of eastern Europe preserved in these two, now widely separated, regions.

6 Finally, with the exception of damage to the genitals, the major divisions seem to lie between east and west. Patrick Wormald draws a differentiation between south and north, with southern legislation more likely to actually be used in court. He postulates that this is because 'the Roman example was more alive in southern than in northern Europe. In Italy, Spain and Southern Gaul, written acta remained central to legal procedure. Roman law was not here a "ghost story," as, in Vinogradoff's words, it was to the north ... It was thus the environment that made the crucial difference to the scope and character of legislation for the southern German kingdoms.'[1] Once again, however, we must make the distinction between the laws as a whole, and those which were specifically created for the Germanic territories by their own peoples. These latter clauses are the personal injury tariffs. And in these, we find that the divide falls between west and east rather than north and south. We find this in the regulation of anatomical functions, in which the east tends to adhere more closely than the west to physiological verity (Fig. 9.2); in the middling specificity of the anatomical breakdown (Fig. 9.3); in either equating the value of arms and legs, or assigning higher fines for damage to legs (Fig. 9.4); and in the names of fingers (Fig. 9.5).

As a final note, then, we find both geographic proximity and political influence at work in the setting of the laws. This is not surprising, as the two are often related. For example, the area of Francia included the territories

---

1 Wormald, '*Lex Scripta* and *Verbum Regis*,' in *Legal Culture* #1, at 24.

of the Salian, Ripuarian, and Chamavan Franks. Not only were these adjacent but they were also all under the dominion of the Salian Franks. The connections between Alamannia and Bavaria can be attributed as much to their contiguity as to the fact that they were both under Frankish domination when the laws were set. The Frisian influence on the laws of Wessex is purely political: Frisians are known to have been in residence at the court of Alfred, and it is clear from the data above that they contributed to the setting of his laws. Finally, the general east/west divide may be attributed to areal diffusion.

Conclusion

My brother Bim suggested that this conclusion follow the pattern of many modern movies, which examine what the lives of the various characters were like ten years later. Unfortunately, this is not an option for the individuals we have met in the preceding pages: they remain to us only in the brief snapshots that literature provides of crucial moments in their lives, or in artistic representations in visual or plastic arts, or in the enduring record their bones have left in archaeological records.[1] Adding to these the evidence of legal rulings allows us to extend our picture of early medieval society beyond the contemporary fragments from these literary, artistic, and archaeological traces. Although the addition of this data helps flesh out the lives of victims and aggressors in the various social strata of medieval Europe, we cannot definitively arrive at the description of any single incident of assault from initial motive to final resolution.

Thus I would instead like to conclude this study by reconsidering the questions posed in the introduction. The first series is directly pertinent to the personal injury tariffs, and I will provide answers drawn solely from this data. Personal injury lawyers, insurance adjustors, and disability advocates, take note: these questions and answers are the foundation upon which your professions are based. The responses provided by the written law may, however, provide only an incomplete picture of the totality of legal knowledge, as discussed further on.

---

1 Fleming, 'Bones for Historians,' pulls off the feat of reconstructing lives from the traces of disease left in the archaeological records.

1. What is the value of the left arm? Is it worth less than the right arm? Is it worth more or less if the victim is left-handed?
The written laws never distinguish between predominant and non-predominant limbs. Only occasionally is profession taken into account: in Frisia, a harpist or goldsmith, whose profession depends upon full use of his hands, is assigned a greater recompense for his maiming. Even in this instance, presumably the plucking hand would be more crucial to the harpist's ability to perform than the harp-holding hand. A modern parallel might be seen in theatrical wig-makers, who crucially rely on both hands and all fingers to accomplish their craft. But the predominant hand accomplishes most of the fine detail work, and thus should be assessed more highly in law.

2. Is it worse to lose an arm than a leg?
According to most Germanic laws, these are either equated, or the leg is valued more highly. I do not believe that this proportion was any more appropriate then than it would be now. Most professions rely on the function of the arm with the attached hand. A leg, conversely, is generally supportive, but not irreplaceable. As the archaeological data adduced earlier demonstrates, a successful prosthesis can now, and could then, replace the function of the leg and foot. Far more flexibility is available in modern times with advanced technology, such as the motorized wheelchair. Although medical science has made great strides in reproducing the function of a missing hand with mechanical substitutes, the loss of a hand still seems more devastating than the loss of a leg. The wig-maker introduced above could still produce brilliant confections with two functional hands and a missing leg, but would be far more constricted were it a hand that had been maimed.

3. An eye?
Consistently, the Germanic territories place the highest valuation on the loss of an eye. Another of my brothers, Gus, lost the sight in his left eye in his early teens as the result of poor medical treatment. He later went on to summer jobs teaching tennis; clearly he had been able to compensate for the partial loss of vision. In fact, our family had mostly forgotten this disability until he was called up for the draft in the Vietnam war, where he was classified as 4F (disabled) due to blindness in one eye. Obviously, he would have received a similar classification had he lost his leg. But the body compensates better for the loss of physical perception than the loss

of functional ability. The high assessment of the eye in medieval law may be an instance of additional payment for visible damage to the face with attendant insult to honour.

4. The sense of smell, with concomitant loss of taste?
Some of the Germanic territories regulate against damage to the sense of smell, but none of them associate it (at least in writing) with the related loss of taste. This combination, however, is far more dangerous than many realize. The loss of smell precludes, for example, the ability to sense dangerous odours such as smoke or (in more modern times) chemical elements released in an enclosed space. The combined loss of the senses of taste and smell presents the possibility of eating spoiled food, perhaps causing temporary or even fatal illness. The latter danger seems to have been one early medieval societies did not take into (at least legal) consideration. We might, however, consider the possibility that their digestive systems were simply more accustomed to processing food that we, in these times of ubiquitous refrigeration, might consider no longer edible.

5. To what extent should cosmetic damage be valued?
All Germanic territories rule visible damage more highly than injuries which are hidden by hair or clothing. These rulings demonstrate the importance that early medieval society placed on honour. An obviously visible injury adds a resultant wound to your reputation in the community. Honour-price is no longer given the same consideration in current law. Although some modern cases have provided payment for plastic surgery to repair cosmetic damage, the underlying motivation seems to be to mend appearance rather than to maintain status within the community.

6. How does an injury affect the ability of the wounded to provide for the family?
This consideration is addressed in only two of the Germanic laws. Those of Kent are the only ones to regulate for the period that a wounded free-born man must lie in bed: the fine stipulated is a flat fee of thirty shillings. This seems a bit odd, since differing wounds will take differing amounts of time to heal. Perhaps this sum represented a maximum fine, which could be lowered if the recuperation time were short. The Lombard laws concern not lasting injury to free-born men, but to freedmen and slaves. Here the restitution is defined as the amount that the owner (or former owner) lost while his worker was incapacitated. This clearly represents a sliding

scale, depending on the time needed for convalescence sufficient to allow the wounded person to resume his or her duties.² Many workers today buy disability insurance, which will provide payment during the period of recuperation. This practice shifts responsibility from governmental authority to the individual, and favours the wealthier section of the population, who can afford to buy such insurance.

This first series of questions and answers are based on a selection of the rulings directly addressing injury and the required recompense. But the previous chapters have also raised some more global questions, the ramifications of which are considered below.

*1. When should a fetus be considered a child in its own right?*³
The fourth-century doctor Vindicianus claims that the soul is assigned to the fetus in the third month:

> In the first month the ejaculation of our semen is gathered in the umbilic: this is the gathering together. In the second month the body is expressed. In the third month, because the body was formed earlier, soul is given to it ...⁴

This makes sense, as most miscarriages occur in the first trimester of pregnancy. Not until this dangerous period has passed does the fetus change to the status of child *in utero*. *Lex Salica* requires a 600 *solidi* fine for killing a pregnant woman. Since the normal wergild was 200 *solidi*, the penalty must include payment of her wergild, that of the child, and another 200 *solidi* for the horror of the offence. (The premium placed on male children is demonstrated by the 600 *solidi* surcharge if the unborn child was male.) Both Salian Francia and Ripuaria assess an additional 100-*solidi* fine if the baby is killed in the womb or in the first nine days, before it has a name (thus before baptism). The baby thus has yet to be relieved of original sin by the sacrament of baptism. An unbaptized child would likely go to the

---

2 Oliver, 'Sick-Maintenance in Anglo-Saxon Law.'
3 An overview of this issue is provided by Niederhellmann, *Arzt- und Heilkunde*, 124–8; I do not always agree with her analysis.
4 'Primo mense iactus semenis nostri in utero materno congregator in umbilicum, in hoc est congregatio. Secundo mense expressio est corporis. Tertio mense, quia priore formatum est corpus, ei tribuitur anima ...' Wellmann, *Fragmente der Sikelische Ärtzte*, 218–19. On the assignment of the soul, see also Niederhellmann, *Arzt- und Heilkunde*, 134–8.

Limbo Infantium – a sort of Garden of Eden where it would experience natural but not supernatural happiness since it would be deprived of the Beatific Vision.[5] The added surcharge, then, might be to penalize the killer for taking away the unborn infant's opportunity for the supernatural happiness of the Beatific Vision. Crucially, it is baptism and not birth that marks the change when a child takes its own place in society and is legally assigned its own wergild according to rank. An interesting variation is provided by the Alamann laws, in which a child assumes legal status after he has lived outside the womb *unius horae, ut possit aperire oculos et videre culmen domus et quatuor parietes*, 'one hour, so that it can open its eyes and see the roof of the house and the four walls.'[6]

No question is more fraught with anxiety in the United States today than the concerns raised above. Two differing approaches to these difficult issues are provided in the medieval laws. On the one hand, a fine (such as we might see for property damage or injury) is assigned for killing a fetus. On the other hand, a child possesses its own wergild, with the accompanying sense that it will grow to adulthood and participate in the workings of society. Medieval texts thus indicate that although the fetus becomes human at three months by being infused with a soul, it only becomes a part of the community after baptism. Do these analyses answer the problems facing legal scholars in the United States today? Sadly, no. Should we define a human being as a formed fetus with the concomitant infusion of a soul, or as a baby possessing the ability to exist independently outside the womb? The same questions recur in contemporary religion and politics, and they are, then as now, probably and unfortunately, not reconcilable.

2. Are the effects of all rapes equivalent? What if the woman is pregnant? Married? Underage?
As a rule in Germanic law, the fine for rape is equated with the fine for murder. Some territories distinguish between raping either married or unmarried women, although the proportion is not consistent: some regions give more value to a woman of child-bearing years, while others assign a greater fine for raping a virgin. The clauses which distinguish medieval rape laws from modern practice are those addressing abducting (and presumably raping) a maiden who has been betrothed to another. This

---

5 See *Catholic Encyclopedia Online*, http://catholic.org/encyclopedia, s.v. Limbo.
6 *Lex Ala* §89; see discussion in Niederhellmann, *Arzt- und Heilkunde*, 125–6.

distinction is economic. When a man betroths himself to a virgin girl, he pays a bride-price to the head of her kin-group. She will now be responsible for carrying on her future husband's family line. If she is subsequently abducted and raped, he loses his investment: she is now damaged goods, and any child she bears him within the next nine months must be suspect. The laws recompense him for the down payment he has put on an unsullied virgin. Today, at least in the western legal offspring of the Germanic laws – the United States and Europe – no similar economic strictures apply.

The archaeological record in early medieval Europe suggests a perception that somehow the victim of rape may have brought it upon herself. Regrettably, this interpretation persists from the early Middle Ages until the present time. How else can we account for the fact that in the modern press rape victims' names are not released? If they were not somehow culpable, why should their identities be hidden? Rape is a violent, not a sexual, crime. But throughout history, women have often been unfairly considered complicit in the action.

3. What is lost when oral transmission is converted to writing? To what extent does inherited wisdom continue to be transmitted from master to apprentice?[7]

This question provides a fitting conclusion to this study, as it extends far beyond the field of law to encompass the mechanisms of human memory, and to open the philosophical inquiry as to what advantages are produced by the technology of writing. No written record can recreate the actual remembrance of any particular event, as not only the details of the happening, but also the concomitant aromas, sounds, and general ambiance are committed to memory. It is very different to read the National Anthem than to hear it sung at the ballpark. In the former instance, I am likely sitting inside, isolated from the world at large. In the latter, I am standing in Fenway Park as one of a multitude, smelling with them hotdogs, popcorn,

---

7 The tension between orality and literacy has recently seen some excellent studies. An overview can be found in Havelock, *The Muse Learns to Write*. Particularly relevant to the period discussed in this monograph are Innes, 'Memory, Orality and Literacy in an Early Medieval Society'; and 'Orality and Literacy in Frankish Society,' in Rio, *Legal Practice and the Written Word in the Early Middle Ages*, chap. 1. For (semi-)contiguous periods of later medieval England, see Clanchy, *From Memory to Written Record*; and Stock, *The Implications of Literacy*; Gellrich, *Discourse and Dominion in the Fourteenth Century*.

and beer; hearing with them planes overhead and the occasional cry of 'Yankees suck!'; feeling with them the sun beating down on the bleachers; and sharing with them the communal anticipation of the game to come. Overall atmosphere, at least, can only be transmitted in an oral recounting: by gesture, facial expression, and tone of voice. Words on a page cannot convey the wealth of extra-verbal impressions provided by any spoken narrative; while the former could be considered a ground-plan, the latter could be viewed as the constructed entity. However, we would be mistaken to assume that oral relations are therefore more accurate than written accounts. A good analogy is provided by the children's game 'Telephone,' in which the first child whispers something to the second, who passes it on to the third, and thus around the circle. The last in line then speaks aloud the received utterance, to accompanying gales of laughter when everyone hears how the statement has changed from initial input to final output. Each listener becomes an active participant in the transmission process, adding his individual interpretation to the data.

I would like to return to a type of oral transmission more directly pertinent to the present study – that of the legal strictures of pre-literate Germanic society. Here we find a functionary known in Iceland as the *løgsøgumaðr* or in Saxony as the *êosago*, 'lawspeaker,' who was responsible for the accurate memorization and proclamation of the law.[8] In Iceland, the entire body of law would be recited aloud over three summer parliaments. In modern times, when we rely heavily on written aids to memory, this might seem a prodigious feat. However, the training that now goes into teaching composition and computer skills was then focused on techniques of memorization. The Indic *Rig Veda* was transmitted for years using precise memorization methods that preserved archaic linguistic forms for centuries. An Icelandic saga presents us with the vignette of a dying hero who wishes to compose one last (very long) poem. He ranges his household on either side of his bed, instructing those on the right to memorize the odd-numbered verses, and those on the left the even-numbered ones. None of his kin seem to have found this assignment difficult or peculiar. The talents of the lawspeaker were not unique, although they were probably more highly developed than those of the layman. Furthermore, the lawspeaker focused his attention and skills specifically on the preservation of legal texts.

---

8 Oliver, *The Beginnings of English Law*, 35.

Conclusion 245

It seems unlikely, however, that these oral versions of the laws were simply transferred intact to the new medium of writing. First, there needed to be an impetus to switch technologies: such an incentive was often provided by an individual ruler who would naturally want to add his own rulings to the existing law. Second, this technology was expensive: many sheep gave their lives so that the Salic laws could be preserved on parchment. Probably only what were considered the most important clauses were committed to writing; others remained live in judicial memory. Certainly the request by a litigant that a *iudex* 'speak to us the Ripuarian law' implies legislation beyond that which exists in the books. The appeal that the *iudex* speak and not read the law indicates that the written legislation gives a selected outline of the totality of legal practice.

Similarly, the records of actual cases provide only brief fragments of the full narrative of an incident from the first infraction of the law to the final issuance of the quit-claim in court. Reconsider, for example, the case from Sens in which a woman fell upon a man and his wife, broke the man's knee, and killed the couple's daughter. These details provide the sum of the evidence left to us; their fragmentary nature serves rather to arouse than to assuage our curiosity. Without doubt, this narrative survived in the community in oral form with considerably more elaboration – in fact, it was likely embellished over the years. What, then, was the purpose of committing this scant outline to writing? Such limited accounts must, at least sometimes, have been produced in the settlement of disputes. Records of specific cases could be turned into formulaic documents, to provide models upon which later, similar actions would be judged. (Here names of people and places are represented in the document by X, to be substituted with the name appropriate to the case.)

These formularies lead naturally into the question of what might be the advantage of committing law to writing? Written records standardize the core of procedure throughout a widespread territory. A case from Tours can be brought into a court in Lyons, which is governed by a very different communal memory. The *rachimburgi* in Lyons now have access to precedents established according to the same written *lex*, but in an area with different remembered *mores*. Customary law, then, can spread beyond the regional boundaries established by family or community interchange.

Does written law, then, supersede oral transmission? Not at all. Let us return once again to the savage attack discussed above. In Lyons or Tours, the courts have access only to the particulars captured in the written records. But in Sens, the memory of the attack may still be fresh, even generations later. Once again, the 'Telephone' effect comes into play:

'I heard the woman was the man's aunt.'

'No, he married his aunt; she was his childhood sweetheart who felt jilted by the economically advantageous marriage.'

'Actually, the attack was aimed at the daughter, who fed the killer's children rotted meat while babysitting, causing them days of severe intestinal distress.'

Whatever the actual circumstances of the case were, they would be coloured through the process of narrative repetition. The further removed the intellectual community is from the pre-literate days of training in memorization, the more dissimilar the account of a previous assault may be from the actual event. In a Germanic court, judgment was a communal process, undoubtedly taking into account both written strictures (*lex*) and local precedent (*mores*). The more distant geographically and chronologically the precedent was from the event itself, the more likely the rulings were to be standardized based on the recorded formula.

In a day in which technology permits almost instant purveyance of information around the world, we might suppose that law has become standardized internationally. Of course, this is not the case. Although the parameters of *mores* may have stretched, communal memory – both written and recounted – still plays a part in adjudicating cases. Both the legal structure and the precedents adduced in a Japanese court remain very different from those brought before a court in England. The laws and precedents that apply in federal courts in the United States differ from those which apply in state laws. But most crucially, no matter how extensive these written records may be, they still lack the ability to provide a full picture of the ramifications of any case. This failure provides job security for trial lawyers, whose responsibility it is to add life to the mute words of the texts. Both now and in the past, the records contained in lawbooks are analogous to what we find in the cemeteries of early medieval Europe: bones that can tell us a great deal but can never represent a living figure.

This discussion completes my series of queries with a long – although not nearly extensive enough – treatment of an issue pertinent both to modern scholars and to practitioners of law: the comparative advantages and disadvantages of orality and writing. I hope that it serves as a model for my readers, who are hereby enjoined to set and answer their own questions pertaining to their specific interests. To the best of my ability, I have laid out the data on personal injury and assault in early medieval law. It is now up to you to apply this in your own fields. This final discussion, then, represents not a conclusion, but a commencement.

Appendix

Charts of Wergild Values in Germanic Injury Laws.

The following charts collect the data on fines for assault from each territory in descending order of amount. These fines should be evaluated as percentages of the wergild listed at the top of each page. Schematics representing these data more completely are available on the webpage of University of Toronto Press. The tables in this appendix are presented in order of the chronological setting of the laws:

Salic Francia (507 x 511)	248
Burgundy (517)	248
Kent (c. 600)	249
Alamannia (beginning of 7th century)	250
Ripuarian Francia (623)	252
Lombardy (643)	253
Visigothic Spain (654)	254
Bavaria (745)	255
Saxony (785)	256
Frisia (785 x 803)	257
Thuringia (802 x 803)	259
Chamavan Francia (c. 813)	259
Wessex (890 x 901)	260

Appendix

Lex Salica 507 x 511 (Wergild = 200 *solidi*)

Wergild (%)	Fine	Head	Torso	Hands/feet
100	200		• penis off	
50	100	• eye out • ear off • nose off • tongue off so cannot speak	• penis pierced/maimed	• hand off • foot off
31.25	62.5	• eye gouged • ear gouged • nose gouged	• continuously running wound	• hand cut through • hand maimed • foot off
25	50			• thumb off • great toe off
22.5	45		• binding freeman and taking to another place	• foot maimed
17.5	35			• forefinger off
15	30	• 3 bones out of skull	• ribcage pierced • stomach pierced • binding freeman	• thumb maimed
7.5	15	• blood from head runs to ground • brain shows • tooth out	• blood from blow with stick • wound with iron weapon	• middle finger off • ring finger off • little finger off
1.5	3		• 1st 3 bloodless blows from stick each • 1st 3 blows with closed fist	

Liber Constitutionum Burgundy 517 (Wergild = 200 *solidi*)

Wergild (%)	Fine	Head	Torso	Hands/feet
50	100	• eye	• arm off	
10	20		• arm broken; healed without scar • tibia broken; healed without scar	
5	10	• tooth		
2	4	• hair pulled two hands [+6]		
1	2	• hair pulled with one hand [+6]		

Domas Æðelbirhtes Kent c. 600 (Wergild = 100 shillings)

Wergild (%)	Fine	Head	Torso	Hands/feet
300	300		• genital organ damaged	
50	50	• eye out		• foot off
30	30		• shoulder maimed • wound causing bedridden • wound requiring doctor's care	
25	25	• ear unable to hear		
20	20	• both *tabula* broken • jawbone broken		• thumb off
12	12	• eye maimed • ear off; no deafness • mouth maimed • speech damaged	• abdomen wounded • abdomen pierced through • thigh broken	
11				• little finger off
10	10	• outer *tabulum* broken		• great toe off
9	9	• nose gashed		• shooting finger off
6	6	• greater disfigurement of face • nose pierced • both cheeks pierced • throat pierced • incisor	• collarbone broken • arm pierced • arm broken • genital organ pierced through • genital organ stabbed into • thigh stabbed into	• goldfinger
5	5			• small toe off
4.5	4.5			• 2nd toe off
4	4	• ear gashed • canine	• cut bone	• middle finger off
3	3	• lesser disfigurement of face • ear pierced • cheek pierced • premolar and molars	• blow with fist to nose • exposed bone • rib broken • thigh wound over 3 inches	• thumbnail off • fourth toe off
2	2		• thigh wound over 2 inches	• middle toe off
1.5	1.5		• bruise outside clothing	• big toenail off
1	1		• blow with raised hand • bruise covered by clothing • thigh wound over 1 inch	• fingernail off
1/2	1/2	• seizing of hair		• toenail off

Appendix

Lex Alamannorum early 7th century (Wergild = 200 *solidi*)

Wergild (%)	Fine	Head	Torso	Hands/feet
40	80		• arm off at shoulder • leg off at thigh	• foot off
20	40	• brain appears in skull; surgery required • eye torn out • ear struck off; deaf • nose struck off • tongue struck out	• arm off at elbow • intestine damaged so excrement comes out	
12	24		• side pierced through	
10	20	• eye damaged; vitrium remains • tongue half off; semi-intelligible	• arm maimed, useless • penis unable to have erection	
6	12	• hair cut against will • brainpan broken; brain appears • lower eyelid cannot hold tears • ear struck off; not deaf • nose tip off; cannot hold mucus • lower lip cut; cannot hold saliva • middle four upper teeth out	• elbow maimed, cannot carry or lift hand • side pierced, organs wounded • thigh pierced • knee lamed so foot drags	• thumb off • little finger off
5.5	11			• index finger off
4	8			• ring finger off
3	6	• spall sounding across street • upper eyelid cannot close • ear sliced • nose pierced • upper lip cut; teeth appear • beard cut against will • bruise to face not covered by beard or hair • middle four upper teeth struck • canine tooth out	• collarbone • arm pierced above elbow • arm broken above elbow, skin intact • side pierced, organs intact • tibia below knee (alt.3)	• 1st joint thumb off • middle finger off • 1st joint little finger off • great toe off

Lex Alamannorum early 7th century (Wergild = 200 *solidi*) *(Continued)*

Wergild (%)	Fine	Head	Torso	Hands/feet
2.5	5			• 2nd joint index finger off
1.5	3	• brainpan scraped	• arm pierced below elbow • arm broken below elbow, skin intact • hernia expressed • tibia below knee (alt. 6)	• vein on hand pierced • 2nd joint middle finger off • 2nd joint ring finger off • all but great toe off
1	2			• 1st joint index finger off • 1st joint ring finger off
.75	1.5			• hand pierced, veins intact • 1st joint middle finger off
.5	1	• molar out	• blow in anger • blood spilled to ground	

Appendix

Lex Ribuaria 623 (Wergild = 200 *solidi*)

Wergild (%)	Fine	Head	Torso	Hands/feet
100	200		• castration	
50	100	• eye out • ear off, deafness • nose off; cannot hold mucus		• hand off
25	50	• eye remains; cannot see • ear off; no deafness • nose off; holds mucus		• hand maimed • foot off • thumb off
18	36	• skull-bone sounding in shield	• ribcage pierced • blood spilled to ground • bone broken • body pierced	• foot maimed • forefinger off • toe off
	30		• binding	
12.5	25			• thumb maimed
9	18			• forefinger maimed
1.5	3		• 3 blows	
1	2		• 2 blows	
.5	1	• each subsequent sounding skull bone	• 1 blow	

Edictus Rothari Lombardy 643 (Wergild = 200 *solidi*)

Wergild (%)	Fine	Head	Torso	Hands/feet
66		• striking out eye from one-eyed man	• binding	
50		• eye out • nose off	• ambush and beating without king's order	• hand off • foot off
25		• ear off		• hand maimed • foot maimed • thumb off
10	20	• lip cut so teeth show	• chest pierced	
8	16	• wound scar on ear • wound scar on nose • cut lip • wound in face • tooth that appears in smile	• arm pierced through • thigh pierced through	• forefinger off • little finger off • great toe off
6	12	• each of first 3 spall bones from skull		
4	8	• each molar	• arm pierced, not through • thigh pierced, not through	• ring finger off
3	6	• each of first 3 wounds to head covered by hair • slap		• 2nd toe off
				• middle finger off
1.5	3		• 1st 4 blows at sudden fight causing bruise or wound • blow with fist	• 3rd toe off • 4th toe off
1	2			• small toe off

Forum Iudicum Visigothic Spain 654 (Wergild = 200 *solidi*)

Wergild (%)	Fine	Head	Torso	Hands/feet
		• 30 lashes for blow to head in which blood does not flow • 10 lashes for premeditated slap	20 lashes for blow with fist or kick	
	Judge decides penalty	• ear • lip • nostrils		
	1 pound gold	• eye maimed, can still see	• breaking leg	
50	100	• broken bone in head • nose entirely destroyed	• hernia • slap or blow arising from quarrel	• hand struck off or useless • foot struck off or useless
25	50			• thumb struck off or useless • great toe off or useless
20	40			• forefinger off or useless • 2nd toe off or useless
15	30			• middle finger off or useless • 3rd toe off or useless
10	20	• head wound to bone		• ring finger off or useless • 4th toe off or useless
6	12	• any tooth		
5	10	• head wound with skin broken		• little finger off or useless • small toe off or useless
2.5	5	• bruise to head		

Appendix 255

Lex Baiuariorum 745 (Wergild = 200 *solidi*)

Wergild (%)	Fine	Head	Torso	Hands/feet
20	40	• eye struck out • ear wounded; deafness		• hand off • foot off
10	20	• eye maimed • ear struck off; no deafness		• hand maimed • foot maimed
8	16			• thumb maimed so cannot hold weapon
6	12	• brain appears in skull • canine tooth out	• foot drags in dew • internal organs wounded	• thumb off • forefinger maimed so cannot hold weapon • little finger maimed so cannot hold weapon
4.5	9			• forefinger off • little finger off
3.66	7 + 1 trem			• middle two fingers maimed so cannot hold weapon
3	6	• bone from skull • lower eyelid cannot hold tears • ear pierced • ear visibly maimed • nose pierced • lower lip cut; cannot hold saliva • non-canine tooth out	• vein torn so blood will not clot • swelling from wound • bones from arm above elbow • arm pierced above elbow	
2.5	5			• 2 middle fingers off
1.5	3	• upper eyelid maimed • upper lip maimed	• laying hand on another • arm pierced below elbow	
.75	1 ½		• blood spilled to ground	
.5	1		• blow in anger	

Lex Saxonum 785 (Wergild = 1440 *solidi* for noble)

Wergild (%)	Fine	Head	Torso	Hands/feet
100	1440	• both eyes out • both ears off; cannot hear	• both testicles off	• both hands off • both feet off
50	720	• one eye out • one ear off; cannot hear • nose off	• one testicle off	• one hand off • one foot off
25	360	• eye useless in place • ear useless in place • nose useless in place		• hand hangs useless • foot hangs useless • thumb off
16.66	240	• disfigurement of countenance	• arm pierced through • body pierced through • thigh pierced through • bone broken • disfigurement of countenance	• little finger off
12.5	180	• eye partially utile • ear partially utile • nose partially utile	• bone laid bare	• hand maimed but moveable • foot maimed but moveable • thumb half off • index finger off • great toe off
11	160			• 2nd joint little finger off
8.33	120	• seizing hair	• blood spilled	• 2nd joint index finger off • middle finger off • ring finger off
5.6	80			• 1st joint little finger off • 2nd joint middle finger off • 2nd joint ring finger off
4.17	60		• bruise and swelling	• 1st joint index finger off • 3 middle toes off
2.6	40			• 1st joint middle finger off • 1st joint ring finger off
2.08	30		• blow against noble	• small toe off

Appendix 257

Lex Frisionum 785 x 803 (Wergild = Variable; generally 100 *solidi*)
(Note: Some of the comparative values in this chart seem very odd; perhaps there was a conflation of two versions?)

Wergild (%)	Fine	Head	Torso	Hands/feet
100			• penis off • both testicles off	
	80		• leg off above knee	
	53		• arm off at shoulder • leg off at hip	
50		• eye struck out	• one testicle off	
	45			• hand cut off at wrist
	41			• all five fingers off
	40			• foot off
	24	• brain laid bare • nose struck off • blow causing deafness • nose struck off	• *praecordium* pierced • *peritoneum* pierced • abdomen pierced	
	26 1/2		• arm maimed • leg maimed	
	22 1/2			• hand maimed
	20 +2	• eye struck; vision destroyed		
	20			• foot maimed
	18	• dura mater touched • blow causing dumbness	• praecordium touched • peritoneum wounded • abdomen wounded	
	15	• nose pierced • cheeks and tongue pierced	• hip and scrotum pierced	• ankle
	13 1/3			• thumb off
	12	• skull bone pierced • ear struck off	• arm broken above elbow • breast pierced • both bones broken below elbow • bone fractured above knee • leg fully-cut below knee • belly wounded • abdominal area wounded	
	8			• ring finger off • great toe off
	7			• index finger off

258 Appendix

Lex Frisionum 785 x 803 (Wergild = Variable; generally 100 *solidi*) (*Continued*)

Wergild (%)	Fine	Head	Torso	Hands/feet
	7 -1tre			• thumb maimed • middle finger off • 2nd toe off
	6	• jawbone pierced	• arm pierced through • one bone broken below elbow • leg pierced through • leg half-cut below knee	• little finger off • third toe off
	5			• 4th toe off
	4	• middle forehead wrinkle cut • throat pierced • molar	• shoulder struck so fluid emerges • elbow struck so fluid emerges • testicle emerges but put back • lung emerges from wound • bowel emerges; put back • fat emerges from abdominal wound; cut off • 1st bone sounding in shield	• wrist struck so fluid emerges • palm struck off • juncture of thumb and arm struck • ring finger maimed • small toe off • big toe maimed
	3 1/2			• index finger maimed • 2nd toe maimed
	3 1/3			• middle finger maimed
	3	• canine		• lower joint thumb struck • little finger maimed • 3rd joint of fingers/ toes struck • 3rd toe maimed
	2 1/2			• 4th toe maimed
	2 [+4]	• hair seized in anger		
	2	• skull laid bare • topmost forehead wrinkle cut • forehead wrinkle closest to eye cut • eyebrow cut • upper or lower eyelid cut • mustache cut off • incisor	• ribcage pierced • 2nd bone sounding in shield	• top joint thumb struck • 2nd joint of fingers/ toes struck • small toe maimed
	1	• blow spilling blood	• 3rd bone sounding in shield	• top joint of fingers/ toes struck
	1/2	• blow causing lump		

Appendix 259

Lex Thuringorum 802 x 803 (Wergild = 200 freeman; 600 noble)
All fines listed as for freeman

Wergild (%)	Fine	Head	Torso	Hands/feet
50	100	• eye out • ear off • causing deafness • nose off • tongue out	• penis off • testicle off	
25	50	• disfigurement of countenance		
16.7	33.3			• thumb off • forefinger off • middle finger off • ring finger off • little finger off
15	30		• bone broken • arm pierced through	• toe off
5	10		• blow • blood spilled • body pierced • hip pierced through • binding	• hand off • foot off
2.5	5			• hand maimed • foot maimed

Lex Francorum Chamavorum c. 813 (Wergild = 200 [+66 2/3 to public peace])

Wergild (%)	Fine	Head	Torso	Hands/feet
25	50 [+4]	• eye out		• hand off • foot off
6	12 [+4]	• seizing hair	• binding • spilling blood	

Appendix

Domas Alfredes Wessex 890 x 901 (Wergild = 200)

Wergild (%)	Fine	Head	Torso	Hands/feet
50	100		• permanent laming	
40	80		• testicles; cannot create children • arm and hand off beneath elbow • leg struck off below knee	
33 1/3	66+2/3	• eye out • tongue out		• hand struck off • foot struck off
30	60	• hair cut like priest while bound • nose off	• shoulder (if man is alive); fluid out • abdomen wounded • both lower arm bones broken • loin struck off	
20	40	• hair cut like priest; not bound	• abdomen pierced; for each opening	• hand struck half off
15	30	• both tabula of skull broken • ear unable to hear	• one arm bone broken beneath elbow • loin pierced through • thigh broken • thigh pierced • large sinew; causes lameness • shank broken below knee	• thumb off
1/9	22+	• eye in head; no sight		
	20	• beard sheared	• shoulder cut off	• hand struck part off; can be cured • great toe off
	17			• ring finger off
7 1/2	15	• outer tabulum of skull broken • ear off; no deafness • cheek pierced • canine tooth	• shoulder cut into • rib and skin broken • loin pierced into	• shooting finger off • 2nd toe off
6	12	• jawbone broken • Adam's apple pierced	• large sinew; curable • shank pierced below knee	• middle finger off

Domas Alfredes Wessex 890 x 901 (Wergild = 200) *(Continued)*

Wergild (%)	Fine	Head	Torso	Hands/feet
5	10	• hair cut	• rib broken; skin unbroken	• thumbnail off • small toe off
4.5	9			• little finger off • middle toe off
4	8	• incisors		• nail of ring finger off
3	6		• small sinew	• nail of shooting finger off • 4th toe off
1 1/2	3	• molar		
1	2			• nail of middle finger off
1/2	1			• nail of little finger off

Bibliography

Primary Sources

Legal Sources: Barbarian Laws

Listed in chronological order of publication.
Editions primarily cited in this volume are marked by *.

MONUMENTA GERMANIAE HISTORICA (MGH)

LEGUM
Vol. 3. ed. Georg Heinrich Pertz
  I. *Leges Alamannorum*, ed. Johan Merkel, 1–182.
  II. *Leges Baiuwariorum*, ed. Johan Merkel, 183–496.
  III. *Leges Burgundionum*, ed. Friedrich Bluhme, 497–630.
  IV. *Lex Frisionum*, ed. Karl von Richthofen, 631–711.
Vol. 4. ed. Georg Heinrich Pertz
  Edictus Langobardorum, ed. Friedrich Bluhme, 1–225.
Vol. 5. ed. Societas Aperiendis Fontibus Rerum Germanicarum Medii Aevii.
  I. *Leges Saxonum*, ed. Karl von Richthofen and Karl Friedrich von Richthofen.
  II. *Lex Thuringorum*, ed. Karl Friedrich von Richthofen.
  III. *Lex Ribuaria*, ed. Rudolph Sohm.
  IV. *Lex Francorum Chamavorum*, ed. Rudolph Sohm.

LEGES NATIONUM GERMANICARUM
Vol. 1. *Leges Visigothorum*, ed. Karl Zeumer. 1902. Repr. 2005.
Vol. 2,1. *Leges Burgundionum*, ed. Ludwig Rudolf von Salis. 1892. Repr. 1973.

Vol. 3,2. *Lex Ribuaria*, ed. Franz Beyerle and Rudolf Buchner. 1954. Repr. 1997.
Vol. 4,1. *Pactus legis Salicae*, ed. Karl August Eckhardt. 1962. Repr. 2002.
Vol. 4,2. *Lex Salica*, ed. Karl August Eckhardt. 1969.
Vol. 5,1. *Leges Alamannorum*, ed. Karl Lehmann. 1888.
2nd edition ed. *Karl August Eckhardt*. 1966. Repr. 1993.
5,2. *Lex Baiwariorum*, ed. Ernst von Schwind. 1926. Repr. 1997.

ALAMANNIA

*Merkel, Johann, ed. *Leges Alamannorum*. MGH *Legum*. Vol. 3, 1–182. Hannover: Hahn, 1898. Repr. 1965.
Eckhardt, Karl, ed. and trans. *Die Gesetze des Karolingerreiches, 714–911*. Vol. 2, *Alamannen und Bayern*, 1–71. Germanenrechte, Band 2.II. Weimar: Verlag Hermann Böhlhaus Nachfolger, 1934.

BAVARIA

*Merkel, Johann, ed. *Leges Baiuwariorum*. MGH *Legum*. Vol. 3, 183–496. Hannover: Hahn, 1898. Repr. 1965.
Von Schwind, Ernst, ed. *Lex Baiwaiorum*. MGH *Leges nationum Germanicarum*. Vol. 5. Hannover: Hahn, 1926. Repr. 1992.
Eckhardt, Karl, ed. and trans. *Die Gesetze des Karolingerreiches, 714–911*. Vol. 2, *Alemannen und Bayern*, 75–109. Germanenrechte, Band 2.II. Weimar: Verlag Hermann Böhlhaus Nachfolger, 1934.

BURGUNDY

Von Salis, Ludwig Rudolf, ed. *Leges Burgundionum*. MGH *Leges nationum Germanicarum*. Vol. 2,1. Hannover: Hahn, 1892.
*Bluhme, Friedrich, ed. *Leges Burgundionum*. MGH *Legum*. Vol. 3, 497–630. Hannover: Hahn, 1898. Repr. 1965.
Beyerle, Franz, ed. *Die Gesetze der Burgunden*. Germanenrechte, Band 10. Weimar: Hermann Böhlhaus Nachfolger, 1936.
Drew, Katherine Fischer, trans. *The Burgundian Code*. Philadelphia: University of Pennsylvania Press, 1972.

CHAMAVAN FRANCIA

*Sohm, Rudolph, ed. *Lex Francorum Chamavorum*. MGH *Legum* Vol. 5, 103–42. Hannover: Hahn, 1875–89. Repr. Kraus, 1965.
Eckhardt, Karl August, ed. *Die Gesetze des Karolingerreiches, 71–911*. Vol. 3, *Sachsen, Thüringer, Chamaven und Friesen*, 49–59. Germanenrechte, Band 2. III. Weimar: Verlag Hermann Böhlhaus Nachfolger, 1934.
Eckhardt, Karl August, ed. *Lex Francorum Chamavorum*, 87–94. Germanenrechte: Neue Folge. Westgermanisches Recht II. Weimar: Böhlhaus, 1934. Repr. 1966.

FRISIA
*Von Richthofen, Karl, ed. *Lex Frisionum*. MGH *Legum*. Vol. 3, 631–711. Hannover: Hahn, 1898. Repr. Kraus, 1965.
Eckhardt, Karl August, ed. *Die Gesetze des Karolingerreiches, 714–911*. Vol. 3, *Sachsen, Thüringer, Chamaven und Friesen*, 60–127. Germanenrechte, Band 2.III. Weimar: Verlag Hermann Böhlaus Nachfolger, 1934.
Eckhardt, Karl August, and Albrecht Eckhardt, eds and trans. *Lex Frisionum*. MGH Fontes Iuris Germanici Antiqui 12. Hannover: Hahn, 1982.

KENT
Thorpe, Benjamin, ed. and trans. *Ancient Laws and Institutions of England; Comprising Laws Enacted under the A-S Kings from Aethelbirht to Cnut, with an English Translation of the Saxon ... also, Monumenta Ecclesiastica Anglicana from the Seventh to the Tenth Century*, 1–10. London: Public Records Office, 1840.
Schmid, Reinhold, ed. and trans. *Die Gesetze der Angelsachsen*, 2–11. Leipzig: Brockhaus, 1858.
Liebermann, Felix, ed. and trans. *Die Gesetze der Angelsachsen*. Vol. 1, 3–8. Halle: Niemeyer, 1897.
Attenborough, F.L., ed. and trans. *The Laws of the Earliest English Kings*, 2–17. Cambridge: Cambridge University Press, 1922.
*Oliver, Lisi, ed. and trans. *The Beginnings of English Law*, 60–71. Toronto: University of Toronto Press, 2002.
Wormald, Patrick, trans. *The First Code of English Law*. Medway, Kent: Canterbury Commemoration Society, 2005.

LOMBARDY
*Bluhme, Friedrich, ed. *Leges Langobardorum*. MGH *Legum*. Vol. 4. Hannover: Hahn, 1868. Repr. Kraus, 1965.
Beyerle, Franz, ed. *Leges Langobardorum, 643–866*. Witzenhausen: Deutschrechtlicher Instituts-Verlag, 1962.
Beyerle, Franz, trans. *Die Gesetze der Langobarden*. Vol. 1, *Edictus Rothari*. Witzenhausen: Deutschrechtlicher Instituts-Verlag, 1962.
Drew, Katherine Fisher, trans. *The Lombard Laws*. Philadelphia: University of Pennsylvania Press, 1973.

RIPUARIAN FRANCIA
Sohm, Rudolf, ed. *Lex Ribuaria*. MGH, *Legum*. Vol. 5, 1–102. Hannover: Hahn, 1875–89. Repr. Kraus, 1965.
*Beyerle, Franz, and Rudolf Buchner, eds. *Lex Ribuaria*. MGH *Leges nationum Germanicarum*. Vol. 3,2. Hannover: Hahn, 1964.

Eckhardt, Karl August, ed. *Lex Ribuaria*, 1–86. Germanenrechte: Neue Folge. Westgermanisches Recht II. Weimar: Böhlhaus, 1934.Repr. 1966.

Rivers, Theodore John, trans. *Laws of the Salian and Ripuarian Franks*, 167–214. New York: AMS Press, 1986.

SALIC FRANCIA

*Eckhardt, Karl August, ed. *Lex Salica, 100 Titel-Text*. Germanenrechte Neue Folge. Westgermanisches Recht. Göttingen: Musterschmidt, 1953.

Eckhardt, Karl August, ed. *Pactus legis Salicae*. MGH *Leges nationum Germanicarum*. Vol. 4,1., 1962.

Eckhardt, Karl August, ed. *Lex Salica*. MGH *Leges nationum Germanicarum*. Vol. 4,2. Hannover: Hahn, 1969.

Rivers, Theodore John, trans. *Laws of the Salian and Ripuarian Franks*, 39–112. New York: AMS Press, 1986.

Drew, Katherine Fischer, trans. *The Laws of the Salian Franks*. Philadelphia: University of Pennsylvania Press, 1991.

SAXONY

*Von Richthofen, Karl, and Karl Friedrich von Richthofen, eds. *Leges Saxonum*. MGH *Legum*. Vol. 5, 1–102. Hannover: Hahn, 1875–89. Repr. Kraus, 1965.

Von Schwerin, Claudius, ed. *Leges Saxonum und Lex Thuringorum*. Fontes Iuris Germanici Antiqui in Usum Scholarum. Hannover: Hahn, 1918.

Eckhardt, Karl August, ed. *Die Gesetze des Karolingerreiches, 714–911*. Vol. 3, *Sachsen, Thüringer, Chamaven und Friesen*, 3–33. Germanenrechte, Band 2.III. Weimar: Verlag Hermann Böhlaus Nachfolger, 1934.

THURINGIA

*Von Richthofen, Karl Friedrich, ed. *Lex Thuringorum*. MGH *Legum*. Vol. 5, 103–142. Hannover: Hahn, 1875–89. Repr. Kraus, 1965.

Von Schwerin, Claudius, ed. *Leges Saxonum und Lex Thuringorum*. Fontes Iuris Germanici Antiqui in Usum Scholarum. Hannover: Hahn, 1918.

Eckhardt, Karl August, ed. *Die Gesetze des Karolingerreiches, 714–911*. Vol. 3, *Sachsen, Thüringer, Chamaven und Friesen*, 35–47. Germanenrechte, Band 2.III. Weimar: Verlag Hermann Böhlaus Nachfolger, 1934.

VISIGOTHIC SPAIN

*Zeumer, Karl, ed. *Leges Visigothorum. Leges nationum Germanicarum*. Vol. 1. Hannover: Hahn, 1902. Repr. Kraus, 2005.

Wohlhaupter, Eugen, ed. and trans. *Gesetze der Westgoten.* Germanenrechte, Vol. 11. Weimar: H. Böhlaus Nachf., 1936.
Scott, S.P., trans. *The Visigothic Code (Forum judicum).* Boston : Boston Book Co., 1910. Consulted at *The Library of Iberian Sources Online,* http://libro.uca.edu/vcode/.

WESSEX

Thorpe, Benjamin, ed. and trans. *Ancient Laws and Institutions of England; Comprising Laws Enacted under the A-S Kings from Aethelbirht to Cnut, with an English Translation of the Saxon . . . also, Monumenta Ecclesiastica Anglicana from the Seventh to the Tenth Century,* 20–43. London: Public Records Office, 1840.
* Liebermann, Felix, ed. and trans. *Die Gesetze der Angelsachsen.* Vol. 1, 16–89. Halle: Niemeyer, 1897.
Attenborough, F.L., ed. and trans. *The Laws of the Earliest English Kings,* 62–93. Cambridge: Cambridge University Press, 1922.
Whitelock , Dorothy, trans. *English Historical Documents.* Vol. 1, *c. 500–1042*, 372–80. London: Eyre & Spottiswoode, 1955.
Eckhardt, K.A., ed. and trans. *Leges Anglo-Saxonum 601–925,* 58–135. Göttingen: Musterschmidt-Verlag, 1958.

Other Legal Sources

Binchy, D.A., ed. 'Bretha Déin Chécht.' *Ériu* 12 (1934), 1–77.
– ed. *Críth Gablach.* Dublin: Institute for Advanced Studies, 1979.
W.J. Buma, ed. *De Eerste Riustringer Codex.* S-Gravenhage: Martinus Nijhoff, 1961.
Hübner, Rudolf, trans. *Gerichtsurkunden der Fränkischen Zeit, Erste Abtheilung: Die Gerichtsurkunden aus Deutschland und Frankreich bis zum Jahre 1000. Zeitschrift der Savigny-Stiftung für Rechtsgeschichte: Germanistische Abteilung* (1891): B. 12.
– trans. *Gerichtsurkunden der Fränkischen Zeit, Zweite Abtheilung: Die Gerichtsurkunden aus Italien, bis zum Jahre 1150. Zeitschrift der Savigny-Stiftung für Rechtsgeschichte: Germanistische Abteilung* (1893): B. 14.
Rio, Alice, trans. *The Formularies of Angers and Marculf: Two Merovingian Legal Handbooks.* Translated Texts for Historians 46. Liverpool: Liverpool University Press, 2008.
Roberts, Sara Elin, ed. and trans. *The Legal Triads of Medieval Wales.* Cardiff: University of Wales Press, 2007.
Zeumer, Karl, ed. *Formulae Merowingici et Karolingi aevi.* MGH *Legum,* Vol. 5. Hannover: Hahn, 1882.

Non-Legal Primary Sources

[Alfred] *King Alfred's West-Saxon Version of Gregory's Pastoral Care*. Ed. Henry Sweet. London: Oxford University Press, 1871.

[Alexander Trallianus] Langslow, D.R., ed. and trans. *The Latin Alexander Trallianus: The Text and Transmission of a Late Latin Medical Book*. Journal of Roman Studies Monograph 10. London: Society for the Promotion of Roman Studies, 2006.

Ambrose: Patrilogiae Latinae. Vol. 14. Paris: J.-P. Migne, 1882.

[Ambrose] *Some of the Principal Works of St. Ambrose*, trans. H. de Romestin. A Select Library of Nicene and Post-Nicene Fathers of the Christian Church, 2nd ser. Volume 10. Grand Rapids: Wm. B. Eerdmans, 1955.

Anglo-Saxon and Old English Vocabularies. Ed. Thomas Wright. 2 vols. 2nd ed. Darmstadt: Wissenschaftliche Buchgesellschaft, 1884, repr. 1968.

Anglo-Saxon Remedies, Charms, and Prayers from British Library MS Harley 585. Ed. and trans. Edward Pettit. Lampeter, Wales: Edwin Mellen Press, 2001.

The Annals of St.-Bertin. Trans. Janet R. Nelson. Manchester: Manchester University Press, 1991.

Aristotle's Ethica Nicomachea. Trans. William David Ross. Oxford: Clarendon Press, 1908.

[*Ars Medicinae*] Laux, Rudolf, ed. 'Ars medicinae: Ein frühmittelalterliches Kompendium der Medizin.' *Kyklos* 3 (1930): 417–34.

Augustin, *City of God and Christian Doctrine*. Trans. Philip Schaff. Christian Classics Ethereal Library. http://www.ccel.org/.

[Basil] *The Treatise De Spiritu Sancto: The Nine Homilies of the Hexaemeron and the Letters of Saint Basil the Great*. Ed. and trans. Rev. Blomfield Jackson. Grand Rapids: Wm. B. Eerdmans, 1955.

Bede's Ecclesiastical History of the English People. Ed. and trans. Bertram Colgrave and R.A.B. Mynors. Oxford: Clarendon Press, 1969.

Biblia Sacra, Iuxta Vulgatam Versionem. Ed. Robert Weber. Stuttgart: Deutsche Bibelgesellschaft, 1969.

Cassius Felix: De la Médicine. Ed. and trans. Anne Fraisse Paris: Les Belles Lettres, 2002.

[Chaucer] Benson, Larry, gen. ed. *The Riverside Chaucer*. Boston: Houghton Mifflin, 1987.

'*Coneigius duib geissi ulchai.*' Ed. and trans. Brian O'Looney. Royal Irish Academy Irish Manuscript Series 1, Part 1. Dublin, 1870.

The Exeter Book. Ed. George Philip Krapp and Eliot van Kirk Dobbie. New York: Columbia University Press, 1936.

Godman, Peter, ed. and trans. *Poetry of the Carolingian Renaissance*. London: Duckworth, 1985.

[Helidore] Sigerist, Henry E., ed. 'Die "Chirugia Eliodori."' *Archiv für Geschichte der Medizin* 12 (1920): 1–9.
– 'Die "Lecciones Heliodori."' *Archiv für Geschichte der Medizin* 13 (1921): 145–56.
Hrabanus Maurus. *Patrologiae Latinae*. Vol. 111. Paris: J.-P. Migne, 1852.
[Irish] *Ancient Irish Tales*. Trans. Tom Peete Cross and Clark Harris Slover. New York: Harry Holt, 1936.
[Irish] *The Irish Penitentials*. Ed. and trans. Ludwig Bieler. Dublin: The Dublin Institute, 1963.
[Isidore] *The Etymologies of Isidore of Seville*. Trans. Stephan A. Barney, W.J. Lewis, J.A. Beach, and Oliver Berghof, with the collaboration of Muriel Hall. Cambridge: Cambridge University Press, 2006.
Isidori Hispalensis episcopi Etymologiarum sive Originum libri xx. Ed. W.M. Lindsay. Oxford: Clarendon Press, 1911, repr. 1978.
[*Lacnunga*] Cockayne, Thomas Oswald, ed. and trans. *Leechdoms, Wortcunning and Starcraft of Early England*. First printed, 1864–6. London: Holland Press, 1961.
[Marie de France]. 'Bisclavret.' In *The Lais of Marie de France*, trans. Glyn S. Burgess and Keith Busby, 68–72. London: Penguin, 1986.
The New Oxford Annotated Bible. Ed. Bruce M. Metzger and Roland E. Murphy. New York: Oxford University Press, 1994.
[Penitentials] Fulk, Rob, and Stefan Jurasinski. *The Old English Canons of Theodore*. London: Early English Text Society. Forthcoming.
[Penitentials] MacNeill, John T., and Helena M. Gamer, trans. *Medieval Handbooks of Penance*. New York: Columbia University Press, 1938, repr. 1990.
[Penitentials] Kottje, R., ed. *Paenitentialia minora franciae et italiae saeculi viii–ix*. Corpus Christianorum 156. Turnout: Brepols, 1994.
[Sidonius Apollinarus] *The Letters of Sidonius*. Trans. O.M. Dalton. Oxford: Clarendon Press, 1915.
Sidonius Apollinaris, Poems and Letters. Ed. and trans. W.B. Anderson. Cambridge, MA: Harvard University Press, 1936.
Wellmann, M. *Die Fragmente der Sikelische Ärtzte: Akron, Philistion, und des Diokles von Karystos*. Berlin: Weidmannische Buchhandlung, 1901.

Secondary Sources

Abels, Richard. *Alfred the Great: War, Culture and Kingship in Anglo-Saxon England*. New York and London: Longman, 1998.
Allingham, Margery. *Mystery Mile*. Aylesbury and Slough: Penguin Books, 1930, repr. 1959.

Amundsen, Darrel W. 'Visigothic Medical Legislation.' *Bulletin of the History of Medicine* 45 (1971): 553–69.

Ariès, Phillipe, *Western Attitudes toward Death: From the Middle Ages to the Present*. Baltimore: Johns Hopkins University Press, 1974.

– *The Hour of Our Death*. Boston: Knopf, 1981.

Autry, Robert, et al., eds. *Lexicon des Mittelalters*. Munich and Zürich: Artemis-Verlag, 1977–.

Baader, Gerhard. 'Anatomie.' In *Lexikon des Mittelalters*, ed. Autry et al. 575–7.

– 'Early Medieval Adaptations of Byzantine Medicine in Western Europe.' *Dumbarton Oaks Papers* 38, *Symposium on Byzantine Medicine* (1984): 251–9.

Baesecke, Georg. 'Die deutschen Worte der germanischen Gesetze.' *Beiträge zur Geschichte der Deutschen Sprache und Literatur* 59 (1935): 1–101.

Barker, Juliet. *Agincourt: Henry V and the Battle That Made England*. Boston: Little Brown, 2005.

Barmires, Alcuin, ed. *Woman Defamed and Woman Defended: An Anthology of Medieval Texts*. Oxford: Clarendon Press, 1992.

Bartlett, Robert. *Trial by Fire and Water: The Medieval Judicial Ordeal*. Oxford: Clarendon Press, 1986.

Bass, Bill, and Jon Jefferson. *Beyond the Body Farm*. New York: HarperCollins, 2007.

Bassett, Steven, ed. *The Origins of Anglo-Saxon Kingdoms*. Studies in the Early History of Britain. London and New York: Leicester University Press, 1989.

Baumgartner, René. 'Fussprothese aus einem frühmittelalterlichen Grab aus Bonaduz.' *Helvetia Archaeologica* 13.51 (1982): 155–62.

Beccaria, Augusto. *Codici de Medicina del Periodo Presalernitano*. Rome: Edizioni di Storia e Letteratura, 1956.

Becher, Matthias. *Charlemagne*. New Haven and London: Yale University Press, 2003.

Behnke, Robert S. *Kinetic Anatomy*. Champagne, IL: Human Kinetics, 2001.

Bergmann, Werner. 'Untersuchungen zu den Gerichtsurkunden der Merowingerzeit.' *Archiv für Diplomatik, Schriftgeschichte, Siegel- und Wappenkunde* 22 (1976): 1–186.

Bevin, James. *A Pictorial Handbook of Anatomy and Physiology*. New York: Barnes and Noble, 1996.

Beyerle, Franz. 'Die Malberg-Glossen der Lex Salica.' *Zeitschrift der Savigny-Stiftung für Rechtsgeschichte, Germanistische Abtheilung* 89 (1972): 1–33.

Bloch, Marc. *La Société Féodale: La Formation des Liens de Dépendance*. Paris: Éditions Albin Michel, 1942.

– *Esquisse d'une histoire honétaire de l'Europe*. Paris: Librairie Armand Colin, 1954.

Bonser, Wilfred. *The Medical Background of Anglo-Saxon England: A Study in History, Psychology and Folklore*. London: Wellcome Historical Medical Library, 1962.
Bosworth, Joseph, and T. Northcote Toller, eds. *An Anglo-Saxon Dictionary*. Oxford: Oxford University Press, 1898.
Boyle, David. *The Troubadour's Song: The Capture and Ransom of Richard the Lionheart*. New York: Walker, 2005.
Brennessel, Barbara, Michael D.C. Drout, and Robyn Gravel. 'A Reassessment of the Efficacy of Anglo-Saxon Medicine.' *Anglo-Saxon England* 34 (2005): 183–95.
Bright, W. *Chapters in Early English Church History*. Oxford: Clarendon Press, 1897.
Brown, Warren. *Unjust Seizure: Conflict, Interest and Authority in an Early Medieval Society*. Ithaca: Cornell University Press, 2001.
Brunner, Heinrich. *Deutsche Rechtsgeschichte: Sytematisches Handbuch der deutschen Rechtswissenschaft*. Leipzig: Duncker und Humblot, 1887–92.
Buck, C.D. *A Dictionary of Selected Synonyms in the Principal Indo-European Languages*. Chicago: University of Chicago Press, 1949.
Burke, Peter. 'The New History: Its Past and Its Future.' In *New Perspectives on Historical Writing*, ed. Burke, 1–24.
– ed. *New Perspectives on Historical Writing*. University Park, PA: University of Pennsylvania Press, 2001.
Burns, Thomas S. *Rome and the Barbarians, 100 B.C. – A.D. 400*. Baltimore and London: Johns Hopkins University Press, 2003.
Bury, J.B. *The Invasion of Europe by the Barbarians*. New York and London: Norton, 1967.
Butler, Judith. *Excitable Speech: A Politics of the Performative*. New York and London: Routledge, 1997.
Butler, Sara M. *The Language of Abuse: Marital Violence in Later Medieval England*. Leiden and Boston: Brill, 2007.
Campbell, James, Eric John, and Patrick Wormald. *The Anglo-Saxons*. London: Phaidon, 1982.
Carroll, Robert. *The Skeptic's Dictionary: A Collection of Strange Beliefs, Amusing Deceptions, and Dangerous Delusions*. New York: Black Dog and Leventhal Press, 2003.
Catholic Encyclopedia Online. http://catholic.org/encyclopedia.
Charles-Edwards, Thomas. *Early Irish and Welsh Kinship*. Oxford: Clarendon Press, 1993.
– 'The Penitential of Theodore and the *Iudicia Theodori*.' In *Archbishop Theodore*, ed. M. Lapdige, 141–74. Cambridge: Cambridge University Press, 1995.

Clanchy, Michael. *From Memory to Written Record: England 1066–1307.* 2nd ed. Oxford: Oxford University Press, 1993.

Clarke, Bob. 'An Early Anglo-Saxon Cross-Roads Burial from Broad Town, North Wiltshire.' *Wiltshire Archaeological and Natural History Magazine* 97 (2002): 89–94.

Collins, Roger. *Early Medieval Europe 300–1000.* 2nd ed. New York: Palgrave, 1999.

Costambeys, Marios. *Power and Patronage in Early Medieval Italy: Local Society, Italian Politics and the Abbey of Farfa, c. 700–900.* Cambridge: Cambridge University Press, 2007.

Czarnetzki, Alfred, Christian Uhlig, and Rotraut Wolf, eds. *Menschen des Frühen Mittelalters im Spiegel der Anthropologie und Medizin.* Stuttgart: Württembergisches Landesmuseum Stuttgart, 1982.

Davies, Wendy. 'Disputes, Their Conduct and Their Settlement in the Village Communities of Eastern Brittany in the Ninth Century.' *History and Anthropology* I (1985): 289–312.

– 'People and Places in Dispute in Ninth-Century Brittany.' In *Settlement of Disputes*, ed. Davies and Fouracre, 65–84.

Davies, Wendy, and Paul Fouracre, eds. *The Settlement of Disputes in Early Medieval Europe.* Cambridge: Cambridge University Press, 1986.

De Jong, Mayke. 'Religion.' In *The Early Middle Ages: Europe 400–1000*, ed. McKitterick, 131–66.

De Jorio, Andrea. *Gesture in Naples and Gesture in Classical Antiquity.* 1832. Trans. Adam Kendon. Bloomington and Indianapolis: Indiana University Press, 2002.

Devroey, Jean-Pierre. 'The Economy.' In *The Early Middle Ages: Europe 400–1000*, ed. McKitterick, 97–130.

Diepgen, Paul. *Deutsche Volksmedizin: Wissenschaftliche Heilkunde und Kultur.* Stuttgart: Ferdinand Enke Verlag, 1935.

Drew, Katherine Fischer. *Law and Society in Early Medieval Europe: Studies in Legal History.* London: Variorum Reprints, 1988.

Du Cange, Domino. *Glossarium Mediæ et Infimæ Latinitas.* Paris: Librairie de Sciences et des Arts, 1678 ; repr. 1937.

Dutton, Paul Edward. *Charlemagne's Mustache and Other Cultural Clusters of a Dark Age.* New York and Hampshire: Palgrave Macmillan, 2004.

Edmunds, Flora, Christian Kay, Jane Roberts, and Irené Wotherspoon, eds. *Thesaurus of Old English Online.* http://libra.englang.arts.gla.ac.uk./oethe-saurus: 2008.

Elsakkers, Marianne. 'Raptus ultra Rhenum: Early Ninth-Century Saxon Laws on Abduction and Rape.' *Amsterdamer Beiträge zur Älteren Germanistik* 52 (1999): 27–53.

- 'Genre Hopping: Aristotelian Criteria for Abortion in Germania.' In *Germanic Texts and Latin Models: Medieval Reconstructions*, ed. Karin E. Olsen, Antonina Harbus, and Tette Hofstra, 73–92. Germania Latina 4. Leuven, 2001.
- 'Abortion, Poisoning, Magic and Contraception in Eckhardt's *Pactus Legis Salicae*.' *Amsterdamer Beiträge zur Älteren Germanistik* 57 (2003): 233–67.
- 'Inflicting Serious Bodily Harm: The Visigothic Antiquae on Violence and Abortion.' *Legal History Review* 71.1–2 (2003): 55–63.
- '*Her anda neylar*: An Intriguing Criterion for Abortion in Old Frisian Law.' *Scientarium Historia* 30 (2004): 107–54.
- 'Gothic Bible, Vetus Latina and Visigothic Law.' *Sacris Eruditi* 44 (2005): 37–76.

Fagan, Brian. *Time Detectives: How Scientists Use Modern Technology to Unravel the Secrets of the Past.* New York: Simon and Schuster, 1995.

Falk Moore, Sally. *Law as Process: An Anthropological Approach.* London and Boston: Routledge and Kegan Paul, 1978.

Faust, Drew Gilpin. *A Riddle of Death: Mortality and Meaning in the American Civil War.* Gettysburg: Gettysburg College, 1995.

- *This Republic of Suffering: Death and the American Civil War.* Boston: Knopf, 2008.

Fell, Christine. *Women in Anglo-Saxon England and the Impact of 1066.* Bloomington: Indiana University Press, 1984.

Field, Bruce F. 'Foot.' *World Book* Online Reference Center, 2009, http://www.worldbookonline.com.libezp.lib.lsu.edu/wb/Article?id=ar203660.

Fleming, Robin. 'Bones for Historians: Putting the Body Back into Biography.' In *Writing Medieval Biography, 750–1250: Essays in Honour of Professor Frank Barlow*, ed. David Bates, Julia Crick, and Sarah Hamilton, 29–48. Woodbridge: Boydell, 2006.

Fletcher, Richard. *Bloodfeud: Murder and Revenge in Anglo-Saxon England.* Oxford: Oxford University Press, 2003.

Fouracre, Paul. '"Placita" and the Settlement of Disputes in Later Merovingian Francia.' In *Settlement of Disputes*, ed. Davies and Fouracre, 23–44.

Frantzen, Alan J. *The Literature of Penance in Anglo-Saxon England.* New Brunswick, NJ: Rutgers University Press, 1993.

Frassetto, Michael. *Encyclopedia of Barbarian Europe: Society in Transformation.* Santa Barbara: ABC-Clio, 2003.

Fruscione, Daniela. 'Eine philologische Schlussbemerkung.' In *Leges – Gentes – Regna: Zur Rolle von germanischen Rechtsgewohnheiten und lateinischer Schrifttradition bei der Ausbildung der frühmittelalterlichen Rechtskultur*, ed. Gerhard Dilcher and Eva-Marie Distler, 525–35. Berlin: Erich Schmidt Verlag, 2006.

- 'Zur Rolle von Ethnologie, Missionsgeschichte und angelsächsischen Rechtsquellen für die Erforschung germanischer Rechtsvorstellungen im Frühmittelalter.' *Zeitschrift der Savigny-Stiftung für Rechtsgeschichte/ Germanistische Abteilung* 125 (2008): 399–410.
Fulk, Rob, and Stefan Jurasinski. *The Old English Canons of Theodore*. Early English Text Society, Forthcoming.
Gabrieli, Francesco. *Arab Historians of the Crusades* (1957). Trans. E.J. Costello. Berkeley and Los Angeles: University of California Press, 1984.
Ganshof, F.L. 'La Preuve dans le Droit Franc.' *La Preuve, IIme Partie: Moyen Age et Temps Modernes. Recuils de la Societe Jean Bodin pour L'Histoire Comparative des Institutions* 17 (1965): 71–98.
Gaudemet, Jean. 'Les Ordalies au Moyen Age: Doctrine, Legislation et Pratique Canoniques.' *La Preuve, IIme Partie: Moyen Age et Temps Modernes. Recuils de la Societe Jean Bodin pour L'Histoire Comparative des Institutions* 17 (1965): 99–135.
Geary, Patrick J. 'Ethnic Identity as a Situational Construct in the Early Middle Ages.' *Mitteilungen der Anthropologischen Gesellschaft in Wien* 113 (1983): 15–26.
- *Before France and Germany: The Creation and Transformation of the Merovingian World*. New York and Oxford: Oxford University Press, 1988.
- *The Myth of Nations*. Princeton: Princeton University Press, 2002.
- *Women in the Beginning: Origin Myths from the Amazons to the Virgin Mary*. Princeton: Princeton University Press, 2006.
- 'Judicial Violence and Torture in the Carolingian Empire.' In *Law and the Illicit in Medieval Europe*, ed. Ruth Mazo Karras, Joel Kaye, and E. Ann Matter, 79–88. Philadelphia: University of Pennsylvania Press, 2008.
Gellrich, Jesse. *Discourse and Dominion in the Fourteenth Century: Oral Contexts of Writing in Philosophy, Politics, and Poetry*. Princeton: Princeton University Press, 1995.
Glaze, Florence Eliza. *The Perforated Wall: The Ownership and Circulation of Medical Books in Medieval Europe, ca. 800–1200*. Ann Arbor, MI: UMI, 2005.
Goebel, Julius, Jr. *Felony and Misdemeanor: A Study in the History of Criminal Law*. Philadelphia: University of Pennsylvania Press, 1937, repr. 1976.
Goetz, Hans-Werner. *Frauen im frühen Mittelalter: Frauenbild und Frauenleben im Frankenreich*. Weimar: Böhlau Verlag, 1995.
Goetz, Hans-Werner, Jörg Jarnut, and Walter Pohl, eds. *Regna and Gentes: The Relationship between Late Antique and Early Medieval Peoples and Kingdoms in the Transformation of the Roman World*. Leiden and Boston: Brill, 2003.
Goffart, Walter. *Barbarian Tides: The Migration Age and the Later Roman Empire*. Philadelphia: University of Pennsylvania Press, 2006.

Gourevitch, Danielle. 'The Paths of Knowledge: Medicine in the Roman World.' In *Western Medical Thought from Antiquity to the Middle Ages*, ed. Mirko D. Grmek, trans. Antony Shugaar, 104–38. Cambridge, MA: Harvard University Press, 1998.

Green, Monica H. 'Documenting Medieval Women's Medical Practice.' In *Practical Medicine from Salerno to the Black Death*, ed. Luis García-Ballester, Roger French, Jon Arrizabalaga, and Andrew Cunningham, 322–52. Cambridge: Cambridge University Press, 1994.

Grimm, Jacob. *Deutsche Rechtsalterthümer*. Göttingen: Dieterich, 1828. Repr. Darmstadt: Wissenschaftliche Buchgesellschaft, 1983.

Hammer, C.I. *A Large-Scale Slave Society of the Early Middle Ages: Slaves and Their Families in Early Medieval Bavaria*. Aldershot: Ashgate, 2002.

Hamonic, Paul Louis Marie. *La chirugie et la medicine d'autrefois d'aprés une premiére série d'instruments anciens renfermés dans mes collections*. Paris: A. Maloine, 1900.

Hansard, George Agar. *The Book of Archery*. London: Henry C. Bohn, 1845.

Harries, Jill. 'Violence, Victims, and the Legal Tradition in Late Antiquity.' In *Violence in Late Antiquity: Perceptions and Practices*, ed. H.A. Drake et al., 85–102. Aldershot: Ashgate, 2006.

Havelock, Eric Alfred. *The Muse Learns to Write: Reflections on Orality and Literacy from Antiquity to the Present*. New Haven: Yale University Press, 1986.

Hebermann, Charles George, et al., eds. *The Catholic Encyclopedia*. New York: The Encyclopedia Press, 1913.

Hedemann, Markus. *Zahn- und Kieferbefunde an Schädeln des frühmittelalterlichen Gräberfeldes Schwanenstadt/Oberösterreich*. Dissertation, Fachbereich Humanmedizin, Philipps-Universität Marburg, 1988.

Higham, Nicholas. *Rome, Britain and the Anglo-Saxons: The Archaeology of Change*. London: Seaby, 1992.

Hines, John, ed. *The Anglo-Saxons from the Migration Period to the Eighth Century: An Ethnographic Perspective*. Studies in Historical Archaeoethnology 2. Woodbridge: Boydell, 1997.

– 'Lies, Damned Lies, and a Curriculum Vitae: Reflections on Statistics and the Populations of Early Anglo-Saxon Inhumation Cemeteries.' In *Burial in Early Medieval England and Wales*, ed. Lucy and Reynolds, 88–103.

Hirst, Susan M. *An Anglo-Saxon Inhumation Cemetery at Sewerby, East Yorkshire*. York Archaeological Publications 4. University of York: Department of Archaeology, 1985.

Holder, Alfred. *Die Handscrhiften der Grossherzoglich Badischen Hof- und Landesbibliothek in Karlsruhe*. Leipzig: Teubner, 1906.

Hough, Carole. 'A Reappraisal of Æthelberht 84.' *Nottingham Medieval Studies* 37 (1993): 1–7.
- 'A New Reading of Alfred, Ch. 26.' *Nottingham Medieval Studies* 41 (1997): 1–12.
- 'Alfred's Domboc and the Language of Rape: A Reconsideration of Alfred, Ch. 11.' *Medium Ævum* 64.1 (1997): 1–27.
- 'Two Kentish Laws Concerning Women: A New Reading of Æthelberht 73 and 74.' *Anglia* 119.4 (2001): 554–78.

Hyams, Paul. *Rancor and Reconciliation in Medieval England: Wrong and Its Redress from the Tenth to the Thirteenth Centuries*. Cornell: Cornell University Press, 2003.

Hyde, Alan. *Bodies of Law*. Princeton, Princeton University Press, 1997.

Hüpper-Dröge, Dagmar. 'Schutz- und Angriffswaffen nach den Leges und verwandten fränkischen Rechtsquellen.' In *Wörter und Sachen in Lichte der Bezeichnungsforschung*, ed. Schmidt-Wiegand, 107–127.

Innes, Matthew. 'Memory, Orality and Literacy in an Early Medieval Society.' *Past & Present* 158 (1998): 3–36.
- *Introduction to Early Medieval Western Europe, 300–900: The Sword, the Plough and the Book*. Oxford: Routledge, 2007.

Jaaska, Arne Alexander. 'Raetia and Alamannia: The Mixed Cultural World of a Former Roman Province in the Middle Ages.' Dissertation, University of California at Los Angeles, 2004.

Joffrey, René. *Le cimetière de Lavoye (Meuse): Nécropole Mérovingienne*. Paris: Éditions Picard, 1974.

Jurasinski, Stefan. 'The Continental Origins of Æthelberht's Code.' *Philological Quarterly* 80.1 (2002 for 2001): 1–15.
- 'Germanism, Slapping and the Cultural Contexts of Æthelberht's Code: A Reconsideration of Chapters 65–8.' *Haskins Society Journal* 18 (2006): 51–71.
- 'Madness and Responsibility in Anglo-Saxon England.' In *Peace and Protection in the Medieval West*, ed. David Rollason and Tom Lambert, 99–120.

Jurasinski, Stefan, Lisi Oliver, and Andrew Rabin, eds. *Law Before Magna Carta: Felix Liebermann and* Die Gesetze der Angelsachsen. Leiden: Brill, 2010.

Kay, C.J., L. Grundy, and J. Roberts, eds. *Thesaurus of Old English* online http://libra.englang.arts.gla.ac.uk/oethesaurus/.

Keil, Baldur. 'Chirug, Chirugie.' In *Lexikon des Mittelalters*, ed. Robert Autry et al., 1845–59.

Keil, Gundolf. 'Eine Prosthese aus einem fränkischen Grab von Greisheim.' *Fundberichte aus Hessen* 178 (1977–8): 195–211.

- 'Roger Frugardi und die Tradition langobardischer Chirugie.' *Sudhoff's Archiv* 86.1 (2002): 1–26.
Kent, J.J. 'The Number and Location of Rings Worn in Different Cultures.' http://www.jjkent.com/articles/number-location-rings-worn.htm: 2004.
Klinck, Anne L. '"To Have and to Hold": The Brideweath of Wives and the Mund of Widows in Anglo-Saxon England.' *Nottingham Medieval Studies* 51 (2007): 231–45.
Köbler, Gerhard. *Neuenglisch-Althochdeutsches Wörterbuch*. www.koeblergerhard.de/germanistischewoerterbuecher: 2006.
Kraus, Bertram S., Ronald E. Jordan, and Leonard Abrams. *Kraus's Dental Anatomy and Occlusion*. St Louis: Mosby Year Book, 1992.
Langbein, John H. *Torture and the Law of Truth: Europe and England in the ancien régime*. Chicago: University of Chicago Press, 1977.
Langslow, D.R. *Medical Latin in the Roman Empire*. Oxford: Oxford University Press, 2002.
Lehmann-Nitsche, Robert. *Beiträge zur Prähistorischen Chirugie nach Funden aus Deutscher Vorzeit*. Buenos Aires: Fessel & Mengen, 1898.
Lendinara, Patrizia. 'The Kentish Laws.' In *The Anglo-Saxons from the Migration Period to the Eighth Century*, ed. Hines, 211–44.
Liebermann, Felix. 'Kentische *hionne*: Hirnhaut.' *Archiv für das Studium der neueren Sprachen und Literaturen* 115 (1905): 177–8.
Liebeschuetz, Wolf. 'Violence in the Barbarian Successor Kingdoms.' In *Violence in Late Antiquity: Perceptions and Practices*, ed. H.A. Drake et al., 37–46. Aldershot: Ashgate, 2006.
Liebs, Detlaf. 'Sklaverei aus Not im germanisch-römischen Recht.' *Zeitschrift der Savigny- Stiftung für Rechtsgeschichte: Römisches Abtheilung* 118 (2001): 286–311.
Lucas, Peter W. *Dental Functional Morphology: How Teeth Work*. Cambridge: Cambridge University Press, 2004.
Lucy, Sam. 'Burial Practice in Early Medieval Eastern Britain: Constructing Local Identities, Deconstructing Ethnicity.' In *Burial in Early Medieval England and Wales*, ed. Lucy and Reynolds, 72–87.
Lucy, Sam, and Andrew Reynolds. 'Early Medieval Burial.' In *Burial in Early Medieval England and Wales*, ed. Lucy and Reynolds, 1–23.
Lucy, Sam, and Andrew Reynolds, eds. *Burial in Early Medieval England and Wales*. London: Society for Medieval Archaeology, 2002.
Lupoi, Maurizio. *Alle radici del mondo giuridico europeo*. 1994. Trans. Adrian Belton as *The Origins of the European Legal Order*. Cambridge: Cambridge University Press, 2000.

Mayr-Harting, Henry. *The Coming of Christianity to Anglo-Saxon England*. 3rd ed. London: Batsford, 1972, repr. 1991.
McIlwain, J.T. 'Does OE *ex* for Brain Lie behind an Instance of *eaxl* in Leechbook III?' *Notes and Queries* 51 (2004): 339–41.
McKinney, Loren C. *Early Medieval Medicine*. Baltimore: Johns Hopkins University Press, 1937.
McKitterick, Rosamond. 'Some Carolingian Law-Books and Their Function.' In *Authority and Power: Studies on Medieval Law and Government Presented to Walter Ullmann on His Seventieth Birthday*, ed. Brian Tierney and Peter Linehan, 13–27. Cambridge: Cambridge University Press, 1980.
– *The Frankish Kingdoms under the Carolingians, 751–987*. New York and London: Longman, 1983.
'Politics.' In *The Early Middle Ages: Europe 400–1000*, ed. McKitterick, 21–68.
– ed. *The Early Middle Ages: Europe 400–1000*. Oxford and New York: Oxford University Press, 2001.
Meaney, Audrey L. *A Gazatteer of Early Anglo-Saxon Burial Sites*. London: Allen & Unwin, 1964.
Memmler, Ruth L., Barbara Janson Cohen, and Dena Lin Wood, eds. *Structure and Function of the Human Body*. Philadelphia and New York: Lippincott, 1996.
Morris, Rosemary. 'Byzantine Provinces in the Tenth Century.' In *Settlement of Disputes*, ed. Davies and Fouracre, 125–49.
Mosby, C.V. *Mosby's Medical Encyclopedia*, Version 2.1 (CD-Rom). San Fransciso and Cedar Rapids: Broderbund Properties, LLC, 1997.
Murray, Alexander C. *Germanic Kinship Structure: Studies in Law and Society in Antiquity and the Early Middle Ages*. Studies and Texts 65. Toronto: Pontifical Institute for Mediaeval Studies, 1983.
Murray, K.M. Elisabeth. *Caught in the Web of Words: James A.H. Murray and the Oxford English Dictionary*. New Haven and London: Yale University Press, 1977.
Nehlsen, Hermann. *Sklavenrecht zwischen Antike und Mittelalter. Germanisches und römisches Recht in den germanischen Rechtaufzeichnungen*. Göttingen: Musterschmidt, 1972.
Nehlsen-von Stryk, Karin. *Die boni homines des frühen Mittelalters unter besonderer Berücksichtigung der frankischen Quellen*. Berlin: Duncker und Humbolt, 1981.
Nelson, Janet L. 'Dispute Settlement in Carolingian West Francia.' In *Settlement of Disputes*, ed. Davies and Fouracre, 45–64.
Niederhellmann, Annette. 'Heilkundliches in den *Leges*: Die Schädelverletzungen und ihre Bezeichnungen.' In *Wörter und Sachen in Lichte der Bezeichnungsforschung*, ed. Schmidt-Wiegand, 74–90.

- *Arzt- und Heilkunde in den frühmittelalterlichen Leges*. Berlin: de Gruyter, 1983.
O'Brien O'Keeffe, Katherine. 'Body and Law in Late Anglo-Saxon England.' *Anglo-Saxon England* 27 (1998): 209–32.
O'Flanagan, J. Roderick. *The Lives of the Lord Chancellors and the Keepers of the Great Seal of Ireland*. London: Longmans, Green, 1870.
Oliver, Lisi. 'Towards Freeing a Slave in Germanic Law.' In *Mír Curad: Papers Presented to Calvert Watkins*, ed. J. Jasanoff, C. Melchert, and L. Oliver, 549–60. Innsbruck: Innsbrucker Beiträge zur Sprachwissenschaft, 1998.
- *The Beginnings of English Law*. Toronto: University of Toronto Press, 2002.
- 'Who Was Æthelberht's *læt*?' In *Confrontation in Late Antiquity*, ed. Linda Hall, 153–66. Cambridge: Orchard Academic Press, 2003.
- 'Lex Talionis in Barbarian Law.' *Journal of Indo-European Studies* 52 (2006): 197–218.
- 'Sick-Maintenance in Anglo-Saxon Law.' *Journal for English and Germanic Philology* 107.3 (2008): 319–42.
- 'Protecting the Body in Early Medieval England.' In *Peace and Protection in the Medieval West*, ed. David Rollason and Tom Lambert, 60–77.
- 'Æthelberht's and Alfred's Two Skulls.' *Heroic Age*, forthcoming.
Pantos, Aliki. '"In medle oððe an þinge": The Old English Vocabulary of Assembly.' In *Assembly Places and Practices in Medieval Europe*, ed. Aliki Pantos and Sarah Semple, 181–201. Dublin: Four Courts Press, 2004.
- 'The Location and Form of Anglo-Saxon Assembly Places: Some "Moot Points."' In *Assembly Places and Practices in Medieval Europe*, ed. Aliki Pantos and Sarah Semple, 155–80. Dublin: Four Courts Press, 2004.
Park, Katherine. 'Medicine and Society in Medieval Europe.' In *Medicine in Society: Historical Essays*, ed. Andrew Wear, 59–90. Cambridge: Cambridge University Press, 1992.
Pilsworth, Clare. 'Could you just sign this for me, John? Doctors, Charters and Occupational Identity in Early Medieval Northern and Central Italy.' *Journal of Early Medieval Europe* 17.4 (2009): 363–88.
Pokorny, Julius. *Indogermanisches Etymologisches Wörterbuch*. Bern and Stuttgart: Francke, 1959. Rev. ed. 1989.
Pollard, Justin. *Alfred the Great: The Man Who Made England*. London: John Murray, 2005.
Rabin, Andrew. 'Old English *forespeca* and the Role of the Advocate in Anglo-Saxon Law.' *Mediaeval Studies* 69 (2007): 223–54.
- 'Female Advocacy and Royal Protection in Tenth-Century England: The Legal Career of Queen Ælfthryth.' *Speculum* 84.2 (2009): 261–88.

Richards, Mary. 'The Body as Text in Early Anglo-Saxon Law.' In *Naked Before God: Uncovering the Body in Anglo-Saxon England*, ed. Withers and Wilcox, 97–115.
Rio, Alice. *Legal Practice and the Written Word: Frankish Formulae, c. 500–1000*. Cambridge: Cambridge University Press, 2009.
Roberts, C., and J. McKinley. 'Review of Trepanation in British Antiquity.' In *Trepanation: History, Discovery, Theory*. ed. R. Arnott, S. Finger, and C.U.M. Smith, 55–78. The Netherlands: Lisse, 2003.
Roberts, Simon. *Order and Dispute: An Introduction to Legal Anthropology*. New York: St Martin's Press, 1979.
Rollason, David, and Tom Lambert, eds. *Peace and Protection in the Medieval West*. Toronto: Pontifical Institute for Mediaeval Studies, 2009.
Rosenwein, Barbara. *Negotiating Space: Power, Restraint, and Privileges of Immunity in Early Medieval Europe*. Ithaca: Cornell University Press, 1999.
Rubin, Stanley. 'Æthelberht 36: A Medico-Linguistic Discussion on the Word *hion*.' *Nottingham Medieval Studies* 39 (1995): 19–25.
Sayers, William. 'Early Irish Attitudes toward Hair and Beards, Baldness and Tonsure.' *Zeitschrift für celtische Philologie* 44 (1991): 154–89.
Schaaffhausen, B. 'Sur quelques trouvailles faites en Allemagne.' In *Congrès international d'anthropologie et d'archéologie préhistoriques. Compte Rendu de la 7e session* 2: 841–8. Stockholm: Imprimerie central, 1874. Vol. 2: 841–8. Discussion, Franz Virchow, 848–50.
Schmidt, L. *Geschichte der deutschen Stämme bis zum Ausgang der Völkerwanderung: die Ostgermanen*. 2nd ed. Munich: C.H. Beck, 1934, repr. 1969.
Schmidt, M.G. 'Prothese aus dem frühen Mittelalter.' *Kosmos* 73 (1977): 806–7.
– 'Steinzeitmensch im Merovingergrab.' *Kosmos* 74 (1978): 746–9.
Schmitt-Weigand, Adolf. *Rechtspflegedelikte in der fränkischen Zeit*. Berlin: Walter de Gruyter, 1962.
Schmidt-Wiegand, Ruth, ed. *Wörter und Sachen in Lichte der Bezeichnungsforschung*. Berlin: Walter de Gruyter, 1980.
Schneider-Schneckenburger, Gudrun. *Churrätien im Frühmittelalter auf Grund der archäologischen Funde*. Münchner Beiträge zur Vor- und Frühgeschichte 26. Munich: C.H. Beck'sche Verlagsbuchhandlung, 1980.
Schoene, H. 'Zwei Listen Chirugischer Instrumente.' *Hermes* 38 (1903): 280–4.
Schulenberg, Anne Tibbetts. *Forgetful of Their Sex: Female Sanctity and Society, ca. 500–1100*. Chicago: University of Chicago Press, 1998.
Schützeichel, Rudolf. *Althochdeutsches Wörterbuch*. Tübingen: Niemeyer Verlag, 1995.
Schutz, Herbert. *The Germanic Realms in Pre-Carolingian Central Europe, 400–750*. New York: Peter Lang, 2000.

Schwartz, Jeffrey. *What the Bones Tell Us*. Tucson: University of Arizona Press, 1993.
Schwyter, Jürg Rainer. 'L1 Interference in the Editing Process: Felix Liebermann, the *Gesetze* and the German Language.' In *Law Before Magna Carta: Felix Lieberman and Die Gesetze der Angelsachsen*, ed. Jurasinski, Oliver, and Rabin, 43–58.
Sharpe, Richard. 'Dispute Settlement in Medieval Ireland.' In *Settlement of Disputes*, ed. Davies and Fouracre, 169–90.
Sharpe, William. 'An Early Mediaeval Treatise on Bloodletting: A Translation from the Latin of the Venerable Bede *De Minutione Sanguinis Sive de Phlebot*.' *Quarterly of the Phi Beta Pi Medical Fraternity* 52 (1955–6): 82–7.
Shklar, Gerald, and David Chernin. *A Sourcebook of Dental Medicine: Being a Documentary History of Dentistry and Stomatology from the Earliest Times to the Middle of the Twentieth Century*. Dental Classics in Perspective 3. Waban, MA: Maro, 2002.
Siraisi, Nancy G. *Medieval and Early Renaissance Medicine*. Chicago: University of Chicago Press, 1990.
– 'Early Anatomy in Comparative Perspective: Introduction.' *Journal of the History of Medicine and Allied Sciences* 50.1 (1995): 3–10.
Skinner, Patricia. *Health and Medicine in Early Medieval Southern Italy*. Leiden: Brill, 1997.
Smith, O.C., E.J. Pope, and S.A. Symes. 'Look until You See: Identification of Trauma in Skeletal Material.' In *Hard Evidence: Case Studies in Forensic Anthropology*, ed. D.W. Steadman, 138–54. NJ: Palgrave MacMillan, 2003.
Smyth, Alfred P. *King Alfred the Great*. Oxford: Oxford University Press, 1995.
Stanley, Eric Gerald. 'Anglo-Saxon Trial by Jury.' In *Imaging the Anglo-Saxon Past*, 111–47. Cambridge: D.S. Brewer, 1975.
Stenton, Frank. *Anglo-Saxon England*. Oxford: Oxford University Press, 1943.
Stock, Brian. *The Implications of Literacy: Written Language and Models of Interpretation in the Eleventh and Twelfth Centuries*. Princeton: Princeton University Press, 1983.
Stoodley, Nick. 'Multiple Burials, Multiple Meanings? Interpreting the Early Anglo-Saxon Multiple Interment.' In *Burial in Early Medieval England and Wales*, ed Lucy and Reynolds, 103–21.
Strohmaier, Gotthard. 'Dura Mater, Pia Mater: Die Geschichte zweier anatomischer Termini.' *Medizinhistorisches Journal* 5 (1970): 201–17.
Sudhoff, Karl. *Ein Beitrag zur Geschichte der Anatomie im Mittelalter*. Leipzig: Barth, 1908.
– *Beiträge zur Geschichte der Chirugie im Mittelalter*. 2 vols. Leipzig: Verlag von Johann Abrosius Barth, 1918.

Turner, Bryan S. *The Body and Society*. 3rd ed. Los Angeles: Sage, 2008.
von Baldur, Keil. 'Eine Prothese aus einem fränkischen Grab von Griesheim, Kreis Darmstadt-Dieburg: anthropologische und medizinhistorische Befund.' *Fundberichte aus Hessen* 178 (1977–8): 195–211.
von Olberg, Gabriele. 'Soziale Schichtung im Spiegel volksprachiger Wörter der Leges.' In *Wörter und Sachen in Lichte der Bezeichnungsforschung*, ed. Ruth Schmidt-Wiegand, 91–106.
Vorwahl, Heinrich. *Deutsche Volksmedizin in Vergangenheit und Gegenwart. Studien zur religiösen Volkskunde*, Heft 9. Leipzig and Dresden: Verlag C. Ludwig Ungelenk, 1939.
Wallace-Hadrill, J.M. *The Barbarian West 400–1000*. Rev. ed. Oxford: Blackwell, 1985.
– *The Long-Haired Kings*. Toronto: University of Toronto Press, 1962. Repr. 1989.
– *Early Germanic Kingship in England and on the Continent*. The Ford Lectures, 1970. Oxford: Clarendon Press, 1971.
Watermann, Rembert. *Medizinisches und Hygenisches aus Germania Inferior: Ein Beitrag zur Geschichte der Medizin und Hygiene der römischen Provinzen*. Neuss: Gesellschaft für Buchdruckerei, 1974.
Watkins, Calvert, ed. *The American Heritage Dictionary of Indo-European Roots*. 2nd ed. Boston: Houghton Mifflin, 2000.
Wickersheimer, Ernest. *Dictionannaire Biographique des Médecins en France au Moyen Age*. Paris: Librairie E. Droz, 1936.
Wickham, Chris. 'Land Disputes and Their Social Framework in Lombard-Carolingian Italy, 700–900.' In *Settlement of Disputes*, ed. Davies and Fouracre, 105–24.
– 'Society.' In *The Early Middle Ages: Europe 400–1000*, ed. McKitterick, 59–96.
Williams, Howard. 'Artefacts in Early Medieval Graves: A New Perspective.' In *Debating Late Antiquity in Britain AD 300–700*, ed. R. Collins and J. Gerrard, 89–102. Oxford: Archeopress, 2004.
– *Death and Memory in Early Medieval Britain*. Cambridge: Cambridge University Press, 2006.
Williams, John, ed. *The Archaeology of Kent to AD 800*. Woodbridge: Boydell, 2007.
Wilson, Colin. *Written in Blood: A History of Forensic Detection*. Philadelphia: Running Press, 2003.
Winfield, Percy H. 'The Myth of Absolute Liability.' *Law Quarterly Review* 42 (Jan. 1926): 37–51.
Withers, Benjamin C., and Jonathon Wilcox, eds. *Naked Before God: Uncovering the Body in Anglo-Saxon England*. Morgantown: University of West Virginia Press, 2003.

Wlaschky, M. '*Sapientia artis medicinae*: Ein frühmittelalterliches Kompendium der Medizin.' *Kyklos* 1 (1928): 103–13.
Wood, Ian. 'Disputes in Late Fifth- and Sixth-Century Gaul: Some Problems.' In *Settlement of Disputes*, ed. Davies and Fouracre, 7–22.
- *The Merovingian Kingdoms: 450–751*. London and New York: Longman, 1994.
Wormald, Patrick. '*Lex Scripta* and *Verbum Regis*: Legislation and Germanic Kingship from Euric to Cnut.' In *Early Medieval Kingship*, ed. P.H. Sawyer and I.N. Wood, 105–38. Leeds: Leeds University Press, 1977. Repr. in Wormald, *Legal Culture*, 1–44.
- 'Charters, Law and the Settlement of Disputes in Anglo-Saxon England.' In *Settlement of Disputes*, ed. Davies and Fouracre. Repr. in Wormald, *Legal Culture*, 289–312.
- 'In Search of King Offa's "Law Code."' In *People and Places in Northern Europe, 500–1600: Studies Presented to P.H. Sawyer*, ed. I. Wood and N. Lund, Woodville: Boydell Press, 1991. Repr. in Wormald, *Legal Culture*, 201–23.
- '"Inter Cetera Bona Genti Suae": Law-Making and Peace-Keeping in the Earliest English Kingdoms.' *Settimana di Studio del Centro Italiano di Studi sull' alto Medioevo* 42 (Spoleto, 1995): 963–96. Repr. in Wormald, *Legal Culture*, 179–200.
- '*Exempla Romanorum*: The Earliest English Legislation in Context.' In *Rome and the North*, ed. Alvar Ellegård and Åkerström-Hougen, 15–28. Studies in Mediterranean Archaeology and Literature 135. Jonsered, Sweden: Paul Astroms Verlag, 1996.
- *Legal Culture in the Early Medieval West: Law as Text, Image and Experience*. London and Rio Grande, OH: Hambledon Press, 1999.
- *The Making of English Law: King Alfred to the Twelfth Century*. Oxford: Blackwell, 1999.
- 'The *Leges Barbarorum*: Law and Ethnicity in the Medieval West.' In *Regna and Gentes*, ed. Goetz et al., 21–55.
- *The First Code of English Law*. Medway, Kent: Canterbury Commemorative Society, 2005.
Yorke, Barbara A.E. *Kings and Kingdoms of Early Anglo-Saxon England*. London: Seaby, 1990.

Index

Vernacular terminology for body parts is listed under specific languages: thus, for example: Old English: *gekyndlice lim*, 'penis'; *hion*, '*tabulum* of the skull'; etc. Law texts are listed under territories: thus, for example, Lombardy: *Lex Langobardorum*. Individual grave finds are listed under cemeteries.

abbess, 179, 192
abbot, 72, 157, 192
abdomen/abdominal, 114, 116, 129, 133, 233, 235, 249, 257–8, 260. *See also* stomach
abduction, 59, 170, 172n30, 184–5, 187–91, 201, 224
abortion, 180, 195–9, 202. *See also* miscarriage
absolute liability, 63
accident(al), 62–7, 76, 107, 121, 127, 141, 162
accuse(r)/accusation, 32, 34, 38–43, 45, 50, 55–6, 58–61, 65–6, 95, 102, 108, 142, 150, 170, 178, 183, 192, 206, 240
Adam's apple, 96, 101, 260
adjourn(ment), 37, 39–40, 58, 65. *See also* continuance
adulterer/adultery, 179, 184, 192, 224

Ælfthryth, queen of Anglo-Saxons, 29n13
Æthelbald, king of West Saxons, 186n27
Æthelberht, king of Kent, 11, 16–17, 23, 24n34, 61, 67, 79–80, 82, 96, 96n53, 102, 106, 134, 140–1, 155, 161–2, 167, 169, 205, 221; laws of (specific clauses), 37n55, 72n1, 106n70, 112n1, 116n9, 129n43, 130n49, 137n1, 165n1, 167n60, 169n19, 181n73, 188n29, 204n2, 205n6, 206n9, 207n10, 212n15. *See also, crucially for discussion of laws,* Kent
Æthelwulf, king of West Saxons, 186n27
afterlife, 46, 153
aire 'freeman' (OI), 31n23
Alamann(ia)/Alemann, 12–14, 17, 19, 21, 24, 37, 45, 47–8, 51, 53, 56, 69,

76, 77n14, 93–9, 102, 104, 106, 108, 112–14, 116–17, 120, 123–4, 128–35, 138, 138n5, 139–41, 143, 150, 152–3, 156, 161, 166, 168, 181–2, 188, 197, 201, 208–9, 222–3, 225, 227, 230, 231, 233, 235, 237, 242, 247; *Lex Alamannorum*, 17, 21–2, 24, 47, 76, 51, 86, 133, 200, 221, 250–1; *Lex Alamannorum*, specific clauses, 34n40, 37n55, 42n81, 45n96, 47n105, 56n140, 72n1, 84nn27, 29, 112n1, 116nn6, 8, 117n11, 123n30, 124nn31, 32, 128n37, 129nn43, 44, 46, 130n49, 131n52, 133n61, 137n1, 141n7, 143n13, 166n5, 167n9, 168nn14, 16, 181n4, 182n12, 188nn30, 31, 197n39, 207n10, 212n15, 222n19, 242n6; *Pactus Alamannorum*, 22, 86, 120, 132, 157; *Pactus Alamannorum*, specific clauses, 42n81, 132n56, 197n59; terminology: *hrevovunt/reveunt* 'wounded in the stomach,' 129n43, 233; *marchzand* 'bordertooth,' 104; *scardi* 'sliced,' 233, 235; *taudragil* 'dragging in dew,' 117, 231, 235; *wasilus* 'synovial fluid,' 132, 132nn56, 58

Alcuin, abbot of St Martin's, 35, 52
Alfred, king of West Saxons, 14, 16–17, 23, 24n34, 50–1, 53, 80, 82, 82n23, 92, 98–9, 104, 106, 108–10, 117, 132, 134, 138n5, 140, 152–3, 161–2, 166–7, 183, 186n27, 198, 200, 235, 237 (*see also* Wessex); laws of (specific clauses), 50n114, 64n160, 72n1, 80n21, 96n54, 112n1, 116n6, 117n13, 123n30, 128n36, 129n43, 130n49, 132n55, 137n1, 142n10, 166nn2, 4, 167n8, 170n22, 172n31, 174n41, 182nn13, 14, 183nn17, 18, 192n8, 198n75, 200n85, 212n15
allegation, 62, 130n51
aloarii, 38
altar, 36, 38–9, 42, 44–5, 57–8
ambush, 44, 58–9, 171, 253
amputation, 119, 127–8, 142, 172, 172n30, 175, 209. *See also* exarticulation
anatomical/anatomy, 4–5, 7–8, 25, 80n20, 83, 106, 113, 128, 132n57, 146, 155, 157, 161–2, 170, 217, 230, 235–6
Andrea de Jorio, 111
Angers, 29n13, 30n15, 40, 42, 43n86, 49, 50n112, 53, 56, 58–9, 151n37, 190n38. *See also* formulary; Marculf of Angers
Anglo-Frisian, 19, 95, 98, 99, 113, 130, 140, 230, 231
Anglo-Saxon, 3, 9, 11, 17, 18, 23–4, 24n34, 29n13, 30n14, 31, 33, 33n29, 35n48, 36, 46, 47n104, 50n113, 57, 61n155, 64, 79, 79n16, 82n25, 83–4, 87, 92, 101–2, 106, 108, 129–30, 134–5, 149–52, 171n28, 190n37, 192, 224, 233
ankle, 117, 130, 162, 257
anthropology/anthropological, 3, 6–7, 80, 80n22, 162
Aquitaine, 186n27
archbishop, 45, 52
archaeology/archaeological, 7
archer(y), 143n16, 147–9, 156
Aristotle, 137
arm, 4, 38, 43, 63, 82n23, 108, 112, 114, 116, 122–4, 124n32, 125–8, 131, 134–6

armbands, 151, 169, 172, 199–200, 208, 211, 214, 216, 218, 230, 231–2, 235–6, 239, 248–51, 253, 255–60
army, 114, 176, 225
arrow(s), 147n25, 148, 149n29, 153, 156
assault, 4, 10, 28, 36–7, 53, 55, 59–61, 67, 109, 169–70, 180, 180n1, 181–3, 185, 188, 195, 195n68, 199–203, 205, 217, 222, 222n20, 224, 238, 246–7. *See also* attack
assembly, 30, 31n23, 35, 35n48, 40, 42n84, 62–3, 65–7, 179. See also *mallberg*; *mæþel*; *thing*
atrophy, 120
attack, 38, 54n132, 58, 61–2, 87, 109, 141, 179, 188n29, 195–6, 199, 202, 212, 217, 221, 224, 245–6. *See also* assault
axe, 44n93, 51, 62, 66, 80

Bangor Gospels, 27
baptism, 73, 196, 241–2
barbarian, 3n1, 9–10, 12, 12nn13, 14, 14, 28–9, 50, 61, 61n155, 100–1, 108, 112, 117, 135–6, 153, 167, 171, 179, 193, 207, 212; law(s), 5, 6n3, 8n1, 13, 17–18, 20, 27, 30, 51, 54, 62–3, 66, 74, 84n28, 86–7, 92–4, 98, 99, 107–8, 110, 112, 130, 138, 140–1, 143, 155, 165–6, 171, 175, 178, 182–3, 189, 191–2, 195, 199, 203–4, 207, 210, 212, 220, 226
battery (physical), 55
Bavaria(n), 3, 6, 13–14, 19, 39, 41, 54, 56, 76, 82, 84, 87, 91, 93, 98, 99, 101, 104, 104n69, 106, 112–13, 122–3, 129, 136, 138, 138n5, 139–40, 153, 168, 175, 177–8, 201–4, 224n25, 225–7, 230, 231, 235, 237, 247; law, 17, 36, 51, 86, 113, 117, 140, 146, 172, 178, 202, 207–9, 216–9, 222, 224, 236; law, specific clauses, 72n1, 76n10, 84nn27, 28, 29, 112n1, 123n30, 129n23, 137n1, 143n13, 146n21, 167n9, 168n17, 172n34, 175n44, 181n5, 207n10, 212n15, 222n19, 215, 233; *Lex Bauiuaroum*, 22, 32, 87, 104n69, 178, 207–8, 255; terminology: *hrevavunt* 'wounded in the stomach,' 129, 233, 235; *marchzand* 'bordertooth,' 104; *scarti* 'sliced,' 233, 235; *taudragil* 'dragging in dew,' 117, 231, 235
beak, 98–9
beard, 108, 110, 166–7, 250
Bede, 72
Beowulf, 109
Berhthun, abbot of Beverly, 72
Bible/biblical, 27, 39, 99, 120n23, 137, 197
bishop, 32, 35n44, 45, 52, 72–3, 136, 157n54, 178, 200, 222, 222nn20, 21, 223–4
blinking (of the eye), 100
blood, 37, 62, 76, 84, 84n28, 86–7, 112n1, 122, 143, 179, 187, 199, 207, 217, 248, 251–2, 254–6, 258–9; bloodline/rank, 182, 223
bloodfeud. *See* feud
Bobbio, 20
body, 4–5, 7, 72, 74, 106, 112, 112n2, 113–16, 118, 128–30, 133–6, 143, 165, 169–70, 172, 174–5, 192–3, 204n4, 207, 230, 239, 241, 252, 256, 259. *See also* torso; *individual listings of body parts*
bone(s), 3, 67, 74, 74n6, 75–8, 80, 80n22, 82, 82n23, 84–8, 90–1,

91n43, 92–4, 101, 104, 117–18, 121–3, 123n27, 124–8, 130, 130n51, 131, 134–6, 158, 158n55, 164, 167, 172, 208, 211, 214, 216–18, 238, 238n1, 248–50, 252–60
boni homines/boni viri, 'good men,' 30–1, 33, 35–6, 46. *See also* jurors; *rachimburgi*
bow (weapon), 119, 141, 147n29, 148, 149n29
bowels, 129, 133, 258
brain, 67, 74, 74n4, 76–7, 79–80, 84, 86–9, 91–2, 94, 208–9, 216, 218, 220, 248, 250–1, 255, 257
breast(s), 90, 178, 199–200, 202, 224, 257
bribe(s), 34, 39, 52, 52n124, 76, 170, 189
bride, 179, 185, 189, 191, 194, 201
bridegroom/groom, 187–9, 191, 201
bride-price, 183, 185, 187–9, 201, 243. *See also* dowry
Britain/British, 3, 12n14, 18–19, 87, 91, 98–9, 144, 206. *See also* Welsh
Brittany, 28n9, 31, 34n39, 47n106
Broca, 91n43
bruise/bruising, 37, 37n55, 57–8, 61, 84, 86–7, 112n1, 165–7, 171, 199, 215, 217, 222, 249–50, 253–4, 256
Brunhild, queen of Merovingians, 108
Burgundy/Burgundian, 9n6, 12, 16, 19, 102, 104, 106, 109, 112–13, 116, 122–3, 166, 172, 185, 200–2, 205, 209, 213, 217, 225, 227, 230, 231; law, 17, 35–6, 40, 42–4, 52n124, 53, 53n129, 92–3, 109, 116, 122, 133, 136, 138, 142, 166, 169, 181, 185–6, 188, 200, 204, 210, 213, 217, 235, 247–8; law, specific clauses, 37n55, 52n125, 72n1, 112n1, 116n7, 142n11, 166n6, 169n20, 172n32, 181n6, 185n26, 187n28, 200nn82, 86, 204n2, 207n10, 212n15; *Lex Burgundionum*, 21–2, 24; *Lex Romana Burgundionum*, 22; *Liber Constitutionem*, 185, 248
burial(s), 5, 35, 47, 78, 82, 82n25, 102, 108, 144–5, 145nn19, 20, 150–1, 153, 173, 192–4. *See also* grave
Byzantine Empire, 19, 109

cane (with which to walk), 120–1
canines/canine teeth, 82n23, 102, 102n67, 104n69, 106, 216, 218, 249–50, 255, 258, 260
canon law, 178
Carolingian, 27n4, 28n9, 35, 39, 52, 110–11, 177; capitulary/capitularies/decrees, 35–6, 45; Francia/Franks, 12, 20, 51n117; laws, 33, 44
case (legal), 3–4, 25–7, 27n3, 28–9, 29n13, 30–3, 33n29, 34–47, 47n106, 49–51, 51n117, 52–3, 53n129, 54–6, 56nn139, 141, 57–66, 66n165, 67–70, 79, 87, 170, 177, 182–7, 198n76, 204, 230, 240, 245–6. *See also* hearing (legal)
castration, 90, 128, 173, 173n39, 216, 252
Celts/Celtic, 9, 12, 12n14, 47n104. *See also* Brittany; Ireland; Old/Early Irish; Welsh
cemetery/cemeteries, 77n14, 107, 118, 122–3, 145, 150–1, 162, 192, 246
ceorl 'freeman' (OE), 183
Chamavan Francia, 13–14, 17, 19, 93, 101, 109, 112, 135, 138, 138n5, 140–2, 172–209, 212, 225–7, 230, 235, 237, 247, 258; law, specific clauses, 72n1, 137n1, 142n9,

172n30, 204n2, 207n10, 212n15, 224n26; *Lex (Francorum) Chamavorum*, 205, 220, 225, 254
character witnesses, 65. See also oath: oath-swearers
Charlemagne, king of Franks, 9n3, 33, 36, 45, 45n97, 52, 54–5, 110–11, 129
Charles the Bald, king of Western Francia, 186n27
chastity, 179, 184, 193; chaste, 150, 190, 201
Chaucer, 193, 226
cheek, 82n23, 101, 177, 249, 257, 260
chest, 84n28, 90, 114, 128–9, 211, 214, 216, 253
child(ren), 39, 42–3, 110, 134, 192, 194–9, 209, 226, 241–3, 260
child-bearing/birth, 158, 182, 194–5, 202, 220–1, 242
chin, 101. See also jaw
Christ, 137, 174, 179, 201; bride of, 179, 201, 224
Christian, 11, 31, 109, 142, 173, 193, 224
church, 27, 30–1, 31n20, 36, 49, 53, 54n132, 56–7, 110, 142, 172–3, 197, 206, 219, 221–2
churchman/men, 34, 190, 198n38, 222, 224–5. See also cleric; clergy
Cirugia Eliodori. See Heliodorus
clergy, 27, 49, 72, 222. See also churchman; cleric
cleric(al), 32, 49, 59, 73, 177, 190n38, 193, 203, 223–4. See also churchman; clergy
Codex Theodosianus, 29. See also Theodosian Code
collarbone, 128, 130, 130n51, 131, 134–5, 249–50
combat, 12, 42, 45, 181
comes 'count,' 35–6, 38

compensation, 4, 7, 9–10, 13, 28, 44–5, 49, 51, 57, 59–60, 62, 64, 69, 84, 87, 93–4, 97, 117, 140–3, 145, 153, 155–6, 161, 166–7, 169, 171, 180–3, 189, 192, 194, 198–9, 201, 203–4, 204n4, 205, 208, 210–12, 214–220, 222–6
conlaudantes. See oath: oath-swearers
continuance, 36. See also adjourn(ment)
contraception, 199n79
cornea, 100
corporal punishment, 87, 97. See also public: lashing/scourging
court (of law), 26–7, 29, 29nn12, 13, 30–3, 33n29, 34, 34n39, 35–40, 42, 49–51, 53, 53n129, 54–5, 59–61, 63, 63n156, 64–6, 69–70, 87, 126, 170, 174, 177–8, 205, 236, 245–6
cow(s), 9, 48, 190, 226
cremation, 108
crime, 10, 30, 33, 38, 49, 51, 59–60, 82, 170, 172–3, 178, 186–7, 190, 195–6, 198, 206, 224, 243
crutch, 120–1
cure, 5, 24–5, 67–8, 72–4, 79, 89, 91, 136, 164, 260
custom(ary law), 13, 28, 32, 38, 51–2, 57, 70n169, 71, 148, 196, 245

damage, 4, 10, 25, 37n55, 42, 55, 59, 66–9, 80, 82–4, 86, 93–8, 101, 106–9, 112–14, 116–17, 120–4, 127–32, 132n57, 133–6, 139–42, 145, 156, 160, 162, 164–9, 171, 173, 175, 180, 190, 183, 199, 201, 203, 207–9, 215–20, 230, 231–3, 235–6, 240, 242–3, 249–50
damages, 4, 10, 42, 51, 181, 191, 199, 209, 212, 217, 220, 225;

compensatory, 10, 50, 165, 167, 170; punitive, 10, 165, 169–70. *See also* fine
deacon, 72, 148, 222–4, 224n22
deafness, 93–4, 168, 171, 216, 218, 249–50, 252, 255, 257, 259–60
death, 5n2, 26, 38, 43, 49, 52n124, 55, 57–60, 64, 77, 91n43, 93, 119, 127, 162, 170, 178, 184–6, 186n27, 187, 191–3, 196, 202, 207, 210, 223, 225
defendant, 32, 34, 36, 38, 40–4, 47, 50, 53, 55–9
deformity, 51, 97, 122
dentist, 107. *See also* tooth
dew, 117, 108–9, 216, 218, 233, 235, 255
diabetes, 162
diploe, 80, 82, 82n24
disfigurement, 101, 165, 167, 171, 176, 233, 249, 256, 259
dismemberment, 178
doctor, 5, 42, 67–9, 73, 76, 79, 81, 88–9, 123n27, 126, 129, 151, 156–7, 157n54, 207, 210, 241, 249. *See also* medical; *medicus*; surgeon
dowry, 186n27, 190–1. *See also* bride-price
duel, 45–6, 102, 198
dura mater, 79n17, 86, 87n31, 257
dux 'duke,' 35

Eadric, king of Kent, 16n21, 24n34, 36, 50n113, 205
ear, 90, 92–5, 97–8, 129, 138, 141, 143, 153, 168, 171, 173–4, 177, 211, 214, 216, 218, 227, 230, 233, 248–50, 252–7, 259–60. *See also* hear(ing) (sense of)
East Germanic. *See* Germanic
Edictus Rothari. *See* Lombard

elbow, 82n23, 114, 123–6, 131–2, 132n56, 142, 199–200, 208, 218, 250–1, 255, 257–8, 260
England/English, 11–12, 18–20, 23, 24n24, 30, 33, 35n48, 36, 46, 47n104, 59, 74–5, 79, 82n25, 86–7, 91–3, 98–9, 101–2, 108, 116, 123, 128, 132, 138, 146–9, 152, 155–6, 159, 170, 171n28, 175n47, 179, 186n27, 187, 224, 243n7, 246
eorl, 205
esne/esnas 'servant(s)' (OE), 57, 210n13, 221
ethnic/ethnicity, 8n1, 11–12
ethnogenesis, 11, 11n11
exarticulation, 119, 162, 164. *See also* amputation
execution, 178, 187, 195
Exodus, 120, 137n2, 197
eye, 4, 63, 72–3, 92–5, 97–101, 109, 137, 137n2, 138–141, 143, 152, 167, 169–74, 177, 182, 195, 208–10, 210n13, 211, 214–17, 220, 227, 230, 236, 239–40, 242, 248–50, 252–60; eyebrow, 101, 258; eyelash, 101; eyelid(s), 69, 99–101, 216, 218–19, 250, 255, 258. *See also* cornea; vision
eye-witness(es), 65, 192

face, 73, 94–5, 101–2, 114, 166–7, 179n62, 192, 211, 214, 216, 233, 236, 240, 249–50, 253
femur, 90, 119, 121–2
fertile/fertility, 194, 222
fetus, 195–7, 197n66, 198, 202, 241–2
feud, 13, 13n16, 36–7, 47, 57, 69
fibula, 122–3
fine(s), 3, 8–10, 30–6, 40–1, 45–7, 49–52, 52n124, 53, 53n129, 55–6, 58–61, 63–6, 68–9, 76–7, 79, 82,

82n23, 84, 87, 89, 93, 95–7, 99, 101, 104, 106, 108–9, 112, 114, 116–17, 120, 123–4, 128–9, 133–6, 140–3, 146, 153, 156, 161, 165–71, 175–6, 181–3, 185, 186n27, 188–92, 194–204, 204n4, 205–10, 212, 215, 217, 219–220, 220n16, 221–7, 230, 231, 233, 235–6, 240–2, 247–61. *See also* damages; *mid wite*
finger(s), 51, 63, 69, 82n23, 112, 114, 117, 131–2, 140–1, 143, 143n16, 144, 144n17, 145–7, 147n22, 148–9, 149n29, 150, 150n32, 151, 151n38, 152, 152n39, 153–60, 169–70, 199, 208–9, 212, 215, 217, 219–20, 229–30, 233–6, 239, 248–61; fingernails, 156, 197n66, 249, 261
foot/feet, 63, 69, 74, 76, 79, 90, 112–14, 116–19, 123, 130, 137, 137n2, 138–42, 151, 158–9, 162, 164, 172, 174, 177, 179, 182, 198, 208–10, 210n13, 211, 214–16, 218, 220, 227, 233, 239, 248–50, 252–60
forearm, 124, 127
forehead, 90, 102, 167, 258
foreign(er), 10, 43, 203, 224–5
forgery, 27, 142, 172
formulary/formularies, 32, 50, 56, 189, 190n38, 205, 245. *See also* Angers
Forum Iudicum. See Visigoth
fracture, 25, 69, 73, 77, 82n35, 83, 94, 122–4, 130, 135, 257
France, 92, 94, 107, 120, 130
Francia. *See* Carolingian; Chamavan Francia; Merovingian; Ripuaria(n): Francia/Franks; Salian Francia
Frank(ish)/Franks, 11–12, 12n13, 13–14, 16–17, 28, 30–1, 33–4, 46,
49n111, 50, 60, 101, 108–9, 118, 123, 204–6, 223, 225, 230, 231, 235, 237 (*for specific regions, see* Chamavan Franks; Salian Francia; Ripuaria(n): Francia/Franks; Carolingian); cases, 40, 53–5; decree, 35–6, 55 (*see also* Carolingian: capitulary/capitularies/decrees); dialects/language, 19, 35, 58, 75, 79, 147, 147n22, 149–50, 152; *Edict of Chilperic*, 39, 49; laws/capitularies, 22, 33, 36, 45, 52, 52n124, 95, 171, 177, 212n15 (*see also* Carolingian: capitulary/capitularies/decrees); terminology: *allatamo/ *alathumo* 'thumb,' 147; *briorotero* 'forefinger,' 149; *gisifrit* '?wounded in internal organs,' 133; *hlinôn* 'support,' 152, 153n42; *mahelvingerlîn* 'the engagement finger,' 151 (*see also* Alamann(ia)/Alemann; Bavaria(n); Thuringia(n): terminology)
Franks Casket, 144, 149
Fredegar, 108
free-born, 212, 219–21, 223, 225–6, 240. *See also* freeman; free woman
freedman, 182n8, 203, 207–12, 214–15, 217–21, 226, 236, 240
freedom, 31, 60, 207
freedwoman, 207, 210, 212, 220
freeman/men, 31n23, 33–4, 36, 42, 42n83, 87, 110, 117, 142, 168, 170, 172–4, 180–1, 190, 194, 198, 204, 204n4, 205, 207–12, 215, 218–19, 220n16, 221–2, 222n21, 223, 226, 248, 259
free woman/women, 180–4, 194, 196, 197–8, 201, 203, 220–2
Frisia(n), 13, 18, 95, 101, 106, 113, 140, 156, 161, 173, 183–4, 200–1,

292   Index

225, 227, 230, 231, 233, 235, 237, 239, 247; language, 19; law, 14, 17, 19, 23, 44, 51, 59, 69, 84, 86–7, 96–7, 99, 101, 104, 106, 109–12, 112n2, 116, 123, 128–34, 138, 138n5, 140–2, 147, 150, 153, 161, 166–70, 172–3, 183, 197n66, 198, 200, 208, 215, 355–6; laws, specific clauses, 72n1, 84nn27, 28, 29, 112n1, 116nn6, 8, 9, 123n30, 124n31, 128nn36, 38, 41, 129n44, 130n49, 131n53, 133n62, 137n1, 141n8, 166n3, 167nn9, 13, 170n22, 173n38, 183n16, 184n19, 199n77, 200n84, 204n2, 207n10, 212n15; *Lex Frisionum*, 45, 106, 116n5, 198, 200, 257–8, 263, 265; terminology: *granones* 'mustache,' 18, 111; *lidu uuagi* 'synovial fluid,' 131

Gaiseric, king of Vandals, 95
gangrene, 162
Gaul, 236
gender: grammatical, 59, 80, 80n20, 156, 178; physical, 96, 108, 156, 178, 180, 180n2, 182, 203
genital(s), 104, 114, 116, 128–9, 134–6, 178, 200, 230, 232, 235–6, 249. See also loin(s); scrotum; testicles
German(y), 10, 12, 29, 77–8, 83, 85, 91, 92, 94, 95, 102, 118, 121, 125–7, 151n38, 193; Middle High, 151; Modern, 24, 33n29, 79, 80n20, 104n69, 132, 149; Old High, 132, 152
Germanenrechte, 24
Germania, 12, 171, 206
Germanic, 4–5, 8, 8n1, 9, 9n2, 10–11, 11n11, 12, 12n14, 13–14, 14n20, 17, 18, 20–5, 28, 29n12, 31n23, 33n29, 39, 52, 55, 61n155, 69, 78, 91, 106, 109, 111, 114, 117, 145, 150, 166–8, 207, 210, 212, 225, 227, 233, 236, 239–40, 244, 246 (see also Germania); dialect(s)/language, 3n1, 9, 9n7, 12, 19, 21, 75, 80, 101, 111, 147 (see also German[y]: Middle High, Modern, Old High); East, 19–20; vernacular, 18, 30, 38n61, 104, 129, 132, 227, 233, 235; West, 19–20; law(s)/legal codes/ legislation, 4, 6, 8, 8n1, 10, 10nn2, 10, 13, 18, 21, 24–5, 44, 44n93, 47n104, 69, 138, 143, 149, 180, 183, 197, 203, 227, 239–40, 242–3, 247; runes, 9; tradition(s), 8, 10n2, 117n12, 186n27
Gesellschaft für ältere deutsche Geschichtskunde, 24
gloss(es), 18, 35, 132n58, 146, 149, 151, 151n38, 153, 155, 188, 233. See also *mallberg*
God, 30, 38, 41, 46, 54n132, 72–4, 174, 178, 193, 205–6, 223–5
gods, 31n20, 173
gold, 9, 47, 52, 97, 107, 151–2, 155, 190, 254; *goldfinger*, 150, 153, 155–6, 170, 249
goldsmith, 48, 51, 141, 213, 239
grafio 'count,' 35, 204–5. See also *comes*
grave(s), 3, 39, 60, 77, 77nn13, 14, 78, 82–3, 85, 91–2, 107–8, 118–23, 123n27, 124–7, 130–1, 144–5, 150, 150n34, 151, 156, 162–3, 172, 192. See also burial
Greek(s), 12, 19, 90–1, 98, 110, 152n39 (see also Byzantine Empire); terminology, 90, 152n39; *odoùs mulítes* 'chewing teeth,' 168;

prosōpōi 'damage to countenance,' 167; *rhis* 'nose,' 98
Gregory, bishop of Tours, 43, 108, 156
Grendel, 109
groom. *See* bridegroom
guilt(y), 34, 40–1, 44, 46, 50, 55–8, 66, 142, 170, 178, 184, 193, 195, 198, 206. *See also* innocence
Gundobad, king of Burgundians, 42

habeas corpus, 33
hair, 84, 86, 95, 99, 102, 108, 108n74, 109–11, 142
hand, 4, 26, 38, 42–6, 51–2, 57, 62–6, 69, 73–4, 109, 112–14, 116, 123–4, 126n32, 128, 130–1, 137, 137n2, 138–44, 144n18, 146–8, 150–1, 151n38, 152n39, 158–61, 165, 169–70, 172, 172n30, 173–4, 177, 199–200, 204–5, 207–8, 210–11, 214–15, 217–19, 220, 227, 239, 248–61; scribal, 21–2
handspan, 145, 158
harpist, 51, 141, 239
head, 52, 69, 72, 72n1, 73–4, 76, 79–81, 82n23, 84, 84n28, 86–92, 101, 109, 112–13, 143, 167, 176, 179, 199, 208, 211, 214, 216, 218, 248–61; headache, 67–9
heal(ing)/healer(s), 3–5, 8, 24, 69, 73–4, 76–8, 82, 91, 91n43, 92, 94, 117, 119, 121–2, 123n27, 125–8, 130, 135, 156–7, 157n54, 158, 164, 169, 211, 214, 216, 240, 248
hear(ing) (sense of), 63, 74, 93, 96–8, 170, 186. *See also* ear
hearing (legal), 29, 30, 32, 34n39, 35–7, 39–42, 45, 52–3, 53n129, 55, 57–8, 65, 68, 205, 249, 256, 260. *See also* case

heart, 52, 133, 150–2
heel, 158
Heliodorus: *Cirugia Eliodori*, 89; *Lecciones Heliodori*, 89, 152n39
herbaria 'woman skilled in herbal medicine,' 137
Herebald, abbot of Tynemouth, 72–4
hernia, 129–30, 133, 251, 254
Hincmar, archbishop of Rheims, 52
hip(s), 90, 116–17, 120–1, 128, 134, 257, 259
Hlothere, king of Kent, 24n34, 36, 50n113, 205
homicide, 39, 47n106, 49–50, 55–6, 56n141, 57–60, 63n156, 64, 139, 176, 182, 184, 196–7, 202
honour, 10, 102, 108, 168, 175, 209, 225, 233, 240; honour-price, 102, 171, 240 (*see also* Old/Early Irish: face-price)
humerus, 124
husband, 39, 53, 58, 157n50, 176, 180, 182–4, 186, 188–9, 195, 197–8, 198n76, 201, 221, 226, 243

Iceland(ic), 30, 207, 244; saga, 244; *thing* (see *thing*)
immunity/immunities, 55, 89, 184
incest, 55
incisor(s), 102, 102n67, 104, 106–7, 168, 249, 258, 261
Indo-European, 9n7, 75, 98, 132, 143
Ine, king of West Saxons, 142
infant, 242
infanticide, 196
infection, 25, 92, 122
inherit, 4, 10, 18, 106, 243
inherit(ance) (legal), 55, 60, 70n169, 151n37, 198n76

injure/injury, 3–5, 7–9, 9n6, 10, 13–14, 14n20, 16, 16n21, 17–19, 21, 25–6, 28–9, 37, 41–2, 51, 51n118, 52n124, 53, 55, 58–9, 61, 61n154, 62–5, 67–9, 72–4, 79, 80n20, 82, 82n25, 83–8, 91–2, 94, 96–8, 100–2, 104, 106, 109–10, 112–19, 121–6, 128–32, 134–5, 140–2, 160, 162, 165–70, 180–4, 191–2, 196, 199, 201–4, 207, 209–10, 215, 217, 219–20, 222, 225–7, 235–6, 238, 240–2, 246–7

innocence/innocent, 40–1, 43–5, 142, 170. *See also* guilt

insular, 16, 18, 23, 83–7, 95, 101

insult, 10, 101–2, 106, 108, 142, 150, 165–6, 168, 170–1, 171n28, 181–2, 217, 240

intermarriage, 12

internal bleeding, 76, 92, 199

internal organs, 59, 133–5, 199, 208, 216, 218, 220, 230, 231–2, 235, 255

intestines, 129, 133

Ireland/Irish, 3, 9, 31n23, 44, 93, 101–2, 108n74, 109–10, 129, 133, 207

iron, 44n93, 45n97, 63, 130, 143, 144n18, 145, 152, 162, 198, 213, 248

Isidore, bishop of Seville, 13, 32, 70, 143, 147n24, 150–1, 153, 224

isogloss, 147, 151–2, 233

Italy, 26, 27n4, 34, 41, 47, 53, 59, 111, 151, 236. *See also* Lombard

iudex 'judge'/*iudices*, 35, 51–2, 57–8, 70, 245. *See also* judge

jaw(bone), 101–2, 104, 249, 258, 260

Jew, 142, 173

John, bishop of Hexham, 72–3

joint (of the body), 69, 117–18, 122, 126, 130–2, 132n57, 133–4, 136, 153, 156, 162, 233, 250–1, 256, 258

judge, 29n13, 31–2, 34–5, 41, 43, 51–2, 52n124, 53, 55, 70–1, 97, 174, 176–8, 195, 205, 230, 236, 254. *See also iudex;* judgment

judgment, 34–5, 40, 46, 70–1. *See also* judge

Judith of Flanders, 186n27

jurors/jury, 33n29, 34, 34n37, 43. *See also boni homines; rachimburgi*

Juvenal, 90

Kent(ish), 11–12, 14, 16–17, 19, 23, 30–1, 37, 39, 42n83, 50, 61, 68, 75, 85–6, 95, 96–7, 99, 101, 104, 106, 109, 112, 114, 116–18, 129–30, 134, 138, 140, 147, 151, 155, 161–2, 165, 167, 181, 181n3, 186n27, 187–8, 188n29, 203, 205, 207, 209, 210n13, 221, 222n20, 230, 231, 233, 235, 240, 247, 249. *See also* Æthelberht. *For specific clauses, see* Æthelberht: laws of

kin(ship), 10, 39, 46, 47n104, 49–50, 57, 60, 64, 175, 183–5, 188, 192, 194, 198, 201–2, 207, 225, 243–4

king, 8n1, 10–11, 14, 14n20, 17, 35–6, 42, 42n84, 50–1, 51n117, 53–4, 60–1, 95, 108–9, 114, 171, 182–3, 186n27, 187–8, 192, 206, 222, 222n20, 224, 253; king's ban/coffer, 36, 50, 60, 109 (*see also* public: coffer, peace); those in king's service, 41, 190, 203–6, 206n9, 219, 221, 225

kingdom(s), 3, 8n1, 14, 16, 23, 30, 85, 95, 98, 113, 140, 142, 179, 186n27, 195, 207, 230, 236

knee(s), 5, 58, 117–19, 123, 131–2, 135, 166, 200, 220, 245, 250–1, 257–8, 260

Lacnunga, 24, 24n35
laet 'freedman' (OE), 207, 210n13
Langobardia. *See* Lombard
Latin, 9–10, 18–21, 24, 38n61, 59, 74, 79, 90, 98, 107, 111, 116, 123, 128, 146, 155, 167, 170, 171n27, 233, 235; terminology: *auricularis* 'earfinger, little finger,' 153; *brachium* 'arm,' 63n158, 123, 131, 169n20; *capsum* 'chest,' 128; *caput* 'head,' 74, 74n6, 90n39; *cerebrum*, 'brain, skull,' 79, 84; *corpus* 'body,' 128, 241n4; *costa* 'ribcage,' 128; *cubitum* 'elbow,' 131; *decalvare* 'to scalp,' 176; *digitus anullaris* 'ring finger,' 150, 153, 155; *folliculo testium* 'scrotum,' 128; *inpudicus digitus* 'unchaste finger,' 150, 156; *iunctura manus et brachii* 'joints of hands and arms,' 131; *iunctura scalpulae* 'shoulder joints,' 131; *labri superioris capilli* 'hairs of the upper lip,' 111; *latus* 'side,' 128; *minimus (digitus)* 'smallest finger,' 152; *pectus* 'chest,' 128; *plaga in facie* 'damage to countenance,' 167, 233; *praecordium* 'area around the heart,' 133, 257; *peritoneum* 'membrane lining the abdominal cavity,' 133, 257; *proximus a police* 'closest to the thumb,' 147; *saggitarius/sagittur* 'arrow finger,' 147–8, 153, 155–6; *virilia, viricula, vectis, veretrum*, 'penis,' 128; *vulnus* 'wound,' 123
lawspeaker, 13, 244
Lecciones Heliodori. See Heliodorus
leg, 4, 108, 112, 114, 116–23, 128, 130, 132–6, 162, 164, 177, 210, 230, 231–2, 235–6, 239, 250, 254, 257–8, 260; leggings, 48

Leges Visigothorum. See Visigoth
legislate/legislation/legislators, 5, 7, 10, 12, 16, 22, 28, 76, 84, 87, 93, 101, 104, 106, 108–9, 112–14, 117, 123, 128–31, 133, 141, 156, 161–2, 166, 168, 170, 178, 201–2, 204n4, 217, 220–1, 227, 230, 233, 236, 245
leod 'wergild.' *See* Frank
Lex Alamannorum. See Alamann
Lex Bauiuaroum. See Bavaria
Lex Burgundionum. See Burgundy
Lex Chamavorum. See Chamavan Francia
Lex Francorum Chamavorum. See Chamavan Francia
Lex Frisionum. See Frisia
Lex Langobardorum. See Lombardy
Lex Ribvaria. See Ripuaria
Lex Romana Burgundionum. See Burgundy
Lex Romana Visgothorum. See Visigoth
Lex Salica. See Salian Francia
Lex Salica emendate. See Salian Francia
Lex Saxonum. See under Saxon
Lex Talionis, 137n2
Lex Thuringorum. See Thuringia
liable/liability, 50, 56, 61, 63–4, 76, 82, 123, 142, 170, 181–2, 185, 190, 199, 206
Liber Constitutionem. See under Burgundy
Liebermann, Felix, 24, 24n34, 79n17, 96, 117
Life of St Emmeran, 178
limb, 63, 69, 76, 90, 112, 116, 118–19, 133–8, 138n5, 139–42, 169, 172, 172n30, 174, 178, 209–10, 215, 217, 220, 227–9, 235, 239; artificial, 118–19 (*see also* prosthesis)

296   Index

limp, 82, 121
linguistic(s), 18–20, 27, 147n22, 148, 167, 188, 231, 235, 244
lip, 96–7, 111, 168, 174, 179, 211, 214, 216–8, 250, 253–5
literacy/literate, 8, 13, 27, 32n27, 177, 243n7, 244, 246. *See also* non-literate
litigant, 29–30, 32, 33n29, 34, 36, 38–41, 43, 45, 52–3, 53n129, 55–6, 65, 70, 176, 245
litigation, 3, 30, 61
Liutprand, king of Lombards, 64, 244
Liuva, king of Visigoths, 142
livestock, 47, 68, 215. *See also* cow
loin(s), 128–9, 260. *See also* genitals; scrotum; testicles
Lombard(s)/Lombardy (*also* Langobardia), 3, 12, 16, 18–20, 33, 35, 35n47, 37, 46–7, 59, 64, 83–4, 95, 203n1, 210–17, 226; case(s) (legal), 26, 33–4, 53, 59–60; *Edictus Rothari*, 20; law, 14, 16–17, 19, 33, 34n37, 35, 43, 43n87, 53n129, 63–4, 74–5, 86, 95, 96–8, 106, 112–14, 117, 128, 136, 138, 140–1, 153, 158–9, 166–8, 170–1, 181, 198, 203, 209–17, 224, 224n25, 226, 230, 231, 233, 235, 240, 247, 253; specific clauses, 74n6, 64n160, 72n1, 84n27, 112n1, 117n10, 128n38, 137n1, 158n55, 166n3, 167nn9, 12, 168n14, 169n18, 170n24, 171n27, 198n70, 207n10, 212n15; *Lex Langobardorum*, 24; *See also* Greek: terminology
London, 36, 158
lot (judicial), 43–4, 44n93, 45
Lucca, 32
lung, 133, 258
Lupus, bishop of Ferrières, 22

Lyons, 245

machtiern 'presider' (Breton), 34n39. *See also* preside
maid(en), 181–2, 187–8, 188n29, 189–90, 195, 198, 221, 242. *See also* virgin(ity)
maim/maimed/maiming, 63, 97, 114, 116, 124, 130, 135, 137, 141–2, 153, 168–9, 174, 177, 180, 208–11, 218–20, 222, 239, 248–50, 252–9
mallberg 'legal language' (Frankish), 18, 35, 133, 143, 149, 151n38, 153, 155–6, 185, 188, 188n29, 233. *See also* Frankish: terminology
mallus 'assembly,' 30, 35, 38–9, 49–50, 53, 53n129, 55. *See also* assembly; *mæþel*; *thing*
manuscript(s), 10, 20–1, 21n26, 22–4, 24n35, 25, 27, 32, 38n61, 47, 58, 80n20, 89, 89n36, 90–1, 104n69, 147, 151–2, 152n39, 202, 219
Marculf of Angers, 29n13, 30n15, 41, 42n84, 50n112, 56n141, 58n149, 70n169, 151n37, 189, 190nn37, 38, 205, 206n7. *See also* Angers; formulary
marriage, 12, 17, 51n118, 182, 185, 186n27, 187–9, 191, 191n44
massaricae 'serf-holdings' (L), 49
master(s), 4, 30, 43, 60, 172, 174, 206, 209–10, 212, 215, 217, 220–1, 225–6, 243
Matthew, Gospel of, 137, 174
'Matthew limbs,' 137–8, 138n5, 139–41, 172, 227–8
mælan 'to speak' (OE), 30
mæþel 'assembly' (OE), 30–1, 36, 62, 64, 67. *See also* assembly; *mallberg*

medical, 5–6, 6nn3, 4, 7, 24–5, 61, 65, 68, 73n3, 74, 76, 87–8, 91, 136, 152n39, 157, 157nn50, 54, 175n45, 239 (*see also* doctor; medicine); assistance, 162; attention, 86, 117, 122; fee(s), 61, 67–9, 215; instruments, 90; intervention, 76, 79, 88–9, 91, 118–19, 127, 143, 159n58, 162; treatment, 58, 123n27, 158, 239
medicine, 6, 158n54
medicus, 89n34, 151, 151n38, 152, 155–7, 157n50, 158. *See also* doctor
membrane, 67, 79n17, 86–7, 92, 131–3, 143
Merovingian(s), 12, 17, 28n9, 31, 34n39, 41, 44, 52n124, 70, 78, 82, 107–9, 111, 123, 150
mid were 'with wergild,' 50
mid wite 'with fine,' 50
midwives, 156, 199n79
miscarriage (of fetus), 195–6, 241. *See also* abortion
missus 'envoy,' 35, 35n44, 42n84, 52
molar(s), 102, 103n67, 104, 104n69, 106–7, 117, 168, 211, 214, 216, 247, 249, 253, 258, 261
monastery, 26, 49, 54n133, 61, 110, 179
monk, 54n132, 61, 110, 223
Monumenta Germaniae Historica, 18, 24, 263
mos 'customary law,' 13, 57, 70
mouth, 92, 95–8, 102, 102–3n67, 106, 124n32, 141, 167–8, 177, 249
mucus, 93, 98, 168, 250, 252
mund 'protection,' 36, 205–6, 217
murder(er), 33, 40, 42, 56, 60, 82n25, 178, 182, 196, 198, 201, 242
muscle, 120, 122
mustache, 18, 110–11, 167, 167n7, 258

mute, 96
mutilation, 46, 57, 100–1, 130, 142, 170–1, 171n28, 172, 172n30, 173–4, 177–8, 201, 220

neb 'beak, nose,' 98–9
neck, 90, 99, 122, 177
nerve, 124, 132, 132n57, 164
noble(man), 35, 53, 108, 129, 198, 203–4, 204n4, 205, 206n9, 207, 221, 223, 225–6, 256, 259
noblewoman, 183, 186n27, 194, 198
non-literate, 13
non-sensory organs, 100
North Sea, 101, 235
Norway, 119
nose, 92–9, 131, 148, 168, 171, 173–4, 177–9, 179n62, 201, 211, 214, 216, 218, 227, 230, 248–50, 251–7, 259–60
nostrils, 51, 97, 254
nun, 32, 178–9, 192, 195, 200–2, 224

oath, 27n3, 29n13, 33n29, 41–2, 42n84, 43, 46, 65, 76, 172n30, 187; false, 142 (*see also* perjury); oath-helpers, 45–6, 57–8, 187; oath-supporters, 39, 57–9, 65; oath-swearers/swearing, 33n29, 34, 38, 41, 42n83, 43, 43n86, 46; oath-takers, 41
obgrafio 'viscount,' 204–5
Oenund Ofeigsson, 119
ogham, 9
Old English, 6, 11, 18–20, 30, 74–5, 79, 93, 98, 101, 116, 123, 128, 132, 146–8, 155, 170, 187; laws, 156; terminology: *earm* 'arm,' 123; *gebrocen* 'broken,' 80, 88; *gekyndlice lim* 'child–creating member,'

128, 134; *geweald* 'power, ?spinal cord,' 117; *goldfinger* 'gold/ring finger,' 150, 153, 155–6, 170, 249; *heafod* 'head,' 74, 88; *heafodban* 'headbone,' 80; *hion* '*tabulum* of the skull,' 79, 79n17, 80; *hrifwund* 'wounded in the abdomen,' 129, 233; *læce-finger* 'leech-finger,' 151; *lytel finger* 'little finger,' 152; *lyðseaw* 'synovia,' 132; *swinglung*, 'vertigo,' 93; *þirel* 'pierced,' 80; *þrot*, 'throat,' 9; *þrotbolla* 'Adam's apple,' 96; *waeltwund* 'wound that causes a welt,' 169; *wlitewam* 'damage to the face,' 101–2, 167, 233

Old/Early Irish, 44n93, 102, 110, 129, 133 (see also Celts/Celtic); law, 3n1, 9, 44, 101, 108n74, 109, 207; terminology: *aire* 'freeman,' 31n23; *airecht* 'assembly,' 31n23; *cumal* 'slave-girl, unit of payment,' 9; *enech* 'face-price, honor price,' 102; *foltgál* 'seizing by the hair,' 109

Old Norse, 147

oral(ity), 4, 8, 13, 19, 29, 32n27, 70–1, 122, 243, 243n7, 244–6

organ(s), 74, 100, 202, 249; internal, 59, 133–4, 135–6, 208, 216, 218, 220, 230, 235, 250, 255; sensory, 92–3, 95, 97–9, 138, 227–9, 231–2, 235

osteomyelitis, 122, 162

overlord, 10, 14, 114

Pactus Alamannorum. See under Alamann(ia)

Pactus Lex Salicae. See under Salian Francia

Pactus pro tenore pacis, 21

palm (of the hand), 140–1, 258

Paris, 23–4, 89–90

pegleg, 119–20

penal servitude, 53, 184, 201

penalty, 10, 30, 34, 35n47, 36, 46, 49–52, 55, 61–2, 64–6, 76–7, 93, 96–7, 109, 168, 172–3, 175–7, 181–2, 184–5, 195, 195n58, 198, 203, 219–22, 241, 254

penis, 128, 134–5, 248, 250, 257, 259

penitential(s), 33, 33n32, 49

peritoneum, 133, 257

perjury, 33–4, 42, 45–6, 142, 172. See also oath: false

personal injury, 4, 7–8, 9n6, 10, 13–14, 14n20, 16, 16n21, 17–19, 21, 25–6, 28–9, 37, 42, 51n118, 53, 55, 59, 61n154, 69, 74, 79, 80n20, 92, 101, 104, 106, 114, 123, 160, 165–6, 170, 181, 201, 203, 227, 235–6, 238, 246; cases, 41, 61, 65; lawyers, 4, 238

Phoenix (OE poem), 98

pia mater, 79n17, 87, 87n31

plaintiff, 29, 29n13, 36, 40–2, 53

plotting, 95, 108

poison/poisoning, 33, 59, 95, 147n25, 198, 221

politics, 12, 65, 242

power of attorney, 30, 55

praecordium, 133, 257

pray(er), 72–3, 136, 193

pregnancy/pregnant, 4, 43, 194–9, 241–2

pre-molars, 102

presbyter, 223–4

preside(r) (over lawsuits), 34, 34n39, 35, 35n47, 36, 39, 46–7, 50, 52–4, 65–6, 70, 97, 177, 183, 230

priest, 5, 34, 42n83, 44–5, 73, 108–9, 137, 222–4, 260

property, 9, 26–9, 32–3, 41, 45, 47, 49–50, 51n117, 52–3, 54n132, 55, 57, 59, 172, 175–6, 184–5, 190–2, 198n76, 205, 213, 217, 219, 221, 242
prosecute/prosecutor, 40, 47, 191
prosthesis, 119, 119n16, 119–20, 162–4, 239
protection, 31n20, 36, 38, 43, 119, 180, 182–4, 187–8, 195, 200, 205–6, 220–2, 225. See also *mund*
Proto-Germanic, 9
public, 3, 21, 30–1, 34, 37–8, 55–7, 64–5, 69, 102, 109, 166, 175–6, 178, 183, 187–8, 195, 209; beating, 175–6; coffer, 50, 138n5, 139, 142, 200–1, 209, 217, 221, 222 (*see also* king: king's ban); decency, 200; lashing/scourging, 53, 87, 174, 176, 178, 190–1, 236; peace, 64, 181, 188, 201, 209, 213, 225, 259; protection/security, 211, 221; service, 55
punish(ment), 31n20, 32, 73, 84, 87, 97, 109, 141–2, 171–2, 172n29, 173–5, 175n45, 178, 186–7, 191–2, 196–7, 199, 204, 217, 224
purgatory, 52

quitclaim, 55–6, 56nn139, 140, 57–8, 66–7, 69. *See also* security

rachimburgi 'judgment finders,' 30, 33–5, 70, 245. See also *boni homines*
radius (arm-bone), 125–7
rank, 29, 54, 57, 108, 110, 157–8, 167, 180, 183, 190, 198, 203–4, 206–7, 210–13, 251, 219–22, 222n21, 223, 224n22, 225–6, 242. *See also* status

rape/rapist, 4, 59, 172n30, 178, 180, 182, 182n8, 183–5, 188, 190–4, 201, 212, 221, 224, 242–3
reges crinati, 108
relics, 42, 42n84, 44–5
restitution, 4, 37, 47, 49, 59, 61–5, 69, 88, 95, 102, 123, 126, 138n5, 140, 156, 168, 171, 180, 183, 188–90, 192, 197, 201, 240
rib(cage), 82n23, 114, 116, 128–9, 133–6, 248–9, 252, 258, 260–1
ring(s), 43, 145–6, 150, 150n24, 151, 151nn37, 38, 152–3, 155–6, 169–70, 212, 215, 217, 235, 248, 250–1, 253–4, 256–61
Ripuaria(n), 19, 22, 43, 48, 98, 101, 147, 153, 161, 194, 200, 222, 230, 241; Francia/Franks, 13–14, 189–90, 194, 219, 225, 233, 235, 237; law(s), 17, 23, 43, 63, 70, 76, 86, 93, 98, 113, 138, 146, 168, 188–9, 194, 216–17, 219, 222–3, 241, 245, 247; laws, specific clauses, 42n81, 43n87, 47, 47n105, 63n158, 70n168, 72n1, 76, 84n28, 112n1, 137n1, 146n21, 168n15, 170nn25, 26, 184n23, 188n32, 190nn38, 39, 194nn54, 55, 196n64, 200n83, 204n2, 205n5, 212n15, 222n19, 224n26; *Lex Ribuaria*, 17, 21, 21n26, 22–3, 44, 47, 76, 123n52, 170, 184, 188, 196, 200, 205, 221–2, 225, 252
Roman(s), 9, 9n6, 10, 12, 16, 29, 110, 154, 225, 236; Empire, 8, 12, 18, 111, 144n18; law/legislation, 9, 10, 10n10, 13, 14n20, 18, 28–9, 30, 44n93, 175n45, 183, 197, 227, 236; monetary system, 9
Rome, 12, 18, 186n27, 227

300 Index

rotator cuff, 130
runes, 9

Sabbath, 175
saga, 3, 119–20, 244
Salian/Salic Francia, 14, 16, 19, 30, 35n48, 37, 84, 101, 104, 106, 113–14, 147, 155, 185, 194–5, 241, 247; law(s), 14, 17–18, 38, 43–4, 70, 70n169, 75–6, 86, 93–4, 113, 123, 133, 138, 146–7, 149, 151, 153, 182, 188, 194, 196–7, 200–1, 213, 227, 230, 231, 233, 235, 237, 245, 247; laws, specific clauses, 37n55, 42n81, 59n152, 72n1, 84nn28, 29, 89n35, 112n1, 123n29, 129n44, 133n60, 137n1, 170n25, 182nn8, 10, 185n25, 188n29, 190n39, 194n53, 196nn60, 62, 200n81, 204n2, 212n15, 224n26; *Lex Salica*, 10, 12n13, 17, 21–3, 35, 40, 44, 59, 75, 89, 123, 129, 147, 170, 182, 184, 188n29, 195, 199, 204–5, 215, 220, 233, 241, 248; *Lex Salica emendata*, 22; *Pactus Lex Salicae*, 34n37, 70
saliva, 96–8, 156, 250, 255
Saxon(s)/Saxony, 3, 13–14, 16, 19, 44, 48, 93, 98, 101, 113, 141–2, 147, 150–1, 166, 172, 206, 231, 233, 235, 244; law(s), 17, 23, 30, 63–4, 93, 98, 109, 112–13, 117, 128, 136, 138, 141–2, 153, 156, 161, 166–7, 172, 189, 201–2, 206, 225, 231, 247; laws, specific clauses, 30n18, 47n104, 64nn159, 160, 72n1, 112n1, 117n10, 128n37, 137n1, 142n9, 166n3, 167n11, 172n30, 189n33, 191n44, 194n56, 204n2, 207n10, 212n15, 222n19; *Lex Saxonum*, 22, 47, 188, 194, 223, 256; terminology: *derbhi* 'expressing disapproval,' 150; *wlitivam* 'damage to countenance,' 167
scalp, 81, 84, 86–7, 167, 176, 211, 214, 216
scalping, 175–6, 176n5
scar(s), 102, 127, 169, 171, 175–6, 211, 248, 253
scourging, 87, 175–6, 178
scribe/scribal, 9, 21, 41, 59n151, 75, 79n17, 80n20, 90, 147n22, 149–51, 153, 173, 202, 204n4, 233
scrotum, 82n23, 128, 257. *See also* genitals; loin(s); testicles
seax 'dagger' (OE), 102
Second Germanic Sound Shift, 147
security, 206, 217, 221, 225, 246
security (legal)/*securitas*, 56, 172n30. *See also* quitclaim
seduction, 178
self-defence, 37–9, 57–8, 62, 65. *See also* self-preservation
self-mutilation, 178, 201
self-preservation, 57. *See also* self-defence
Sens, 37, 39, 41, 57–9, 245
sense of smell, 4, 93, 240
sensory organs, 92, 97–9, 138, 227–9, 235
sensory perception, 93
sentence (legal), 49, 51, 52n124, 53, 174–5, 187, 191, 223
serf, 43, 49
servant, 47, 56–7, 60, 190, 203–6, 219, 223–5. *See also esne*
servitude, 50, 53, 110, 184, 201, 226. *See also* slavery
settle(ment of disputes), 6, 26, 31–2, 36–7, 46–7, 50, 65–6, 187, 245
sex, 39, 96, 127, 156, 178, 180–1, 185, 196–7, 199–202, 243

sexual assault, 181; harassment, 193; intercourse, 193; misconduct, 183
shank (of the leg), 260
shearing (of hair), 108–9, 166, 176, 200, 202, 260. *See also* tonsure
shield, 45, 58, 74, 74n6, 76, 85, 144n18, 145, 158, 158n55, 252, 258
shilling(s), 39, 64, 66–9, 74–5, 79, 82, 82n23, 85–6, 117, 128, 138, 138n5, 142, 165, 167–9, 183, 187–8, 193, 200, 205, 207, 209, 221, 240, 249
shin bone, 123n27
shoulder, 63, 82n23, 88, 114, 116, 124, 130–2, 134–5, 144n17, 249–50, 257–8, 260
sinew, 260–1
skeletal/skeleton, 25, 118, 123n27, 124–5, 162, 172, 192
skin, 84, 86–7, 124, 143, 167, 200, 250–1, 254, 260–1
skull, 5, 66–9, 73–4, 74n5, 76–9, 79n16, 80–2, 82n25, 83–8, 90–1, 91n43, 92, 94–5, 118, 167, 208, 211, 218, 248, 250, 252–3, 255, 257–8, 260
slander, 96, 173, 175, 200, 210, 222
Slav, 12
slave(s), 7, 9, 29, 39, 47, 56–7, 60, 87, 110, 142, 172–3, 173n39, 174–6, 180n2, 182, 182n8, 184–5, 190, 190n39, 191, 195, 200–1, 203, 206, 206n9, 207, 209–12, 212n15, 213–20, 220n16, 221–2, 225–6, 236, 240
slavery, 33. *See also* servitude; slave
solidi/solidus, 9, 9n3, 33–4, 36, 40, 45, 47–50, 53, 53n129, 56, 59, 76, 84–90, 97, 123, 133, 138, 138n5, 139–143, 146, 167–8, 170, 172, 176, 181–2, 185, 186n27, 187–90, 194–200, 204–7, 209–10, 212, 215, 219–23, 225, 241, 248, 250–8
Spain. *See* Visigoth
spall, 76, 79–81, 84, 86, 250, 253. *See also* splinter
spear, 45, 48, 63, 144–6, 149n29, 153
speech, 12, 81, 96–8, 233, 249
spinal column, 117
splinter(s) (of bone), 76–8, 80, 84, 90. *See also* spall
status, 29, 43, 43n86, 50, 54, 56, 76, 145n19, 151, 153, 157, 180, 180n2, 181, 187, 203–4, 207, 209, 212, 213, 215, 219, 211–12, 224–6, 240–2. *See also* rank
statute of limitations, 122
stelzia 'crutch' (L), 120–1
stomach, 133–6, 248
subdeacon, 222–4, 224n22
surgeon/surgery/surgical procedures, 5, 25, 67, 89, 89n36, 90–2, 94, 119, 122, 157n54, 158, 162, 240, 250. *See also* doctor; medical
swinglung 'vertigo' (OE). *See* vertigo
Switzerland, 92, 104n69, 130, 162–3, 172
sword(s), 48, 57, 63, 85, 118, 127, 144, 144n18, 145, 186
synovia, 131–4, 145

tabula/tabulum, 'bone plate(s) of skull,' 66–8, 80, 82, 82nn24, 25, 83–4, 86–7, 249, 260
Tacitus, 12, 156
Tassilo, duke of Bavaria, 54
taste (sense of), 4, 74, 93, 98, 152, 240
taudragil 'dragging in the dew' (Ala; Bav), 117, 231, 235
teeth. *See* tooth/teeth

temple(s) (of head), 94, 143
testicle(s), 128–9, 134, 230, 256–60.
    See also genitals; loin(s); scrotum
testimony, 29, 41–2, 65
theft, 43, 49, 55, 59, 95, 142, 156,
    171–2, 172n30, 173, 222n20. *See
    also* thief
Theodosian Code, 108. See also
    Codex Theodosianus
Theodore, archbishop of Canterbury,
    6, 33
Theodulf, bishop of Orléans, 39, 52,
    177
thief, 95, 142, 170–3, 177
thigh, 116–17, 121, 129, 192, 210–11,
    214, 216, 249–50, 253, 256, 260
thing 'Assembly' (OIc), 30. *See also*
    assembly; *mallberg*; *mæþel*
throat, 96, 101, 249, 258
thumb, 73, 141, 143, 145–8, 152n39,
    153, 156, 158–9, 208, 212, 215, 217,
    219–20, 248–50, 252–61
thumbnail, 249, 261
Thuringia(n), 13, 98, 147, 150–1, 156,
    206, 233, 235; law, 14, 17, 51, 63,
    93–4, 96, 101, 112–14, 128, 138,
    153, 156, 167, 182, 194, 198, 230,
    231, 233, 247, 259; law, specific
    clauses, 63n157, 64n160, 72n1,
    112n1, 128n37, 137n1, 156n46,
    167n11, 182n9, 194n54, 198n74,
    204n2, 212n15; *Lex Thuringorum*,
    22, 204n4, 259; terminology:
    wlitewam 'damage to counten-
    ance,' 101, 167, 233
tibia, 112, 116, 122–3, 130, 135, 169,
    214, 216, 248, 250–1
toe, 82, 82n23, 112, 153, 159–62, 210,
    212, 215, 217, 229–30, 235, 248–54,
    256–61

toenail, 160, 249
tongue, 38, 96, 173–4, 178, 248, 250,
    257, 259–60
tooth/teeth, 82n23, 91, 96–8, 102,
    102n67, 103–4, 104n69, 105–7, 119,
    137n2, 167–8, 179, 205, 211–14,
    216–18, 229, 235–6, 248, 250,
    253–5, 260
tonsure, 109–10. *See also* shearing
torso, 112–17, 119, 121–3, 125, 127–9,
    131, 133, 135, 169, 178, 208, 211,
    214, 216, 218, 230, 231, 248–61
torture, 43, 52, 108, 176, 178
Tours, 30, 38, 43, 57–8, 108, 156, 245
treason, 55
trepanation, 67–9, 91, 91n43, 92
trial, 10, 28n9, 33n29, 37, 40, 42,
    42n85, 45, 45n97, 110, 170, 246
Twelve Tables, 13

ulna(e), 125–7
uxoricide, 198

Vandals, 95
vein, 143, 151, 207, 217, 251, 255
verdict, 32, 34–5, 37–8, 40, 54, 58, 66
vernacular, 3n1, 18–10, 30; Germanic,
    18, 72n1, 75, 79, 104, 129, 132nn54,
    56, 147; Old English, 18, 74, 151
vertigo, 93
victim, 4, 10, 49, 56, 63, 67, 76, 89,
    93–6, 100, 109–10, 114, 120, 123–4,
    124n32, 125–6, 141, 166–9, 173,
    183–4, 192–3, 201, 205, 210, 225,
    238–9, 243
Vikings, 179
vineyard, 55, 59, 190
vintner, 213
violence, 38, 121, 167, 174, 178, 181,
    181n3, 195, 199, 202, 222, 243

Index   303

virgin(ity), 179, 183–5, 187–8, 190, 194, 200–1, 224, 242–3. *See also* maid(en)
Visigoth(ic)/Visigoth(s), 3, 12, 14, 19, 30, 32–3, 84, 87, 95, 113, 142, 157, 167, 175, 177, 184, 190–1, 201–2, 220, 222, 230, 231, 236; *Forum Iudicum*, 10, 29n12, 37, 63n156, 72, 84, 173, 176–7, 190–1, 195, 201, 206, 254; law, 9n6, 10, 14n20, 29n12, 35n47, 38, 40, 51–2, 52n124, 64, 84, 86–7, 95, 97, 106, 112–13, 129, 138, 152–3, 157, 161, 167, 172–5, 175n45, 176–7, 196, 199, 201–2, 206, 220, 230, 247, 254; law, specific clauses, 31n19, 33n31, 33n35, 37n58, 38n62, 40n71, 51n116, 53n126, 63n156, 64n162, 72, 72n1, 84n28, 95n50, 112n1, 129n47, 137n1, 157n52, 170n23, 173nn35, 36, 40, 174n43, 175n46, 176nn49–54, 184nn 20–2, 190n40, 191nn 41–2, 192n45, 195n59, 196, 204n2, 206n8, 207n10, 212n15; *Leges Visigothorum*, 24; *Lex Romana Visigothorum*, 22
vision, 93–4, 96–8, 100, 239, 257
Vulgate. *See* Bible

waist, 119
Wales, 27. *See also* Welsh
wargengum 'foreigner' (OF), 225
water on the knee, 5, 132. *See also synovia*
weapon(s), 47, 114, 144–7, 144n18, 145n19, 147n25, 153, 181, 205, 208–9, 219, 248, 255. *See also* arrow; bow; shield; spear; sword
Welsh, 11, 84n28, 148. *See also* Celts/Celtic; Wales
wergild, 33–4, 35n47, 36, 39, 47, 47n107, 50–2, 56–8, 60, 63–4, 66, 68–9, 76–7, 85–6, 89, 96, 116–17, 116n5, 123–4, 128, 133–6, 138, 138n5, 139–42, 153, 168–9, 171–2, 174, 182–3, 187–8, 190, 194, 198–9, 201, 203–6, 206n9, 207, 209, 210–13, 222–3, 225, 227, 241–2, 247–61. See also *leod*
Wessex, 14, 16–17, 19, 23, 85–6, 95, 96–7, 99, 102, 104, 106, 108, 112, 116–17, 123, 128–30, 132, 134, 138, 140, 147, 160, 165, 168–9, 172–3, 176, 182–4, 186n27, 192, 194, 198, 200–2, 206, 221, 224, 230, 231, 235, 237, 247, 260–1, 267 (*see also* West-Saxon); laws of (*see* Alfred)
West Germanic, 19–20
West-Saxon, 19, 133, 144, 183. *See also* Wessex
widow, 186n27, 190
wife, 42, 50, 51n118, 53, 58, 67–8, 94, 109, 176, 182–4, 188, 190–1, 193, 198, 198n76, 201, 221, 245
Wihtred, king of Kent, 16n21, 24n34, 35, 42n83, 46, 87
witness, 32–4, 36–43, 45–6, 58, 62, 64–6, 68, 76, 169, 172, 184, 192
Witteric, king of Visigoths, 142
woman/women, 4, 6–7, 29, 29n13, 34n39, 40, 43, 58–9, 69, 82, 96, 101, 108, 128, 145–6, 156–8, 157n50, 172n30, 178, 180, 180n1, 181n3, 182–4, 187–90, 190n38, 191, 191n44, 192–202, 207, 209–10, 212, 220–3, 207, 210, 212, 220–2, 224–6, 241–3, 245–6. *See also* abduction; abortion; fertile; maid; marriage; pregnancy; rape; wife; womb
womb, 196–7, 199, 241–2

work (physical labour), 49, 61, 67–9, 82, 87, 99, 107, 116, 124, 134, 156–7, 161–2, 174–5, 185, 210, 213, 215, 220, 220n16, 221, 223, 226, 239–41

wound, 4–5, 25, 27, 42, 51, 54n132, 58, 63, 67, 69, 74, 74n5, 75–82, 82nn23, 25, 83–4, 84n28, 84–92, 94, 96, 102, 112, 112n1, 113–14, 116–18, 120–3, 123n27, 124, 127–33, 135, 142–3, 162, 165–71, 203–5, 207–12, 214–18, 220, 230, 231, 233, 235–6, 240–1, 248–50, 253–5, 257–8, 260

wrist, 62, 125–7, 130–2, 257–8

Toronto Anglo-Saxon Series

General Editor
ANDY ORCHARD

Editorial Board
ROBERTA FRANK
THOMAS N. HALL
ANTONETTE DIPAOLO HEALEY
MICHAEL LAPIDGE

1 *Preaching the Converted: The Style and Rhetoric of the Vercelli Book Homilies*, Samantha Zacher

2 *Say What I Am Called: The Old English Riddles of the Exeter Book and the Anglo-Latin Riddle Tradition*, Dieter Bitterli

3 *The Aesthetics of Nostalgia: Historical Representation in Anglo-Saxon Verse*, Renée Trilling

4 *New Readings in the Vercelli Book*, edited by Samantha Zacher and Andy Orchard

5 *Authors, Audiences, and Old English Verse*, Thomas A. Bredehoft

6 *On Aesthetics in* Beowulf *and Other Old English Poems*, edited by John M. Hill

7 *Old English Metre: An Introduction*, Jun Terasawa

8 *Anglo-Saxon Psychologies in the Vernacular and Latin Traditions*, Leslie Lockett

9 *The Body Legal in Barbarian Law*, Lisi Oliver

www.ingramcontent.com/pod-product-compliance
Lightning Source LLC
Chambersburg PA
CBHW030304080526
44584CB00012B/439